Corporate Accountability in the Context of Transitional Justice

Corporate Accountability in the Context of Transitional Justice explores how corporations can be held accountable for their role in past human rights violations when a country is making a transition from conflict or repression to peace and democracy. It breaks new ground in theorizing the linkages between the areas of transitional justice and corporate accountability and in analyzing problems frequently arising where the two fields meet in practice: for example where the role of corporations in past human rights violations is examined by truth and reconciliation commissions or in the course of litigation.

The book provides an overview of the current trends in law and in legal and political discussion relating to both areas, as well as in-depth analysis of how tools of corporate accountability and transitional justice can complement each other in order to achieve the best outcomes for bringing justice to victims and lasting peace to societies. The authors bring extensive experience from diverse professional backgrounds and jurisdictions to provide the first sustained attempt to address this link. The book will be of interest to scholars, practitioners, policymakers and activists working in the areas of transitional justice, corporate accountability, and business and human rights.

Sabine Michalowski is Professor of Law at the University of Essex. Her research interests include the economic and social dimensions of transitional justice as well as corporate complicity. Her recent publications include articles on corporate complicity and on the link between sovereign debt and transitional justice.

Transitional Justice
Series Editor: Kieran McEvoy
Queen's University Belfast

The study of justice in transition has emerged as one of the most diverse and intellectually exciting developments in the social sciences. From its origins in human rights activism and comparative political science, the field is increasingly characterized by its geographic and disciplinary breadth. This series aims to publish the most innovative scholarship from a range of disciplines working on transitional justice related topics, including law, sociology, criminology, psychology, anthropology, political science, development studies and international relations.

Titles in this series:

Transitional Justice, Judicial Accountability and the Rule of Law
Hakeem O. Yusuf (2010)

The Era of Transitional Justice: The Aftermath of the Truth and Reconciliation Commission in South Africa and Beyond
Paul Gready (2010)

The Dynamics of Transitional Justice
Lia Kent (2012)

Corporate Accountability in the Context of Transitional Justice
Sabine Michalowski (2013)

Identity, Reconciliation and Transitional Justice
Nevin T. Aiken (2013)

Forthcoming titles in the series:

The Judiciary and the Politics of Transition: Saviours, Scoundrels, Scapegoats
Marny Requa

Truth, Denial and Transition: The Contested Past in Northern Ireland
Cheryl Lawther

Families of the Missing
Simon Robins

Gender Politics in Transitional Justice
Catherine O'Rourke

The Concept of the Civilian
Claire Garbett

Transitional Justice and the Arab Spring
Edited by Kirsten Fisher and Robert Stewart

Transitional Justice Theories
Edited by Susanne Buckley Zistel, Teresa Koloma Beck, Christian Braun, Friederike Mieth

Corporate Accountability in the Context of Transitional Justice

Edited by
Sabine Michalowski

Routledge
Taylor & Francis Group
a GlassHouse Book

First published 2013
by Routledge
2 Park Square, Milton Park, Abingdon, Oxon OX14 4RN

Simultaneously published in the USA and Canada
by Routledge
711 Third Avenue, New York, NY 10017

Routledge is an imprint of the Taylor & Francis Group, an informa business

British Library Cataloguing-in-Publication Data
A catalogue record for this book is available from the British Library

Library of Congress Cataloging-in-Publication Data
Corporate accountability in the context of transitional justice /
[edited by] Sabine Michalowski.
pages cm. — (Transitional justice)
1. Transitional justice. 2. Human rights. 3. Political crimes and offenses. 4. Restorative justice. 5. Corporate governance—Law and legislation. 6. Social responsibility of business. I. Michalowski, Sabine.
K5250.C67 2013
343.07—dc23

2013001783

ISBN: 978-0-415-52490-2 (hbk)
ISBN: 978-0-203-33809-4 (ebk)

Typeset in Garamond
by Keystroke, Station Road, Codsall, Wolverhampton

Contents

Acknowledgments

This book is largely the product of two international seminars entitled "Linking Corporate Complicity and Transitional Justice," which took place at the University of Essex, UK, in September 2010 and the University of Palermo, Argentina, in April 2011. The seminars and the book's copyediting were funded by the British Academy under its UK-Latin American/Caribbean Link Scheme.

I would like to thank all participants of the two seminars, quite a few of whom have also written chapters for this book, for their stimulating contributions to the discussions. In particular, I would like to thank Leonardo Filippini, who was my co-investigator in the British Academy-funded project and the co-organizer of the two seminars, and Clara Sandoval, without whose support neither the seminars nor the book would have been possible. All authors of this book deserve my gratitude for the patience with which they endured my editing.

Morgan Stoffregen did a fantastic job copyediting this book. Many thanks also go to Diana Guarnizo for editing the footnotes and providing other assistance.

Contributors

Charles P. Abrahams is senior director of Abrahams Kiewitz Incorporated, a South African boutique law firm specializing in class actions, public interest law, and litigation in the area of business and human rights.

Sylvain Aubry is a consultant in economic, social and cultural rights. He has carried out research, training and advocacy on the right to food, the right to education, and the right to housing with, inter alia, the Right to Education Project, ActionAid, FIAN International, EuropAfrica and Amnesty International.

Juan Pablo Bohoslavsky holds a PhD in law from the University of Salamanca and has also studied in Latin and North America. He is currently sovereign debt expert at the United Nations Conference on Trade and Development and has widely published in the area of corporate accountability and lending.

Darren Calley holds a PhD in law from the University of Essex, where he is a lecturer in law. His research interests are in the area of public international law (especially the living marine environment), animal welfare, and tort law.

Ruben Carranza is director of the Reparative Justice Program at the International Center for Transitional Justice in New York. He has carried out transitional justice work in Asia (Timor-Leste, Nepal, Cambodia, Indonesia, and the Philippines), the Middle East and North Africa (Palestine, Iraq, and Morocco), and Africa (Liberia, Sierra Leone, Kenya, Ghana, and South Africa).

Youseph Farah holds a PhD in law from the University of Essex, where he is a lecturer in law and an associate of the Essex Business and Human Rights Project. His expertise lies in international commercial arbitration, contract law, international investment law, and business and human rights.

Leonardo Filippini is a professor of law at the Universidad de Buenos Aires and the Universidad de Palermo in Buenos Aires.

Wolfgang Kaleck is a solicitor and secretary general of the European Center for Constitutional and Human Rights in Berlin. He is the author of numerous publications on corporate accountability and on transitional justice in Argentina.

Sabine Michalowski holds a PhD in law from the University of Sheffield and is a professor of law at the University of Essex, where she directs the research area on economic and social dimensions of transitional justice within the Essex Transitional Justice Network.

David M. Ong is professor of international and environmental law at the Nottingham Law School, Nottingham Trent University. His main research interests are on the intersection of public international law, environmental law (including European environmental law), and, more recently, transnational investment law.

Geneviève Paul is program officer at the Globalisation and Human Rights Desk of the International Federation for Human Rights (FIDH).

Nelson Camilo Sánchez is coordinator of the Area of Transitional Justice at the Center for the Study of Law, Justice and Society (DeJusticia) and an associate professor at the Universidad Nacional de Colombia in Bogotá.

Clara Sandoval holds a PhD from the University of Essex, where she is a senior lecturer in law, the director of the Essex Transitional Justice Network, and responsible for directing the research area on reparations.

Judith Schönsteiner is director of the Human Rights Centre at the Diego Portales University, Santiago, Chile. She holds a PhD in law from the University of Essex and is a project associate of the Essex Business and Human Rights Project.

Gill Surfleet is a solicitor at Leigh Day and Co., London, where she works on the Mau Mau case on torture in Kenya.

Tara L. Van Ho is a lawyer licensed in the state of Ohio, United States. She is a project associate with the Essex Business and Human Rights Project and provides consultations and trainings on business and human rights, particularly in the extractive industries.

Roberto Vidal is a professor of law at the Universidad Javeriana in Bogotá.

Introduction

Sabine Michalowski

This book makes a groundbreaking and original contribution to the almost non-existent analysis of the links between corporate accountability and transitional justice. In recent years, both transitional justice—that is, how best to achieve a transition to peace and democracy in the aftermath of armed conflict or oppressive and violent regimes—and corporate accountability for human rights violations have received a lot of academic and political attention. While corporations often operate in countries affected by conflict or repression, the resulting problems are usually not conceptualized as part of transitional justice. Indeed, there is hardly any literature exploring the link between the two fields. In the academic transitional justice debate, the role of corporations is sometimes mentioned as one of the topics to consider in the context of transitional justice,[1] and the issue of transitional justice on rare occasions finds its way into the academic discussion of corporate complicity and/or accountability.[2] What is missing is a conceptualization of the particular issues that might arise when attempting to hold corporations to account in the context of transitions.

There are good reasons for exploring the linkages between the two fields. Transitional justice aims to establish an account of the truth regarding the past, to achieve justice and reparations for victims, and to accomplish institutional reforms, all with the goal of preventing the recurrence of conflict or repression. Corporate accountability for human rights violations aims to prevent such violations from occurring by encouraging policies that assist

1 See, for example, N. Roht-Arriza and K. Orlovsky, 'A Complementary Relationship: Reparations and Development', in P. de Greiff and R. Duthie (eds), *Transitional Justice and Development. Making Connections*, Social Science Research Council, New York, 2009 (170–213); and E. Harwell and P. Le Billon, 'Natural Connections: Linking Transitional Justice and Development through a Focus of Natural Resources', *ibid.* (282–330).

2 See, for example, D. Gray, 'Devilry, complicity and greed: transitional justice and odious debt', 70 *Law and Contemporary Problems* 137 (2007); S. Michalowski and J.P. Bohoslavsky, 'Ius cogens, transitional justice and other trends in the debate on odious debts: A response to the World Bank discussion paper on odious debts', 48 *Columbia Journal of Transnational Law* 59–113 (2009).

with identifying and addressing relevant risks, and to provide victims with remedies if violations took place. Linking the two fields can potentially enhance and strengthen both transitional justice and corporate accountability.

The contributions to this book are based on discussions that took place in two international seminars that were funded by the British Academy under its UK-Latin American/Caribbean Link Scheme. The seminars centered on the following questions: (i) the role of liability for corporate complicity in achieving the objectives of transitional justice; (ii) the mechanisms through which this liability can be achieved; and (iii) whether the remedies for complicity need to be adapted to the special circumstances of the transitional context. While the original project focused specifically on the link between corporate complicity and transitional justice, it quickly became clear that the topic needed to be broadened to encompass corporate accountability more generally in order to get away from the narrow legal connotations of the term "complicity" and make it possible to consider extralegal mechanisms for holding corporations to account for their role in the context of transitional justice.

The central objective of this book is to explore the possible integration, in both theory and practice, of the two domains of corporate accountability and transitional justice. This involves a discussion of conceptual concerns as well as of selected practical issues that may well be approached differently if the links between corporate accountability and transitional justice are clear to those applying corporate accountability mechanisms to transitional justice situations or using transitional justice mechanisms to hold corporations accountable for their role in the violations committed during a conflict or repression. The clarification of these problems is important to further an understanding of the role of corporations for successful transitions, and it will help relevant stakeholders design adequate processes that take due account of corporate responsibility while being sensitive to the particular demands of the specific transitional justice context in which the responsibility arises.

Some of the authors of this book have a background in transitional justice, others in corporate accountability, and some in both areas. They range from academics to practicing lawyers to practitioners of non-governmental organizations, and they live and work in a variety of jurisdictions. This guarantees a rich assortment of perspectives. Authors were encouraged to consider a set of questions, including what they regard as the value added of linking transitional justice and corporate accountability, instead of dealing with both areas separately; potential problems and limitations of linking transitional justice and corporate accountability; potential future trends regarding the issues explored in their contributions; and open questions that need to be addressed by future research.

The book is divided into two parts. Part I, "Transitional justice and corporate accountability: exploring current trends and potential linkages," contains conceptual and theoretical analyses of various questions around the relationship between corporate accountability and transitional justice (chapters 1 to 7).

As its title indicates, part II, "Linking transitional justice and corporate accountability: examples and case studies," provides reflections on particular country experiences and specific corporate activities that give rise to corporate responsibility in the context of transitional justice (chapters 8 to 12).

The book starts with two chapters that present an overview of the main mechanisms and tools, as well as philosophies and trends, in the areas of transitional justice and corporate accountability. In chapter 1, Clara Sandoval, Leonardo Filippini, and Roberto Vidal introduce the main transitional justice processes and mechanisms—truth, justice, reparations, and institutional reform—and identify the primary features of traditional approaches to transitional justice. They also explore current trends that allow for, and in fact might call for, broadening the field from being largely state-centered to incorporating non-state actors, including corporations, and addressing root causes and consequences of conflict and repression. The authors sketch out the possibilities and challenges of using various transitional justice mechanisms to achieve corporate accountability, thereby setting the scene for the discussions that follow in other chapters.

Similarly, in chapter 2, Youseph Farah provides an overview of the main mechanisms of corporate accountability. Since other chapters deal with the United Nations (UN) Guiding Principles on Business and Human Rights and the United States Alien Tort Statute (ATS), chapter 2 focuses primarily on other important mechanisms of corporate accountability. After providing a discussion of the concept of accountability, it evaluates the possibilities of achieving accountability through several soft-law (in particular, corporate social responsibility and the OECD Guidelines for Multinational Enterprises) and hard-law (tort law and contractualization of human rights) tools. Farah assesses the strengths and weaknesses of these mechanisms in the context of transitional justice and demonstrates how they can complement one another.

Chapters 3 to 7 then discuss potential linkages between corporate accountability and transitional justice, each focusing on a particular topic or mechanism. In chapter 3, Tara L. Van Ho analyzes the possibilities of using transnational litigation to hold corporations accountable for their role in atrocities that were committed prior to transitions to peace and democracy. She highlights the challenges of both criminal and civil transnational litigation and shows the limited role of criminal prosecutions, given that the International Criminal Court lacks jurisdiction over corporations and that many countries either do not provide for corporate criminality or are reluctant to apply it in practice. The main focus of chapter 3 is on transnational civil litigation. Litigation under the ATS, which has proved to be the main tool in this context over the past few years was used as an example to discuss the potential and problems of such litigation in the context of transitional justice. Discussing the potential and problems of such litigation in the context of transitional justice, Van Ho makes a strong plea for the need to approach transnational civil litigation with a transitional justice background clearly in mind.

Chapter 4 introduces the UN Guiding Principles on Business and Human Rights and provides a critical analysis of the extent to which they might be used to achieve corporate accountability in the context of transitional justice. Geneviève Paul and Judith Schönsteiner discuss, in particular, the extent to which the Guiding Principles need to be clarified and refined for their application to corporate operations in conflict zones, and analyze the potential and challenges of the Guiding Principles' approach to remediation and reparations. This chapter highlights the tension between the advantages of soft-law principles that establish corporate responsibilities that go beyond corporations' legal obligations, and potential drawbacks of leaving these processes largely to the discretion of the corporations involved, which might lead to inhibiting transitional justice goals rather than enhancing them.

In chapter 5, Clara Sandoval and Gill Surfleet approach the linkages between corporate accountability and transitional justice from the perspective of reparations and redress. At the beginning of this analysis stands an examination of the extent to which corporations have an obligation, or at least a responsibility, to provide reparations for violations of human rights. They then examine how some truth and reconciliation commissions have evidenced corporate responsibility for human rights violations, and introduce some of the often innovative recommendations that these bodies have issued. While acknowledging the importance of these developments, Sandoval and Surfleet show how governments have been slow to implement these recommendations. This leads to an examination of how other mechanisms—in particular litigation, but also corporate remediation processes—might be used to obtain reparations for victims of corporate human rights violations in countries in transition. The chapter highlights the need to adapt corporate reparations that are obtained outside transitional justice mechanisms to the transitional justice context.

Chapter 6 introduces a theoretical framework, as well as specific examples from the transition in Colombia, to argue that while reparations must provide corrective justice to victims, they must also take considerations of distributive justice into account to avoid restoring victims to a situation of poverty and inequality. Applying this framework to corporate accountability, Nelson Camilo Sánchez suggests that corporate responsibility for reparations, including transformative reparations, must be differentiated according to the degree of corporate involvement. He argues that in transitional justice contexts, this responsibility needs to go beyond corporate liability in the strictly legal sense. He then suggests that a redistribution of wealth might sometimes be justified based on the principle of solidarity, even where corporations only benefited from operating in the context of conflict or repression, without holding direct or indirect responsibility for violations that occurred.

To finish the theoretical discussion of linkages between corporate accountability and transitional justice, chapter 7 draws attention to an area that is largely neglected both in the field of corporate accountability and in that of transitional justice: violations of economic, social, and cultural rights (ESCR). Sylvain Aubry introduces an interesting and innovative mechanism for achieving the inclusion of these violations—namely, the Optional Protocol to the International Covenant on Economic, Social and Cultural Rights. Aubry shows how a mechanism aimed at achieving state accountability can potentially be used to establish and address, though indirectly, wrongdoings committed by corporations, thereby providing a tool to investigate corporate responsibility regarding the violation of ESCR in the context of transitional justice.

The second part of the book discusses the linkages between corporate accountability and transitional justice by looking at specific examples and case studies. In chapter 8, Charles P. Abrahams presents an analysis of the South African approach, from both a legal and a political angle. He argues that South African transitional justice prioritized, particularly in the context of corporate accountability, truth and reconciliation over justice and reparations. According to the South African Truth and Reconciliation Commission, corporations had a clear responsibility for their role in apartheid, which resulted in the recommendation to impose corporate reparations. This is contrasted with the view of the democratic government, which regarded reparations as a matter for the state, while encouraging corporations to make voluntary contributions to a trust fund and to invest in the new South Africa in order to foster development and social reconstruction. Abrahams demonstrates how the victims' frustration with corporate impunity and the lack of corporate reparations led to litigation under the ATS and discusses some of the problems of such litigation from a transitional justice perspective.

Chapter 9 moves to Latin America and explores the challenges of bringing corporate accountability into Argentina's transitional justice debate. Wolfgang Kaleck argues that the Argentinean repression cannot properly be understood without taking account of its economic and social context, as unionists and members of workers' councils were particular targets of the repression. He shows the challenges faced when attempting to carry out criminal prosecutions against corporate directors, both in Argentina and elsewhere, for their responsibility for the persecution of unionists. The chapter thus demonstrates the problems with trying to broaden transitional justice from prosecuting those directly responsible for blood crimes to prosecuting their corporate accomplices. He also shows the transformative value of litigation, whether or not it leads to criminal convictions, in making corporations' role in the repression part of the transitional justice narrative.

Staying in Latin America, chapter 10 looks at Uruguay as an example of the importance of establishing the role of banks in financing repressive regimes. Making the case that without private funding, the Uruguayan military regime could not have confronted the serious political and economic challenges it faced, strengthened the military and police apparatuses, and carried out the repression to the extent that it did, Juan Pablo Bohoslavsky suggests that the role of financiers of conflict and repression needs to be made more transparent in the context of transitional justice processes. He argues that establishing the accountability of lenders would further the goals of transitional justice by allowing for a fuller narrative of the occurrences during the repression, obtaining justice and reparations for victims, and contributing to non-recurrence.

Chapters 11 and 12, while very different from each other, move the discussion from corporate accountability for past violations into the realm of accountability for corporate activities in transitional and often weakened states. Chapter 11 uses the example of Kosovo to discuss the challenges of pursuing a post-conflict reconstruction, in which private corporations play an important role, in a way that is respectful of international human rights and environmental standards and sensitive to the particular transitional context. David M. Ong suggests that transitional societies often present a combination of investor-friendly institutional frameworks and privatization policies, and weak enforcement of environmental justice mechanisms. He proposes a framework for transitional environmental justice that would help avoid such an adverse impact—and that would include corporate accountability where it nevertheless occurs. Ong also emphasizes the challenges faced by such a framework, particularly given the limits of holding corporations to account under international law.

In chapter 12, Darren Calley discusses a corporate activity that has not yet been linked to transitional justice: the flag of convenience (FOC) industry. He shows how corporations take advantage of the legal possibilities of registering vessels in weak states, which often happen to be transitional or post-transitional states, in order to circumvent international fishery agreements. While acknowledging that engagement with the FOC industry might seem to many transitional states an attractive and easy short-term solution to meet their pressing needs for foreign investment, Calley argues that it is the corporations, not the countries in transition, that benefit from the often weak institutional context in which maritime registries are opened up to non-indigenous vessels. He demonstrates that this practice is harmful to the relevant states, which risk international sanctions and isolation. While acknowledging the limited possibilities of holding corporations to account in this context, Calley introduces some recent initiatives in this direction.

Part I

Transitional Justice and Corporate Accountability: Exploring Current Trends and Potential Linkages

Chapter 1

Linking Transitional Justice and Corporate Accountability

Clara Sandoval with Leonardo Filippini and Roberto Vidal

Introduction

Armed conflicts and repressive regimes constitute a potential threat to the international community since they have damaging spillover effects, such as the commission of massive atrocities, the migration of people, the expansion of terrorism, arms production and proliferation, drugs proliferation, organized crime, environmental damage, poverty, and lack of development. This threat makes it imperative to help states in such situations undergo important political and social change that enables them to build systems where the rule of law, democracy, and human rights protection can flourish. Transitional justice is one of the mechanisms designed to achieve such political and social changes. Nevertheless, if it fails to address all causes of conflict and repression, a relapse into conflict is the most likely consequence.[1]

Addressing the causes and consequences of conflict and repression requires considering the role of all actors that caused or contributed to the commission of mass atrocities—even if they are not state actors, as in the case of corporations. Nevertheless, as the chapters in this book demonstrate, whether or not corporations should be included in the work of transitional justice mechanisms is a much debated question to which there is no clear-cut answer. Indeed, the issue requires careful consideration. First, transitional justice is a field with particular goals, mechanisms, and processes whose adequacy for dealing with corporations needs to be examined, and cannot be taken for granted. Second, when using transitional justice mechanisms to hold corporations to account, consideration must be given to the role of other mechanisms that deal with corporate accountability, such as arbitration tribunals, the regulation of corporations, and economic agreements.

Therefore, to begin the discussion about the possible linking of transitional justice with corporations, and the extent to which doing so is desirable, this

1 P. Collier, A. Hoeffler and M. Söderbom, 'On the duration of civil war', 41 *Journal of Peace Research* 253–273 (2004); and P. Collier and A. Hoeffler, 'Greed and grievance in civil war', 56 *Oxford Economic Papers* 563–595 (2004).

chapter starts by introducing the concept of transitional justice and providing an overview of its different components (justice, truth, reparations, and institutional reform). It then notes some of the key challenges faced by those working in this area when considering the responsibility of corporations in the commission of serious crimes or their possible role in the aftermath of mass atrocities and in social reconstruction projects. The chapter concludes by challenging a narrow understanding of transitional justice and its processes in order to provide some fertile terrain for the discussions taking place in the rest of this book.

Defining transitional justice

The term "transitional justice" was coined in 1995, as a result of the publication of *Transitional Justice: How Emerging Democracies Reckon with Former Regimes*, edited by Neil Kritz.[2] Today, almost two decades later, the concept of transitional justice has influenced the legal, social, and political discourse of societies undergoing fundamental social change, as well as that of the international community. The key assumption in such periods of change is that any state where mass atrocities have taken place should engage in processes (judicial and non-judicial) that provide justice for past crimes, peace, a democratic society, and an established rule of law.[3]

This assumption underpins the UN's working definition of transitional justice. For the UN, transitional justice refers to "the full set of processes and mechanisms associated with a society's attempts to come to terms with a legacy of large-scale past abuse, in order to secure accountability, serve justice and achieve reconciliation."[4] This definition, all-encompassing as it seems, leaves important issues unresolved. Among them are the relationship between international law and transitional justice; whether countries that move from authoritarian regimes toward democracy, but where gross human rights violations did not take place, should also engage with transitional justice processes; whether a transition can take place only after conflict or oppression

2 N. Kritz, *Transitional Justice: How Emerging Democracies Reckon with Former Regimes*, United States Institute for Peace Press, Washington DC, 1995.

3 N. Roht-Arriaza and J. Mariezcurrena, *Transitional Justice in the Twenty-First Century: Beyond Truth versus Justice*, Cambridge University Press, New York, 2006; R. Teitel, *Transitional Justice*, Oxford University Press, Oxford, 2001; M. Minow, *Between Vengeance and Forgiveness: Facing History After Genocide and Mass Violence*, Beacon Press, US, 1998; P. Arthur, 'How "Transitions" Reshaped Human Rights: A Conceptual History of Transitional Justice', 31 *Human Rights Quarterly* 321–367 (2009); C. Turner, 'Delivering Lasting Peace, Democracy and Human Rights in Times of Transition: The Role of International Law', 2 *International Journal of Transitional Justice* 126–151 (2008).

4 UN Secretary General, *The Rule of Law and Transitional Justice in Conflict and Post-Conflict Societies*, U.N. Doc. S/2004/616, 24 August 2004, p.4.

has ceased to exist; how to come to terms with large-scale past abuse; and what mechanisms should be used.

Other definitions of transitional justice complement and enrich the one used by the UN. Naomi Roht-Arriaza, for example, defines transitional justice as the "set of practices, mechanisms and concerns that arise following a period of conflict, civil strife or repression, and that are aimed directly at confronting and dealing with past violations of human rights and humanitarian law."[5] According to this concept, transitions can take place only when conflict or repression has ended, and transitional justice processes could include abuses of all human rights, as opposed to violations of just certain civil and political rights. This concept was not followed by stakeholders involved in transitional justice processes in Argentina, Chile, and South Africa, for example, where a choice was made to limit the transitional justice process to serious and systematic violations of civil and political rights.[6]

Other definitions prefer to focus on the set of actors behind such processes rather than on the substance of transitional justice. Paige Arthur, for example, defines transitional justice as a "field" constituted by "an international web of individuals and institutions, whose internal coherence is held together by common concepts, practical aims, and distinctive claims for legitimacy,"[7] most of which are articulated as a result of the need to resist and respond to mass atrocities in contexts of significant political change. In contrast, others, like Christine Bell, challenge the idea that transitional justice is a "field," preferring to think of it as a "label or cloak that aims to rationalize a set of diverse bargains in relation to the past as an integrated endeavor, so as to obscure the quite different normative, moral and political implications of the bargains."[8] For her, understanding transitional justice as a field denies its very nature.

Despite important differences among these concepts, they all highlight the fact that transitional justice implies a particular set of approaches to deal with the legacy of gross human rights violations, serious breaches of international humanitarian law and international crimes. Some of these approaches are driven by the international law paradigm, meaning international human rights law, international humanitarian law, international criminal law, and international refugee law, which provide "the normative foundation" of

5 Roht-Arriaza and Mariezcurrena, n.3, p.2.

6 In Argentina, for example, the focus was on disappearances (Comisión Nacional sobre la Desaparición de Personas (CONADEP), *Nunca Más*, 1984); in Chile, it was on disappearances, killings, and torture (Comisión Nacional de Verdad y Reconciliación, *RETTIG Report*, 1991, p.XIX and Decreto Supremo N355/1990, article 1); and in South Africa, it was on killing, abduction, and torture or severe ill-treatment (South African Truth and Reconciliation Commission, *Final Report*, Volume 1, Chapter 2, 1998, p.29).

7 Arthur, n.3. p.324.

8 C. Bell, 'Transitional Justice, Interdisciplinarity and the State of the Field or Non-Field', 3 *International Journal of Transitional Justice* 5–27 (2009), p.6.

transitional justice.[9] Nevertheless, not all approaches to transitional justice accept this normative basis.[10] In any case, and regardless of the approach that is followed, there appears to be some consensus about the role of transitional justice as aiming to deal with the legacy of mass atrocities, achieving justice, and moving toward a democratic society where the rule of law and human rights are respected. This guiding principle, which provides some flexibility, has given rise to different processes and mechanisms.

Processes of transitional justice

Four processes are believed to constitute the core of transitional justice, even if there is disagreement about what each of them entails and about the relationship that should exist between them. Usually, a transition encompasses a *justice process*, to bring perpetrators of mass atrocities to justice and to punish them for the crimes committed; a *reparations process*, to redress victims of atrocities for the harm suffered; a *truth process*, to fully investigate atrocities so that society discovers what happened during the repression or conflict, who committed the atrocities, and where the remains of the victims lie; and an *institutional reform process*, to ensure that such atrocities do not happen again.[11]

In addition to these core processes, others have become part of the transitional justice agenda: primarily, *national consultations*, which have been strongly recommended by the Office of the High Commissioner for Human Rights (OHCHR) and the UN Peacebuilding Commission, which emphasize that "meaningful public participation" is essential for the success of any transition.[12] National consultations should take place in relation to different aspects of transitional justice and nowadays are considered a *sine qua non* of the traditional transitional justice mechanisms described above. Lastly, in cases of conflict, *disarmament, demobilization, and reintegration* (DDR), which usually take place parallel to rather than as part of the transitional justice processes, actively interact with and complement transitional justice mechanisms and policies. DDR focuses on helping ex-combatants stop fighting and reintegrate into society.[13] While all these processes are important, this chapter focuses on

9 UN Secretary General, n.4, and OHCHR, *Analytical Study on Human Rights and Transitional Justice*, U.N. Doc. A/HRC/12/18, 6 August 2009, p.5.

10 Bell, n.8.

11 OHCHR, n.9, p.9.

12 *Ibid.* and UN Secretary-General, *Report of the Secretary General on Peacebuilding in the Immediate Aftermath of Conflict*, U.N. Doc. A/63/881-S/2009/304, 11 June 2009, para.71.

13 N. Ball and L. van de Goor, *Disarmament, Demobilization and Reintegration: Mapping Issues, Dilemmas and Guiding Principles*, 2006, www.clingendael.nl/publications/2006/20060800_cru_paper_ddr.pdf; United Nations Department of Peacekeeping Operations and Office of Rule of Law and Security Institutions, *DDR in Peace Operations: A Retrospective*, 2010, www.un.org/en/peacekeeping/documents/DDR_retrospective.pdf.

the core processes of transitional justice—namely, justice, truth, reparations, and institutional reform.

Justice process

A key belief of transitional justice is that alleged perpetrators of genocide, crimes against humanity, and war crimes should be prosecuted, tried, and, if found guilty, punished for the atrocities they committed. This approach is supported by three main arguments: (i) the international law paradigm obliges states to investigate, prosecute, and punish such crimes; (ii) adequate reparations under international law include bringing perpetrators to account; and (iii) accountability for past crimes is crucial to preventing such atrocities in the future. This belief covers both state and non-state actors. Indeed, any individual who commits or helps commit a serious crime must be held accountable.[14]

Important developments, at both the domestic and international levels, support the need to fight impunity: domestic trials are taking place in countries such as Argentina, Colombia, and Chile, not only as a response to victims' demands and in order to protect and enforce their rights, but also to comply with what the justice sector in these countries considers to be binding international obligations.[15] For example, article IV of the 1948 UN Convention on the Prevention and Punishment of the Crime of Genocide and article 4 of the 1984 UN Convention against Torture and Other Cruel, Inhuman or Degrading Treatment or Punishment establish an international obligation to investigate genocide and torture. This obligation is claimed to have the status of customary international law in relation to such crimes.[16] Therefore, states are obligated to investigate cases of torture and genocide regardless of who carried them out.

Equally, although human rights treaties—such as the International Covenant on Civil and Political Rights, the European Convention for the Protection of Human Rights and Fundamental Freedoms, and the American

14 J. Mendez, 'Accountability for Past Abuses', 19 *Human Rights Quarterly* 255–288 (1997); D. Orentlicher, 'Settling Accounts: The Duty to Prosecute Human Rights Violations of a Prior Regime', 100 *Yale Law Journal* 2537 (1991); D. Orentlicher, 'Settling Accounts Revisited: Reconciling Global Norms and Local Agency', 1 *International Journal of Transitional Justice*, 10–22 (2007).

15 A good account and discussion of the trials taking place in Argentina is the book co-authored by CELS and ICTJ, *Hacer Justicia: Nuevos Debates Sobre el Juzgamiento de Crímenes de Lesa Humanidad en la Argentina,* Buenos Aires, 2012, www.cels.org.ar/documentos/?info=publicacionesTpl&ids=3&lang=es&ss=126.

16 For a detailed analysis of the status of customary law on the prohibition of genocide, see J. Quingley, *The Genocide Convention: An International Law Analysis*, Ashgate, Hampshire, 2006, p.80; and Committee Against Torture, General Comment No.2: *Implementation of article 2 by States parties*, U.N. Doc. CAT/C/GC/2, 24 January 2008, para.1.

Convention on Human Rights—do not expressly incorporate such an obligation, all of them include the right to an effective remedy, which has been understood by their respective monitoring bodies to raise an obligation to provide reparations in relation to human rights violations, such as disappearances, torture, and arbitrary killings.[17] The key legal precedent for this approach is the *Velásquez Rodríguez v Honduras* judgment, where the Inter-American Court on Human Rights considered that "States must prevent, investigate and punish any violation of the rights recognized by the [American] Convention and, moreover, if possible attempt to restore the right violated and provide compensation as warranted for damages resulting from the violation."[18] These treaties are also understood to require states to investigate crimes against humanity.[19]

Besides these sources of international human rights law, international criminal law has also developed in important ways to fight impunity. Ad hoc tribunals have been established by the UN Security Council to deal with the atrocities committed in the former Yugoslavia and Rwanda (the International Criminal Tribunal for the former Yugoslavia and the International Criminal Tribunal for Rwanda). The Rome Statute establishing the International Criminal Court (ICC) was agreed to and entered into force in 2002. To date, the Statute has 121 ratifications. It grants jurisdiction to the ICC over individuals who commit any of the following international crimes: crimes against humanity, war crimes, genocide, and aggression.[20] Also, hybrid tribunals have been established, such as the Special Court for Sierra Leone, the Crime Panels of the District Court of Dili in East Timor, the War Crimes Chamber in the Court of Bosnia and Herzegovina, and the Extraordinary Chambers in the Courts of Cambodia.[21] These developments all show an important domestic and international trend toward fighting impunity. This means that if states fail to fulfill their international obligation to hold the perpetrators of such crimes to account within their own jurisdictions, the international community can take action to ensure that justice is achieved.

17 Orentlicher (1991), n.14.

18 Inter-American Court of Human Rights, *Velásquez Rodriguez v Honduras*, Merits, Series C No 4 (1988), para. 166.

19 Orentlicher (1991), n.14.

20 Rome Statute of the International Criminal Court, articles 5–8.

21 These tribunals often employ international and national staff, and apply international and national substantive and procedural law. They are usually set up by agreement—for example, between the UN and the country concerned. Some, but not all, of these tribunals are part of the local judiciary. They normally depend on voluntary contributions. For information on these tribunals, see C. Romano, A. Nolkaemper and J. Kleffner, *Internationalized Criminal Courts: Sierra Leone, East Timor, Kosovo and Cambodia (The International Courts and Tribunals Series)*, Oxford University Press, Oxford, 2004; C. Tofan and F. Mouloudi (eds), *The Special Court for Sierra Leone: History, Work and Future*, International Court Association, Nijmegen, 2011.

With regard to holding corporations to account, however, international practice appears to suggest that corporations are not to be held criminally accountable for their role in such crimes. This is partly explained by the general belief that prosecutions could be an obstacle to peace, truth, and/or reconciliation in the aftermath of conflict or repression. Those who support this view often claim that in such periods of change the international law paradigm is not applicable given the exceptional circumstances faced by states. In such situations, according to them, international law does not fully rule out amnesties or certain immunities for past crimes.[22] It is then believed that peace (or any of the other goals mentioned) must be sought first, even at the expense of justice. Therefore, it could, for example, be appropriate to limit criminal prosecutions to those who committed the most serious crimes, or provide amnesties (and also apply statutes of limitation) to allow a society to move forward, even if this potentially results in a breach of the international obligation to investigate, prosecute, and, if applicable, punish. This argument also applies to corporations because countries undergoing transitions are often in a state of economic collapse, and the work of corporations is seen as critical for economic progress. Thus, a trade-off appears to be required: in exchange for their contributions to a country's economic recovery, corporations and their CEOs are not prosecuted.[23]

That corporations are not responsible under international criminal law can be shown by looking at the jurisdiction of international criminal tribunals. For example, the ICC, the world court on criminal justice, lacks jurisdiction to prosecute corporations, given that the topic was excluded from the Rome Statute during its negotiations.[24]

While corporations are not criminally liable before the ICC and in many domestic jurisdictions,[25] individuals working for corporations, if implicated in the commission of crimes under its jurisdiction, could be prosecuted, tried, and punished. However, prosecuting directors of corporations is only one dimension of seeking accountability for the wrongdoings of corporations. Prosecuting corporations directly is crucial to dismantling the economic

22 L. Mallinder, *Human Rights and Political Transitions: Bridging the Peace and Justice Divide*, Hart Publishing, London, 2008.

23 R. Carranza, 'Plunder and Pain: Should Transitional Justice Engage with Corruption and Economic Crimes?', 2 *International Journal of Transitional Justice* 310–330 (2008), pp.325–326.

24 M.C. Bassiouni, *The Statute of the International Criminal Court: A Documentary History*, Ardsley, New York, 1998, p.55; A. Clapham, 'The Question of Jurisdiction Under International Criminal Law Over Legal Persons: Lessons from the Rome Conference on an International Criminal Court', in M.T. Kamminga and S. Zia-Zarifi (eds), *Liability of Multinational Corporations Under International Law*, Kluwer, The Hague, 2000 (139–195), p.140.

25 M. Pieth and R. Ivory (eds), *Corporate Criminal Liability: Emergence, Convergence and Risks*, Springer, Germany, 2011.

structures that make such crimes possible and preventing such situations from recurring in the future.[26]

At the same time, while criminal liability of corporations should be sought, it needs to be used together with the enforcement of applicable domestic law—for example, the law governing commercial transactions. Legal avenues such as those offered by commercial law are not exceptional mechanisms created to deal with the very unique circumstances faced by a state involved in a transitional justice moment. Rather, they are mechanisms geared toward dealing with the work carried out by corporations, and they provide important tools to investigate corporate wrongdoing. From this point of view, they might be more effective than transitional justice mechanisms in getting corporations to be more cooperative with investigations and their outcomes.

Another tool to be explored is civil liability. Non-transitional-justice mechanisms, such as ordinary domestic courts, could either order corporations to pay compensation for civil wrongs or support the reaching of settlements in relation to situations that took place during conflict or repression and that arguably caused serious crimes. Most of these developments have taken place using tort law.[27] A good example is the case of *Doe v Unocal*,[28] where Unocal agreed to a confidential settlement and even to provide funds for programs in Burma to improve the living conditions of victims.[29] These civil-law mechanisms, which seek redress for victims rather than punishment of the perpetrators, can complement criminal proceedings.

Truth process

Transitional justice processes are also built on the belief that individual victims and their societies need to know what happened. Since most of the atrocities committed in periods of repression or conflict take place in secrecy, there is an inherent need to clarify what happened and who was responsible, and to find the whereabouts of beloved ones.[30] This finds strong support in

26 M. Kremnitzer, 'A Possible Case for Imposing Criminal Liability on Corporations in International Criminal Law', 8 *Journal of International Criminal Justice* 909-918 (2010), p.912.

27 M. Koebele, *Corporate Responsibility under the Alien Tort Statute*, Martinus Nijhoff, The Netherlands, 2009; R. Meeran, 'Tort Litigation against Multinational Corporations for Violation of Human Rights: An Overview of the Position Outside the United States', 3 *City University of Hong Kong Law Review* 1 (2011). See also chapters 2 and 3 of this book.

28 *Doe v UNOCAL Corp.*, 395 F.3d 932 (9th Circuit, 2002); 395 F.3d 978 (9th Circuit, 2003).

29 R. Chambers, 'The Unocal Settlement: Implications for the Developing Law on Corporate Complicity in Human Rights Abuses', 13 *Human Rights Brief* 1 (2005), www.wcl.american.edu/hrbrief/13/unocal.pdf.

30 OHCHR, *Rule of Law Tools for Post-Conflict States: Truth Commissions*, HR/PUB/06/1, 2006, p.1, www.ohchr.org/Documents/Publications/RuleoflawTruthCommissionsen.pdf.

international law, at least in relation to certain crimes, such as disappearances. For example, Protocol I to the Geneva Conventions indicates, in articles 32, 33, and 34, that families of missing persons have the right to know the fate of their loved ones, and it establishes the obligations to be fulfilled by each party to the conflict in this respect. Similarly, the International Convention for the Protection of All Persons from Enforced Disappearance establishes, in article 24, the right of victims to "know the truth regarding the circumstances of the enforced disappearance, the progress and results of the investigation and the fate of the disappeared person." The UN Working Group on Disappearances has recently confirmed the existence of this right under international law, and not only in relation to disappearances.[31]

Aside from judicial proceedings, other mechanisms have been used to enforce the right to know the truth. These mechanisms can achieve a more comprehensive reconstruction of the past than that which can be achieved judicially. The most common way to deal with the truth of past atrocities is through a truth and reconciliation commission (TRC). A TRC is a commission of inquiry created by the state (usually the executive or parliament) to investigate heinous crimes committed during conflict or repression and to produce recommendations for dealing with the consequences.[32] The mandates of TRCs are very diverse. For example, the South African TRC had the power to investigate crimes committed during apartheid, including the use of subpoena and seizure powers; to have public hearings; and to recommend the granting of an amnesty for perpetrators in exchange for full disclosure. This commission was also allowed to award interim reparations and make recommendations in this respect.[33] In contrast, the Argentinian National Commission on the Disappeared was mandated only to investigate the disappearances that took place in the country between 1976 and 1983, without subpoena or seizure powers.[34]

TRCs have been the main transitional justice mechanism used to consider the role and responsibility of corporations. This is because they are generally able to create a historical account of what happened, the violations that took place, the root causes of conflict and repression, who was responsible, and how a society reached that situation. In this context, a few TRCs have used their mandates to look at the role and responsibility of corporations. For example,

31 UN Working Group on Enforced or Involuntary Disappearances, *General Comment in Relation to the Right to the Truth in Relation to Enforced Disappearances*, 22 July 2010, www.ohchr.org/Documents/Issues/Disappearances/GC-right_to_the_truth.pdf.

32 M. Freeman, *Truth Commissions and Procedural Fairness*, Cambridge University Press, New York, 2006.

33 Promotion of National Unity and Reconciliation Act 34/1995, sections 5 and 6, www.justice.gov.za/legislation/acts/1995-034.pdf.

34 R. Alfonsín (then Argentinian President), Decree 157/83, 15 December 1983, www.derechos.org/ddhh/arg/ley/conadep.txt.

the South African TRC was established by the Promotion of National Unity and Reconciliation Act in 1995 to clarify "the nature, causes and extent of gross violations of human rights"[35] that happened during apartheid. To carry out this mandate, the TRC considered the role of corporations and concluded that "business was central to the economy that sustained the South African state during the apartheid years."[36] The Commission extensively documented corporations' involvement in apartheid and even held a special hearing on businesses, labor, and apartheid. The Liberian TRC also looked at the role of all state and non-state actors. Part of its mandate was to look at economic crimes, which allowed it to examine particular features of the role played by corporations.[37] Equally, the Sierra Leonean TRC found that "successive political elites plundered the nation's assets, including its mineral riches, at the expense of the national good."[38] The Commission's final report understood that Sierra Leone's political elite was constituted, among others, by the business elite. The TRC also looked into the role of diamonds in fuelling the conflict.[39] These examples illustrate that, in practice, TRCs have been looking at the role of corporations and particular industries. Furthermore, these commissions have made important recommendations in their final reports, as discussed in the next section.

While TRCs have looked into the role of corporations, this does not mean that they are functionally able to address the role and responsibility of corporations or that the ones that have done so to date have been successful. TRCs are politically weak institutions, with few economic and human resources and with expertise most often linked to violations of certain civil and political rights for which states are responsible.[40] All of these factors have an impact on the work that TRCs can do to deal with corporations. For example, despite the work carried out by the South African TRC, its treatment of corporations was problematic. As described by Sampie Terreblanche, a leading South African academic:

> in the end the TRC devoted only three days of its life span of two and a half years to public hearings on the role of business in the apartheid era. Not surprisingly, the hearings were conducted in a way that obscured the systemic character of apartheid, and offered business people an undeserved

35 Preamble to the Act.

36 South African Truth and Reconciliation Commission, *Final Report*, Volume Four, Chapter Two, 1998, p.58.

37 Truth and Reconciliation Commission of Liberia, *Final Report, Preliminary Findings and Determinations*, 2009, Volume 1, pp.2–3.

38 Sierra Leone Truth and Reconciliation Commission, *Final Report*, 2004, Volume II, p.27.

39 *Ibid.*, p.12.

40 OHCHR, n.30, pp.9, 13 and 24.

> opportunity to clear themselves and their corporations of any guilt in respect of or responsibility for the legacy of apartheid.[41]

He carried out a similar analysis of the TRC's final report and recommendations on the subject.

Despite the fact that several TRCs have tried to document corporate abuse and establish accountability, some questions remain unanswered. Should corporations carry out their own truth processes—for example, by disclosing the supporting documents of negotiations with abusive regimes? Is this an issue of corporate ethics and image, or is it a public issue? Should there be a corporate duty to actively cooperate with truth efforts? Should corporations lead and fund these efforts, and, if so, would that threaten the independence or impartiality of the proceedings? If corporations cooperate with truth efforts, could they and/or their directors be exonerated from criminal responsibility?

Reparations process

Transitional justice is also based on the assumption that serious harm caused to victims should be redressed. This assumption is widely upheld in relation to both state responsibility and individual criminal responsibility. First, under customary international law, any state that breaches its international obligations (by action or omission) has the obligation to produce reparations.[42] Thus, for example, when states are involved in the commission of human rights violations (such as disappearances or torture), as in Chile and Argentina during their periods of repression, the state is liable under international law to provide reparations for its victims if, at the time of the commission of such atrocities, it was bound by international law (treaty or custom) not to commit these violations.[43] Second, as stated above, international law recognizes individual criminal responsibility for crimes against humanity, war crimes, genocide, and aggression. Perpetrators of such crimes should also repair the harm they caused to their victims.[44]

These two forms of reparations (state and individual) are thus well founded in international law. International law is, however, silent about the obligation of corporations to provide redress to victims of such serious crimes.

41 S. Terreblanche, *A History of Inequality in South Africa: 1652–2002*, University of Natal Press and KMM, South Africa, 2003, p.128. For a more in-depth discussion of how the South African TRC dealt with businesses, see chapters 5 and 8 of this book.

42 International Law Commission, *Draft Articles on Responsibility of States for Internationally Wrongful Acts with Commentaries*, A/56/10, 2001, 2001, article 1.

43 International Covenant on Civil and Political Rights, article 2.2(a) and American Convention on Human Rights, articles 8, 25, and 1.1. Both Argentina and Chile have ratified these treaties.

44 Rome Statute of the International Criminal Court, article 75.

Nevertheless, corporations are liable for their wrongdoing in tort and should provide redress, as ordered by courts, for harms caused. Depending on the circumstances, wrongful acts can engage the responsibility of the corporation itself, its directors, or other persons working for the corporation.[45] These examples indicate that there is a common principle across international law and domestic law according to which those who commit harm should provide redress to their victims.

Reparations should be adequate, effective, and prompt, according to UN General Assembly Resolution 60/147, and the Basic Principles and Guidelines on the Right to a Remedy and Reparation for Victims of Gross Violations of International Human Rights Law and Serious Violations of International Humanitarian Law.[46] They could include, as appropriate, restitution, compensation, rehabilitation, satisfaction, and guarantees of non-repetition.[47] The primary aim of reparations is to return victims to the status quo ante. However, in periods of transition, this is very difficult—if not impossible—to achieve, given the nature of the violations that might have been committed, the scarcity of economic resources in the state, the frequently alleged insolvency of the perpetrators, and the lack of a clear institutional and normative framework to design and implement reparations policies.

Indeed, transitions take place in countries where a significant portion of the population has been targeted and has suffered as a result. Consider the case of Rwanda, where 800,000 people (approximately 10 per cent of the total population) were killed within 100 days in 1994.[48] The country was left bankrupt after the genocide. Many victims and perpetrators fled the country. In a case such as this, how can redress be provided to so many victims? Clearly, the state bears responsibility for the human rights violations that took place and should therefore redress them. Individual perpetrators, such as Hutus involved in the genocide and those helping them, also bear criminal responsibility and therefore are in principle liable to provide reparations for the harm they caused. However, if perpetrators do not redress the harm they were responsible for, the state is obligated to ensure that the victims nevertheless receive adequate reparations—an obligation that a state lacking economic resources might struggle to fulfill.[49]

In this context, corporations can play an important role in the reparations process. First, to continue with the example of Rwanda, if corporations aided

45 Meeran, n.27.

46 UN General Assembly, *Basic Principles and Guidelines on the Right to a Remedy and Reparation for Victims of Gross Violations of International Human Rights Law and Serious Violations of International Humanitarian Law*, Resolution 60/147, 16 December 2005.

47 *Ibid.*, Principle IX.18.

48 UN, *Report of the Independent Inquiry into the Actions of the United Nations During the 1994 Genocide in Rwanda*, S/1999/1257, 16 December 1999.

49 Basic Principles and Guidelines, n.46, Principle IX.15.

and abetted those who committed the genocide—for example, by providing the machetes that made it possible[50]—they are directly or indirectly responsible for genocide and, at the very least, have a moral duty to redress surviving victims.[51] Second, there is an argument to be made related to the place that corporations, depending on their role in the commission of the crime or as beneficiaries thereof, should have in the reconstruction of a country like Rwanda. Even if they do not bear any criminal responsibility for the genocide, they should assist in the country's reconstruction by helping finance reparations—for example, by contributing to a special fund for reparations or paying an annual tax to the authorities. It is, after all, in their economic interest to make sure that the country, and its people, move toward recovery and that the path is paved for the reconciliation of victims and perpetrators, as this is believed to have a positive impact on economic recovery.

Reparations to victims have also generated important discussion regarding their transformative potential. Given that victims of heinous crimes are usually discriminated against and poor, reparations can be seen as a means to move toward development and to challenge structures of discrimination that can be left unaltered if victims are simply returned to the status quo ante.[52] This potential reach of reparations has helped challenge the traditional understanding of transitional justice as being limited to the achievement of retributive justice for past atrocities, paving the way toward a broader concept of justice that encompasses the achievement of distributive justice. Under this assumption, corporations could play an important role in the reconstruction of the country, in development, and in helping eradicate discrimination and poverty.[53]

That corporations should play a role in reparations processes is not just an academic proposal. As indicated earlier, TRCs have made important recommendations on reparations of corporations, even if these recommendations have not been fully implemented. The South African TRC, for example, discussed various proposals with the business sector, including, among others: (i) a wealth tax; (ii) a once-off levy on corporate or private income; and (iii) a retrospective surcharge on corporate profits extending back to a date to be agreed on.[54] In the end, it was agreed that a business

50 L. Melvern, *Conspiracy to Murder: The Rwandan Genocide*, Verso, London, 2004, p.56.

51 For a discussion of such moral duties, see also chapter 6 of this book.

52 Inter-American Court on Human Rights, *Cotton Field v Mexico*, Preliminary exceptions, merits, reparations and legal costs, 16 November 2009, para. 450; Nairobi Declaration on Women's and Girls' Right to a Remedy and Reparation, Principle 3.H and UN General Assembly, *Report of the Special Rapporteur on Violence against Women, its Causes and Consequences*, Rashida Manjoo, U.N. Doc. A/HRC/14/22, 23 April 2010, para. 31.

53 For a further discussion of whether and to what extent this is and should be their task, see chapter 6 of this book.

54 South African Truth and Reconciliation Commission, *Final Report*, Volume six, Section two, Chapter 5, 2003, p.143.

trust would be created so that corporations in South Africa would contribute to the country's reconstruction and to reparations. Approximately 140 corporations have contributed R1.2 billion[55] (about US$143,734,000) to the fund. This amount of money has been considered to be insufficient for providing redress to the victims and not to have been used in the most effective way.[56] Nevertheless, this example demonstrates that corporations can play an active role in achieving reparations, even if their engagement is on a purely voluntary basis.

It is important to note that reparations by corporations should not be limited to compensation, as this will not have a deterrent impact on them. For reparations to be truly effective, they should be about expropriation, providing restitution of lands, terminating contracts, forbidding companies' participation in new biddings, and so forth. These forms of reparations would constitute a real threat to companies, thereby discouraging them from aiding and abetting human rights or humanitarian law violations. Such forms of reparation, though, are possible only if the corporation's criminal or civil responsibility is established.

Lastly, considering reparations from corporations also invites to think about those forms of reparations that only corporations can provide, such as the rehiring of unfairly dismissed workers or the construction of a memorial within private facilities, and to analyze how they would contribute to transitional justice.[57]

Institutional reform process

Reforming state institutions involved in, or that failed to prevent, the commission of heinous crimes is an essential element of the transitional justice processes. Without the reform of institutions, transitional justice would be unable to prevent such crimes and human rights violations from occurring again, for the structures that facilitated those violations would continue to exist.[58]

Institutional reform is closely linked to guarantees of non-repetition (reparations process), an obligation imposed by the international community on states that have breached international obligations as an assurance that what happened will not happen again. The key concern of such measures is

55 The South African Business Trust, www.btrust.org.za/resources.html.

56 P. de Vox, 'Khulumani Welcomes Call for a Wealth Tax', *Constitutionally Speaking (Blog)*, 6 August 2011, http://constitutionallyspeaking.co.za/khulumani-welcomes-call-for-a-wealth-tax/.

57 For more on reparations and corporations, see chapter 5 of this book.

58 Economic and Social Council, *Updated Set of Principles for the Protection and Promotion of Human Rights through Action to Combat Impunity*, U.N. Doc. E/CN.4/2005/102/Add.1, 8 February 2005, Principles 35 to 38.

prevention. In particular, but not exclusively, the process of institutional reform aims to transform the security sector and the justice sector. The security sector refers to "the structures, institutions and personnel responsible for the management, provision and oversight of security in a country."[59] It includes the police; military personnel; intelligence services; customs; certain segments of the justice sector; and non-state actors with security functions, some of which are corporations.

Even though the justice sector is not fully included in this concept, it is also an element of institutional reform that should be at the heart of transitional justice processes. Indeed, one of the key aims of transitional justice, from a human rights perspective, is to bring to account those responsible for the atrocities. To this end, both the security and justice sectors are essential. If they are not up to the challenge, impunity and corruption will prevail. The Organisation for Economic Co-operation and Development prefers the term "security system," which not only integrates the security and justice sectors but also includes other sectors, such as prison reform, democratic oversight and accountability, and civil society.[60]

Common institutional reforms include vetting, meaning the "processes for assessing an individual's integrity as a means for determining his or her suitability for public employment."[61] If an individual lacks integrity, the person should be removed from public office or not be appointed to any public position. Equally, clear rules should be enacted—from constitutional and legislative norms to the enactment of codes of conduct—to regulate wrongful behavior so that those who engage in gross and systematic human rights violations cannot commit such atrocities again. Also, both disciplinary and criminal procedures should be established to process those involved in the commission of serious crimes and impunity.[62] Furthermore, adequate educational training of security sector and justice sector personnel is essential, to ensure that they understand the rights of all individuals, that certain conducts are forbidden, and that a culture of impunity will not be tolerated. Legislative reform is particularly relevant with regard to corporations. Lack of legal regulation of their work only facilitates the commission of abuses and further engages the international responsibility of the state, as it fails to take the necessary measures, legal and otherwise, to make sure that people can

59 UN General Assembly Security Council, *UN Secretary General, Securing Peace and Development: The Role of the United Nations in Supporting Security Sector Reform*, U.N. Doc. A/62/659-S/2008/39, 23 January 2008.

60 OECD DAC, *Handbook on Security System Reforms: Supporting Security and Justice*, OECD, Paris, 2007.

61 R. Duthie, 'Introduction', in A. Mayer-Rieckh and P. de Greiff (eds), *Justice as Prevention: Vetting Public Employees in Transitional Societies*, Social Science Research Council, New York, 2007, p.17.

62 L. Davis, *Transitional Justice and Security System Reform, Initiative for Peacebuilding*, ICTJ, New York, 2009.

enjoy the rights protected under international law. Further, legislation related to corruption, white-collar crimes, and the like is essential to preventing corporations and those representing them to act beyond the law.[63]

Institutional reform measures recommended by TRCs or agreed to by governments do not go very far in addressing the business sector and trying to reform it. This area is usually considered to fall outside the purview of transitional justice. Of all transitional justice processes, institutional reform is one of the most needed measures to stop businesses from feeling that they have immunities that protect them. Yet, it is the area of transitional justice where the least is done in practice. Institutional reform is the area that all relevant political parties want to avoid so that the transition does not produce lasting change.

States in processes of transition must deal not only with the atrocities that were committed but also with the structures that made them possible. The business sector should be required to do the same. It is essential to first transform the state so that it is able to reform the business sector and establish the necessary measures to that end. This should then be followed by adopting guarantees of non-repetition that are applicable to the business sector. For example, lustrating the board of directors of a company responsible for violations could be an effective measure to prevent the company concerned, as well as other companies, from carrying out such acts in the future. It would also provide shareholders the opportunity to know what has been done in their name (i.e. find out the truth of what happened).

Role of corporations

Human rights law and principles have been designed to address states' duties, and the same applies to the transitional justice processes mentioned above. However, progressive developments are increasingly including non-state actors as possible human rights violators. Although states remain the key violators in the context of human rights law, they are no longer the only actors at stake. In relation to corporations, for instance, some previously absent principles and norms are being built within the UN, which specify that corporations can be held responsible for violating human rights.

It is significant that in July 2011, the UN Human Rights Council endorsed the UN Guiding Principles on Business and Human Rights. This set of principles, developed by Special Representative of the United Nations Secretary-General on Business and Human Rights, Professor John Ruggie, is designed "to ensure that companies do not violate human rights in the course of their transactions and that they provide redress when infringements

63 UN Convention Against Corruption, General Assembly Resolution 58/4, 31 October 2003, article 12.

occur."[64] The groundbreaking UN Guiding Principles outline how states and businesses should implement the UN's "Protect, Respect and Remedy" Framework in order to better manage business and human rights challenges. They highlight what steps states should take to foster businesses' respect for human rights; provide a blueprint for companies to know and show that they respect human rights, and reduce the risk of causing or contributing to human rights harm; and constitute a set of benchmarks for stakeholders to assess business respect for human rights.[65] While the principles do not refer to transitional justice processes in particular, they do recognize that in certain situations, such as those of conflict, corporations are more likely to violate human rights and that they have a duty of due diligence and an obligation to provide redress.[66] Therefore, the UN Guiding Principles are also applicable in transitional justice processes, and they provide a window of opportunity for linking corporate behavior and accountability with transitional justice.

Conclusion

Dealing with the legacy of mass atrocities and with the root causes of conflict or repression in a period of change is a complex task. Transitional justice has emerged as a possible response to this dilemma. It is a way to articulate the different processes considered necessary to help a society move from a period of repression or conflict, where mass atrocities took place, to one in which human rights, democracy, and the rule of law can prevail. Nevertheless, transitional justice processes have usually ignored the root causes of conflict and failed to look at all parties responsible for the crimes, making it difficult to achieve their aims. However, important developments have taken place in recent years that question the scope and normative limitations of transitional justice work. This opens new windows of opportunity for dealing with root causes of conflict and repression, the atrocities that took place, and the role of non-state actors, such as corporations.

The developments considered in this chapter show how some transitional justice mechanisms, even if in an incipient manner, have attempted to address the role of corporations. This is particularly true for TRCs and reparations mechanisms. An assessment of their work in this respect is a pending task, but what this chapter has shown is that the corporate element could and must

64 'UN Human Rights Council endorses principles to ensure businesses respect human rights', *UN News Centre*, 16 June 2011, www.un.org/apps/news/story.asp?NewsID=38742&Cr=human+rights&Cr1.

65 J. Ruggie, Report of the Special Representative of the Secretary-General on the Issue of Human Rights and Transnational Corporations and Other Business Enterprises, *Guiding Principles on Business and Human Rights: Implementing the United Nations "Protect, Respect and Remedy" Framework*, U.N. Doc. A/HRC/17/31, 21 March 2011.

66 For more on the UN Guiding Principles, see chapter 4 of this book.

be addressed by transitional justice mechanisms. TRC and reparations practices to date also highlight the challenges they face: a lack of political, human, and economic support that translates into subsequent obstacles to achieving the aims of transitional justice.

Equally important to note is that transitional justice is state-centered. It is built around the belief that the primary target of its mechanisms is the state and its agents, and that its work is confined to the territory of the state where the atrocities occurred. While these assumptions remain true for some aspects of transitional justice, the close interaction between states and other important international actors, such as multinational corporations, and between people across borders, calls for a more comprehensive approach to truth, justice, reparations, and institutional reform that transcends state boundaries. Therefore, transitional justice faces the challenge of catching up with a changing world that is affecting its most basic premises.

Similarly crucial is the recognition that transitional justice actors go beyond the state, demobilized groups, and the military. Indeed, transitional justice processes are conducted by diverse actors that need to figure more openly and visibly in them, such as regional human rights courts (as opposed to criminal tribunals), local and traditional courts, international cooperation agencies, non-governmental organizations (local and international), and transnational corporations. Furthermore, transitional justice goes beyond international human rights law, international humanitarian law, international refugee law, and international criminal law: if it aims to include corporate behavior and accountability, transitional justice and its stakeholders should be ready to deal with other branches of law, such as private law and commercial law. Nevertheless, transitional justice stakeholders should be mindful of the complexities of dealing with corporations and of the limitations of transitional justice mechanisms to do so. Careful consideration of these issues is crucial to helping stakeholders understand the potential and limitations of transitional justice to deal with corporations—and to seize the opportunities, even if small, that it provides in this respect.

Chapter 2

Toward a Multi-Directional Approach to Corporate Accountability

*Youseph Farah**

Introduction

This chapter identifies the routes, mechanisms, and processes by which a multinational corporation (MNC)[1] may be held accountable to individuals for its human rights violations. An important objective is to assess how hard law and soft law, individually or when combined, can bring proactive compliance with human rights or serve as a reactive tool of accountability to individuals who were harmed by MNCs' non-compliance. Some reflections will be offered on what the outcome of this analysis might contribute to the debate on corporate accountability in the particular context of transitional justice where, it will be argued, a multi-directional approach to accountability is particularly important to guarantee relevant, timely, and effective remedies to individuals who have suffered harm or loss because of MNCs' non-compliance with soft and hard law. The chapter relates MNCs' actions or inactions to the traditional concept of "accountability." There are many ways in which an MNC could be held to account for the harm it has caused to individuals. One source of corporate accountability, for example, can be found in the criminal law.[2] This chapter, however, focuses on three normative sources of corporate accountability that arise in the private sphere.

The first source of accountability is based on soft law, such as a corporation's commitment to ethical behavior and philanthropy as reflected in the UN Guiding Principles on Business and Human Rights,[3] corporate

* I would like to thank Sheldon Leader, Sabine Michalowski, and Chris Willett for their comments on and conversations about the ideas expressed in this chapter.

1 Most of the discussion in this chapter is relevant to corporations, whatever their base, size, or context. However, the term "MNC" occupies a particular role in relation to the scope of the OECD Guidelines.

2 See chapter 3 of this book.

3 J. Ruggie, Report of the Special Representative of the Secretary-General on the Issue of Human Rights and Transnational Corporations and Other Business Enterprises, *Guiding Principles on Business and Human Rights: Implementing the United Nations "Protect, Respect and Remedy" Framework*, U.N. Doc. A/HRC/17/31, 21 March 2011.

social responsibility (CSR),[4] and the OECD Guidelines for Multinational Enterprises.[5] While not the strongest form of accountability, soft law can assist in establishing an imperfect form of accountability through a corporation's internal processes and mechanisms. These processes have been strengthened, moreover, by the gradual recognition of corporations' responsibility to respect international human rights.[6]

The second source of accountability relates to civil wrongs. Accountability here is based on established doctrines and laws that are commonly referred to as tort law, civil wrong, or delict.

The third source of accountability in the private sphere is a product of the contractualization of human rights obligations in agreements between host states and corporations or between corporations and other institutions, such as under the Equator Principles. In this respect, this chapter will show that while such contractual obligations appear to be at odds with the traditional concept of accountability, the contractualization of human rights may ultimately make an MNC accountable to individuals.

Meaning of accountability

Before identifying MNCs' accountability in the three normative sources mentioned above, it is essential first to explore the meaning of accountability. Most authors agree that the traditional meaning of accountability is "associated with the process of being called 'to account' to some authority for one's actions."[7] Under this meaning, one could locate three essential components that must be established in order to say that an MNC is accountable. First, the MNC must be held accountable to an independent and impartial external party or body; second, the MNC is subordinate as a matter of right and authority to the external party; and, third, the MNC must act in accordance with the instruction of the external party.

Accountability, however, may have an internal aspect. Internal accountability refers to an MNC's policy or rules that set a code of conduct for its employees, and possibly contractors. It is not the employee's own professional judgment that holds the employee to account but rather the corporation through its internal structures. Thus it can be argued that the employee is

4 See, for example, Boots Ltd CSR policy, www.boots-uk.com/Corporate_Social_Responsibility.aspx.

5 *OECD Guidelines for Multinational Enterprises*, 2011 edn, www.oecd.org/daf/internationalinvestment/guidelinesformultinationalenterprises/48004323.pdf.

6 The UN Guiding Principles, n.3, may have this effect, for example, through the due diligence requirement and, more importantly, the acknowledgment that corporations have the responsibility to respect human rights; see, in particular, principles 11 and 17. See also chapter 4 of this book.

7 R. Mulgan, '"Accountability": an ever expanding concept?', 78 *Public Administration* 555–573 (2000), pp.555–556.

accountable to the company's own objective standards, which are external to the employee.[8] However, the main problem with this form of accountability is its lack of neutrality, as the corporation holds the employee, who acted on its behalf and might have caused harm in the process, to account according to its own—rather than objectively imposed—standards. From the perspective of the harmed party, internal accountability thus means that the corporation is a judge of its own cause.

Soft law and MNC accountability

For our purpose of assessing MNCs' accountability, the distinction between hard law and soft law is useful. It facilitates comparing the efficiency between certain norms that are described as "hard law" and "soft law," on the one hand, and between different sets of soft law that vary with regard to their degree of softness or hardness, on the other. The proposition of this part of the chapter is that hard law is more likely to exhibit the traditional features of the concept of accountability than soft law. Nevertheless, as will be seen, soft law is better positioned at times to respond to the needs of particular contexts such as transitional justice.

It is important from the outset to express the view that the distinction between hard law and soft law is not a binary one.[9] Further, and logically following from this, it is hard to agree on a definition of the concept of soft law or to delineate its boundaries with hard law. In fact, the term "soft law" is often criticized for being somewhat misleading and antagonistic to the traditional normative value that is attached to law, in particular its binding nature.[10] Others argue that much turns on the efficiency of the law rather than on the narrow criterion of its binding force.[11]

Even though it is at times difficult to distinguish between hard law and soft law, a process of exclusion could help in identifying soft law. According to Kenneth Abbott and Duncan Snidal's paradigm, hard law is made up of "legally binding obligations that are precise, and that delegate authority to a third party for interpreting and implementing the law."[12] In the context of international legislation, they see the law as consisting of a spectrum of three factors: (i) precision of rules; (ii) obligation; (iii) and delegation to

8 *Ibid.*

9 K. Abbott and D. Snidal, 'Hard and Soft Law in International Governance', 54 *International Organization* 421 (2000), p.424.

10 J. Klabbers, 'The Undesirability of Soft Law', 67 *Nordic Journal of International Law* 381 (1998).

11 I. Duplessis, 'Soft international labour law: The preferred method of regulation in a decentralized society', in International Institute for Labour Studies, *Governance, International Law & Corporate Social Responsibility*, 2008, www.ilo.org/public/english/bureau/inst/download/116.pdf, p.15.

12 Abbott and Snidal, n.9, p.437.

a third-party decision maker.[13] Soft law thus is a law that is weak along any of the three factors. Accordingly, what is not hard law is soft law; and the degree of softness varies according to the degree of conformity with the factors listed above.

There are of course other ways of seeing soft law—for example, as a form of regulation that refers to "the normative processes which frame relations between actors but without any legal constraint."[14] Yet soft law is often dismissed because it lacks an independent judiciary and supportive institutions to enforce it. Even international law did not escape being criticized as soft law due to its lack of proper enforcement mechanisms.[15]

Why choose soft law?

It is easier to create soft law than hard law. Soft law can reduce contracting costs, particularly if there are differences between the contracting states. States may also be reluctant to forfeit their sovereign autonomy on certain issues. Some observers stress that "state interests are formed through socialization processes of interstate interaction which soft law can facilitate. They thus favor soft law instruments for their capacity to generate shared norms and a sense of common purpose and identity."[16] Furthermore, other proponents of soft law see the efficiency of the law as the principal consideration. Hard law could, for example, command certain behavior, without having any practical force.[17] There is, however, an immediately visible problem in this view when assessed in relation to corporate accountability: there is a possibility of a clash between the various sources of law,[18] whether soft or hard. Furthermore, priority or hierarchy between the various norms could dissolve in the quest for efficiency, and thus may lead to unintended fragmentation of international law. This clash could also lead to inconsistency. For example, a company may find itself signed to a trust seal or to an industry standard that qualitatively falls below the standard applicable under internationally recognized human rights law. The threat of this has been mitigated, however, by principle 12 of the UN Guiding Principles, which confirms businesses' responsibility to respect internationally recognized human rights, and by greater convergence among different soft-law instruments, such as the OECD Guidelines, CSR policies, and International Labour Organization (ILO) instruments.

13 *Ibid.*
14 Duplessis, n.11, p.7.
15 *Ibid.*, p.11.
16 G. Shaffer and M. Pollack, 'How Hard and Soft Law Interact in International Regulatory Governance: Alternatives, Complements and Antagonists' 2008, http://papers.ssrn.com/sol3/papers.cfm?abstract_id=1156867, p.2.
17 *Ibid.*
18 See *ibid.* for further details on the concept of antagonism.

The proposition is that "softer forms of legalization will be more attractive to states as contracting costs increase."[19] The failure to give legal effect to the UN sub-commission draft norms is a good example.[20] The Draft Norms on the Responsibilities of Transnational Corporations and Other Business Enterprises with Regard to Human Rights (UN Draft Norms), presented to the UN in 2003, were initially meant to be binding rules. However, the norms were highly specific and carried obligatory language commanding MNCs to observe certain rules. This, of course, made the norms resemble hard law more than soft law. General principle 1 of the UN Draft Norms, for example, stated that "transnational corporations and other business enterprises have the *obligation* to promote, secure the fulfillment of, respect, *ensure respect of*, and *protect* human rights recognized in international as well as national law" (emphasis added). Also, there was a great degree of precision, particularly in section D. With diverse views regarding the approach for holding MNCs accountable, it was very difficult to pass these norms as binding international law.[21] The greater demand for precision may lead states to avoid hard law, as it may be costly and difficult to create precise legal obligations.

Before we begin to analyze the relationship between soft law and accountability, it will be helpful to introduce two of the most important forms of soft law that have been used in order to define MNCs' commitment to human rights, namely CSR and the OECD Guidelines. These examples will identify the bidirectional relationship between soft law and contract law. It will be shown how this interrelation can transform soft law from non-binding norms into legally binding obligations. It is important to note here that the UN Guiding Principles are important for this debate and will be addressed from time to time. However, this chapter will not discuss the UN Guiding Principles in detail because they are the specific subject of chapter 4 of this book.

CSR

It is extremely difficult to conceptualize CSR or define its content. Because CSR policies are usually internally drafted documents, the scope and reach of

19 Contracting costs are higher where the legalization is binding. Since the cost of infringement is high, states will exercise caution when drafting the agreement. Contracting costs include, among other things, review and approval by expert committees; the cost of ratification by parliaments; usual negotiation costs between states; and arriving at acceptable detail. See Abbott and Snidal, n.9, p.436.

20 Sub-Commission on the Promotion and Protection of Human Rights, *The Norms on the Responsibilities of Transnational Corporations and Other Business Enterprises with Regard to Human Rights*, E/CN.4/Sub.2/2003/12/Rev.2, 26 August 2003.

21 For a critical discussion of the UN Draft Norms see, J. Ruggie, 'Business and Human Rights: The evolving International Agenda', 101 *American Journal of International Law* 819 (2007), p.825.

CSR varies from one corporation to another and from one context to another. Despite this, a broad consensus on general principles exists because many companies have acceded to internationally recognized principles such as the UN Global Compact, aligning themselves to universally accepted principles in the areas of labor law, human rights, environment, and anticorruption.[22]

While CSR is exclusively voluntary, many of the documents acknowledge the relevant legal obligations of corporations, for example in the areas of labor law, environmental regulations, and health and safety. Ethical CSR, on the other hand, consolidates a corporation's response to what is considered just and fair, but often in a way that would advance the corporation's own interests, and usually lying within the corporation's direct or indirect economic activities.[23] CSR could also encapsulate the corporation's moral obligations toward the environment and the community, which goes beyond fulfilling the corporation's economic goals, and where the corporation does not directly benefit.[24] Clearly in these instances, the main motive is philanthropy.[25] CSR has a wide scope that can encompass responsibility to consumers, workers, society, and the environment. Thus, CSR influences a wide range of relationships, including with employees, suppliers, consumers, and civil society.[26]

Corporate governance and CSR

The main argument in this section is that the traditional doctrine of corporate governance, which prioritizes accountability to shareholders over accountability to external stakeholders, undermines soft law measures designed to hold MNCs to account in relation to a breach of internationally recognized human rights.

While it is difficult to come up with a universal definition of corporate governance, it could be described as:

> a set of relationships between a company's management, its board, its shareholders and other stakeholders. Corporate governance also provides the structure through which the objectives of the company are set, and the means of attaining those objectives and monitoring performance are determined.[27]

22 *United Nations Global Compact*, www.unglobalcompact.org/ParticipantsAndStakeholders/un_agencies/index.html.

23 D. Jamali and R. Mirshak, 'Corporate Social Responsibility (CSR): Theory and Practice in a Developing Country Context', 72 *Journal of Business Ethics* 243–262 (2007), p.260.

24 *Ibid.*

25 *Ibid.*

26 See J. Zerk, *Multinationals and Corporate Social Responsibility, Limitations and Opportunities in International Law*, Cambridge University Press, Cambridge, 2011, p.31.

27 See OECD, *Principles of Corporate Governance*, 2004, www.oecd.org/daf/corporateaffairs/corporategovernanceprinciples/31557724.pdf.

The prevailing view in the UK and the United States is that corporations are accountable only according to the company's legal and economic obligations. According to this school of thought, a corporation's primary objective is the maximization of profit for its shareholders, and while doing so it must obey the law.[28] This approach was epitomized by Milton Friedman's famous statement that "the social responsibility of business is to increase its profits."[29] The principle of the maximization of wealth obliges board directors to act exclusively in the economic interests of shareholders. Accordingly, decisions that reduce the wealth of the corporation—such as philanthropy and in some respects CSR— are not permissible.[30]

A competing school of thought sees the private sector as the primary creator of wealth and growth, and thus argues that corporations must contribute to growth and opportunity. Like their shareholders, corporations are organs of society and therefore must bear the "obligations and duties of any good person or citizen."[31] Out of this grew the stakeholder[32] approach, where directors of the corporation, when exercising their powers, must take into account the interests of various stakeholders, including employees, creditors, and the community. Under this approach, the corporation is accountable to shareholders and other stakeholders.

Furthermore, while CSR is conceptually and legally distinct from corporate governance,[33] practice exhibits relational interdependence between the two

28 See F.H. Easterbrook and D.R. Fischel, *The Economic Structure of Corporate Law*, Harvard University Press, 1991, pp.35–39.

29 M. Friedman, 'The Social Responsibility of Business Is to Increase its Profits', *New York Times Magazine*, 13 September 1970.

30 See V. Harper Ho, '"Enlightened Shareholder Value": Corporate Governance Beyond the Shareholder-Stakeholder Divide', 36 *Iowa Journal of Corporate Law* 59 (2010), p.73.

31 See Jamali and Mirshak, n.23, p.245, where a good summary of this view is provided.

32 According to Freeman, "A stakeholder in an organization is (by definition) any group or individual who can affect or is affected by the achievement of the organization's objectives." R.E. Freeman, *Strategic Management: A Stakeholder Approach*, Cambridge University Press, Cambridge, 1984, p.46.

33 While the meaning of corporate governance may vary from one system of law to another, it was defined by the Cadbury Report in the UK as "the system by which business corporations are directed and controlled. The corporate governance structure specifies the distribution of rights and responsibilities among different corporate participants in the corporation, such as, the board, the managers, shareholders and other stakeholders, and spells out the rules and procedures for making decisions on corporate affairs. By doing this, it also provides the structure through which the company objectives are set, and the means of attaining those objectives and monitoring performance." See G. Barwick, 'Controlling Business', 153 *New Law Journal* 674 (2003), p.674. See also A. Gill, 'Corporate Governance as Social Responsibility: A Research Agenda', 26 *Berkeley Journal of International Law* 452 (2008), p.456, according to whom corporate governance is "the set of processes, customs, policies, laws and institutions affecting the way in which a corporation is directed, administered or controlled."

that may de facto have influence on the decision making of the corporation.[34] In addition, a company cannot have effective corporate governance without responding to the needs of its external stakeholders, such as the community.[35] Thus there are "clear complementarities between corporate governance and CSR by considering business as responsible *vis a vis* a complex web of interrelated stakeholders that sustain and add value to the corporation."[36] In the UK, for example, this approach has been enforced by the Companies Act 2006. According to section 172(4), a company's director, in addition to looking after the interest of shareholders, must take into consideration a corporation's impacts on the community and the environment.[37] While the principle of the primacy of shareholders (maximization of wealth to shareholders) continues to dominate UK corporate law, it can be argued that section 172 creates an indirect accountability by directors to stakeholders.[38] It is, however, indisputable that a corporation's legal obligations to shareholders override any voluntary responsibility toward external stakeholders.

CSR generates a weak form of accountability

It is important to note that when following Abbott and Snidal's definition of hard law, it is not difficult to see the voluntary nature of most CSRs. In particular, most CSR initiatives do not provide for a neutral third party with the authority to hold the MNC to account.[39] Thus, CSR will struggle to conform to the traditional meaning of accountability.[40] However, it is possible for an MNC to adhere to a group-based or industry-wide code of conduct, such as agreeing to standards set by a trade association.[41] This type

34 See Zerk, n.26 pp.31–32, where the author argues that CSR and corporate governance are distinct. This author holds the view that while the two are conceptually different, some overlap and complementariness between the two concepts nevertheless exist.

35 D. Jamali, A. Safieddine and M. Rabbath, 'Corporate Governance and Corporate Social Responsibility Synergies and Interrelationships', 16 *Corporate Governance* 443–459 (2008), p.457.

36 *Ibid.*, p.446. See Jamali and Mirshak, n.23 for a general discussion of the interrelation between corporate governance and CSR.

37 See also OECD Guidelines, n.5, article IV.

38 Harper Ho, n.30, p.79.

39 Rio Tinto, for example, has a very detailed CSR policy that takes into account human rights and environmental risk. However, the policy lacks any form of obligation outside the corporate structure. Indeed, the accountability in this instance is greatly internal. See www.riotinto.com/ourapproach/6009_corporate_social_responsibilty_csr_related_memberships.asp.

40 Mulgan, n.7.

41 See a detailed review of this approach in S.P. Sethi, *Setting Global Standards, Guidelines for Creating Codes of Conduct in Multinational Corporations*, John Wiley & Sons, Hoboken, NJ, 2003.

of self-regulation could empower an administrative body to investigate and take actions against MNCs that have breached the terms of the code.[42] This way, the MNC may be obliged to adhere to the code of conduct and it may be subject to monitoring by that association and possibly a form of external authority.[43]

Holding corporations to their CSR policies

Despite the clear soft nature of CSR, it may nonetheless create some binding obligations. An MNC might, for example, under certain circumstances be held to its promises to consumers or other traders,[44] such as in the decision of the Supreme Court of California in the *Kasky v Nike* case.[45] The case concerned the publication of articles in the *Financial Times* and the *New York Times*, among others, arguing that Nike breached its own CSR policies in factories where Nike products were made. Allegedly, in these factories, workers were paid less than the applicable local minimum wage; worked overtime; were subjected to verbal, physical, and sexual abuse; and worked under dangerous health and safety conditions.[46]

In response to this adverse publicity, Nike advertised and made statements to the California consuming public that the allegations were false and misleading. Nike claimed the following:

(a) workers who make NIKE products are protected from and not subjected to corporal punishment and/or sexual abuse;
(b) NIKE products are made in accordance with applicable governmental laws and regulations governing wages and hours;
(c) NIKE products are made in accordance with applicable laws and regulations governing health and safety conditions;
(d) Nike pays average line-workers double-the-minimum wage in Southeast Asia;
(e) workers who produce NIKE products receive free meals and health care;
(f) the GoodWorks International (Andrew Young) report proves that NIKE is doing a good job and "operating morally"; and

42 See Zerk, n.26, p.38.
43 *Ibid.* in relation to ABTA (a travel association) code of conduct. R. Baldwin and M. Cave, *Understanding Regulation: Theory, Strategy and Practice*, OUP, Oxford, 1999, pp.45–46; here, the authors pertain that self-regulation is characterized by low precision while benefiting from the overview of "general law."
44 See C. Glinski, 'Self-Regulation of Transnational Corporations; Neither Meaningless in Law Nor Voluntary', in S. MacLeod (ed.), *Global Governance and the Quest for Justice*, Volume 2, Hart Publishing, Oxford, 2006 (197–220), pp.198–202.
45 45 P.3d 243 (2002).
46 *Ibid.*

(g) NIKE guarantees a "living wage" for all workers who make NIKE products.[47]

These statements, designed to boost or at least maintain Nike's strong financial performance, were later shown to be misleading. For example, the claimant submitted evidence that corporal punishment was widely used in factories where Nike products were made; there was sexual harassment against women; workers worked long hours and received wages in breach of national regulation; and Nike violated health and safety regulations. Nike agreed to settle the case for US$1.5 million and made an undertaking to monitor workplace conditions in factories where its products are made.[48] Therefore, CSR policies, while in principle voluntary, can lead to accountability where they are violated and the corporation uses them to create a false image of itself.

Beyond *Kasky* and on the other side of the Atlantic, European Union (EU) law may hold corporations accountable for misleading CSR policies. Under article 5(4)(a) of the EU Unfair Terms Commercial Practices Directive, which prohibits unfair business practices, a business's practice is unfair if it is misleading to consumers. Article 6(2)(b) states:

> A commercial practice shall also be regarded as misleading if, in its factual context, taking account of all its features and circumstances, it causes or is likely to cause the average consumer to take a transactional decision that he would not have taken otherwise, and it involves:
>
> . . .
>
> (b) non-compliance by the trader with commitments contained in *codes of conduct* (emphasis added) by which the trader has undertaken to be bound, where:
>   (i) the commitment is not aspirational but is firm and is capable of being verified, and
>   (ii) the trader indicates in a commercial practice that he is bound by the code of conduct.[49]

A code of conduct is defined in article 2(f) as

> an agreement or set of rules not imposed by law, regulation or administrative provision of a Member State which defines the behaviour

47 *Ibid.*, pp.247–248. See also www.corpwatch.org/article.php?id=3448.

48 See www.business-humanrights.org/Categories/Lawlawsuits/Lawsuitsregulatoryaction/LawsuitsSelectedcases/NikelawsuitKaskyvNikeredenialoflabourabuses for more details.

49 Directive 2005/29/EC of the European Parliament and of the Council concerning unfair business-to-consumer commercial practices in the internal market and amending OJ L 149, 11.6.2005, pp.22–39.

of traders who undertake to be bound by the code in relation to one or more particular commercial practices or business sectors.

This definition encompasses CSR.[50]

Kasky and the EU Directive on Unfair Commercial Practices demonstrate that MNCs are bound to comply with laws that protect consumers from unfair commercial practices. Thus, MNCs must not falsely pretend to be committed to CSR and must ensure full compliance with their promise to be socially responsible.

OECD guidelines

The OECD Guidelines are a form of soft law that is addressed to multinational enterprises "operating in or from adhering countries."[51] They are in essence an expression of the shared values of OECD members, and represent an aspiration that multinational enterprises contribute to social and economic development in the countries where they operate. The OECD Guidelines express commitment to core labor standards of the ILO, the Global Compact, and the Universal Declaration of Human Rights.

The first guidelines were introduced in 1976. They underwent a number of revisions, most recently in 2011. The new edition of the OECD Guidelines is divided into two parts. Part I contains general concepts and principles, and specific sections dealing with MNCs' responsibilities in relation to human rights, environment, combating bribery, and taxation, among other things. Part II contains detailed implementation procedures. Of particular importance to corporate accountability is the National Contact Point (NCP) mechanism established under section I of part II. In this section, adhering countries are asked to establish NCPs, which will be responsible for "undertaking promotional activities, handling enquiries, and contributing to the resolution of issues that arise relating to the implementation of the Guidelines in specific instances."[52]

The OECD Guidelines are modeled on internationally recognized principles and have implemented the UN's "Protect, Respect and Remedy Framework."[53] This should, in theory, incentivize corporations to adopt best practice.[54] However, the guidelines suffer from two weaknesses. First, their implementation procedures do not empower NCPs to make interim orders to

50 O. de Schutter, A. Ramasastry, M. Taylor and R. Thompson, *Human Rights Due Diligence: The Role of States*, A Project of: International Corporate Accountability Roundtable, European Coalition for Corporate Justice, and Canadian Network on Corporate Accountability, 2012, p.40.

51 See OECD Guidelines, n.5.

52 *Ibid.*, Part I.

53 *Ibid.*

54 RAID, *Fit for purpose?* 2008, http://oecdwatch.org/files/raid-fit-for-purpose-report.

prevent imminent threats to environment and human rights resulting in breach of the guidelines.[55] Second, victims of an MNC's breach would struggle to compel the corporation to repair his or her loss. For example, a study evaluating the effectiveness of existing systems of redress to victims of human rights abuse by UK corporations found the NCP procedure a poor investment of resources due to enforcement and procedural weaknesses.[56] Furthermore, victims have no standing before NCPs and therefore are unable to approach them directly in relation to human rights violations that they have suffered at the hand of an MNC. Practice under the previous versions of the OECD Guidelines moreover showed that NCPs had not been effective. In as many as 85 reported cases between 2000 and 2008, except for five cases, NCPs failed to reach a "meaningful and effective" resolution of the alleged environmental law and/or human rights violations that were raised by the complainants.[57]

Failure to make final statements jeopardizes the probability of resolving the dispute. According to Human Rights Watch, "an impending NCP final statement" and its recommendations can push contending parties to resolve their dispute, even without binding legal force. Final statements typically recount events leading to the complaint, positions of the parties, actions of the NCP, and recommendations or final outcomes of the case. By assessing companies' performance under the guidelines, NCP final statements hold global firms accountable for their behavior.[58]

Some suggest that the OECD Guidelines and the NCP system have been developing from a formally non-binding system to a system exhibiting the "characteristics of a binding governance system."[59] In order to differentiate it from the discussion above relating to soft law, it is argued that the OECD system functions in a:

> regulatory context in which municipal and international law converge within hybrid systems of regulation that are not formally law but provide

55 See OECD Guidelines, n.5, Part II.

56 London School of Economics and CORE, *The Reality of Rights, Barriers to Accessing Remedies when Business Operate beyond Borders*, London, 2009. Referenced in OECD Watch, *Assessing the Contribution of the OECD Guidelines for Multinational Enterprises to Responsible Business Conduct*, June 2010, p.9, http://oecdwatch.org/publications-en/Publication_3550/?searchterm=Assessing%20the%20contribution%20of%20the%20OECD%20Guidelines%20for%20Multinational%20Enterprises%20to%20Responsible%20Business%20Conduct.

57 RAID, n.54.

58 See statement of A. Ganesan before the US Bureau of Economic, Energy, and Business Affairs, *US: Review of US National Contact Point for the OECD Guidelines for Multinational Enterprises*, www.hrw.org/news/2010/11/08/us-review-us-national-contact-point-oecd-guidelines-multinational-enterprises.

59 For an excellent discussion, see L.C. Backer, 'Rights and Accountability in Development ("raid") v Das Air and Global Witness v Afrimex: Small Steps towards an Autonomous Transnational Legal System for the Regulation of Multinational Corporations', 10 *Melbourne Journal of International Law* 258 (2009), pp.284–289.

> a functionally similar normative framework. . . . Ultimately, under the guise of "soft" law, the OECD may be able to construct a system of customary law and practice as binding as any hard law system.[60]

The above construction should be viewed with some suspicion. First, the evidence substantiating the convergence between domestic and international law is based on a limited sample from the practice of the UK NCP, which is not representative of the work of other NCPs. Second, the prospect of a convergence between international and domestic law may lead to inconsistency of decisions and a clash between competing norms, whether domestic, international, or soft law. For example, in *Global Witness v Afrimex* (28 August 2008), the UK NCP panel found that Afrimex, which was incorporated in the UK, exercised sufficient control over a company in the Democratic Republic of Congo (DRC) to allow the NCP to attribute an unlawful act of the affiliated DRC company to Afrimex (paying tax to rebels, which ultimately contributed to the conflict in the DRC),[61] despite both companies being separate corporations. This de facto amounted to an avoidance of the corporate veil, which is a departure from the DRC's principles of corporate law.

While this is welcomed by individuals who are harmed by corporate non-compliance with human rights, it nonetheless amounts to an unjustified departure from basic principles of corporate law. Under the principle of "corporate entity," which the NCP in Afrimex ignored, an incorporated company has a legal personality that is separate from its members.[62] In correlation to this, the corporate veil can be pierced only "where special circumstances exist indicating that it is a mere facade concealing the true facts."[63] Whether or not the DRC entity was a mere facade concealing the true facts, it is clear from at least the jurisprudence of the English courts that piercing the corporate veil should be exercised with caution, and only after careful reasoning and consideration of the facts, an approach that was not followed in Afrimex.

Relationship between accountability and soft law

There are two possible dimensions in which soft law may have a bearing on the ability of the law to manage corporate behavior. The first dimension, which is essentially preventive, relates to managing the MNC's behavior in the strict sense. This is where the corporation must be proactive through impact assessment, due diligence, and overall commitment to internationally

60 *Ibid.*, p.287.

61 For further details, see the UK NCP final statement, http://oecdwatch.org/cases/Case_114?searchterm=global+witness.

62 B. Pettet, *Company Law*, Pearson Longman, Harlow, 2nd edn, 2005, pp.23–25.

63 *Adams v Cape Industries plc* [1990] BCC 786, p.822.

recognized human rights. For example, the OECD Guidelines stipulate in general principles 1 and 2 that corporations should "[c]ontribute to economic, environmental and social progress with a view to achieving sustainable development" and should "respect the internationally recognised human rights of those affected by their activities." The human rights due diligence promoted by the UN Guiding Principles equally emphasize this preventive dimension.[64]

In the second dimension, which is more reactive, soft law may require an MNC that has acted contrary to its responsibilities under soft law, and has caused harm, to offer a remedy to the victims. For example, principle 22 of the UN Guiding Principles stipulates that "[w]here business enterprises identify that they have caused or contributed to adverse impacts, they should provide for or cooperate in their remediation through legitimate processes." Principle 29 of the UN Guiding Principle requires corporations to "establish or participate in effective operational-level grievance mechanisms for individuals and communities who may be adversely impacted."

The use of soft law could be as effective as the use of hard law in terms of prescribing the behavior of the corporation, but would need certain adjustments to make it as effective in controlling infringements of the law. Soft law struggles to conform to the traditional concept of accountability and may lack an external authority that could hold the corporation to account and command it to repair past or prevent imminent breaches of the law. Even where some form of external authority exists, as with the NCPs, the lack of individual complaints mechanisms plus the lack of providing and enforcing remedies mean that some soft law falls short of remediating affected individuals.

Moreover, individuals harmed by an MNC's conduct would be astonished to learn that the satisfaction of their remedy is dependent on the voluntary action of the MNC. Therefore, to the victim, soft law represents uncertainty about available remedies and the failure of his or her home state to protect or fulfill the person's human rights[65] where adequate reparation is not voluntarily forthcoming.

However, soft law, such as CSR, can still play an important role in supporting the remediation of victims. Despite their voluntary nature, the UN Guiding Principles may yet place significant pressure on corporations to express their CSR in more binding and precise language. Furthermore, principle 29 of the UN Guiding Principles stipulates that MNCs should establish grievance mechanisms accessible by individuals harmed by an MNC's

64 UN Guiding Principles, n.3, particularly principles 17–19.

65 On the state's duty under international law, see, for example, Basic Principles and Guidelines on the Right to a Remedy and Reparations for Victims of Gross Violations of International Human Rights Law and Serious Violations of International Humanitarian Law, adopted and proclaimed by the UN General Assembly resolution 60/147 of 16 December 2005, title VIII.

conduct. In accordance with principle 31(f) of the UN Guiding Principles, this envisaged grievance mechanism should be "right-compatible"—in other words, "ensuring that outcomes and remedies accord with internationally recognized human rights." An MNC can expressly commit itself to adhering to its CSR when engaging its grievance mechanism. With this, CSR is transformed from soft law to an instrument exhibiting some of the values of hard law. But in order to make sure that the mechanism adheres to basic principles of legality, equality before the adjudicator, and due process, a grievance mechanism would need to be impartial and independent of the MNC and all concerned parties. Therefore, such a grievance mechanism would be more forceful if administered by an independent and impartial external authority. Under this construction, soft law could be as effective as hard law in providing a remedy to victims of MNC human rights violations.

Corporate accountability under tort law

An MNC may find itself accountable under ordinary principles of civil wrong. The most basic form is founded in national law. Under tort law, an individual is entitled "so far as money can achieve this, to be restored to the position he would have been in if he had not suffered the injury of which complaint is made."[66]

In the United States, federal courts have dealt with cases brought under the ATS in relation to torts committed in breach of the law of nations. MNCs have been found liable for a direct tort (primary liability), such as in the case of *Pfizer Inc. v Abdullahi*,[67] where Pfizer, a US-based pharmaceutical company, violated a customary international law norm prohibiting non-consensual medical experimentation on humans in Nigeria. Secondary liability is also possible under the ATS, where US courts have found MNCs liable for aiding and abetting torts committed in breach of the laws of nation.[68] This body of law, including the doctrine of complicity, is thoroughly discussed elsewhere in this book[69] and therefore falls outside the scope of this chapter.

Numerous cases have been brought before national courts in claims for compensatory damage for a harm that was caused directly or indirectly by the MNC. Examples spawn from claims in relation to environmental harm causing irreparable harm to individuals[70] or causing damage to the livelihood of local communities, breach of health and safety conditions at work, and

66 *Anufrijeva v Southwark London BC* [2003] EWCA Civ 1406, [2003] 3 FCR 673, paras.54–55.

67 562 F.3d 163 (2nd Circuit, 2009).

68 See, for example, *Khulumani v Barclay Nat'l Bank Ltd.*, 504 F.3d 254 (2nd Circuit, 2007).

69 See chapter 3 of this book.

70 *Yao Essaie Motto & Ors v Trafigura Ltd* [2009] EWHC 1246 (QB). The case was settled out of court.

occupational injury or disease from an MNC's negligence.[71] For example, in *Yao Essaie Motto & Ors v Trafigura Ltd*,[72] a lawsuit was brought before the English High Court in relation to the unlawful dumping of toxic waste in the Ivory Cost by the company Trafigura. Over 30,000 victims who lived near the disposal site suffered serious bodily harm, such as nausea, skin illnesses, and breathlessness. The case settled out of court and Trafigura agreed to pay each victim approximately US$1,500. In parallel to the court proceedings, criminal charges were brought against Trafigura in the Netherlands, where it was charged with the offense of illegally exporting hazardous waste outside the Netherlands. The company was found guilty and was ordered to pay a fine of US$1 million.[73]

Another case brought before the English High Court concerned a claim for reparation in relation to harm suffered by farmers in Colombia that was allegedly caused by a consortium led by BP during the construction of an oil pipeline. The farmers alleged that BP benefited from paramilitaries who were employed to guard the pipeline. The paramilitaries, according to the claimants, engaged in unlawful activities that caused distress to the local population and suppressed their natural right to oppose the construction of the pipeline. Farmers claimed that BP's unlawful conduct destroyed "their way of life leading to destitution for them and their families." BP and the claimants settled the case out of court.[74]

Almost exclusively, the above listed tortious or delictual causes of action had their jurisprudential basis in national law. This has made human rights litigation highly dependent on the peculiarities of the legal system under which the claim is brought. This might cause problems in that human rights usually receive only incidental protection under national tort law in an action brought between private parties. For example, common law holds a corporation accountable for any harm that it negligently caused to individuals in breach of its duty of care. A claimant must demonstrate a duty of care owed to him by the MNC, a breach of that duty, and causality between the harm caused to him and the unlawful act of the tortfeasor.[75] Only to the extent that a claim fits into these narrow legal constraints can violations of human rights be the subject of claims for redress under tort law.

71 See the House of Lords' decision in *Lubbe and Others v Cape Plc* [2000] All ER 268 in relation to injuries caused to employees of the defendant at its South African asbestos mining and milling activities, and diseases sustained by communities living near Cape's asbestos operation.

72 [2009] EWHC 1246 (QB).

73 See *Trafigura* lawsuits which were brought before the English High Court. For further details, see www.business-humanrights.org/LegalPortal/Home/Countrywherelawsuitfiled/EuropeCentralAsia#86277.

74 Business and Human Rights Resource Centre, *Case Profile: BP lawsuit (re Colombia)*, www.business-humanrights.org/Categories/Lawlawsuits/Lawsuitsregulatoryaction/LawsuitsSelectedcases/BPlawsuitreColombia.

75 *Donoghue v Stevenson* [1932] AC 562.

The majority of tortious claims involve a tortfeasor and a victim domiciled in the same state, and concern a local harm. For example, in the *AngloGold Ashanti* silicosis lawsuit, a South African miner brought a lawsuit against his former employer in relation to a lung disease that he developed while working at one of the defendant's mines. The claimant passed away a few weeks before the final decision was made, which was in his favor.[76] Many causes of action, however, are brought at the MNC's place of incorporation or domicile, by individuals located outside that forum, for a harm that was sustained where the claimant is normally domiciled.

The *Cape* case is a good example of a case pursued outside the country in which the harm occurred. Claims were brought against the parent company in England by employees of its South African subsidiaries, who accused it of being directly responsible for breaching its duty of care owed to the claimants. The facts of the case concerned South African claimants who had suffered from asbestos-related disease caused by the operation of the company's subsidiary in South Africa. They argued that Cape's operations generated asbestos dust 30 times the British legal limit and constituted a breach of its duty of care since the workers were not provided with adequate protective gear.[77]

Thus, one could see the importance of tort litigation in ensuring MNCs' accountability to victims of human rights violations. The content of tort law, however, may vary from one jurisdiction to another, and often victims must litigate at a foreign forum. Crucially, tort law is able to capture only a human rights violation that fits into narrow legal constraints of what jurisprudentially qualifies as an actionable claim in tort. Tort law will normally offer compensatory damages to victims, a limitation with important ramifications for MNC accountability in the context of transitional justice.

Improving accountability through the contractualization of human rights

Contracts play an important role in making corporations accountable for violations of human rights. This section explores two types of relationships that can normatively influence MNCs' accountability under contract law. The first type concerns a direct contractual relationship between the host state and the MNC. This starts at the pre-contractual phase, where the MNCs and host states identify human rights risks. Here, host states and MNCs must "integrate the management of human rights risks into investment project contract negotiations."[78] Thus, the parties should refrain from including

76 *Mankayi v AngloGold Ashanti Ltd* (CCT 40/10) [2011] ZACC 3.

77 *Lubbe and Others v Cape Plc* [2000] All ER 268.

78 See J. Ruggie's Report to the UN Human Rights Council, *Principles for Responsible Contracts: Integrating the Management of Human Rights Risks into State-Investor Contract Negotiations: Guidance for Negotiators*, A/HRC/17/31/Add.3, 25 May 2011, para.1.

contractual obligations that could have a chilling effect on the protection and respect of human rights, such as the use of stabilization clauses that:

> if used, should be carefully drafted so that any protections for investors against future changes in law do not interfere with the State's bona fide efforts to implement laws, regulations or policies, in a nondiscriminatory manner, in order to meet its human rights obligations.[79]

Or the investment contract can include investors' promises to abide by health and safety regulations, ILO labor standards, and the responsible use of security forces. For example, in the Chad pipeline project, the investor agreed that its use of water resources would not prejudice water supplies for the local community.[80]

Another point of entry for human rights can be seen in MNCs' positive contractual obligations to realize human rights. In some investment contracts, MNCs commit themselves to fulfilling social and environmental obligations. Examples include promises to provide adequate education, health clinics, railways, and adequate housing to employees and their families. Contracts can thus have the effect of both reinforcing corporations' responsibility to respect and refrain from harming human rights, and creating proactive obligations to promote human rights that go beyond even the most far-reaching soft-law standards.

Moreover, support for the contractualization of human rights can be achieved under national law, as in articles 101 and 102 of the proposal for the Minerals Law in Afghanistan, which require mining companies to prepare a community development agreement with affected communities before their license can be approved by the mining ministry.[81] There are two advantages to this approach. First, a community development agreement enables an MNC to understand the needs of the local community and respond to the risks of the investment from the view point of the local community. Second, accountability is reinforced because Afghanistan's Mining Ministry can refuse to award a license to the mining MNC that has not complied with the community development agreement. Without a license, an MNC would not be able to engage in mining operations in Afghanistan.

The second type of relationship concerns a separate contract between a project finance bank or an export credit agency on the one hand and an MNC on the other, under which the corporation undertakes to comply with

79 *Ibid.*, para.30.

80 See *Consortium—Chad Convention for the Development of Oil Fields*, article 4.3, in S. Leader, 'Human Rights, Risks, and New Strategies for Global Investment', 9 *Journal of Economic and International Law* 657 (2006), p.680.

81 A proposal for Minerals Law 1391, Islamic Republic of Afghanistan, chapter 16, articles 101 and 102.

social and environmental obligations. For example, under the Equator Principles,[82] which were established in 2003 and have been endorsed by many commercial and public banks, MNCs wishing to borrow from member banks to finance an investment project must complete an environmental and social impact assessment, and must promise to comply with certain social and environmental commitments.[83] The Equator Principles are "based on World Bank and IFC (International Finance Corporation) environmental and social policies and guidelines."[84] Accountability is strengthened by requiring, under principles 8 and 9, that an independent third party monitor the MNC's compliance with the principles and that the MNC promise, in the project finance documents, to respect certain social and environmental commitments.[85] This is important because banks can treat the corporation's breach of the covenants as an event of default under the loan agreement.[86] However, despite the accountability measures put in place, receiving project finance from adoptees of the Equator Principles is not a guarantee of compliance with environmental and social standards. In the Baku-Tbilisi-Ceyhan pipeline project, for example, non-governmental organizations found "127 violations of the IFC Policies on environmental assessment, natural habitats, indigenous peoples, involuntary resettlement and cultural property."[87]

Challenges of the contractualization of human rights

While contractualization of human rights must be encouraged, it may nonetheless pose a few challenges. First, contracts that primarily create *in personam* rights and that are essentially individualistic are being used in order to create obligations that are not easily described in contractual terms. A similar debate was captured in relation to whether human rights and private law are compatible;[88] some argued that the "insertion of fundamental rights into private law engenders problems of . . . translation."[89] This is

82 For detailed information on the Equator Principles, see www.equator-principles.com/.

83 R.P. Alford, 'Arbitrating Human Rights', 83 *Notre Dame Law Review* 505 (2008), p.534.

84 N. Affolder, 'Cachet Not Cash: Another Sort Of World Bank Group Borrowing', 14 *Michigan State Journal of International Law* 141 (2006), p.154.

85 Alford, n.83, p.535.

86 Equator Principles, *Guidance to Epfis on Incorporating Environmental and Social Considerations into Loan Documentation*, www.equator-principles.com/resources/ep_loan_document_guidance_note.pdf.

87 Baku-Ceyhan Campaign, *Evaluation of the Compliance of the Baku-Tbilisi-Ceyhan (BTC) Pipeline with the Equator Principles*, October 2003, www.bakuceyhan.org.uk/publications/Equator_Principles.pdf, cited in Affolder, n.84, p.157.

88 F. Raday, 'Privatising Human Rights and the Abuse of Power', 13 *Canadian Journal of Law and Jurisprudence* 103–137 (2000), p.103.

89 See C. Hugh, *On the (In)compatibility of Human Rights Discourse and Private Law*, LSE working Paper 2012, www.lse.ac.uk/collections/law/wps/WPS2012-07_Collins.pdf, in relation to the transplant of human rights into the private sphere.

relevant here because human rights have traditionally been invoked against a state[90] and have been interpreted bearing in mind its wider socioeconomic objectives. When applied in the private context, human rights obligations might be interpreted differently, and to a lower standard than that which is required under international law. The problem may be exacerbated if the investment contract calls for an application of the contractualized human rights in accordance with acceptable industry standards. For example, Sheldon Leader has argued that:

> the requirements of health and safety, respect for land rights; gender rights; and environmental standards can then adjust up and down in accordance with commercial pressures, so long as the bulk of projects around the world stay in step with one another.[91]

However, given that an investment contract should be treated as subordinate to human rights, in principle it should not dilute the content of the contractualized human rights or the methods and standards of redress in case of a violation.[92] One way of averting such an undesirable result is to include a choice-of-law agreement in the investment contract that would subject the human rights commitment to international human rights standards and, where applicable, ILO standards and those contained in other relevant treaties.

Besides the translation problems associated with the contractualization of human rights, a contract may not have sufficient tools to give full effect to human rights. For example, the type of remedy could be limited to those normally available under contract law, such as damages. Following the reasoning above, which submits that contracts should be viewed as subordinate to human rights, the remedy that is available for a breach of an internationally recognized human right should be available for a breach of the contractualized human right, and if in doubt, the investment contract could make express provisions for the realization of this objective.

Accountability, contractualization, and safeguarding third parties' rights

When returning to the main theme of this chapter, it is difficult to locate in contractualization all features of the traditional concept of accountability. This is explained in part by the autonomous nature of a contract. In the majority of instances, parties adhere to those obligations as a matter of

90 See Raday, n.88.
91 See Leader, n.80, p.676.
92 *Ibid.*, p.668.

self-interest. Further, there is no competent external authority that could sanction the MNC for an action or inaction unless a judicial action or a claim under arbitration is brought by one of the contractual parties.

It is important here to identify to whom the corporation is accountable. Under the contractualization of human rights, accountability operates between the contractual parties, each owing obligations to the other. The contract creates rights and obligations between the host state and the MNC. Under common-law torts, on the other hand, accountability is owed to a reasonably foreseeable victim or group of victims. Under the latter, therefore, individuals harmed by an MNC's conduct could seek to impose this standard in national courts, administrative bodies, or special tribunals. Under contractualization, unless there is an external obligatory rule that empowers the beneficiary to do so, third-party beneficiaries may be barred under the doctrine of privity to enforce the benefits bestowed on them by the investment contract.[93] The host state, however, can exceptionally sue the corporation for the breach and require compensation to cover the loss to third parties, or demand specific performance of the contract, requiring the MNC to confer the promised benefits on individuals or the community.[94]

It is therefore important to safeguard the rights of third-party beneficiaries by ensuring that the body of law that governs the contract permits them to hold the MNC accountable to its obligations under the contract, such as in the approach in England and Wales under the Rights of Third Parties Act.[95] This can be done by expressly stipulating in the investment contract that third-party beneficiaries will be able to enforce the terms of the contract.[96] An example where third-party empowerment was not achieved can be found in the "Human Rights Undertaking" commitment of the Baku-Tbilisi-Ceyhan pipeline project, which stated that nothing in the Human Rights Undertaking:

> express or implied, shall confer a benefit on, or grant any right to enforce any of its terms to, any Person other than each of the Government of the Azerbaijan Republic, the Government of Georgia and the Government of the Republic of Turkey and the Contracts (Rights of Third Parties) Act 1999 shall not apply.[97]

93 For English law, see *Tweddle v Atkinson* (1861) 1 B & S 393, p.398.

94 *Panatown Ltd v Alfred McAlpine Construction Ltd* [2001] 1 AC 518 (HL).

95 See UK Contracts (Rights of Third Parties) Act 1999.

96 *Ibid.*, section 1(1)(a).

97 Host Government Agreement between Turkey and the Consortium led by British Petroleum (2000), Human Rights Undertaking, article 4.

Corporate accountability and transitional justice

It remains to be discussed what the features and trends of corporate accountability identified so far may contribute when thinking about how corporations can be held to account in the context of transitional justice. Transitional justice is not a special kind of justice but rather an approach to achieving justice in times of transition. One of its objectives is to repair victims of past human rights violations and provide a framework for accountability.[98] This section will demonstrate the relevance of corporate accountability to the four processes of transitional justice: justice process, reparation process, truth-telling process, and institutional reform process.[99] Most of the emphasis is placed on the reparation process, which requires MNCs to be accountable to victims for the violation of their human rights. Furthermore, it will be shown how soft law and contract law, if well drafted, can be sensitive to transitional justice conditions and needs.

Where corporations played a role in the commission of mass atrocities during conflict or repression, the reactive nature of human rights-related tort litigation could make an important contribution to establishing an MNC's potential role in the reparation and truth-telling processes. Damages, which are the usual remedy under tort causes of action, could provide reparation to victims and help communities cope with their basic needs. They might also contribute to promoting reconciliation and long-term peace.[100] Moreover, deterrence, one of the *raisons d'être* of civilian accountability, can inhibit the repetition of a similar unlawful conduct or atrocity.[101] Because civil wrong claims strengthen the truth-telling process through establishing the violations in court, this might eventually support the institutional reform process by leading, for example, to stronger regulation and control of corporations.

The *Cape* case[102] demonstrates the importance of tort as a source of accountability. The defendant in this case benefited financially by operating in a state where the health and safety of black workers was of little value, and tort law was used by the victims to substantially complement the reparations owed by the state to the victims at a time when transitional justice mechanisms struggled to achieve corporate accountability in South Africa.[103]

98 P. de Greiff, *Report of the Special Rapporteur on the promotion of truth, justice, reparation and guarantees of non-recurrence*, 21st session, A/HRC/21/46, 9 August 2012, paras.19–20.

99 See chapter 1 of this book.

100 E. Harper, 'Delivering Justice in the Wake of Mass Violence: New Approaches to Transitional Justice', 10 *Journal of Conflict and Security Law* 149 (2005).

101 D. Hollywood, 'The Search for Post-Conflict Justice in Iraq: A Comparative Study of Transitional Justice Mechanisms and their Applicability to Post-Saddam Iraq', 33 *Brooklyn Journal of International Law* 59 (2007), p.92. See also, E. Posner and A. Vermeule, 'Transitional Justice as Ordinary Justice', 117 *Harvard Law Review* 761 (2004), p.792.

102 *Lubbe and Others v Cape Plc* [2000] All ER 268.

103 For further discussion of the South African approach to corporate accountability in the context of transitional justice, see chapter 8 of this book.

Tort law, however, has its limits. First, since the available remedy under tort is usually a financial measure, tort law does not offer the full range of remedies that are particularly important to transitional justice, such as guarantees of non-repetition, rehabilitation policies, memorial initiatives, and formal apologies.[104] Moreover, human rights litigation frequently concerns a local harm litigated in a foreign forum or fora against the ancillary accomplice, but not the principal tortfeasor—in most cases, the state.[105] Thus, in this scenario, and particularly in causes of action based on complicity, the process of reparation might be strengthened through tort actions but must be complemented by other transitional justice mechanisms, such as the investigation of crime and criminal prosecution, and reparation by the state. It is important to note here that a foreign jurisdiction seized of the tortious action may not fully appreciate the context of transitional justice at the place where the harm occurred. For example, a US court seized of a claim under the ATS in relation to a tort committed in South Africa may not fully understand the implications of its decision and reasoning for the transitional justice processes in South Africa.

Soft law could strengthen democratic values, such as the ability of businesses and all stakeholders to cooperate in reaching a resolution, instead of framing their dispute within the coercive nature of hard law. It could furthermore encourage truth telling and ultimately lead to institutional reform, and thereby help achieve the goals of transitional justice.

It needs to be borne in mind that the effect of MNC accountability on transitional justice is not yet well established; it is an area of law that conceptually and normatively continues to evolve. According to the UN Special Rapporteur on Transitional Justice, there exist "bidirectional relations between reparations and the other transitional justice measures" that still require a better understanding.[106] The degree of uncertainty is thus particularly high, not just regarding the relationship among different transitional justice mechanisms but also when it comes to conceptualizing the role of corporate accountability in this context. Soft law might then be better suited than hard law to adapt as the understanding of how best to integrate corporate accountability in the transitional justice processes develops.[107] Soft law potentially could combine a number of initiatives that may contribute to achieving coherency when holding corporations to account in the context of transitional justice. For example, soft law could support the creation of an alternative dispute resolution that is committed to reparation

104 See chapter 5 of this book.

105 Alford, n.83, p.506.

106 de Greiff, n.98, paras.22–27.

107 Abbott and Snidal, n.9, p.444; V. Petrova, 'At the Frontiers of the Rush for Blue Gold: Water Privatization and the Human Right to Water', 31 *Brooklyn Journal of International Law* 577 (2006), p.606 and fn.193.

and truth telling. Such a dispute resolution mechanism could allow for proactive remedies to victims while not losing track of the importance of reconciliation and guarantees of non-recurrence.[108] In relation to the latter, according to principle 31(g) of the UN Guiding Principles, an institution that administers the dispute resolution should be a "source of continuous learning" by "regular analysis of the frequency, patterns and causes of grievances." This should allow it to identify and influence policies that can be used in order to avert future harm.

Another advantage of soft law relates to the type of remedy that can be offered to victims. Civil wrongs usually allow courts to repair the victim's economic loss. Soft law, on the other hand, could offer additional and more imaginative remedies, which are important to transitional justice. MNCs under principle 29 of the UN Guiding Principles should, for example, establish or participate in "effective operational-level grievance mechanisms" directly accessible to individuals and communities "who may be adversely impacted by a business enterprise." This could be interpreted to include a responsibility to focus on dialogue in order to resolve grievances, including a dialogue with all stakeholders concerning the design and performance of the chosen grievance mechanism.[109] Such responsibility could include the disclosure of important documents that would help in truth seeking and, ultimately, reconciliation. Moreover, MNCs could issue public apologies,[110] which are not normally available under civil wrong actions.

However, soft law has not yet optimized its potential. For example, the majority of CSR commitments do not specifically refer to the goals of transitional justice, a shortcoming that should be remedied. Furthermore, the OECD Guidelines have not been effective in holding MNCs accountable for their non-compliance with internationally recognized human rights. In relation to transitional justice, this has meant that, except for their proactive potential, the OECD Guidelines have been slow in supporting the reparation and truth-telling processes. Even where some form of external authority exists, as with the NCPs, the lack of individual complaint mechanisms plus the lack of providing and enforcing remedies mean that they could be useful for truth seeking, but not necessarily for remediation.

Contract law may have a limited role in supporting the processes of transitional justice. Having said that, following the logic of the UN Principles for Responsible Contracts,[111] a host state and an MNC should take into consideration the transitional justice objectives when entering into investment contracts; they should make sure that any risk to transitional justice is identified and averted before and at the time of the contract. Equally,

108 See de Greiff, n.98, Section E.
109 See UN Guiding Principles, n.3, principle 31(h).
110 See Basic Principles, n.65, principle 20 of title VIII.
111 Ruggie, n.78.

stakeholders to a project finance should require full consideration of the goals of transitional justice when performing the human rights impact assessment and action plan.

Furthermore, contracts can play an important role in strengthening the effectiveness of soft law. In particular, if well drafted, contracts can turn soft-law instruments into binding obligations. We have seen, for example, that a breach of the Equator Principles by an MNC financed by an adhering bank can be treated as an event of default under the loan agreement. While this may be of little benefit to individuals harmed by the MNC's non-compliance, who may lack the ability to hold MNCs to their promises under the Equator Principles, it nonetheless can play a proactive role in ensuring compliance with international human rights and environmental law.

Conclusion

The concept of accountability captures a range of corporate behavior in the private sphere. The dynamics that have a bearing on how and when an MNC is held to account vary depending on the normative source of the claim. A key finding of this chapter is that none of the three normative sources alone offers an optimal solution to achieving accountability. Rather, it is vital to acknowledge the multi-directional relationship between the three normative sources, as well as their codependence, and to apply a system that combines all three sources.

The pursuit of accountability under civil wrong is arguably a strong mechanism for achieving accountability to victims. The deterring function of civil wrong could persuade many MNCs to improve their human rights standards in order to avoid expensive litigation and civil liability. Equally, contracts, which are an important source of accountability, can achieve proactive compliance with MNCs' responsibility to respect and fulfill human rights. If well drafted, contracts can also ensure reparation for third-party beneficiaries who suffered at the hand of an MNC that was in breach of a contractual commitment.

This chapter has further unraveled a bidirectional relationship both between soft law and contracts, and between hard law and soft law. Further, soft law can be particularly effective when supported by contracts, such as the Equator Principles, or by hard law, such as the case of *Kasky v Nike* and the EU's Unfair Commercial Practices Directive.

We have seen how soft law can align itself to the challenges of a particular context, such as that of transitional justice. Soft law is more dynamic than tort law, and can readily respond to unforeseen challenges. Furthermore, soft law can offer remedies—such as a particular performance or an apology—that are not available under civil wrong mechanisms, where the usual remedy is a monetary compensation. It remains to be seen, however, whether soft law will realize its potential to progressively support the processes of transitional justice.

Chapter 3

Transnational Civil and Criminal Litigation

Tara L. Van Ho

Introduction

Courts in the United States,[1] the UK,[2] the Netherlands,[3] and Canada,[4] among others, have encountered civil claims against corporations for complicity in human rights and humanitarian law violations in other states. "Complicity as an avenue for corporate liability rests on the idea – supported by empirical data – that corporations are rarely the principals or direct perpetrators of international crimes [but] often provide economic assistance."[5] Corporate complicity cases can help victims and activists pursue at least four related goals: (i) raising international awareness about atrocities that have taken place; (ii) raising awareness about the role of corporations in perpetrating abuse and atrocities; (iii) pursuing reparations; and (iv) pressuring corporations to refrain from engaging with oppressive regimes in the future.[6] This final goal can function as a guarantee of non-repetition with a reach extending well

1 See, e.g., *Kiobel v Royal Dutch Petroleum Company*, Slip Opinion, 569 U.S. ___ (2013); *Sarei v Rio Tinto*, 221 F.Supp. 2d 1116 (C.D. California, 2002); 671 F.3d 736 (9th Circuit, 2011); *Presbyterian Church of Sudan v Talisman Energy, Inc.*, 582 F.3d 244 (2nd Circuit, 2009); *Khulumani v Barclay National Bank, Ltd.*, 504 F.3d 254 (2nd Circuit, 2007); *Doe v Unocal Corporation*, 110 F.Supp.2d 1294 (C.D. California, 2000), 248 F.3d 915 (9th Circuit, 2001), 395 F.3d 932 (9th Circuit, 2002); *Wiwa v Royal Dutch Petroleum Company*, 226 F.3d 88 (2nd Circuit, 2000).

2 See, *Bodo Community v Shell Petroleum Development Company of Nigeria, Ltd.*, Claim No. HQ11X01280 (filed 23 March 2012).

3 *Oruma v Royal Dutch Shell Plc.*, Court of the Hague, Docket number 330891 (Judgment, 2009), translation at www.milieudefensie.nl/publicaties/bezwaren-uitspraken/judgment-courtcase-shell-in-jurisdiction-motion-oruma.

4 *Association Canadienne contre l'impunité v Anvil Mining Limited*, Supreme Court of Canada, Docket Number 34733 (application for leave to appeal filed 26 March 2012).

5 W. Huisman and E. van Sliedregt, 'Rogue Traders: Dutch Businessmen, International Crimes and Corporate Complicity', 8 *Journal of International Criminal Justice* 803–828 (2010), pp.805–806.

6 See, generally, T. Harris, 'Settling a Corporate Accountability Lawsuit without Sacrificing Human Rights: Wang Xiaoning v. Yahoo!', 15 *Human Rights Brief* (2008), pp.10, 11, 13, www.wcl.american.edu/hrbrief/15/152.pdf.

beyond the society in which the violations occurred. Truth and reconciliation commissions have recognized the impact of corporations in facilitating the gross violations carried out by oppressive regimes and during armed conflicts,[7] but traditional transitional justice processes have been ineffective in holding corporations responsible for their complicit behavior.[8] It is thus interesting to examine whether transnational litigation can serve as a supplement to these domestic activities and a means of holding corporations accountable.

Many of the civil claims against corporations have been brought in the United States under the Alien Tort Claims Act (ATS), which allows foreign citizens to bring a tort action for violations of customary international law.[9] Only a few cases have resulted in settlements; most have been dismissed on procedural grounds in the early stages of litigation.[10] The jurisprudence developed, though, addresses a range of issues pertinent to transitional justice. These include determining which human rights violations are severe enough to justify litigation against corporations for complicity in actions taken by a foreign state, and how courts should address competing claims by a society that has specific transitional justice processes and those victims who wish to pursue additional claims.

This chapter considers the impact and appropriateness of transnational litigation within the context of transitional justice. In doing so, it focuses on a small subset of ATS jurisprudence. This jurisprudence can shed light on the considerations, benefits, concerns, and hindrances that transnational civil litigation poses in the context of transitional justice. In addition, it might be of some benefit to courts outside the United States that are called on to address claims for their corporations' overseas activities. The chapter was altered at the eleventh hour to take account of the Supreme Court's decision in *Kiobel v Royal Dutch Petroleum Co.,* which held that the ATS does not extend extraterritorially.[11] While the true impact of this decision may not be fully understood for several years, it clearly limits the claims that can be brought to US courts,[12] but it is unlikely to eliminate them. The question will rather turn to

7 See, e.g., Commission for Reception, Truth and Reconciliation in East Timor (CAVR), *Chega! Final Report*, 2005, Chapter 11, pp.4 and 42; Truth and Reconciliation Commission in Liberia, *Final Report*, 2009, Volume 3, Appendices title III: Economic Crimes and the Conflict, Exploitation and Abuse, pp.1–2 and 11–12.

8 See, generally, S. Darcy, 'Truth Commissions, the European Union and Reparations from Business', in F. Medjouba (ed.), *Building Peace in Post-Conflict Situations*, British Institute of International and Comparative Law, London, 2011 (43–60), http://aran.library.nuigalway.ie.

9 28 U.S.C. §1350.

10 K. Gallagher, 'Civil Litigation and Transnational Business: An Alien Tort Statute Primer', 8 *Journal of International Criminal Justice* 745–767 (2010), pp.751 (fn.27) and 753.

11 *Kiobel v Royal Dutch Petroleum Company*, Slip Opinion, 569 U.S. ___ (2013), p.14.

12 *See*, M. Coyle, 'Justices Limit Reach of Alien Tort Law,' *The American Lawyer*, 17 April 2013, http://www.americanlawyer.com.

what provides a connection sufficient to the US to rebut the presumption against extraterritoriality.[13] Despite representing a serious drawback for transnational litigation under the ATS, the decision does not make obsolete to discuss the lessons to be learned from ATS cases for transitional justice.

Civil claims represent only one means of transnational accountability for corporations. The Rome Statute of the International Criminal Court precludes jurisdiction over corporations,[14] but individuals can and have been prosecuted by international tribunals for business activities that supported genocide and war crimes.[15] Corporations and individuals acting on their behalf can be subject to domestic prosecution for complicity in international crimes.[16] The treatment of corporate criminal liability in this chapter is intentionally brief, as the trend in transnational litigation has focused on civil claims, where victims have more control over initiating the proceedings and presenting the case.

The remainder of the chapter is divided into three sections. The first section raises the potential for corporate criminal complicity. The following section outlines ATS jurisprudence while considering the transitional justice implications of these cases. The third section demonstrates that transnational human rights litigation can assist in several transitional justice goals but needs to be managed well by litigants and states alike. Given space constraints, cases are used throughout for illustration rather than an exhaustive discussion of the jurisprudence or individual claims.

Corporate criminal complicity

Since the ICC excludes jurisdiction over legal entities,[17] corporate prosecution needs to occur in domestic courts. A state emerging from conflict or an oppressive regime may be reluctant to pursue such claims during a time in which the international community is encouraging it to be more accommodating to business.[18] Prosecution for complicity in international crimes may be pursued outside the transitional state in jurisdictions that recognize the capacity of corporations to commit crimes and that have adequate

13 A question the Supreme Court will have to consider in *DaimlerChrysler v Bauman,* Docket Number 11-965.

14 Rome Statute of the International Criminal Court, article 35, 2187 U.N.T.S. 90.

15 See, e.g., *Prosecutor v Nahimana*, Case No. ICTR-96-11 (Judgment of 3 December 2003); *Prosecutor v Barayagwiza*, Case No. ICTR-97-19 (Judgment of 3 December 2003); *Prosecutor v Ngeze*, Case No. ICTR-97-27 (Judgment of 3 December 2003).

16 J. Ruggie, 'Business and Human Rights: The Evolving International Agenda', 101 *American Journal of International Law* 819 (2007), pp.830–831.

17 Rome Statute, article 25(1) limits the jurisdiction of the ICC to natural persons.

18 See, e.g., O. de Schutter, 'The Accountability of Multinationals for Human Rights Violations in European Law', in P. Alston (ed.), *Non-State Actors and Human Rights*, Oxford University Press, Oxford, 2005 (227–314), pp.237–240.

jurisdictional statutes.[19] Alternatively, states may pursue prosecutions against individuals associated with the corporation.[20]

Criminal prosecutions complement civil claims. For criminal complicity prosecutions, two questions will always be at the center of the case: what action was or was not taken, and what was the mental state of the relevant actors at the relevant time?[21] For corporate liability, an additional question needs to be asked: can the conduct of the individuals be imputed to the corporation?[22] Not all states provide for corporate criminal responsibility, but "[i]n the majority of those [that do,] companies can be held responsible for both national crimes and crimes under international law."[23] While jurisprudence in this area is limited, two recent Dutch prosecutions shed light on the legal standards applied in such cases. Both involved businessmen accused of supplying weaponry to regimes accused of war crimes.[24]

Frans van Anraat was accused of complicity in war crimes and genocide for selling a mustard gas component to Saddam Hussein's regime after the gas was used against civilians in Iraq and Iran.[25] While neither producing nor stocking mustard gas is a crime under Dutch or international law, the *actus reus* element for both charges was satisfied when expert testimony linked the component supplied to the gas that was actually employed against civilians.[26] The Court of Appeal determined that van Anraat did not have the special intent necessary to commit genocide.[27] However, the court ruled that his knowledge that the component "would serve as a precursor for mustard gas" was sufficient to satisfy the *mens rea* element of the charge of complicity to commit war crimes.[28] He was sentenced to 16 and a half years in prison for the war crimes conviction.[29]

Guus Kouwenhoven was also accused of war crimes, coupled with a violation of Dutch sanctions law, stemming from allegations that he supplied

19 Ruggie, n.16.

20 See, generally, Huisman and van Sliedregt, n.5; M. Zwanenburg and G. den Dekker, 'Prosecutor v. Frans van Anraat, Case No. 07/10742', 104 *American Journal of International Law* 86 (2010); R. van Rossum, 'Adjudication of International Crime in the Netherlands', 39 *International Journal of Legal Information* 202 (2011).

21 International Commission of Jurists (ICJ), *Report of the International Commission of Jurists Expert Legal Panel on Corporate Complicity in International Crimes*, 2008, Volume 2, p.37, http://icj-usa.org/wp-content/uploads/2010/01/Volume2-CriminalLaw_IntCrimes-2.pdf.

22 N. Farrell, 'Attributing Criminal Liability to Corporate Actors: Some Lessons from the International Tribunals', 8 *Journal of International Criminal Justice* 873 (2010), p.876.

23 ICJ, n.18, p.57.

24 Huisman and van Sliedregt, n.5; Zwanenburg and den Dekker, n.17; van Rossum, n.17.

25 Huisman and van Sliedregt, n.5, pp.805 and 807.

26 *Ibid.*, p.809.

27 *Ibid.*, pp.808–809; H. van der Wilt, 'Genocide v. War Crimes in the Van Anraat Appeal', 6 *Journal of International Criminal Justice* 557 (2008), pp.558–559.

28 Huisman and van Sliedregt, n.5, pp.808–809.

29 *Ibid.*, pp.807 and 809.

Charles Taylor's forces with weapons and illegally traded in timber to finance Taylor's conflicts in Liberia and Sierra Leone.[30] Kouwenhoven was named in a 2000 report by the UN Panel of Experts on Sierra Leone Diamonds and Arms.[31] The expert panel found that he was "a member of President Taylor's inner circle" and was "responsible for the logistical aspects of many of the arms deals."[32] The report resulted in UN sanctions "imposing travel restrictions and eventually freezing his assets."[33] The prosecution alleged that the security forces employed by his company were also members of the Liberian armed forces and the National Patriotic Front of Liberia and had committed war crimes in which he was complicit.[34] He was ultimately acquitted of all charges.[35] The district and appellate courts determined that it was unclear whether Kouwenhoven was aware of, let alone sanctioned, the actions of the security forces. As a result, his *mens rea* could not be established.[36] The Supreme Court overturned the dismissal, finding the lower courts wrong to exclude certain witness testimony, and the case is now pending another trial.[37]

These Dutch cases suggest that those who support international crimes knowingly or with intention could face criminal sanctions. Corporate criminal responsibility rests on the recognition that corporations "operate through human beings and some of these human beings have the legal power to reflect the actions and will"[38] of the corporation. The more direct the assistance and the more closely it is tied to the commission of an international crime, the more likely it is that individuals or a company will be found complicit in violations of international law.[39] It is unclear if Dutch prosecutors would pursue a corporate entity for involvement in international crimes, though they have the capacity to do so.[40] Van Anraat's effective prosecution may have rendered prosecution of the corporation unnecessary, and the dismissal of Kouwenhoven's case suggests a prosecution of his corporation may be untenable.

30 *Ibid.*, pp.810–812.
31 Panel of Experts established by resolution 1306 (2000), Report of the Panel of Experts appointed pursuant to Security Council resolution 1306 (2000), paragraph 19, in relation to Sierra Leone, U.N. Doc. S/2000/1195, 20 December 2000, para.215.
32 *Ibid.*
33 Huisman and van Sliedregt, n.5, p.811, citing UN Res. 1343 (2001), 1521 (2003), 1532 (2004) and 1792 (2007).
34 *Ibid.*, pp.811–812.
35 *Ibid.*, pp.810–812.
36 *Ibid.*, pp.810–812.
37 *Ibid.*, pp.812-813.
38 M. Kremnitzer, 'A Possible Case for Imposing Criminal Liability on Corporations in International Criminal Law', 8 *Journal of International Criminal Justice* 909–918 (2010), p.911.
39 See, H. Vest, 'Business Leaders and the Modes of Individual Criminal Responsibility under International Law', 8 *Journal of International Criminal Justice* 851–872 (2010), p.853.
40 Dutch Criminal Code, article 51.

Corporate criminal responsibility may prove necessary, though, where the conduct requires a clear sanctioning of the business activities or where the criminal responsibility stems not from a single individual's actions but from the collective responsibility of several employees or agents.[41] The beneficiary of the illegal activity will often be the corporation, rather than an individual, and the sanctioning of individuals rather than the entity may not adequately address a corporate culture that encouraged the violation.[42] Sanctions against individuals undermine the transitional justice goal of ensuring non-repetition of violations, whereas a prosecution of the corporation may have lasting deterrent effects both within the transitional state and throughout a corporation's global activities. Corporate criminal responsibility can be particularly important for victims, who may consider the corporation as the violator and who may not be able to identify the individuals who took specific actions. If the corporation—perceived as the real culprit—remains unpunished, victims' sense of justice may be left unsatisfied, giving rise to a feeling of impunity.

Criminal prosecution may be beneficial for victims because the state is responsible for the time and resource-intensive investigatory work that in civil claims falls on the victims. A tension could emerge, though, if the prosecutor's choices do not align with the needs of victims or the purposes of transitional justice. Prosecutors may be cautious about pursuing parent corporations for acts of local subsidiaries, whereas victims may see the parent as the real, or at least an important, perpetrator and wish to ensure a global reprimand that can function as a means of guaranteeing non-repetition both locally and internationally. The higher burden of proof generally required for criminal cases over civil ones may discourage prosecutors from pursuing certain claims, may lead them to dismiss some victims' claims as untenable, or may compel them to concentrate on only a few crimes. This can leave a narrow record and a shallow determination of "truth" where victims seek a robust accounting. The general transitional justice approach to prosecutions, which focuses only on those deemed "most responsible," raises this same issue, as victims might feel that justice is only partly pursued and achieved. While corporate prosecutions may not fully satisfy victims' needs, being able to bring such a prosecution may provide some relief to those who find that traditional processes fail to adequately address their needs.

Civil claims and the ATS

The ATS appears to be a global anomaly in that it provides jurisdiction reserved for foreigners only over civil claims arising from "violation[s] of the

41 See, Kremnitzer, n.38, pp.912–913.
42 *Ibid.*, p.912.

law of nations or a treaty of the United States."[43] It was not until the 1992 passage of the Torture Victim Protection Act that US citizens were extended similar rights, though limited to claims of torture and extrajudicial killing.[44] The ATS was used sparingly until 1980,[45] when a federal appellate court determined that torture constituted a violation of the law of nations and could give rise to a civil suit under the statute.[46] In the 1990s, claims started being brought against corporations, and US courts were asked to address allegations as varied as child labor,[47] slavery,[48] aiding and abetting apartheid,[49] and labor rights violations.[50] While the statute allows for cases based on treaty violations, peculiarities in the US legal system have precluded this and limited ATS litigation to violations of customary international law.[51] To date, the Supreme Court has decided only two ATS cases, *Sosa v Alvarez-Machain*,[52] and *Kiobel v Royal Dutch Petroleum Co.*[53] This has left the 12 regional courts of appeals and the district courts to address several important questions regarding the reach and application of the statute. The decisions of the courts of appeals are binding only on those district courts within their circuit and not on one another. This sometimes results in "circuit splits," where the interpretation and application of the ATS varies between regions.

This chapter concentrates on six cases to illustrate the transitional justice concerns raised by ATS litigation: *Doe v Unocal*;[54] *Wiwa v Royal Dutch Shell*;[55] *Kiobel v Royal Dutch Petroleum Co.*;[56] *Presbyterian Church of Sudan v Talisman*

43 28 U.S.C. §1350. Other states recognize extraterritorial tort liability, but it either does not rest on customary international law or is not limited to foreign citizens. See, E. Engle, 'Kiobel v. Royal Dutch Petroleum Co.: Corporate Liability Under the Alien Torts Statute', 34 *Houston Journal of International Law* 499 (2010), p.501 (fn.6).

44 *Wiwa v Royal Dutch Petroleum Company*, 226 F.3d 88 (2nd Circuit, 2000), pp.104–105.

45 But see, *Bolchos v Darrel*, 3 F. Cas. 810 (C.C.D.S.C., 1795); *O'Reilly de Camara v Brooke*, 209 U.S. 45 (1908); *Adra v Clift*, 195 F.Supp. 857 (D. Md., 1961); *Nguyen Da Yen v Kissinger*, 528 F.2d 1994 (9th Circuit, 1975).

46 *Filartiga v Pena-Irala*, 630 F.2d 876 (2nd Circuit, 1980).

47 *Flomo v Firestone*, 643 F.3d 1013 (7th Circuit, 2011).

48 See *Doe v Unocal Corporation*, 110 F.Supp.2d 1294 (C.D. California, 2000), 248 F.3d 915 (9th Circuit, 2001), 395 F.3d 932 (9th Circuit 2002).

49 See *Khulumani v Barclay National Bank, Ltd.*, 504 F.3d 254 (2nd Circuit, 2007).

50 *Aldana v Del Monte Fresh Produce N.A., Inc.*, 578 F.3d 1283 (11th Circuit, 2009).

51 See B. Stephens et al. (eds), *International Human Rights Litigation in U.S. Courts,* Martinus Nijhoff Publishers, Leiden, 2nd edn, 2008, pp.215–227.

52 542 U.S. 692 (2004).

53 Slip Opinion, 569 U.S. ___ (2013).

54 *Doe v Unocal Corporation*, 110 F.Supp.2d 1294 (C.D. California, 2000), 248 F.3d 915 (9th Circuit, 2001), 395 F.3d 932 (9th Circuit, 2002).

55 *Wiwa v Royal Dutch Petroleum Company*, 226 F.3d 88 (2d Circuit, 2000), pp.104–105.

56 *Kiobel v Royal Dutch Petroleum Company*, Slip Opinion, 569 U.S. ___ (2013); 621 F.3d 111 (2nd Circuit, 2010).

Energy, Inc.;[57] *Sarei v Rio Tinto*;[58] and *Khulumani v Barclay National Bank Ltd.*[59] These cases raise important considerations about the role of corporations in armed conflicts and oppressive regimes, and the appropriateness of transnational litigation when domestic processes are ill-equipped to handle claims of human rights and humanitarian law violations. Though many of the cases were brought independent of any transition within the state, they can be seen as a pursuit of transitional justice principles. The cases themselves may be used to establish an early accounting of the situation on the ground. They can also provide a blueprint for the effective use of litigation by those seeking to raise awareness and can empower individuals seeking a transition in pre-transitional societies.

Cases stemming from the long-standing situation in the Niger Delta raise questions about the appropriate boundaries for relationships between militaries engaged in armed conflicts and corporations that operate in areas of conflict. *Wiwa* relates to the infamous execution of indigenous activists from the Niger Delta by the Nigerian government following riots and protests over pollution in the Niger Delta.[60] Shell was alleged to have "instigated, orchestrated, planned, and facilitated" the arrests, torture, and executions.[61] *Kiobel* also addressed claims of complicity between Shell and the Nigerian government, though it involves a greater number of plaintiffs.[62] Claimants allege that Shell aided and abetted numerous human rights violations throughout the Niger Delta, principally through aiding the military.[63]

Unocal concluded before a transition in Myanmar,[64] but the court decisions address the question of when transnational litigation of human rights violations should proceed despite claims of sovereignty and state action.[65] The *Unocal* plaintiffs alleged that while being forced to work for Unocal's benefit, they were subjected to rape and other forms of torture, murder, and forced relocation by the military.[66] *Unocal* and *Wiwa* each settled after the defendants lost motions for summary judgment.[67] Shell group members paid the

57 *Presbyterian Church of Sudan v Talisman Energy, Inc.*, 582 F.3d 244 (2nd Circuit, 2009).

58 *Sarei v Rio Tinto*, 221 F.Supp. 2d 1116 (C.D. California, 2002); 671 F.3d 736 (9th Circuit, 2011).

59 *Khulumani v Barclay National Bank, Ltd.*, 504 F.3d 254 (U.S. 2nd Circuit, 2007); *In re South African Apartheid Litigation*, 617 F.Supp.2d 228 (S.D.N.Y., 2009), p.283.

60 *Wiwa v Royal Dutch Petroleum Company*, 226 F.3d 88 (2nd Circuit, 2000), p.92.

61 *Ibid.*

62 *Kiobel v Royal Dutch Petroleum Company*, 621 F.3d 111 (2nd Circuit, 2010).

63 *Ibid.*, pp.189 and 192.

64 'Unocal pays out on Burma "abuses"', BBC News, 22 March 2005, http://news.bbc.co.uk/1/hi/world/asia-pacific/4371995.stm.

65 See *Doe v Unocal Corporation*, 395 F.3d 932 (9th Circuit, 2002), pp.956–960.

66 110 F.Supp.2d 1294 (C.D. California, 2000), p.1298.

67 See Gallagher, n.10, pp.751 (fn.27) and 753. *Xiaoning v Yahoo!* also settled, but it did so before any decisions were made regarding the merits of the case. Joint Stipulation of Dismissal, Case No. CO7-02151 CW (N.D. California, 2007).

Wiwa plaintiffs US$11 million, though without an admission of liability or wrongdoing,[68] while the amount of the *Unocal* settlement remains undisclosed.[69]

Talisman and *Rio Tinto* stem from allegations of complicity during armed conflicts. The plaintiffs in *Talisman* claimed that the oil company had aided and abetted in the commission of genocide and war crimes. The company had built roads that the military used when carrying out military strikes, provided fuel for military aircraft, and paid royalties to the government.[70] *Rio Tinto* involved allegations that the mining giant's exploitation of copper in Papua New Guinea destroyed the environment, inculcated a policy of racial discrimination, incited a ten-year armed conflict that amounted to genocide, and facilitated the commission of crimes against humanity and war crimes. The company allegedly encouraged the state's actions, providing vehicles for the military and funding its response to protests and sabotage against the company.[71]

Lastly, *Khulumani*, later restyled *In re South African Apartheid Litigation*,[72] addressed claims against numerous corporations for aiding South Africa's apartheid regime.[73] The allegations were wide-ranging. Banks were accused of providing loans that allowed the state to function, technology firms were accused of developing technology specifically for the government to track individuals and institute a policy of denationalization, and automobile companies were accused of selling military vehicles used for extrajudicial killings.[74]

ATS claims face several hurdles, starting with a ten-year statute of limitations,[75] and, in the light of the Supreme Court decision in *Kiobel*,[76] the question of what provides a sufficient connection to the US to withstand the presumption against extraterritoriality. This chapter touches on three issues that both affect the likelihood of success for an ATS claim and illustrate some of the specific concerns about transnational civil claims arising from situations of transitional justice. The first is the narrow scope of claims recognized under the ATS, while the second is the standard for proving aiding and abetting human rights violations under international law. The third is courts' treatment

68 *Wiwa v Shell, Settlement Agreement and Mutual Release*, 8 June 2009, http://ccrjustice.org/files/Wiwa_v_Shell_SETTLEMENT_AGREEMENT.Signed-1.pdf.
69 BBC News, n.60.
70 *Presbyterian Church of Sudan v Talisman Energy, Inc.*, 582 F.3d 244 (2nd Circuit, 2009), pp.261–262.
71 *Sarei v Rio Tinto*, 221 F.Supp. 2d 1116 (C.D. California, 2002), pp.1125–1126.
72 *In re South African Apartheid Litigation*, 617 F.Supp.2d 228 (S.D.N.Y. 2009), p.283.
73 *Khulumani v Barclay National Bank, Ltd.*, 504 F.3d 254 (2nd Circuit, 2007).
74 *In re South African Apartheid Litigation*, 617 F.Supp. 2d 228 (S.D.N.Y., 2009), pp.264–266.
75 See, *Xuncax v Gramajo*, 886 F.Supp. 162 (D. Mass., 1995), p.192.
76 *Kiobel v Royal Dutch Petroleum Company*, Slip Opinion, 569 U.S. ___(2013).

of prudential considerations, including deference to the acts of the foreign state.

Choice of Law: Defining a Specific, Universal, Obligatory Norm

As interpreted by the US Supreme Court in *Sosa v Alvarez-Machain*, the ATS requires plaintiffs to plead a violation of a "specific, universal and obligatory" norm.[77] This is not necessarily coterminous with the international legal concepts of customary international law or with *jus cogens*, the peremptory norms that bind all states and from which there can be no derogation.[78] *Jus cogens* norms will usually be sufficient,[79] but this may not always be the case.[80] Additionally, claims against corporations require a link between the actions of the corporation and a state.[81]

Some claims are easier to establish than others. The *Wiwa* court concluded that torture clearly met the *Sosa* criteria,[82] while the *Unocal* court found that forced labor was a modern form of slavery, and therefore met the *Sosa* criteria.[83] Courts have utilized the standards in international criminal law in recognizing that crimes against humanity, war crimes, genocide, and supporting apartheid can constitute specific, universal, and obligatory norms.[84] Child labor, labor rights violations, environmental degradation, and racial discrimination not rising to the level of apartheid have failed the test.[85] Proving the factual basis for these claims can be difficult, though. The *Rio Tinto* court engaged in an extensive analysis of genocide and crimes against humanity before concluding that the allegation that the government and corporation treated the residents as a collective based on their "native way of life" was sufficient to meet the standard of genocide.[86]

77 See, *Sosa v Alvarez-Machain*, 542 U.S. 692 (2004), p.732.

78 See L. Dhooge, 'Lohengrin Revealed: The Implications of Sosa v. Alvarez-Machain for Human Rights Litigation pursuant to the Alien Tort Claims Act', 28 *Loyola of Los Angeles International and Comparative Law Review* 393 (2006), pp.450–451.

79 *Siderman de Blake v Republic of Argentina*, 965 F.2d 699 (9th Circuit, 1992), pp.717–718.

80 Dhooge, n.78, pp.450–451.

81 *Kadic v Karadzic*, 70 F.3d 232 (2nd Circuit, 1995).

82 226 F.3d 88 (2nd Circuit, 2000), pp.104–105 (occurring before *Sosa* but applying the same standard articulated in the latter case).

83 395 F.3d 932 (9th Circuit, 2002), p.946; see also *Sosa v Alvarez-Machain*, 542 U.S. 692 (2004), p.732.

84 Stephens, et al., n.51, pp.156–167 and 202–204; A. Reggio, 'Aiding and Abetting in International Criminal Law: The Liability of Corporate Agents and Businessmen for "Trading with the Enemy" of Mankind', 5 *International Criminal Law Review* 623 (2005), pp.629–637.

85 See, generally, Gallagher, n.10, pp.753–755.

86 *Ibid.*

The Supreme Court's decision in *Kiobel* leaves some uncertainty as to whether a claim could withstand the presumption against extraterritoriality based solely on the international community's commitment to combat the underlying crime. The majority opinion recognized that piracy would still be justiciable, finding that when the ATS was passed, "[p]irates were fair game whenever found, by any nation, because they generally did not operate within any jurisdiction."[87] It then left unaddressed the modern position, as stated in *Filartiga* and seemingly endorsed by the Supreme Court in *Sosa*,[88] that torturers are like modern day pirates and therefore "fair game" for any nation.[89] Justice Breyer criticized the majority's opinion on this point, noting that "[c]ertainly today's pirates include torturers and perpetrators of genocide. And today, like the pirates of old, they are 'fair game' where they are found."[90]

One advantage of basing liability on a violation of customary international law is that defendants are unable to rely on domestic law as a defense. The *Unocal* defendants invoked Myanmar law to argue that the use of forced labor was akin to "public service" and therefore did not violate international law.[91] The courts rejected this position because the ATS requires the "application of international law—rather than the law of Myanmar, California state law, or our federal common law."[92] The district court decision suggested that while mandatory service may be allowed under international law, the context and gross human rights violations present in this project distinguished it from those instances of acceptable mandatory public service.[93]

Several courts have considered whether corporations can ever violate international human rights law.[94] A circuit split has emerged on the issue of whether corporations can be liable to the same extent as natural persons.[95] *Rio Tinto* relied on the dissolution of I.G. Farben after World War II and jurisprudence from the International Court of Justice to find that the prohibition against genocide extends to corporations,[96] but the Second Circuit *Kiobel* decision found the fact that no international criminal tribunal had ever

87 *Kiobel v Royal Dutch Petroleum Company*, Slip Opinion, 569 U.S. ___ (2013), p.10.

88 *See*, *Filartiga v Pena-Irala*, 630 F.2d 876 (2nd Circuit, 1980) p.890; *Sosa v Alvarez-Machain*, 542 U.S. 692 (2004), p.732.

89 *Kiobel v Royal Dutch Petroleum Company*, Slip Opinion, 569 U.S. ___ (2013), p.10.

90 *Ibid,* (Breyer, J., concurring), p.5.

91 110 F.Supp.2d 1294 (C.D. California, 2000), pp.1308–1309.

92 395 F.3d 932 (9th Circuit, 2002), p.949.

93 110 F.Supp.2d 1294 (C.D. California, 2000), p.1310.

94 671 F.3d p.760 (9th Circuit, 2011) (citing *Sosa v Alvarez-Machain*, 542 U.S. 692, p.732 fn.20).

95 Compare, *Kiobel v Royal Dutch Petroleum Company*, 621 F.3d 111 (2nd Circuit, 2010), pp.132–145, with, *Flomo v Firestone*, 643 F.3d 1013 (7th Circuit, 2011), p.1021; *Sarei v Rio Tinto*, 671 F.3d 736 (9th Circuit, 2011), pp.760–761; *Romero v Drummond Company, Inc.*, 552 F.3d 1303 (11th Circuit, 2008), p.1316; *Doe VIII v Exxon Mobil Corporation*, 654 F.3d 11 (C.A.D.C., 2011), pp.41–43.

96 *Sarei v Rio Tinto*, 671 F.3d 736 (9th Circuit, 2011), pp.760–761.

prosecuted a corporation persuasive in determining that corporations cannot be liable for violations of international human rights.[97] The Second Circuit appears to conflate two distinct fields: international criminal law and international human rights law.[98] It also sits in opposition to conclusions and observations made by both the International Commission of Jurists and the Special Representative of the UN Secretary-General on Business and Human Rights, John Ruggie.[99] Ruggie vehemently condemned Shell for trying "to negate" the usefulness of the ATS and for attempting to "destroy an entire juridical edifice for redressing gross violations of human rights" in its *Kiobel* defense.[100] In its April 2013 decision in *Kiobel*, the US Supreme Court avoided this question, though it had heard oral arguments on it.[101]

Aiding and Abetting under International Law

For the ATS, plaintiffs must show that the corporation aided or abetted a violation of international law, and that the prohibition on aiding and abetting is itself a specific, universal, and obligatory norm.[102] Complicity claims can rest on the theory that either the corporation assisted the state or the state committed a violation on behalf of the corporation.[103] As Sabine Michalowski has noted, "[t]he main difficulty for courts in deciding complicity liability is where to draw the line between acceptable business interactions with regimes that clearly commit gross human rights violations, and activities that make the corporation complicit in these violations."[104] Post-*Sosa* courts have generally relied on international criminal law for defining the relevant liability

97 *Kiobel v Royal Dutch Petroleum Company*, 621 F.3d 111 (2nd Circuit, 2010), pp.132–145.

98 *Ibid.*, pp.151–153 (Leval, J., concurring); O. Murray, D. Kinley and C. Pitts, 'Exaggerated Rumours of the Death of an Alien Tort? Corporations, Human Rights and the Remarkable Case of Kiobel', 12 *Melbourne Journal of International Law* 57 (2011), pp.80–81; A. Mamolea, 'The Future of Corporate Aiding and Abetting Liability under the Alien Tort Statute: A Roadmap', 51 *Santa Clara Law Review* 79 (2011), pp.100-101.

99 See, ICJ, n.21 and J. Ruggie, Report of the Special Representative of the Secretary-General on the Issue of Human Rights and Transnational Corporations and Other Business Enterprises, *Guiding Principles on Business and Human Rights: Implementing the United Nations "Protect, Respect and Remedy" Framework*, U.N. Doc. A/HRC/17/31, 21 March 2011, paras.11–24.

100 J. Ruggie, *Kiobel and Corporate Responsibility*, 4 September 2012, www.business-humanrights.org/media/documents/ruggie-kiobel-and-corp-social-resonsibility-sep-2012.pdf.

101 *Kiobel v Royal Dutch Petroleum Company*, Slip Opinion, 569 U.S. ___ (2013).

102 See *Presbyterian Church of Sudan v Talisman Energy, Inc.*, 582 F.3d 244 (2nd Circuit, 2009), pp.259–260.

103 See, generally, D. Amoroso, 'Moving Towards Complicity as a Criterion of Attribution of Private Conducts: Imputation to States of Corporate Abuses in the US Case Law', 24 *Leiden Journal of International Law* 989–1007 (2011).

104 S. Michalowski, 'No Complicity Liability for Funding Gross Human Rights Violations?' 30 *Berkeley Journal of International Law* 451 (2012), p.452.

standards,[105] but they have not reached a consensus on the applicable *mens rea* test, a byproduct, at least in part, of different interpretations about the *mens rea* standard under international law.

There is now a circuit split on the appropriate *mens rea* standard.[106] The Ninth Circuit applied a "knowledge" standard in *Unocal*.[107] The Second Circuit's *Talisman* decision required the higher "purpose" test, resulting in a dismissal of the claims, as it could not be shown that the corporation had acted with the wish to facilitate human rights violations—only that it had knowledge that its actions would have this effect.[108] The "purpose" standard raises the pleading requirements for plaintiffs, who must demonstrate an intention to assist in an international crime, rather than an intention to generate a commercial interest coupled with knowledge of the state's illegal actions. Meeting this pleading standard represents a particularly difficult evidentiary test and is likely to exclude claims that would succeed if the required *mens rea* was "knowledge."[109]

Courts have consistently determined that the *actus reus* for aiding and abetting is the provision of practical assistance that has a substantial effect on the perpetration of the crime.[110] In *re South African Apartheid Litigation*, the district court faced allegations on a range of activities alleged to have supported apartheid, including financing or the sale of specific goods to the government. The court concluded that the provision of "neutral goods"—those "that are not inherently harmful"—could not give rise to liability.[111] As a result, financial services could not result in liability, but the provision of technological goods deemed "indispensable" to apartheid could meet the *actus reus* standard.[112] Software "specifically designed to produce identity documents" and computer equipment "designed to track and monitor civilians with the purpose of enforcing the racist, oppressive laws of apartheid" both fulfilled the *actus reus*.[113]

105 Gallagher, n.10, p.746 (fn.4).

106 See, e.g., *Presbyterian Church of Sudan v Talisman Energy, Inc.*, 582 F.3d 244 (2nd Circuit, 2009), p.259; *Sarei v Rio Tinto*, 671 F.3d 736 (9th Circuit, 2011), pp.766–767; *Kiobel v Royal Dutch Shell Plc*, 621 F.3d 111 (2nd Circuit, 2010), pp.148–149 (Leval, J., concurring); *Aziz v Alcolac*, 658 F.3d 388 (4th Circuit, 2011), pp.400–401; *In Re: Chiquita Brands International, Inc. Alien Tort Statute And Shareholder Derivative Litigation*, 792 F. Supp. 2d 1301 (S.D. Fla., 2011).

107 *Doe v Unocal Corporation*, 395 F.3d 932 (9th Circuit, 2002), p.953.

108 *Presbyterian Church of Sudan v Talisman Energy, Inc.*, 582 F.3d 244 (2nd Circuit, 2009), pp.264 and 268.

109 S. Bhashyam, 'Knowledge or Purpose? The Khulumani Litigation and the Standard for Aiding and Abetting Liability under the Alien Tort Claims Act', 30 *Cardozo Law Review* 245 (2008), p.248.

110 See *Doe v Unocal*, 395 F.3d 932 (9th Circuit, 2002), p.952.

111 Michalowski, n.104, p.469.

112 *In re South African Apartheid Litigation*, 617 F.Supp.2d 228 (SDNY 2009), pp.265–266.

113 *Ibid.*, p.268. See also Michalowski, n.104, pp.461–462.

Operating in an oppressive regime or in a state with an armed conflict, in and of itself, is likely to be insufficient for corporate liability. The relationship between the state and the corporation must go beyond simple commercial interactions. The corporation must have provided material support to the state that attends to the heart of the illegal conduct. That support must also be provided with a level of knowledge or purpose, and plaintiffs must clearly link the harms suffered with state conduct aided by specific acts of a corporation. These pleading requirements limit the claims that courts will hear and establish a difference between the civil legal process in the US and "traditional" transitional justice processes, which can address not just legal but also moral responsibility for involvement in armed conflicts or oppressive regimes.

"Prudential Justiciability"

The Supreme Court in *Kiobel* determined that complaints under the ATS must be sufficiently connected to the territorial jurisdiction of the United States.[114] Even where this connection exists, though, US courts may dismiss due to prudential considerations. US courts regularly employ the doctrine of *forum non conveniens* to dismiss cases if an alternative state would offer an adequate forum.[115] When considering *forum non conveniens*, one factor that US courts weigh is the interests of the competing jurisdictions in hearing the claim. The *Wiwa* court cautioned against dismissing ATS suits under this doctrine,[116] but the *Kiobel* court seemed to embrace it, suggesting a limited scope for assuming US interest in overseas actions.

Other prudential considerations developed by courts to balance competing interests include the "act of state," "international comity," and "political question" doctrines discussed below. The US Supreme Court has also indicated that plaintiffs may sometimes be required to exhaust domestic remedies in the state where the violation occurred, though the full scope of this requirement is still unsettled.[117] Each of these "prudential considerations" has been raised by ATS corporate defendants, and each gives rise to considerations about the appropriateness of transnational litigation involving civil claims arising from a transitional justice situation.

The environmental, health, and racial discrimination claims in *Rio Tinto*, for example, were each dismissed under the "act of state" doctrine, while

114 *Kiobel v Royal Dutch Petroleum Company*, Slip Opinion, 569 U.S. ___ (2013), p.14.

115 See Stephens *et al.*, n.51, pp.391–392. European law limits the use of similar theories, but courts may still refuse civil claims if they rest on complicated claims of foreign law. See European Council Regulation (EC) No. 44/2001 (22 December 2000). The Dutch courts refused to hear civil claims in the van Anraat case "partly because of the application of foreign law." Van Rossum, n.20, p.202; see also Zwanenburg and den Dekker, n.20, p.89.

116 *Sosa v Alvarez-Machain*, 542 U.S. 692 (2004), p.733, fn.21.

117 *Sosa v Alvarez-Machain*, 542 U.S. 692 (2004), p.733, fn.21.

other allegations were deemed to fall outside the legitimate acts of a state.[118] The "act of state" doctrine precludes a US court from hearing a claim "if it involves (1) an official act of a foreign sovereign, (2) performed within its own territory, and (3) seeks relief that would require the court to declare the sovereign's act invalid."[119] The more official the state action, the more inappropriate it is for US courts to intervene.[120] The district court found that international law protects each state's right to determine the appropriate balance between the benefits and drawbacks of resource exploitation.[121] International environmental law may bind a state but it does not allow other states to sit in judgment of the means taken to meet the competing demands of environmental protection and economic development.[122]

Perhaps the most contentious debate on prudential considerations has taken place in the context of the *Khulumani* litigation. South Africa's government requested that the proceedings be dismissed, asserting "that the South African government regarded [the] proceedings as interfering 'with a foreign sovereign's efforts to address matters in which it has predominant interest.'"[123] The US government concurred, expressing concern that continuation of the case "risk[ed] potentially serious adverse consequences for significant interests of the United States."[124] On appeal, the United States asserted that this case specifically, and aiding and abetting litigation generally, impinged on the "broader foreign policy interests in using trade and investment to promote economic development in other countries as a way of promoting stability, democracy and security."[125] The district court initially dismissed the claims on other grounds, and did not fully analyze the prudential jurisdiction questions.[126] When the Second Circuit Court of Appeals overturned the dismissal, it found that the prudential considerations needed to be more fully addressed by the lower court.[127]

The majority opinion elicited a strongly worded dissent explaining that the doctrine of international comity demanded the case's dismissal.[128] International comity refers to "the degree of deference that a domestic forum must pay to the act of a foreign government . . . [or] a discretionary act of

118 *Sarei v Rio Tinto*, 221 F.Supp. 2d 1116 (C.D. California, 2002), pp.1184–1185; see also 671 F.3d 736 (9th Circuit, 2011), pp.757–758.

119 *Sarei v Rio Tinto*, 221 F.Supp. 2d 1116 (C.D. California, 2002), pp.1184–1185.

120 *Ibid.*, p.1185.

121 *Ibid.*, p.1193.

122 *Ibid.*

123 *Khulumani v Barclay National Bank, Ltd.*, 504 F.3d 254 (2nd Circuit, 2007), p.259.

124 *Ibid.*

125 *Brief for the United States of America as Amicus Curiae*, pp.18–19, www.state.gov/documents/organization/87317.pdf.

126 *Khulumani v Barclay National Bank, Ltd.*, 504 F.3d 254 (2nd Circuit, 2007), p.262.

127 *Ibid.*

128 *Ibid.*, pp.295–306 (Korman, J., dissenting).

deference by a national court . . . in a case properly adjudicated in a foreign state."[129] The dissent, written by Judge Korman, claimed that failure to dismiss the case would undermine the right of South Africa to direct its own internal transitional justice processes.[130] He called the continued litigation of the claims an "affront" to South Africa, "which is justifiably proud of the ability of its legal system to adjudicate legitimate human rights claims."[131] Other states had also expressed an expectation that cases against their corporate nationals should be handled in South Africa.[132] Refusal to dismiss, Judge Korman reasoned, was an imposition on this process and on South Africa's sovereignty.[133] The majority opinion responded by noting that the South African government could have changed its position in the meantime and remanded the case to the district court with a recommendation that the lower court again consult the South African and US governments before deciding the prudential considerations.[134]

On remand, the defendants argued that the case not only undermined South African law and sovereignty but also contradicted the stated purpose of the US government to encourage investment in South Africa.[135] The political question doctrine requires dismissal when a decision would interfere with an action taken by the political branches that is primarily within their constitutional purview.[136] The district court, however, found the political question and international comity doctrines inapplicable.[137] It determined that since apartheid-related litigation was unlikely to deter investment in the new regime, the case would not harm the US executive's goals.[138] On the issue of international comity, the court concluded that it "comes into play only when there is a true conflict between American law and that of a foreign jurisdiction," and that in this case, such a conflict did not exist.[139] The TRC process precluded criminal or civil proceedings "only upon a grant of amnesty."[140] The defendants were ineligible for amnesty because they had "declined to offer testimony to the TRC."[141] Since the TRC had "recognized the possibility of corporate liability," the court found that the exercise of jurisdiction over corporations that were not granted amnesty did not undermine South

129 *Ibid.*, p.298.
130 *Ibid.*, pp.299–304.
131 *Ibid.*, pp.292 and 299.
132 *Ibid.*, p.297.
133 *Ibid.*, p.302.
134 *Ibid.*, p.263 (fn.13).
135 *South African Apartheid Litigation*, 617 F.Supp.2d 228 (S.D.N.Y., 2009), pp.281–282.
136 Stephens *et al.*, n.51, pp.338–349.
137 *South African Apartheid Litigation*, 617 F.Supp.2d 228 (S.D.N.Y., 2009), pp.285–286.
138 *Ibid.*, p.284.
139 *Ibid.*, pp.283 and 285–286.
140 *Ibid.*, p.285.
141 *Ibid.*

Africa's sovereign choices.[142] South Africa did not claim to offer an adequate, alternative forum for the claims, so the court reasoned that dismissal was inappropriate.[143]

During oral arguments for *Kiobel*, the US Supreme Court expressed concern that the ATS was causing tensions with the international community, noting that the Netherlands, the UK, and Germany had filed an amicus curiae brief stating that corporate responsibility for violations of international human rights law is inconsistent with international law. The position of the Dutch government is particularly interesting since the Dutch Criminal Code recognizes corporate liability for international crimes.[144] But many have expressed similar concerns about the impact of the ATS on foreign states' sovereignty and the United States' foreign relations.[145]

The Supreme Court's *Kiobel* decision focused on this issue, though it was presented through the lens of the appropriate territorial scope of the statute.[146] In utilizing the presumption against extraterritoriality, the Court had to contend with its own earlier decision indicating the statute was applicable to piracy.[147] The Court concluded that "[a]pplying U.S. law to piracy does not typically impose the sovereign will of the United States onto conduct occurring within the territorial jurisdiction of another sovereign, and therefore carries less direct foreign policy consequences."[148] The Court's reasoning suggests it was relying on the presumption of extraterritoriality in an effort to avoid difficult cases that could cause diplomatic tension.[149] As Justice Breyer noted, though, this was unnecessary since US courts have other avenues for avoiding cases that pose diplomatic problems.[150] He highlighted the inconsistency of the majority's view by pointing out that piracy actually occurs on the territory of a foreign state if the ship being targeted carries a foreign flag, making it the territory of a foreign state.[151]

The position of the Court ignores evidence that the judicial process itself can alleviate the concerns that lay at the bottom of its desire to limit the

142 *Ibid.*
143 *Ibid.*
144 Dutch Criminal Code, article 51; see also N. Jägers, *The Netherlands: Survey Questions and Responses*, 2006, pp.16–17, www.fafo.no/liabilities/CCCSurveyNetherlands06Sep2006.pdf.
145 See, e.g., R. Knowles, 'A Realist Defense of the Alien Tort Statute', 88 *Washington University Law Review* 1117 (2011), p.1119; T. Adamski, 'The Alien Tort Claims Act and Corporate Liability: A Threat to the United States' International Relations', 34 *Fordham International Law Journal* 1502 (2011).
146 *Kiobel v Royal Dutch Petroleum Company*, Slip Opinion, 569 U.S. ___ (2013).
147 *Ibid.*, p.14.
148 *Ibid.*
149 *Ibid.*, pp.5-6, 8-10.
150 *Ibid.* (Breyer, J., dissenting), p.7.
151 *Ibid.*, p.4-5.

extraterritorial reach of the ATS, and has done so in previous ATS cases. Following the second decision of the district court in the *Apartheid Litigation* case,[152] for example, the Zuma administration reversed the South African government's earlier position, stating that one of the government's concerns had been the continuation of cases based solely on the grounds of doing business with the South African government.[153] Since the district court had dismissed those very claims, the decision "addressed some of the concerns of the Government," and the government was "now of the view that this [US District] Court is an appropriate forum to hear the remaining claims of aiding and abetting in violation of international law."[154] This is not the only time a government has changed its position with regard to ATS claims stemming from its history. The Papua New Guinea and US governments initially opposed the *Rio Tinto* suit but reversed their positions during the decade-plus of litigation.[155]

Considering extraterritorial complicity litigation and transitional justice

The discussions on *Khulumani* and *Kiobel* express deep reservations US courts have about the potential for human rights imperialism. This raises important considerations about the standards that foreign courts should employ when considering whether to hear transnational human rights litigation. The standard of "a specific, universal, obligatory norm" adopted in *Sosa*[156] appeared to be an attempt to avoid that very allegation. The benefit of raising the standard to universal norms is that the ATS provides a forum for hearing human rights claims without relying on complicated considerations of domestic law. As seen in *Unocal*, this pleading requirement also means those who violate human rights cannot circumvent international responsibility by introducing incompatible domestic laws. Claims meeting the *Sosa* standard will generally be those where a state can offer no legitimate justification for the violations that occurred. The *Kiobel* decision suggests, though, that this alone is not sufficient for addressing concerns about international comity and respect for foreign sovereign interests.

The ATS makes it clear that international human rights can govern individual civil responsibility, even if the scope of customary international

152 617 F.Supp.2d 228 (S.D.N.Y., 2009), p.286.

153 Letter from Jeffrey Thamsanqa Radebe, Minister of Justice and Constitutional Development, to the Judge Shira A. Scheindlin, www.khulumani.net/attachments/343_RSA.Min.Justice_letter_J.Scheindlin_09.01.09.PDF.

154 *Ibid.*

155 221 F.Supp. 2d 1116 (C.D. California, 2002), pp.1199–1204; 625 F.3d 561 (9th Circuit, 2010), pp.756–757.

156 542 U.S. 692 (2004), p.732.

human rights law is in dispute. The large number of ATS claims advanced in US courts indicates victims' need for alternative avenues through which to pursue remedies for human rights violations.

Transnational litigation may be particularly beneficial for claims emanating from transitional societies. The judiciary of such states may be inundated with more cases than their domestic courts can handle, while victims may question the impartiality and competence of the judiciary or face pressure from a government concerned about attracting investment. By allowing claims based on international law, the ATS can help realize victims' right to a remedy while using "common" standards. Yet the United States' definition of universal rights is quite limited, excluding most economic, social, and cultural rights. The ATS is therefore still open to criticism of human rights imperialism. This domestication of international law is problematic in that it creates an amalgamation of domestic and international law without fully recognizing the contours of each and assumes, at times, a US understanding as universal.[157] By hearing extraterritorial claims under a proposition of universality, US courts are implicitly determining what claims should be recognized by foreign states.[158]

While there are valid concerns about over-reliance on the ATS and its connection to US interpretations of international law, the ATS could still represent an important means of securing justice for some victims. Transnational litigation is an important supplement to domestic efforts to achieve greater accountability, particularly for transitional societies. Such cases can encourage corporations to more fully participate in domestic transitional justice programs. Transitional justice processes require a "buy in" from the relevant parties. Thus far, though, non-judicial mechanisms have been unable to compel the cooperation or participation of corporations.[159] Failure to secure greater accountability for corporations, and to secure adequate reparations for victims, can feed the desire to seek alternative fora.[160] When determining whether to hear a transnational claim, foreign courts could consider whether a corporation has participated in a transitional justice process, granting legal immunity only if the corporation was or is an active participant in such a process. This may require that courts consult the relevant governments and civil society to determine the sufficiency of corporate participation before dismissing a claim.

157 See K. Knop, 'Here and There: International Law in Domestic Courts', 32 *New York University Journal of International Law and Practice* 501 (2000), pp.505–506.

158 See Roberts, n.154, pp.61–63, 68–72 and 76–77.

159 See, S. Darcy, n.8, 'Truth Commissions, the European Union and Reparations from Business', in F. Medjuba (eds), *Building Peace in Post-Conflict Situations*, British Institute of International and Comparative Law, London, 2011 (46–30), http://aran.library.nuigalway.ie.

160 See also chapters 5 and 8 of this book.

It is also important for courts to consider the balance of rights between the collective, represented through the state-sanctioned process, and the individual victim, who might be dissatisfied with that process and wish to pursue an alternative avenue for redress and remedies. The inclination may be to defer to the rules and processes adopted by a transitional state as recognition of that foreign state's sovereignty. This approach, though, should be taken cautiously to ensure that it does not simply perpetuate human rights violations. While the government or civil leadership may be assumed to speak for all victims, this may not be the case. Of particular consideration should be the representation of, inclusion of, and respect for minorities, women, and the most vulnerable. Courts should also question whether the claims raised in a transnational lawsuit are addressed through the transitional justice process—and if not, why not. These questions should be used solely to ascertain the necessity of transnational litigation by determining how corporations and victims have been included in the process.

Transnational litigation must not be considered a substitute for transitional justice processes. It has significant limitations for the values of transitional justice, starting with substantive and procedural requirements that limit the success of claims in securing financial reparations. These requirements also restrict the completeness of record, and victims who seek a robust determination of historical injustices may be dissatisfied by the judiciary's offer of a limited reflection of the truth.[161] The worth of judicial decisions as a form of "truth" or as a means of reconciliation is therefore limited.

Conclusion

This chapter only touches on two means of holding corporations accountable extraterritorially: civil human rights claims and criminal prosecutions. The ATS has been relied on the most for pursuing such claims, but ordinary tort claims may provide an avenue for pursuing similar goals.[162] Corporations have, thus far, largely escaped criminal responsibility. The prosecution of individuals for their business activities, though, provides a clear precedent as an increasing number of states recognize the potential of corporations to commit international crimes.

Other, less mainstream means of accountability can also prove important. A new rule by the US Securities and Exchange Commission requires companies listed on US stock exchanges and engaged in "the commercial development of oil, natural gas or minerals" to disclose payments made to governments, regardless of the company's nationality, its size, its ownership, "or the extent of business operations constituting commercial development" of these

161 Van Rossum, n.20, p.199.
162 See chapter 2 of this book.

resources.[163] Victims can utilize the reports to understand the nature and extent of a corporation's engagement and potential complicity with oppressive regimes or in an armed conflict. They can also utilize the information to pursue complicity claims after a transition has occurred, or to advocate for adequate budgetary allocations toward reparations. Business groups have sued to halt implementation of the rule.[164]

More still needs to be done, though, to ensure the compatibility of extraterritorial legal avenues with the needs and interests of societies in transition and of individual victims. States other than the United States should consider adopting jurisdictional bases similar to the ATS. Such efforts can provide victims with access to remedies and can dissuade corporations from continuing practices that harm the realization of human rights. Additional avenues will also ensure that other states effectively contribute to the growing jurisprudential dialogue on corporations' human rights responsibilities. In such cases, the lessons raised by ATS litigation and the Dutch criminal prosecutions may prove useful. Regardless of the future availability of the ATS, it is important for victims, advocates, and courts to consider how and to what effect the ATS has provided an important supplement to the traditional transitional justice processes. Its successes should be replicated while its weaknesses discussed, with a view toward encouraging a robust and consistent international response to the responsibility of corporations for violations of international human rights or humanitarian law during armed conflicts or oppressive regimes.

163 Securities and Exchange Commission, *Disclosure of Payments by Extraction Issuers*, Release No. 33-67717 ("SEC"), 2012, pp.13–14, www.sec.gov/rules/final/2012/34-67717.pdf; see, also, Essex Business & Human Rights Project, *Corporate Liability in a New Setting: Shell and the Changing Legal Landscape for the Multinational Oil Industry in the Niger Delta*, 2012, www.essex.ac.uk/ebhr.

164 S. Lynch, 'Business groups sue SEC over Dodd-Frank Anti-bribery Rule', Reuters.com, 10 October 2012, www.reuters.com/article/2012/10/11/us-sec-lawsuit-idUSBRE8991NL20121011.

Chapter 4

Transitional Justice and the UN Guiding Principles on Business and Human Rights

*Geneviève Paul and Judith Schönsteiner**

Introduction

Although issues of transitional justice were not specifically covered by the mandates given to the Special Representative of the United Nations Secretary-General on Business and Human Rights (SRSG), Professor John Ruggie and his team developed several concepts in the "Protect, Respect and Remedy" framework (Framework) and the accompanying UN Guiding Principles on Business and Human Rights[1] that are informative for a discussion of corporate complicity and transitional justice. Additionally, he and his team addressed business activities in conflict zones.[2]

This chapter seeks to critically evaluate some aspects of the work of Special Representative John Ruggie, especially the UN Guiding Principles, in order to assess to what extent they provide useful concepts and mechanisms for tackling corporate accountability in transitional justice contexts. The chapter begins by briefly describing the history, mandate, and process of the SRSG's work. It then analyzes states' obligations and companies' responsibilities in relation to conflict zones in order to identify some of the challenges for the Framework's implementation in the context of transitional justice.

It has been correctly pointed out elsewhere that the UN Guiding Principles were not meant to cover in depth all of the different human rights issues related to corporate accountability.[3] However, weaknesses of the UN

* The authors would like to thank María Belén Saavedra, law student at Diego Portales University, for her research assistance, and Sabine Michalowski for her fine editing.

1 J. Ruggie, Report of the Special Representative of the Secretary-General on the Issue of Human Rights and Transnational Corporations and Other Business Enterprises, *Guiding Principles on Business and Human Rights: Implementing the United Nations "Protect, Respect and Remedy" Framework*, U.N. Doc. A/HRC/17/31, 21 March 2011, endorsed by the UN Human Rights Council in Resolution A/HRC/Res/17/4.

2 See for discussions of Ruggie's work, for example, A. McBeth, *International Economic Actors and Human Rights*, Routledge, Abingdon, 2011.

3 T. Melish and E. Meidinger, 'Protect, Respect, Remedy and Participate: "New Governance" Lessons for the Ruggie Framework', in R. Mares (ed.), *The UN Guiding Principles on Business and Human Rights: Foundations and Implementation*, Brill, The Hague, 2012 (303–336), p.328.

Guiding Principles from an international human rights law perspective, as will be highlighted in this chapter, do have repercussions for transitional justice.

This chapter welcomes the Special Representative's emphasis on the prevention of human rights abuses and related strategies from a human rights perspective[4] and argues that it is especially useful in transitional justice contexts. This emphasis also fits nicely into the governance perspective adopted in the Framework and UN Guiding Principles.[5] However, the sometimes inaccurate representation of international law regarding certain aspects of states' obligation to protect; the lack of clarity on some aspects of the substantive dimension of the corporate responsibility to respect; and the absence of recommendations for effective enforcement mechanisms[6] and of limits set for private reparations initiatives weakens the UN Guiding Principles and raises important challenges to be addressed from a human rights perspective on transitional justice.

History, mandate, and process of the SRSG's work

In 2005, UN Secretary-General Kofi Annan appointed Professor John Ruggie as SRSG on the issue of human rights and transnational corporations and other business enterprises. Ruggie had been a former advisor to Kofi Annan for strategic planning and played a pivotal role in the establishment of the UN Global Compact.[7]

Seeking to respond to the harsh state and corporate criticism of the 2003 Norms on the Responsibilities of Transnational Corporations and Other Business Enterprises with Regard to Human Rights (UN Draft Norms),[8] the SRSG's first mandate focused on the identification and clarification of standards related to corporate responsibility and accountability for businesses with regard to human rights; states' role in regulating companies; and the development of materials and methodologies on human rights impact

4 See also contributions to S. Leader and D. Ong (eds.), *Global Project Finance, Human Rights and Sustainable Development*, Cambridge University Press, Cambridge, 2011.

5 See L.C. Backer, 'On the Evolution of the United Nations "Protect-Respect-Remedy" Project: The State, the Corporation and Human Rights in a Global Governance Context', 9 *Santa Clara Journal of International Law* 37 (2011).

6 See A/HRC/Res/17/4, para. 4, and, for example, N. Jägers, 'UN Guiding Principles on Business and Human Rights: Making Headway Towards Real Corporate Accountability?' 29 *Netherlands Quarterly of Human Rights* 159 (2011), p.163.

7 United Nations Global Compact, www.unglobalcompact.org.

8 Sub-Commission on the Promotion and Protection of Human Rights, Commission on Human Rights, *Norms on the responsibilities of transnational corporations and other business enterprises with regard to human rights*, E/CN.4/Sub.2/2003/12/Rev.2, 26 June 2003.

assessments.[9] Upon starting his mandate, the SRSG decided to set aside the UN Draft Norms.[10]

In his second mandate (2008–2011), the SRSG was mostly tasked with "operationalizing" his framework by providing recommendations and guidance to states and companies, including enhancing access to effective remedies.[11] The SRSG held an extensive consultation process,[12] with financial contributions from public and private donors,[13] which undeniably contributed to creating momentum around business and human rights issues. The outcome was the adoption of the UN Guiding Principles that condense the key points of the Framework and conclusions of the discussion process.

State obligations in conflict zones

The UN Guiding Principles aim to provide guidance for states and businesses. According to the SRSG, the principles elaborate on "the implications of existing standards and practices for states and businesses." The SRSG summarizes the structure of the Framework as follows:

> The Framework rests on three pillars. The first is the State duty to protect against human rights abuses by third parties, including business enterprises, through appropriate policies, regulation, and adjudication. The second is the corporate responsibility to respect human rights, which means that business enterprises should act with due diligence to avoid infringing on the rights of others and to address adverse impacts with which they are involved. The third is the need for greater access by victims to effective remedy, both judicial and non-judicial. Each pillar is an essential component in an inter-related and dynamic system of preventative and remedial measures.[14]

9 Commission on Human Rights, *Human Rights and Transnational Corporations and Other Business Enterprises*, Resolution 2005/69, 20 April 2005.

10 J. Ruggie, *Interim Report of the SRSG the Issue of Human Rights and Transnational Corporations and Other Business Enterprises*, U.N. Doc. E/CN.4/2006/97 (2006), paras.56–61.

11 UN Human Rights Council, *Mandate of the Special Representative of the Secretary-General on the Issue of Human Rights and Transnational Corporations and Other Business Enterprises*, Resolution A/HRC/8/7, 18 June 2008.

12 OHCHR, *Holding Business Accountable for Human Rights*, News and Events, 21 January 2011, www.ohchr.org/EN/NewsEvents/Pages/HoldingbusinessaccountableHRabuses.aspx.

13 The regional consultation held in India was for instance supported by the Danish government and the OHCHR. See Report of the SRSG, *Regional Consultation held by the Special Representative of the Secretary-General on Human Rights and Transnational Corporations and Other Business Enterprises*, 5–6 June 2009, http://198.170.85.29/Report-Ruggie-consultation-Delhi-5-6-Feb-2009.pdf.

14 UN Guiding Principles, n.1, Introduction, para.6.

State responsibility is referred to in the first pillar (sole responsibility) and in the third pillar (shared responsibility). In that sense, the first foundational principle of the UN Guiding Principles seems straightforward: it establishes that "states must protect against human rights abuse within their territory and/or jurisdiction" and are required to take "appropriate steps to prevent, investigate, punish and redress such abuse." The "respect, protect, and fulfill" typology used (by UN treaty bodies, as well as regional human rights bodies) to interpret states' human rights obligations is not mentioned in Ruggie's Framework, which refers to states' responsibility to *protect* without specifically discussing their additional obligations to respect and to fulfill. This could suggest a limited reading of state obligations by the SRSG.

The UN Guiding Principles were endorsed by a UN Human Rights Council resolution, but do not constitute a codification of customary international law. They can therefore not alter, let alone weaken, obligations that states have acquired through ratification or through customary international law. However, even though they formally take into account the paramount status of treaty and customary law,[15] the UN Guiding Principles could turn out to be misleading in practice due to a few shortcomings in terms of international human rights law that could be particularly important in transitional justice situations.

First, and contrary to language of international law, the UN Guiding Principles avoid using the expression "violations of human rights." This gives the misleading impression that states simply confront human rights "challenges"—and obscures the fact that what is really at stake is the risk of committing human rights *violations*, in breach of states' international legal obligations.

Second, the wording of the non-discrimination provision in principle 3 of the UN Guiding Principles does not reflect current international human rights law. Aiming at being general, it misses some of the important elements of the prohibition of discrimination. Most importantly, in mentioning only the discrimination that "women and men" may face, and not other "prohibited categories" of discrimination, the UN Guiding Principles do not correctly reflect international human rights law.[16] This results in a very superficial treatment of indigenous people's rights, which states are bound to protect and which are particularly vulnerable in the context of corporate activities.

Third, the SRSG took an ambiguous position on extraterritorial obligations of home states. The wording of the UN Guiding Principles[17] suggests that states are neither required to nor prohibited from regulating extraterritorial activity of the enterprises incorporated under their jurisdiction. However,

15 *Ibid.*, para.4.

16 UN Human Rights Council, *Resolution on Sexual Orientation and Gender Identity*, A/HRC/17/L.9/Rev.1, 17 June 2011.

17 UN Guiding Principles, n.1, principles 12 and 24.

treaty interpretation by authoritative bodies and experts, as well as jurisprudence, indicates that states do indeed have obligations in this area.[18] Considering the frequent failure of the rule of law in conflict-ridden countries and in countries in transition, a clear statement in the UN Guiding Principles regarding states' extraterritorial obligations would have been desirable both from a human rights perspective and from a practical approach, to effectively address governance gaps identified by the SRSG.

Fourth, the SRSG seems to have minimized state obligations under international humanitarian law. The first Geneva Convention, by way of example, stipulates that:

> [t]he High Contracting Parties undertake to enact any legislation necessary to provide effective penal sanctions for natural persons committing, or ordering to be committed, any of the grave breaches of the present Convention. . . . Each High Contracting Party shall be under the obligation to search for persons alleged to have committed, or to have ordered to be committed, such grave breaches, and shall bring such persons, regardless of their nationality, before its own courts [and] . . . shall take measures necessary for the suppression of all acts contrary to the provisions of the present Convention other than the grave breaches.[19]

It would have been useful if the SRSG had highlighted these state obligations in the commentary to the UN Guiding Principles. He could also have pointed out that states *must*, rather than *should*, comply with them.[20] Corporations do not have these same obligations under international humanitarian law, but corporate actors are nevertheless bound by important norms for non-state actors, such as the proportionality principle and, if taking part in the hostilities, the protection of civilians and non-combatants.[21]

18 See 'The Maastricht Guidelines on Violations of Economic, Social and Cultural Rights', 20 *Human Rights Quarterly* 691 (1998), and, for example, F. Coomans, 'The extraterritorial scope of the International Covenant on Economic, Social and Cultural Rights in the work of the United Nations Committee on Economic, Social and Cultural Rights', 11 *Human Rights Law Review* 1 (2011). See also European Commission, Communication, *A renewed EU Strategy 2011–2014 for Corporate Social Responsibility*, adopted in Brussels on 25 October 2011, COM(2011) 681 final.

19 See, for example, Convention (IV) relative to the Protection of Civilian Persons in Time of War. Adopted in Geneva, 12 August 1949, article 146. See generally on the international humanitarian law obligation to make non-state actors horizontally liable, R. Bismuth, 'Mapping a responsibility of corporations for violations of international humanitarian law sailing between international and domestic legal orders', 38 *Denver Journal of International Law & Policy* 203 (2010), pp.218–221.

20 UN Guiding Principles, n.1, principle 7. Compare with Geneva Conventions of 1949, GC I, article 49, GC II, article 50, GC III, article 129, GC IV, article 146.

21 See also A. Clapham, *Human Rights Obligations of Non-State Actors*, Oxford University Press, Oxford, 2006.

This obligation becomes more concrete in the draft of a possible convention to regulate the activities of private military and security companies,[22] elaborated by the Working Group on the Use of Mercenaries, "to make concrete proposals, including new norms, principles or guidelines to fight this new phenomenon [the activities of private military and security companies]."[23] This initiative, parallel to but independent from the SRSG's work, might contribute to clarifying state and possibly corporate obligations vis-à-vis corporate activities in conflict situations.

Thus, the UN Guiding Principles do not take up all relevant aspects of the treaty bodies' interpretations of state obligations under international human rights law and international humanitarian law.[24] In sum, the UN Guiding Principles could have been more precise in distinguishing states' *legal* obligations from *corporate governance* considerations; this might have helped differentiate obligations from expectations and suggestions for operationalization.

Despite these shortcomings, there is another statement—besides the prevention focus—that should be highlighted as an important contribution to the adaption of state obligations to business and human rights issues: states have obligations, drawn from the UN Charter, with regard to international economic and social cooperation, which has also been recognized as relevant in human rights protection.[25] With respect to conflict zones, the SRSG has made a novel point in highlighting the positive role that neighboring states could play:

> Where transnational corporations are involved, their "home" States therefore have a role to play in assisting both those corporations and *host States* to ensure that businesses are not involved with human rights abuse, while *neighbouring States* can provide important additional support.[26]

22 UN Working Group on the Use of Mercenaries as a means of violating human rights and impeding the exercise of the right of peoples to self-determination, *Use of mercenaries as a means of violating human rights and impeding the exercise of the right of peoples to self-determination*, A/66/317, 22 August 2011, para.64.

23 J.L. Gómez del Prado, Chairperson, UN Working Group on the Use of Mercenaries, *Private Military and Security Companies and Challenges to the UN Working Group on the Use of Mercenaries*, conference paper, 2008, www.havenscenter.org/privatemilitaryconference2008.

24 UN Guiding Principles, n.1, principle 7. On prevention and international humanitarian law, see for example, J. Mendez, 'Preventing, Implementing and Enforcing International Humanitarian Law', in E. Andersen and D.M. Crane, *Proceedings of the First International Humanitarian Law Dialogs*, American Society of International Law, Washington D.C., 2008.

25 Special Rapporteur on the Highest Attainable Standard of the Right to Health, Preliminary note on missions to Uganda and to the offices of the Executive Directors of the Nordic-Baltic countries at the World Bank and the International Monetary Fund, A/HRC/4/28/Add.3, 21 March 2007.

26 SRSG, *Report on business and human rights in conflict-affected regions: challenges and options towards State responses*, A/HRC/17/32, 27 May 2011, para.6, emphasis added.

This wording should be interpreted as recommending cooperation among all states—including, for example, donor states that are of particular importance in transitional justice contexts but were not specifically mentioned by the SRSG—in implementing the UN Guiding Principles.

Corporate human rights responsibilities in conflict zones

The SRSG recognizes that companies' activities may affect all human rights and that—as a "social expectation" —the "baseline responsibility of companies is to respect human rights."[27] Such rights refer to the rights enshrined in the International Bill of Human Rights, as well as principles and rights set out in the ILO Declaration on Fundamental Principles and Rights at Work,[28] and may include additional standards depending on the circumstances. In situations of armed conflict, "enterprises should respect the standards of international humanitarian law."[29]

Defining the meaning of the corporate responsibility to respect

The corporate responsibility to respect requires that companies "[a]void causing or contributing to adverse human rights impacts through their own activities, and address such impacts when they occur"; and "[s]eek to prevent or mitigate adverse human rights impacts that are directly linked to their operations, products or services by their business relationships, even if they have not contributed to those impacts."[30] Since "business relationships" are understood as including "relationships with business partners, entities in [a company's] value chain, and any other non-State or State entity directly linked to its business operations, products or services,"[31] a company should seek to prevent or mitigate human rights impacts directly linked to the operations of its subsidiaries or suppliers.

To address such responsibility, companies must have a "policy commitment to meet their responsibility to respect human rights"; adopt a human rights due diligence process; and undertake measures allowing for the remediation

27 UN Human Rights Council, *Protect, Respect and Remedy: a Framework for Business and Human Rights. Report of the Special Representative of the Secretary-General on the issue of human rights and transnational corporations and other business enterprises*, John Ruggie, A/HRC/8/5, 7 April 2008, para.54.

28 UN Guiding Principles, n.1, principle 12.

29 *Ibid.*, commentary to principle 12.

30 *Ibid.*, principle 13(a) and (b).

31 *Ibid.*, commentary to principle 13.

of "adverse human rights impacts" in which they may have played a role.[32] Measures to be taken will vary according to factors such as the size, sector, operational context, ownership, and structure of the company, as well as the severity of the "human rights impacts."[33]

The SRSG defines due diligence as "the steps a company must take to become aware of, prevent and address adverse human rights impacts."[34] While the concept lacks a uniform content in international law,[35] in both domestic and international contexts it focuses on elements of "prevention" and "prudence" and entails an "obligation of conduct" as opposed to an "obligation of result." The process rests on an ongoing assessment of actual and potential human rights impacts, and possibly violations, that a company may cause through its own activities or as a result of its business relationships, including "meaningful consultation with potentially affected groups and other relevant stakeholders."[36] While due diligence is a laudable goal, it is unclear how a "meaningful consultation with potentially affected groups or other relevant stakeholders"[37] should be conducted, especially in conflict and transitional justice contexts, where stakeholders cannot be expected to form a homogenous group.

The way in which the Framework and the UN Guiding Principles address corporate responsibility poses a number of questions at both the conceptual level and the practical level. Some of the questions that we consider specifically relevant for situations of conflict or transitional justice will be discussed below.

As far as corporations are concerned, the concept of due diligence is often used in domestic corporate law and domestic corporate governance matters, where it is part of the duty of care imposed on the board of directors, which requires them to act in the interests of the shareholders and the company itself.[38]

Considering that the most egregious corporate human rights abuses occur in conflict zones, and given the specific circumstances in such cases, especially the absence of the rule of law,[39] enhanced due diligence is required

32 *Ibid.*, principle 15.
33 *Ibid.*, principle 14.
34 SRSG Report 2008, n.27, para.56.
35 M. Flemme, *Due Diligence in International Law*, Master Thesis, Faculty of Law, University of Lund, 2004, p.41.
36 UN Guiding Principles, n.1, principle 18(a) and (b).
37 *Ibid.*, principle 18(b).
38 B. Loeve, sous la direction de Michel Doucin, Ambassadeur chargé de la bioéthique et de la responsabilité sociale des entreprises, *Analyse des notions de 'due diligence' et de 'sphere d'influence' dans le contexte du respect des droits de l'homme par les entreprises: enjeux de la définition du champ d'application des standards en matière de RSE*, 13 April 2010, p.48.
39 SRSG Report 2008, n.27, para.47.

from companies operating in conflict zones.[40] However, apart from a few recommendations, such as the need to protect company employees,[41] the UN Guiding Principles provide no further guidance to corporations operating in such environments. Rather, the SRSG's recommendations concerning conflict zones focus on state obligations.[42]

Beyond processes that need to be established in order to conduct due diligence, what should reasonably be expected from companies in conflict situations? What elements (such as knowledge, perceptions, and experiences) should be taken into consideration to determine a corporation's responsibility? What type of acts and omissions should be prohibited under a company's responsibility to respect?

Likely related to the process-focused structure of the UN Guiding Principles, the SRSG has avoided defining any specific human rights responsibilities for companies operating in diverse environments (based on the argument that "business can affect virtually all internationally recognized rights"[43]). While this is in principle an important acknowledgment, the SRSG's focus on "deduc[ing] responsibilities on a case-by-case basis with reference to a general principle" may have caused him to miss an opportunity to address core issues.[44] Practically speaking, and unless states take regulatory measures requiring companies to conduct human rights due diligence, this allows each stakeholder to define for itself what the scope of the corporate responsibility to respect is, especially as the SRSG has refrained from using case examples in his work.[45]

One of the best tools of due diligence is human rights impact assessment. While the UN Guiding Principles do not explicitly refer to the methodology of human rights impact assessment, they do refer to the identification of human rights impacts and the need for companies to make sure findings and measures to address identified risks are integrated within companies' structures and management systems. To a certain extent, this process also includes looking at supply chains. Measures to be taken will depend on the

40 See below the discussion of complicity.

41 SRSG Report 2008, n.27, para.63.

42 See for instance, UN Human Rights Council, Report of the SRSG on the issue of human rights and transnational corporations and other business enterprises, John Ruggie, *Business and human rights in conflict-affected regions: Challenges and options towards State responses*, A/HRC/17/32, 27 May 2011.

43 SRSG Report 2008, n.27, para.58.

44 S. Deva, 'Protect, Respect and Remedy?: A Critique of the SRSG's Framework for Business and Human Rights', in K. Buhmann, L. Roseberry and M. Morsing (eds), *Corporate Social and Human Rights Responsibilities. Global Legal and Management Perspectives*, Palgrave, Basingstoke, 2011 (108–126), p.121.

45 Joint Open Letter to UN Special Representative on Business and Human Rights (endorsed by over 240 organizations and individuals), October 2007, www.fidh.org/IMG/pdf/OpenLetter_Ruggie_FINAL_wOct10Endorsements.pdf.

causal link between the human rights abuse and the company,[46] as well as the "leverage" that the company may have in addressing the harm. Also, the severity of the abuse will play a role in deciding whether to continue the relationship with the supplier, as will the question of whether cutting the relationship would have any human rights impact. Leverage is understood as "the ability to effect change in the wrongful practices of an entity that causes harm."[47] Such an entity could be, for example, a subsidiary, a supplier, or the host state. The UN Guiding Principles therefore call on companies to use their leverage if the harm being done is somehow linked to the company's activities.[48] Ruggie does not explicitly require companies to speak out against repressive governments—even if they could effectively do so, and even if they are benefitting from the human rights violations that are committed—though he does suggest that the due diligence responsibility to avoid complicity in human rights violations includes beneficial and silent complicity.[49]

As a final resort, if a company is unable to prevent or mitigate human rights violations, it "should consider ending the relationship" with a contractor or subcontractor if such a decision does not risk further exacerbating human rights abuses.[50] In that sense, a company should use its leverage—in the form of a threat to end the relationship—to prevent human rights abuses. Such a threat is best included in the contract with the supplier itself, accompanied by a specification of the relevant remedies.[51]

While these recommendations are useful, the SRSG does not address other situations in which companies should be using their leverage or acting with due diligence. In this context, the vague concept of complicity that the SRSG uses leaves room for addressing and specifying such issues in the future. The UN Guiding Principles make a distinction between complicity as a legal issue and "extra-legal/social complicity."[52] The SRSG highlights, in a 2008

46 See UN Guiding Principles, n.1, principle 19(b)(i).

47 *Ibid.*, commentary to principle 19.

48 The draft version of the UN Guiding Principles clearly stated that a company should use its leverage to "prevent and mitigate its potential human rights impacts or help remediate any actual impacts for which it is responsible." While not explicitly stated in the final version of the UN Guiding Principles, the interpretation of the use of leverage remains linked to a company's direct or indirect impact. See interpretation of leverage according to Ruggie (presented by David Virjms, former member of his team): www.slideshare.net/compartuser/david-presentation-icco-supply-chains.

49 For a further discussion, see S. Michalowski, 'Due Diligence and Complicity – A Relationship in Need of Clarification', in D. Bilchitz and S. Deva (eds), *Human Rights Obligations of Business: Beyond the Corporate Responsibility to Respect?* Cambridge University Press, Cambridge, 2013 (forthcoming).

50 UN Guiding Principles, n.1, commentary to principle 19.

51 See for analysis pointing in that direction, Leader and Ong, n.4.

52 Michalowski, n.49.

report, that the "[m]ere presence in a country, paying taxes, or silence in the face of abuses is unlikely to amount to the practical assistance required for legal liability."[53]

Direct obligations of corporations under international law?

Since the beginning of his mandate, the SRSG was very cautious—not to say reluctant—toward the idea that corporations may have *direct* obligations under international human rights law.[54] However, there are arguments that corporations are in part subjects of international law and that, therefore, just as individuals, they have both rights and corresponding obligations.[55] At the same time, the SRSG did not argue that these obligations do *not* exist.

Despite a recognition that international crimes (genocide, slavery, torture, war crimes, and grave breaches of the Geneva Conventions)[56] "may fall under customary international law," the SRSG has emphasized that provisions of the Universal Declaration of Human Rights that have entered customary law "currently apply only to States (and sometimes individuals)."[57] The view of the SRSG therefore appears to depart from the opinion taken by some of the UN treaty bodies, which have, albeit to a limited extent, started to address directly private actors' responsibilities.[58] Some UN Special Rapporteurs have also interpreted their mandates as allowing them to make

53 SRSG Report 2008, n.27, para.77. However, from a legal perspective, it should be noted that the SRSG's approach has not developed factors such as proximity (used similarly to the notion of sphere of influence) and the foreseeability of risk, both elements that might prove relevant in assessing these types of situations. Such an approach coincides with the SRSG's general refusal to refer to broader concepts, such as sphere of influence, which would not strictly be tied to a company's own corporate behavior. See also International Commission of Jurists, *Corporate Complicity and Legal Accountability*, Volume 1, 2008, p.9, stressing the importance of: "[g]eographic closeness, or . . . the duration, frequency, intensity and/or of the nature of the connection".

54 UN Guiding Principles, n.2, commentary to principle 12. See also UN Human Rights Council, Report of the SRSG on the issue of human rights and transnational corporations and other business enterprises, John Ruggie, *Business and human rights: Mapping international standards of responsibility and accountability for corporate acts*, A/HRC/4/35, 19 February 2007, para.44: "[i]t does not seem that the international human rights instruments discussed here currently impose direct legal responsibilities on corporations."

55 A. Clapham, *Human Rights Obligations of Non-State Actors*, Oxford University Press, Oxford, 2006, pp.70–84.

56 SRSG, Interim Report 2006, n.10, para.61.

57 SRSG, Report 2007, n.54, para.37.

58 See for instance, CESCR, General Comment No.14: the Right to the Highest Attainable Standard of Health, E/C/12/2000/4, 11 August 2000, para.42.

recommendations to private actors.[59] Additionally, it must be highlighted that private actors do have obligations under humanitarian law.[60]

Adopting the pragmatic outlook of the UN Guiding Principles,[61] the SRSG concludes, in his report on conflict-affected regions, that "there remains a lack of clarity with regard to what innovative, proactive and, above all, practical policies and tools States may have or should acquire for preventing or mitigating corporate-related abuses in situations of conflict."[62] Nonetheless, the SRSG could have highlighted that with respect to serious violations of human rights and grave breaches of humanitarian law, there are *legal* standards that guide companies, as well as states, in such situations, and that such standards constitute a paramount tool for the purposes sought in transitional justice contexts, such as ending impunity, knowing the truth about what happened during the period of conflict, and securing reparations and institutional change.[63]

Can due diligence require leaving a country?

A final question worth considering is whether there may be situations in which a company can comply with its due diligence commitment only by leaving a country. The UN Guiding Principles are silent on this question, and the SRSG has not addressed the issue in his reports. Corporate presence in conflict situations is often assumed to be, in principle, positive at all moments, as it creates employment. However, more balanced views recognize that a company's mere presence in a country might, in certain circumstances, amount to condoning a repressive regime and exacerbating human rights violations. While space constraints prevent a detailed discussion of this question, the following proposal by Lene Bomann-Larsen seems to be a useful standard: a company should "take responsibility for effects that would not have come about had it not been for the presence of the company."[64]

59 See for instance the Special Rapporteur on the Right to Health, Paul Hunt, *Human Rights Guidelines for Pharmaceutical Companies in relation to Access to Medicines.* Report to the General Assembly, A/63/263, 11 August 2008. See also reports from the UN Special Rapporteur on the Right to Food, Olivier de Schutter, *Agribusiness and the right to food*, A/HRC/13/33, 22 December 2009.

60 Common article 3 to the Geneva Conventions, and protocol II to the Geneva Conventions.

61 J.G. Ruggie, 'The construction of the UN "Protect, Respect and Remedy" Framework for business and human rights', 16 *European Human Rights Law Review* 127–133 (2011).

62 SRSG, Report on Conflict Affected Regions, n.42, para.8.

63 C. Sandoval, Office of the High Commissioner for Human Rights, *Special Issue on Transitional Justice and Economic, Social and Cultural Rights*, forthcoming, p.3. See also P. de Greiff, 'Introduction', in P. de Greiff, *Handbook of Reparations*, Oxford University Press, Oxford, 2006 (1–18), p.11, and more generally the various contributions to that book.

64 L. Bomann-Larsen, *Corporate actors in zones of conflict. Responsible engagement*, Confederation of Norwegian Business and Industry and Peace Research Institute of Oslo, Oslo, 2003, p.5.

This seems to indicate that where a company's mere presence can be shown to have a harmful human rights impact, the best—though perhaps not only—way to avoid this adverse impact, as well as resulting liability, might be to leave the country before such a situation occurs. In that sense, more concretely, enterprises could avoid the risk of being complicit by "stay[ing] away from countries where forces that stay in power have a proven record of severe human rights violations such as genocide, ethnic cleansing, torture, rape, induced famine, and deprivation of property."[65]

Challenges for a business and human rights framework in the context of transitional justice

As mentioned above, the due diligence concept of the UN Guiding Principles indicates that the SRSG sees a procedural approach as the solution to corporate human rights responsibilities. This is also evidenced in the way that the third pillar addresses issues of access to justice. This section examines the extent to which the UN Guiding Principles could be relevant for transitional justice situations, while highlighting challenges raised by the third pillar's over-emphasis on company-based grievance mechanisms and its inattention to the implications of the substantive dimension of the right to reparations.

As the commentary to principle 26 of the UN Guiding Principles makes clear, obstruction of justice may well stem from private actors.[66] Transitional justice contexts seem especially prone to this kind of undue influence, whereby companies may try to exercise influence directly (such as through bribery and corruption of judicial officials, strategies to unduly delay proceedings, and judicial harassment of or violence against human rights defenders) or indirectly (such as through threats of divestment). In that sense, corporate actors alleged to have committed human rights violations during conflict might well enjoy impunity during the transition, taking advantage of their economic power.

Generally, human rights law requires states to investigate, prosecute, punish, and repair human rights violations that occur during periods of

65 M. Bazela, 'Corporate Complicity in Human Rights Violations. When is it time to leave a country?' 8 *Información Filosófica* 55–72 (2011), p.65.

66 See notably the well-known case of Chevron in Ecuador, where the company has been accused of fraud and attempts to corrupt the judicial process. See 'Preemptive orders block Chevron-Ecuador judgment', 6 *Global Arbitration Review* 9 (2011); J. Dine and B. Paulsen, 'US Court of Appeals for the Second Circuit declines to stay Chevron's arbitration against Ecuador', 16 *International Bar Association Arbitration News* 137 (2011); J. Kimerling, 'Indigenous peoples and the oil frontier in Amazonia: the case of Ecuador, Chevron Texaco, and Aguinda v. Texaco', 38 *New York University Journal of International Law and Politics* 413 (2006).

conflict just as those that occur in times of peace.[67] This includes violations of all rights, including economic, social, and cultural rights, especially violations of the core content of these rights.[68] Also, for all states where serious violations occur, and especially states in transition, human rights law requires governments to comply with the right to know the truth about human rights violations committed before the transition, and with the obligation to repair human rights damage that occurred.

Access to effective remedies in post-conflict and post-dictatorship situations is considered crucial to ensuring peaceful transitions and stability.[69] The UN Guiding Principles recommend that "where business enterprises identify that they have caused or contributed to adverse impacts, they should cooperate in their remediation through legitimate processes."[70]

As far as companies are concerned, the SRSG has recommended the establishment of company-based or industry-based ("multi-stakeholder") non-judicial grievance mechanisms (referred to as "operational-level grievance mechanisms"), accessible by individuals and communities that may have been affected negatively.[71] For a grievance mechanism to be considered effective, it must meet a series of criteria: it must be legitimate, accessible, predictable, equitable, transparent, rights compatible, and a source of continuous learning and improvement.[72]

Companies may also "take a role" in providing remediation in situations where they could not foresee or prevent human rights violations or in situations where abuses, though not committed by the companies themselves, are directly linked to the companies' operations, products, or services as a result of a business relationship.[73] In other words, companies are recommended to go further than the "legal obligation to pay compensation for complicity in human rights violations," which normally arises where a company at least was

67 UN General Assembly, *Basic Principles and Guidelines on the Right to a Remedy and Reparation for Victims of Gross Violations of International Human Rights Law and Serious Violations of International Humanitarian Law, A/Res.*60/147, adopted without a vote on 16 December 2005. See also, for example, American Convention on Human Rights, article 1.1, as interpreted in, for example, Inter-American Court of Human Rights (IACtHR), *Case of the Ituango Massacres v Colombia*, Preliminary Objection, Merits, Reparations and Costs, Judgment of 1 July 2006, Series C No.148. See also the procedural obligations under European Convention of Human Rights, articles 2 and 3, as interpreted in, for example, *Timurtas v Turkey* (App. No. 23531/94) ECHR 221 (13 June 2000). Lastly, see International Covenant on Economic, Social and Cultural Rights, article 6.

68 K. Young, 'The Minimum Core of Economic and Social Rights: A Concept in Search of Content', 33 *Yale Journal of International Law* 113 (2008).

69 See chapter 5 of this book.

70 UN Guiding Principles, n.1, principle 22.

71 *Ibid.*, principle 29.

72 *Ibid.*, principle 31.

73 *Ibid.*, commentary to principle 22.

or should have been aware of the risk.[74] While these norms apply to all human rights abuses, they may have special relevance in transitional justice contexts, particularly when the state justice system is overburdened or is reluctant or hostile to judging past crimes or cases concerning indemnity for past violations. As this book demonstrates, transitional justice mechanisms rarely extend to corporations. Alternative remediation mechanisms might therefore be particularly welcomed, provided they are effective and satisfactory from a human rights perspective.

Unlike the 2008 "Protect, Respect and Remedy" framework, the UN Guiding Principles explicitly refer to the substantive dimension of the right to an effective remedy and mention the different forms that reparations may take.[75] Yet, the UN Guiding Principles remain largely focused on company-based grievance mechanisms and tend to overlook the complexity of reparations issues, making it difficult to adapt these mechanisms to the challenges of establishing shared responsibilities in transitional justice contexts. Reparations after conflicts often have to take place on a very large scale and are hardly manageable on a case-by-case basis. Governments usually implement reparations laws that define who is regarded as a victim and what types of reparations need to be provided.[76] If private reparations mechanisms step in while public mechanisms are not (yet) functional, or if they are developed to complement public mechanisms, this may have the advantage of providing efficient and prompt relief to certain groups of the population. At the same time, however, such mechanisms can be problematic: if private reparations show disparities with regard to the approaches adopted by other companies or with regard to public reparations mechanisms, these differences might fuel new conflict rather than appeasing tensions, as it might exacerbate root causes that generated conflict in the first place.[77] The same might be true if company-based reparations mechanisms do not award reparations systematically according to generalized criteria, or where the criteria deviate from those adopted by the state reparations program.

Given that international law is usually governed by the principle of non-retroactivity, it is important to mention that the UN Guiding Principles do not exclude due diligence regarding *past* human rights abuses when defining the baseline against which corporate responsibility is to be measured. This is crucial from a transitional justice perspective. While the relevant principles themselves refer to "actual and potential human rights impacts," the commentary explains that actual impacts are "those that have already occurred," which "should be a subject for remediation." The SRSG has also clearly highlighted that "human rights risks . . . may be inherited through

74 Michalowski, n.49.
75 UN Guiding Principles, n.1, commentary to principle 25.
76 See, for example, the different contributions and material in de Greiff, n.63.
77 Sandoval, n.63.

mergers or acquisitions."[78] This is important, as in situations of conflict and transitional justice there are often changes of ownership.

Thus, while periods of transition from one political regime to another may frequently be accompanied by profound changes in business ownership, this does not mean that enterprises may start from a clean slate. Again, however, the SRSG has not been sufficiently clear in distinguishing legal from moral responsibility—leaving it to businesses, states, and other actors involved to decide which concrete obligations exist with respect to past violations. He has, however, specified that remediation of past "adverse impact" must occur through "legitimate processes,"[79] a concern he has repeated with regard to the requirement[80] that "courts [be] independent of economic or political pressures . . . from business actors."[81] This is especially important in transitional justice situations, where the societal framework and institutions are usually weak and adept to reversal of the process of democratization and re-establishment of constitutional rights.

In such contexts, company-based grievance mechanisms might be seen as lacking—and in actual fact may lack—independent and maybe even impartial decision-making processes. Such procedural and legitimacy problems might cause difficulties both with regard to the human rights compliance of the process and with regard to the outcome of reparations proceedings. As long as these difficulties are not resolved, the need for effective and independent judicial, administrative, or public remediation mechanisms remains where corporations caused or contributed to human rights violations. In sum, private grievance mechanisms are a useful complementary tool, particularly where they surpass existing legal obligations—but they cannot replace impartial administration of justice by independent third parties.

Considering these difficulties, the third pillar of the Framework should have established limits for recurring to private non-judicial mechanisms,[82] especially in contexts of gross violations of human rights in conflict situations. Amongst the core effectiveness criteria set forth by the SRSG for non-judicial grievance mechanisms,[83] the necessity for such mechanisms to be compatible with "internationally recognized human rights" should have been further explained, particularly with regard to the internationally recognized right to have access to effective remedies.[84] Furthermore, a mechanism's independence

78 UN Guiding Principles, n.1, principle 17 and commentary.

79 *Ibid.*, principle 22.

80 The SRSG again uses the misleading "should," although the prohibition of corruption is an international obligation.

81 UN Guiding Principles, n.1, commentary to principle 26.

82 A criticism that has also been addressed to the "access to remedy" pillar generally, Jäger, n.6; McBeth, n.2, Deva, n.44.

83 That they be legitimate, accessible, predictable, equitable, transparent, rights compatible, and a source of continuous learning. See UN Guiding Principles, n.1, principle 31.

84 See for example, International Covenant on Civil and Political Rights of 1966, article 14.

does not constitute one of the "effectiveness criteria" of non-judicial grievance mechanisms, nor does the importance of making the outcome of the proceedings publicly available.[85] While this could hamper reparations processes beyond contexts of transitional justice, it remains especially serious in such contexts where truth, trust in institutions and societal actors, and justice must be restored.

The UN Guiding Principles also fail to recognize and address the fact that corporate-related abuses in conflict situations have gone largely unpunished. In this regard, the interrelationship between judicial and non-judicial mechanisms, as well as corporate responsibility not to interfere with or try to undermine ongoing judicial proceedings, should be further elaborated upon. The Texaco/Chevron lawsuit for damage caused in Ecuador— characterized by proceedings in multiple fora (United States, Ecuador, Canada, Brazil, and international investment arbitration proceedings),[86] an aggressive strategy on the part of the company to discredit the Ecuadorian judicial system, and never-ending legal proceedings (it took 18 years to obtain a decision, which has yet to be enforced and continues to be challenged by the company)—sharply illustrates the obstacles that victims face in trying to obtain reparations via judicial proceedings. While the UN Guiding Principles recognize some of these obstacles, they could have elaborated further on measures that states (including home states) need to take to overcome them, as well as on companies' responsibilities not to unduly interfere with or undermine judicial proceedings as part of their obligation to respect human rights. As far as out-of-court settlements (preferred by companies, and sometimes by victims, and where most lawsuits involving corporations end) are concerned, they should have been discussed in light of their compatibility with the right to the truth and, more generally, the right to reparations. This is particularly true when broad clauses of such agreements prevent future claims against a company and do not provide for the public acknowledgment of corporate actors' responsibilities. It would have been useful to address the need to maintain a baseline of rights protection even in negotiated remedies,[87] in order to make the enforcement of the UN Guiding Principles credible.

Considering the paramount importance of the right to the truth after conflict and dictatorial periods, it seems problematic to allow for secrecy regarding the account of the facts, the acknowledgment of responsibilities (including a potential apology) that may come with such an account, and the modalities for reparations to which the parties have agreed. The lack of transparency around the outcome implies a considerable risk that compensation or

85 The criteria on transparency focus on information provided to the involved parties during the process, as well as information on the mechanism's performance.

86 See n.66.

87 M. Freeman, *Truth Commissions and Procedural Fairness*, Cambridge University Press, Cambridge, 2006.

satisfaction programs offered by companies directly to victims or their relatives may not comply with the relevant standards of international law. Secrecy around results, and possibly around process, might also deprive the process of its deterrent effects for future violators. Nevertheless, these risks must be balanced with the advantage that private voluntary remedies can offer in obtaining effective reparations in concrete cases.

Furthermore, the UN Guiding Principles remain weak when it comes to addressing the issue of reparations in cases where the company is not responsible under *domestic* law. Indeed, they suggest that in cases where no legal responsibility has been determined, but where the corporation is nevertheless to some extent responsible for the harm that occurred, it is left to the company to decide whether or not it will play a role in providing for remediation.[88] This assertion, while consistent with the overall approach of the UN Guiding Principles, generates a possible mismatch where, under international law, reparations should be provided, but where domestic law does not sufficiently implement this obligation by providing a legal framework that encompasses corporations' corresponding legal obligations. This mismatch may not necessarily be attributed to a fault of business: if domestic law does not provide for a remedy when it should do so according to international law, a voluntary mechanism might be helpful in ensuring that victims receive reparations. At the same time, the state—including home states—should not feel released from the obligation to adequately regulate simply because the UN Guiding Principles contain provisions that de facto encourage companies to fill some of the gaps. This is especially so because of the reparations disparities and independence problems discussed above. A suggestion might be for the state to define a minimum baseline for reparations based on the public reparations law, with the aim of preventing inadequate reparations payments and mitigating the impact of disparities in negotiation skills and companies' readiness to repair.

In sum, neither the SRSG's Framework nor the UN Guiding Principles provide sufficient orientation regarding the advantages and disadvantages of private voluntary engagement in reparations and redress. Yet, the *preventive* focus of the UN Guiding Principles offers the possibility for reinforcing the fundamental aim of transitional justice: preventing the recurrence of atrocities. If companies are called on to prevent human rights violations through due diligence mechanisms and risk evaluation, they should be especially aware of risks specific to transitional justice contexts and should consider carefully how they employ private security guards, how they relate to military or paramilitary actors, how they deal with corruption, how they affect the land rights of previously displaced individuals or communities, and so forth. What many believe to be an excellent incentive to ensure that

88 UN Guiding Principles, n.1, commentary to principle 22.

such precautions are taken would be to require (which the UN Guiding Principles fail to do) that under the duty to protect, home states regulate and sanction accordingly companies operating abroad, particularly those in conflict situations.

Conclusion

The SRSG's strong insistence on the need to adopt a pragmatic approach and the continuous search for consensus from various stakeholders throughout his two mandates have undoubtedly contributed to the current political uptake of the UN Guiding Principles by all stakeholders, particularly states and companies. While such an approach may have stimulated debates on business and human rights issues and given human rights a higher political profile, this might have been at the expense of much-needed clarity and guidance on states' obligations and businesses' responsibilities regarding human rights.

In general, the preventive focus of the UN Guiding Principles, especially with respect to corporate responsibility, is crucial and to be welcomed. It shows an acute concern that it is better to avoid human rights violations than to repair them (if at all possible). However, while companies' responsibilities are addressed quite clearly and through useful concepts such as human rights due diligence, guidance provided to states and companies operating in conflict zones remains insufficient and not reflective of international humanitarian law.

This chapter has highlighted blurred areas, as well as areas of the UN Guiding Principles that depart from existing and recognized human rights and humanitarian law standards. By emphasizing the fact that the UN Guiding Principles did not create any *new norms of international law*, the SRSG may have implied that the UN Guiding Principles intended to reflect legal accuracy and depth. If, on the contrary, the UN Guiding Principles were meant to be only a "collection of best practices" *in light of* international human rights law, but not representing the latter, then the UN Guiding Principles should certainly not be treated as current codification of international law regarding business and human rights issues. Even the latter interpretation does not justify errors made in the reference to, and interpretation of, states' obligations under international law. These errors are more worrisome given the current considerations of the UN Guiding Principles by the UN Global Compact,[89] and even by the newly formed UN Working Group on Business and Human Rights, as representing the "global authoritative standard."[90]

89 UN Global Compact, *The UN Guiding Principles on Business and Human Rights: Relationship to UN Global Compact Commitments*, July 2011, www.unglobalcompact.org/docs/issues_doc/human_rights/Resources/GPs_GC%20note.pdf.

90 UN Human Rights Council, *Report of the Working Group on the issue of human rights and transnational corporations and other business enterprises*, A/HRC/20/29, 10 April 2012.

Among the notable gaps in the UN Guiding Principles is the lack of guidance for states and companies concerning how to ensure victims' access to effective remedies (including reparation). Similarly, states are provided with little guidance regarding how to regulate corporate activities to effectively prevent human rights abuses. The general emphasis on non-judicial and company-based grievance mechanisms can constitute an important addition to current mechanisms and could be of particular use in transitional justice contexts. However, the lack of attention given to the relationship between judicial and non-judicial remedies and the lack of "red lines" drawn to indicate scenarios in which these mechanisms would not be appropriate pose particular difficulties in transition contexts. In addition, company-based grievance mechanisms cannot claim to be independent—a fact that might constitute a disadvantage in tense and contested transition environments.

The authors of this chapter are conscious that the SRSG's mandate did not specifically call on him to clarify applicable standards regarding transitional justice contexts. This chapter's analysis of the UN Guiding Principles' usefulness in transitional justice contexts shows that further research in law and social sciences is needed to clarify and further elaborate on states' obligations and corporations' responsibilities in this context.

There seems to be room in the future for analyzing how truth commissions and other transitional justice mechanisms have addressed (or failed to address) companies' role in fueling conflict situations and the need to lift corporate-related obstacles to justice that may pose particular problems in transitional justice contexts, such as status limitations or current practices that prevent victims from obtaining adequate forms of reparations.

Generally speaking, it is critical that treaty bodies and human rights tribunals continue developing authoritative interpretations and jurisprudence on human rights obligations,[91] particularly where the UN Guiding Principles present shortcomings and, more importantly, misinterpretations of existing international standards applicable to states. In addition, domestic standards on complicity, negligence, and liability should not be overlooked. It is worth recalling that "further enhancement of standards" was foreseen in the adoption of the mandate of the new UN Working Group on Business and Human Rights. Such a normative development could, as a first step, focus on corporate accountability in conflict and transition situations,[92] attending to the gravity of present challenges.

91 See for example, Committee on the Rights to the Child, *Consultation on Draft Outline of Forthcoming General Comment on Business and Child Rights*, 2012. The documentation of the consultation process is available at www2.ohchr.org/english/bodies/crc/callSubmissions CRC_BusinessSector.htm.

92 UN Human Rights Council, *Human Rights and Transnational Corporations and other Business Enterprises*, A/HRC/RES/17/4, 6 June 2011.

Chapter 5

Corporations and Redress in Transitional Justice Processes

Clara Sandoval and Gill Surfleet

Introduction

It is beyond dispute that corporations cause and are implicated in serious human rights and humanitarian law violations.[1] That corporate violations of human rights and humanitarian law are often more serious and affect more victims in countries undergoing conflict or repression is also well known.[2] Despite this reality, the harm caused by corporations to victims has for the most part been overlooked in transitional justice processes, and, as a consequence, their responsibility to provide reparations has not been given adequate consideration. Instead, attention has centered on making the state accountable and liable for the harm caused, often in circumstances where it lacks economic resources and human capacity to provide justice and redress.

This chapter explores this gap in transitional justice practice and literature and looks at the role that corporations can have in providing redress to victims. In particular, it considers two interrelated questions: whether corporations have an international legal obligation in post-conflict or post-repression situations to provide redress to victims of serious violations of human rights and humanitarian law; and how corporations could best contribute to reparation processes in states undergoing transitions.

International law, transitional justice, and redress

Transitional justice aims to deal with the legacy of past atrocities by applying four different branches of international law: international human rights law, international humanitarian law, international refugee law, and international

1 J. Ruggie, Report of the Special Representative of the Secretary-General on the Issue of Human Rights and Transnational Corporations and Other Business Enterprises, *Guiding Principles on Business and Human Rights: Implementing the United Nations "Protect, Respect and Remedy" Framework*, U.N. Doc. A/HRC/17/31, 21 March 2011, p.3; for a specific example, see Human Rights Watch, *The Curse of Gold: Democratic Republic of Congo*, HRW, US, 2005, pp.1–4.

2 Ruggie, n.1, para.11 and principle 7.

criminal law.[3] Reparation is one of the processes available to remedy serious violations of those laws in times of transition, which could involve gross and systematic human rights violations, serious violations of international humanitarian law, or international crimes.[4] Transitional justice deals with reparations because: (i) under international law, victims have a right to reparation; and (ii) the harm suffered by victims needs to be addressed—otherwise, society will not be able to move forward and deal with the past.

The right to reparation is primarily a right against the state under international human rights law, against the state and non-state actors under international humanitarian law, and against individual perpetrators under international criminal law. This means that any actor, whether state or non-state, who caused harm should redress it, even in periods of transition.

Under international human rights law, when a state violates an international human rights obligation, either by act or omission of its agents or those acting under their acquiescence, the violation triggers the obligation to provide reparation to victims.[5] Most of the law applicable to state responsibility and to reparations has become customary international law[6]—binding on all states—and has been codified in the Draft Articles on Responsibility of States for Internationally Wrongful Acts.[7] Before the 1980s, human rights treaties then in existence did not explicitly refer to a right to reparation. This is the case of the International Covenant on Civil and Political Rights and the International Covenant on Economic, Social and Cultural Rights. Nevertheless, the right to an effective remedy under those treaties has been interpreted to include it.[8] More recently, the right to reparation has been explicitly included in human rights treaties. In particular, the Convention against Torture and Other Cruel, Inhuman or Degrading Treatment or Punishment acknowledges the right of torture victims and their families to redress.[9] This right was also included in the International Convention for the Protection of All Persons from Enforced Disappearance.[10] International

3 UN Secretary General, *Report of the Secretary-General, The Rule of Law and Transitional Justice in Conflict and Post-Conflict Societies*, S/2004/616, 23 August 2004, para.9.

4 *Ibid.*, paras.8, 12, and 54–55.

5 International Law Commission, *Draft Articles on Responsibility of States for Internationally Wrongful Acts, with Commentaries*, A/56/10, 2001, articles 1, 2, 3, and 31.

6 Office of the High Commissioner for Human Rights, *Rule-of-Law Tool for Post-Conflict States, Reparations Programmes*, HR/PUB/08/1, 2008, p.6.

7 *Ibid.*

8 See, for example, International Covenant on Civil and Political Rights, article 2.3, and some of the General Comments of the UN Human Rights Committee, such as *General Comment 31 on the Nature of the General Legal Obligation Imposed on States Parties to the Covenant*, CCPR/C/21/Rev.1/Add.13, 26 May 2004, para.16.

9 UN General Assembly, *UN Convention against Torture and Other Cruel, Inhuman or Degrading Treatment*, GA/Res/39/46, 10 December 1984, article 14.

10 UN Convention on Enforced Disappearances of Persons, Doc.A/61/488, 20 December 2006, article 24.

humanitarian law contemplates the obligation of parties to armed conflict to pay compensation for violations of provisions, specifically in article 3 of the Hague Convention regarding the Laws and Customs of War on Land, and article 91 of the Protocol Additional to the Geneva Conventions relating to the Protection of Victims of International Armed Conflicts.[11]

Despite the existence of legal rules on the right to reparation, it was necessary to flesh out the meaning and scope of this right and its correlated obligations in a separate instrument, the Basic Principles and Guidelines on the Right to a Remedy and Reparation for Victims of Gross Violations of International Human Rights Law and Serious Violations of International Humanitarian Law (the Basic Principles). The Basic Principles:

> do not entail new international or domestic legal obligations but identify mechanisms, modalities, procedures and methods for the implementation of existing legal obligations under international human rights law and international humanitarian law which are complementary though different as to their norms.[12]

The Basic Principles recognize two important dimensions of the right to a remedy and reparation under international law. The *procedural dimension* requires that states have adequate and effective remedies in place, including of a judicial nature, to provide victims with access to reparation. In transitional justice processes, the procedural dimension of reparation takes the form of reparations through courts (civil and/or criminal; national and/or international) and of administrative reparation programs designed by state authorities to provide the same form of redress to great numbers of victims who have suffered certain violations, while providing them with flexible, cheap, and quick procedures to deal with their claims. Administrative reparation programs cannot replace judicial remedies, since the latter should be available to all victims who wish to access redress.[13]

In addition, the right to a remedy and reparation has a *substantive dimension* according to which victims should be given "adequate, effective and prompt reparation for harm suffered"[14] by providing, according to the circumstances, one or a combination of the following five forms of reparation: restitution,

11 Diplomatic Conference on the Reaffirmation and Development of International Humanitarian Law Applicable in Armed Conflicts, *Protocol Additional to the Geneva Conventions* of 12 August 1949, and *Protocol I Relating to the Protection of Victims of International Armed Conflicts*, 8 June 1977.

12 *Basic Principles and Guidelines on the Right to a Remedy and Reparations for Victims of Gross Violations of International Human Rights Law and Serious Violations of International Humanitarian Law*, adopted and proclaimed by the UN General Assembly resolution 60/147 of 16 December 2005, preamble, para.7.

13 *Ibid.*, principles VII, VIII and IX.15.

14 *Ibid.*

compensation, rehabilitation, satisfaction, and guarantees of non-repetition.[15] The Basic Principles do not order that victims be given all of these forms of reparation in each case but rather indicate that reparation should be provided to victims "as appropriate and proportional to the gravity of the violation."[16]

The Basic Principles are concerned mainly with state obligations. Nevertheless, they also make reference to non-state actors. Notably, principle IX.15 states that:

> [i]n cases where a person, a legal person, or other entity is found liable for reparation to a victim, such party should provide reparation to the victim or compensate the State if the State has already provided reparation to the victim.

This paragraph thus recognizes the obligations of entities other than states to provide reparations for victims of violations. The words "person," "legal person," and "other entity" could include senior staff of corporations, such as CEOs, boards of directors, or corporations themselves. The Basic Principles also acknowledge the harm that can be caused by enterprises and call on states to provide guarantees of non-repetition, such as by "[p]romoting the observance of codes of conduct and ethical norms, in particular international standards . . . by economic enterprises."[17]

Within international criminal law, victims' rights to reparation are upheld under article 75 of the Rome Statute, which mandates the Court to award reparations to victims of crimes, against the individual perpetrator.[18] While the Rome Statute recognizes only individuals—and not corporations—as capable of committing crimes under its jurisdiction, it is clear that persons, such as the CEO of a company, can be held accountable for crimes under the jurisdiction of the Court. Article 75 also orders the Court to establish the applicable principles relating to reparations.[19]

All standards applicable to reparations for serious violations of international law agree on some basic principles. They include the following: victims' right to reparation against the state if responsibility is attributable to it and/or against the individual perpetrator of the violation; entitlement to five forms of reparation, including restitution, compensation, satisfaction, rehabilitation, and guarantees of non-repetition; promptness, adequacy, and effectiveness of

15 *Ibid.*, principle IX.18.

16 *Ibid.*, principles IX.15 and 18.

17 *Ibid.*, principle IX.23(f).

18 Rome Statute of the International Criminal Court, U.N. Doc. A/Conf.183/9*, 17 July 1998.

19 The ICC identified the principles applicable to reparations in *Situation in the Democratic Republic of the Congo, in the Case of the Prosecutor v Thomas Lubanga Dyilo*, Trial Chamber I, ICC-01/04-01/06, 7 August 2012, pp.64–85.

reparations; access to justice and other remedies necessary to achieve redress; and proportional reparations to the harm suffered. It is significant that the Basic Principles and the Rome Statute acknowledge that such serious violations can be committed by either state or non-state actors and that in these instances victims should be redressed.

Extending human rights responsibilities to corporations under international law

While, arguably, direct reference to the responsibility of corporations to provide reparation is scarce under international law, important developments have taken place in recent years that recognize corporations' responsibility to redress human rights violations that they have caused or contributed to. Three developments stand out: the Global Compact; the Norms on the Responsibilities of Transnational Corporations and Other Business Enterprises with Regard to Human Rights; and the UN Guiding Principles. Even though not binding, they provide an important framework through which transitional justice actors can seek to hold corporations responsible for providing reparations to victims.

In 2000, the Global Compact, the largest corporate voluntary platform, was launched. Principles I and II of the Global Compact establish that "[b]usinesses should support and respect the protection of internationally proclaimed human rights; and make sure that they are not complicit in human rights abuses."[20] To date, thousands of businesses have joined the Global Compact voluntarily, and by doing so, in particular by accepting the content of principles I and II, they have consented to supporting and respecting human rights. This would include their acceptance of a right to a remedy and reparation and of the notion that if they cause harm, they should support state initiatives to provide redress.

In the aftermath of the Global Compact, and responding to the need to establish human rights standards applicable to corporations, the UN Sub-Commission on the Promotion and Protection of Human Rights prepared the Norms on the Responsibilities of Transnational Corporations and Other Business Enterprises with Regard to Human Rights (2003). The final version of the so-called UN Norms includes a paragraph stating the following:

> Transnational corporations and other business enterprises shall provide prompt, effective and adequate reparation to those persons, entities and communities that have been adversely affected by failures to comply with these Norms through, inter alia, reparations, restitution, compensation

20 *United Nations Global Compact*, human rights principles I and II, www.unglobalcompact.org/AboutTheGC/TheTenPrinciples/humanRights.html.

> and rehabilitation for any damage done or property taken. In connection with determining damages, in regard to criminal sanctions, and in all other respects, these Norms shall be applied by national courts and/or international tribunals, pursuant to national and international law.[21]

As David Weissbrodt and Muria Kruger have commented:

> [the] addition of this principle indicates the working group's intent not only to prevent conduct that violates human rights standards, but also to repair past harms. It can be further read to indicate the group's intent not only to make a statement about the appropriate conduct of businesses, but also to require action on their part.[22]

The UN Norms were the object of serious criticism. In particular, it was said that they could not impose on corporations the same obligations that states have under international law.[23] This led the UN Commission on Human Rights to reject the adoption of the text proposed by the Sub-Commission. Nevertheless, the impact of corporations on the enjoyment of human rights was firmly on the UN agenda, prompting further action.

In 2005, the UN Secretary-General appointed a special representative on human rights and transnational corporations and other business enterprises.[24] After six years of work and various consultations, the Special Representative, John Ruggie, released the UN Guiding Principles, which were endorsed by the Human Rights Council in 2011.[25] They highlight the state obligation to provide redress to victims of human rights abuses in which corporations have been involved[26] and establish the responsibility of corporations to provide redress for the harms they cause.[27] Indeed, principle 11—which reflects principle 1 of the Global Compact—establishes that, "[b]usiness enterprises should respect human rights. This means that they should avoid infringing on the human rights of others and *should address* adverse human

21 Sub-Commission on the Promotion and Protection of Human Rights, *The Norms on the Responsibilities of Transnational Corporations and Other Business Enterprises with Regard to Human Rights*, E/CN.4/Sub.2/2003/12/Rev.2, 26 August 2003, para.18.

22 D. Weissbrodt and M. Kruger, 'Norms on the Responsibilities of Transnational Corporations and Other Business Enterprises with Regard to Human Rights', 97 *American Journal of International Law* 901 (2003), p.913.

23 J. Ruggie, 'Current Development: Business and Human Rights: The Evolving International Agenda', 101 *American Journal of International Law* 819 (2007), p.819.

24 *Ibid.*, pp.819–820; and UN Commission on Human Rights, E/CN.4/Res/2005/69, 20 April 2005.

25 UN Guiding Principles, n.1. endorsed by the UN Human Rights Council in Resolution A/HRC/Res/17/4. See also chapter 4 of this book.

26 UN Guiding Principles, n.1, principle 1.

27 *Ibid.*, principle 11.

rights impacts with which they are involved."[28] The commentary to the principle indicates that "[a]ddressing adverse human rights impacts requires taking adequate measures for their prevention, mitigation and, where appropriate, remediation."[29] Principles 14 and 23 explicitly state that such responsibility exists irrespective of the "operational context" of corporations, which includes the adverse human rights impact in "conflict-affected areas."[30] Furthermore, principle 22, under the heading of remediation, establishes that "[w]here business enterprises identify that they have caused or contributed to adverse impacts, they should provide for or cooperate in their remediation through legitimate processes."

The UN Guiding Principles devote some attention to access to remedies, acknowledging that the state has the obligation to provide victims with effective remedies (judicial and non-judicial) but that corporations should establish or participate in non-state-based grievance mechanisms to ensure that they respond effectively to those who have been adversely affected.[31] While the principles themselves do not establish what kind of mechanism is required to deal with adverse human rights impacts, the commentary to principle 22 suggests that in situations where the impact could amount to an alleged crime, it "would require cooperation with judicial mechanisms."[32] This appears to reinforce the procedural dimension of reparations stated in the Basic Principles. The commentary to principle 25 notes that there are different forms of remedy for human rights violations, such as "apologies, restitution, rehabilitation, financial or non-financial compensation and punitive sanctions (whether criminal or administrative), as well as the prevention of harm through, for example, injunctions or guarantees of non-repetition."[33] This reinforces the substantive dimension of reparations expressed in the Basic Principles.

These three sets of instruments, even if not binding under international law, constitute an important reference framework for transitional justice stakeholders, for they acknowledge the responsibilities that corporations have, particularly that of providing remediation (procedural and substantive) to victims. However, they remain silent on how corporations should deal with redress for serious human rights and humanitarian law violations that they have committed after periods of conflict or repression.

Transitional justice stakeholders dealing with reparations, as in the case of truth commissions, administrative reparations programs, and civil society, have a historical opportunity to interpret these principles to promote

28 *Ibid.* (emphasis added).
29 *Ibid.*, commentary to principle 11.
30 *Ibid.*, principles 11 and 23.
31 *Ibid.*, principles 28 and 29.
32 *Ibid.*, commentary to principle 22.
33 *Ibid.*, principle 25.

accountability of corporations and their responsibility to provide redress. They should do so bearing in mind the international legal framework applicable in transitional justice, especially the Basic Principles. As has been seen, they provide an authoritative tool for dealing with reparations in transitional justice contexts, given their focus on redress for serious human rights violations. Specifically, transitional justice stakeholders need to determine the content of the procedural and substantive dimension of the right to a remedy and reparation that victims have against corporations, beyond the enunciation of generally accepted principles. Some relevant practice already exists and is examined in the next section.

Transitional justice in practice: the legacy of truth commissions

Some transitional justice mechanisms, in particular TRCs, have not ignored the role and responsibility of corporations and have pushed the subject onto the transitional justice agenda. This has generated a small, but relevant, number of transitional justice examples illustrating the role that TRCs could play in pushing corporations to provide redress to victims. Such emerging practice indicates how TRCs have defined the procedural and substantive dimension of the right to a remedy and reparation of victims of corporate abuses in conflict and repressive regimes. Nevertheless, the few TRCs that have made this link have not been very successful in getting corporations to assume responsibility for the harm that they have caused victims or to provide redress for it.

South African TRC

The Promotion of National Unity and Reconciliation Act of 1995, which established the South African TRC, gave the TRC the power to make recommendations to the government on reparations.[34] More specifically, the Act ordered the TRC to recommend reparations to the president. It also provided for the creation of South Africa's Presidential Fund to provide reparations.[35]

The role of corporations under apartheid was the object of a special hearing on business and labor held by the TRC.[36] Because business provided substantial help—financial or otherwise—to the system, the TRC considered that "business was central to the economy that sustained the South African

34 Promotion of National Unity and Reconciliation Act 34, section 3(c) and others.

35 *Ibid.*, sections 4 (f)(i) and 42.

36 South African Truth and Reconciliation Commission, *Final Report*, Volume 4, Chapter 2, 1998, para.161. See also chapter 8 of this book.

State during the apartheid years."[37] At the same time, business benefited from apartheid. During the hearing, different ways in which corporations could contribute to a new South Africa were discussed.[38] The TRC concluded that corporations should contribute to the payment of reparations for victims, recommending different ways in which they could support reparations: a wealth tax, a one-off levy on corporate and private income, a one-off donation of 1 per cent of market capitalization by companies listed in the Johannesburg Stock Exchange, a retrospective surcharge on corporate profits backdated to an agreed time, and responsibility for the payment of the previous government's debt.[39]

The government and corporations rejected these recommendations. Indeed, corporations thought that:

> reparation was not the way to go. . . . [They] decided [that] the best way forward was to show that business was serious about transformation. [They] wanted to establish a project in which business could play a catalytic role to achieve agreed objectives.[40]

This did not mean that all corporations refused to accept responsibility for their role under apartheid. Indeed, some corporations acknowledged that business had "a responsibility to help repair the ravages of apartheid and build South Africa into a modern, democratic and economically successful nation."[41] As a consequence, while reparations were to be paid from the Presidential Fund, a business trust was created to contribute to development and economic prosperity in the country.

The Business Trust was established in 1999, ran until 2011, and received R1.2 billion of financial contributions from 140 companies. Contributions were made with 0.15 per cent of market capitalization in the first phase of the scheme and with 0.7 per cent in the second phase. This permitted companies of different sizes to contribute according to their means. These financial contributions should not be understood as a form of compensation given that they were not a response to the individual harm suffered by victims and were not used to redress victims. The majority of this money (approximately 60 per cent) has been used for tourism and education and has had various

37 *Ibid.*

38 See S. Terreblanche, *A History of Inequality in South Africa: 1652–2002*, University of Natal Press and KMM Review Press, 2003, pp.124–132.

39 South African TRC, n.36, Volume 5, Chapter 8, 1998, p.318.

40 S. Makozoma, 'Winning Trust', in Business Leadership South Africa, National Business Initiative and Business Trust, *Building the Nation: A Business Contribution*, July 2007, p.4, www.businessleadership.org.za/gup/filez/Occassional_Papers_Building_the_Nation_A_Business_Contribution_July_2007.pdf.

41 *Ibid.*, Introduction, p.3.

beneficiaries, including some who could claim to have been acknowledged as victims by the South African TRC. Importantly, while this was meant to be a business trust, the government has also contributed public funding to it, which the trust has used for designated purposes.[42]

Only the President's Fund has been used to provide reparations to victims. However, not all reparations have been paid.[43] This has caused great frustration for victims, who consider that their harm continues to be unaddressed by South Africa and by corporations. As a consequence, the *Khulumani* litigation was put into motion, using the ATS in the United States[44] to achieve accountability of corporations for aiding and abetting apartheid in South Africa and to seek reparations for victims.[45]

While the experience of South Africa has not been entirely satisfactory in terms of achieving reparations for victims, South Africa is a good example of a TRC trying to link corporations and redress, despite the associated political cost of doing so. The TRC considered that access to justice for victims of apartheid against corporations could take place through corporations' contributions to the domestic administrative reparations program and through compensation. Corporations, with the support of the government, opted for a different model, one of financial contributions to a business fund to provide development to the country.

Liberian TRC

The Liberian TRC also dealt with abuses carried out by corporations, focusing in particular on economic crimes and violations of human rights law carried out by corporations. In its consolidated report, the TRC noted that:

> private companies benefited from dealings with corrupt public officials to obtain lucrative natural resource concessions and exclusive licenses and, in many instances, formed corporate entities with perpetrators of grave human rights violations.[46]

While it predominantly investigated economic crimes, the TRC also detailed gross human rights violations in the timber and mining industries. Its report

42 See website of the Business Trust at http://www.btrust.org.za/.

43 C. Colvin, 'Overview of the Reparations Programme in South Africa', in P. de Greiff (ed.), *The Handbook of Reparations*, Oxford University Press, Oxford, 2006 (176–214).

44 *In re South African Apartheid Litigation*, 346 F.Supp.2d 538 (SDNY 2004); *Khulumani v Barclay National Bank, Ltd.*, 504 F.3d 254 (2nd Circuit, 2007); *In re South African Apartheid Litigation*, 617 F.Supp.2d 228 (SDNY 2009).

45 See chapter 8 of this book.

46 Republic of Liberia Truth and Reconciliation Commission, Volume Two, VI, *Recommendations*, 2009, p.1.

clearly linked human rights violations with corporations, holding them directly responsible for their part in the violations:

> [A]ll . . . corporations including shareholders and corporate officers and their agents affiliated with or who aided and abetted warring factions or armed groups share responsibility for the commission of those human rights violations including violations of international humanitarian law, international human rights law, war crimes.[47]

The report failed to explicitly link the human rights violations carried out by corporations with an obligation to provide reparation, but it did recommend that they play a role in providing reparation.[48] The TRC suggested the establishment of a reparation trust fund to compensate victims of economic crimes in Liberia.[49] It did not recommend that corporations pay into this fund on a voluntary basis but rather suggested that monies be received from civil and criminal "judgements against economic criminals."[50] Its funding recommendations included the following:

> (1) recovering tax arrears from timber, mining, petroleum and telecommunications companies that evaded tax liability under the Taylor regime; (2) obtaining funds from economic criminals that are sentenced by Liberian courts to pay restitution or other fees; and (3) utilizing criminal and civil confiscation schemes in foreign jurisdictions to repatriate Liberian assets.[51]

The report recommended that the government "aggressively" seek restitution from corporations and that both criminal and civil laws be used to recover and repatriate stolen assets.[52] It noted that those convicted under Liberian criminal law are required to pay fines—which can be up to twice their illicit gains—to the government and restitution to victims.[53] Perhaps most controversially, the report suggested that restitution paid directly to the victims be rerouted to the Reparations Trust Fund.[54] The TRC encouraged the government to trace, identify, and freeze assets by utilizing processes established by the UN, specifically the Convention against Corruption. It also recommended that any funds frozen under UN sanctions not be

47 *Ibid.*, Volume Two, Title VI, Section 11.4.
48 *Ibid.*, Volume Two, Title VI, Section 17.
49 *Ibid.*, Volume Three, Title III, p.43.
50 *Ibid.*
51 *Ibid.*
52 *Ibid.*, pp.43 and 45.
53 *Ibid.*, p.43.
54 *Ibid.*

released until the new government has had an opportunity to collect tax arrears.[55] This recommendation, if implemented, could contribute significantly to financing reparations. Freezing and recovering stolen assets, as well as collecting tax arrears and rerouting them for the payment of reparations, can have a substantial impact on the state's ability to provide reparation and can consequently contribute to improving victims' standard of living.

The current government of Liberia has not implemented the TRC's recommendations regarding the reparations program.[56] The Independent National Commission on Human Rights, which was mandated by the TRC to implement recommendations, has dissociated itself from the TRC's report,[57] and the country's president has ruled out reparations for individuals, favoring reparations of a collective nature.[58] Although there has been international support for the use of frozen assets in the reparation program, the UN has secured only a tiny percentage of illicit funds.[59] Furthermore, the Liberian government rejected legislation that would have given it the power to freeze assets,[60] arguably because the Liberian government still faces challenges with corruption.[61]

Timor-Leste commission for reception, truth and reconciliation

The final report of the Commission for Reception, Truth and Reconciliation (CAVR) in Timor-Leste noted that corporations have a legal obligation to provide reparations to victims.[62] CAVR made a direct link between the human rights obligations of corporations, the violations they aided and abetted, and their obligation to provide reparation. It stated that the

55 *Ibid.*, pp.44–45.

56 CENTAL Website, 'CENTAL, ITCJ, Action Aid Conduct Reparation Workshop', www.cental.org/index.php?option=com_content&view=category&layout=blog&id=1&Itemid=50&limitstart=5.

57 The work of the Commission has been the object of strong criticism. It has been seen as a political compromise to avoid prosecutions and as lacking impartiality and independence. See P. James-Allen, A. Weah and L. Goodfriend, *Beyond the Truth and Reconciliation Commission: Transitional Justice Options in Liberia*, International Center for Transitional Justice, NY, 2010, p.3.

58 I. Al-bakri Nyei, 'Liberia after the Civil War: Victims Demand for Reparation', 1 *Conflict Trends* 43–49 (2011), pp.46–49.

59 International Center for Transitional Justice, *The Rabat Report: The Concept and Challenges of Collective Reparations*, 2009, p.24.

60 *Ibid.*

61 Zimbabwean Watchdog, 22 August 2012, www.u4.no/publications/overview-of-corruption-and-anti-corruption-in-liberia/.

62 *Chega! Final Report of the Commission for the Reception, Truth and Reconciliation in East Timor, Part 11, Recommendations*, 2006, p.42.

obligation to provide reparation emanates from "the principle of international responsibility recognised in the international customary law of torts" but failed to provide any further explanation regarding the legal grounds of such liability.[63]

CAVR recommended that this obligation be fulfilled through corporate contributions to a domestic reparation program.[64] It suggested that the scheme be jointly funded by a number of actors, including state and privately owned Indonesian businesses, as well as international and multinational corporations that "profited from war and benefited from the occupation" and that profited from selling weapons to Indonesia.[65] The recommendations with regard to reparations were endorsed by the Parliament in Timor-Leste in 2009.[66] However, little progress has been made in implementing the program, and a draft law on compensation to victims awaits enactment by Parliament.[67] Despite the lack of implementation, CAVR provides a good example of a TRC finding corporations liable to provide a remedy and recommending that they provide redress through financial contributions to the domestic reparations program.

Other mechanisms used to obtain redress from corporations

Lack of corporate accountability in transitional justice processes has forced human rights activists and transitional justice stakeholders to consider alternative venues to hold businesses accountable and secure redress for victims. Two such alternatives are litigation under the ATS and other tort litigation.

The ATS has been used to deal with serious violations that have occurred both during conflict/repression and in peace situations.[68] The *Khulumani* litigation in South Africa provides a good example of the way that the ATS has been used to obtain redress for victims of apartheid after great frustration caused to victims given the lack of reparation.[69] Tort litigation in the home

63 *Ibid.*

64 *Ibid.*, p.4.

65 *Ibid.*, p.208.

66 International Center for Transitional Justice, *Timor-Leste. Background: Justice Denied*, http://ictj.org/our-work/regions-and-countries/timor-leste.

67 *Ibid.*

68 The possibilities to use the ATS for such purposes was limited significantly by the recent US Supreme Court decision in *Kiobel v Royal Dutch Petroleum Co.* (2013), 2013 WL 1628935. More information on this decision is found in chapter 3 of this book. Relevant academic work on the ATS prior to this decision includes M. Koebele, *Corporate Responsibility under the Alien Tort Statute,* Martinus Nijhoff, The Netherlands, 2009.

69 M. Swart, 'The Khulumani Litigation: Complementing the Work of the South African Truth and Reconciliation Commission', 16 *Tilburg Law Review* 30–59 (2011), p.31.

state of the parent company allegedly implicated in the violations is also an option. The difference between these methods is that under the ATS, the allegation involves a civil action by an alien alleging the breach of customary international law or a treaty of the United States, allowing a claim, for example, because torture took place.[70] In ordinary tort actions, on the other hand, the allegation is not of a human rights violation with customary or treaty status but of violations involving, for example, a breach of the duty of care owed by the company.[71] Both types of litigation are expensive and time consuming.

The general outcome of ATS and tort litigation in recent years has been that plaintiffs arrive at a settlement.[72] In *Khulumani*, for example, one of the corporations involved, General Motors, agreed to a settlement in February 2012 with the 25 plaintiffs in the case. It agreed to pay US$1.5 million in shares in the company without acknowledging responsibility for apartheid crimes. The shares were to be placed into a trust fund and converted into money to be shared between the 25 plaintiffs and the Khulumani Support Group.[73]

It is important that such settlements not be limited to compensation as a form of reparation; rather, they should take due account of the harm inflicted on groups of people, ethnic groups, and communities. Doing so lessens the focus on providing individual reparation and incorporates a collective dimension. For example, where a corporation is to continue working in the same area after conflict or repression, the company could help provide infrastructure for the community by constructing roads, clean water pipelines, or the like. The company could also provide employment to surviving victims. Settlements are common in this form of litigation, but they are a two-edged sword. On the one hand, they often provide the quickest option for victims to obtain some form of reparation. However, they are problematic because if the case was heard in full and it was established that the corporation had breached its duty of care or any other relevant norm under domestic law, victims may be in a better legal position to raise a claim for reparation. While success in such litigation is incredibly difficult, such a precedent would constitute a milestone in the field of reparations for victims.

The importance of tort litigation to achieve redress cannot be underestimated. Nevertheless, from a transitional justice perspective, it presents

70 See chapter 3 of this book.

71 R. Meeran, 'Tort Litigation against Multinational Corporations for Violation of Human Rights: An Overview of the Position Outside the United States', 3 *City University of Hong Kong Law Review* 1–41 (2011), p.3. See also chapter 2 of this book.

72 Meeran, *ibid.*, p.2. Contrast Meeran's view with that of D. Childress III, 'The Alien Tort Statute, Federalism, and the Next Wave of Transnational Litigation', 100 *Georgetown Law Journal* 709–757 (2012), pp.724–725.

73 OIL Motoring, 'GM to Pay Out for Apartheid Role', 1 March 2012, www.iol.co.za/motoring/industry-news/gm-to-pay-out-for-apartheid-role-1.1246265.

challenges that need to be addressed. First of all, this type of litigation changes the matrix with which transitional justice is familiar. It moves issues of accountability from a domestic—or even regional or international—forum to another state, internationalizing the transitional justice process. This illustrates that transitional justice cannot continue to be sought from a state-centered perspective, since the root causes of conflict and repression go and operate beyond the state. This, in turn, requires familiarizing stakeholders with these tools so that they are seen for what they are: remedies available to victims to achieve redress, even if risky and costly. If these alternative remedies are not adequately taken into account in transitional justice processes, victims will continue to be deprived of even the option of using existing remedies to achieve redress—remedies that could ensure, depending on the specific circumstances of the case, some redress for victims.

Second, since these developments often happen in parallel rather than as part of a more consistent approach toward transitional justice, they could compete with and even undermine transitional processes at the domestic level. For example, if the confidential agreement reached between corporations and plaintiffs in a given case stands in stark contrast to the administrative reparation program set up in the transitional state—for instance, because it provides substantial amounts of money to victims while the administrative reparations program provides symbolic financial reparation—then reparations could create further divisions, rather than reconciliation, within society. In this regard, it is important that lawyers involved in ATS or tort litigation understand transitional justice processes and link with domestic lawyers in the transitional state in order to consider how their litigation could benefit, or at least not undermine, the work of other transitional justice mechanisms. For example, as illustrated in the *Khulumani* settlement, the beneficiaries will not be limited to the plaintiffs in the case but also include victims more generally, such as those who might have been equally harmed but did not meet the requirement to qualify as plaintiffs in the lawsuit.

While litigation has not been effective in securing adequate reparation for victims, at the very least it has given visibility to the role and responsibility of corporations, forcing some of them to settle cases to avoid further economic or reputational damage.

Best procedural remedies to provide redress to victims

As noted, TRCs have been important in documenting the responsibility and role of corporations in conflict and repressive situations and the occurrence of human rights violations. The next question is whether reparations should be given by corporations as a result of the adjudication on the matter by a court or as part of an administrative reparation program. As noted already, corporations' failure to redress the harm they caused during conflict or repression has pushed human rights activists and other stakeholders to seek legal action. Nevertheless, legal action is expensive and time consuming, and it does not provide adequate and effective reparation for victims; in most cases, it is limited to symbolic compensation and to a very limited amount of victims who qualify as plaintiffs under procedural rules.[74] More importantly, courts continue to be uneasy about awarding reparations for such harm. In contrast, domestic reparation programs appear to be more appropriate mechanisms for redressing harm caused by corporations, for a number of reasons.

First, administrative reparation programs often result from recommendations made by TRCs that, as noted above in the cases of Timor-Leste and South Africa, have been the key mechanism linking corporations and transitional justice. This means that well-crafted recommendations on reparations could consider ways in which corporations can provide redress for harm done. Second, domestic reparations programs benefit multitudes of victims while normal adjudication, as a general rule, benefits only the plaintiffs in the case. Therefore, these programs have the potential to reach most victims of corporations and not just a few. This, as a consequence, prevents reparations from producing more harm to victims and communities, for it prevents unequal treatment of reparations. Third, since the state is responsible for managing an administrative reparation program, it could facilitate reparation, since corporations will contribute according to what is stipulated (with economic resources or through other means) but the state will be responsible for implementing the program. Nevertheless, it is important to note that preference for domestic reparation programs or for setting up trust funds does not mean that victims should be deprived of the right to seek justice and reparation through courts.

TRCs are certainly well placed to make recommendations to states on how corporations should contribute to reparations; and they have already, in some instances, risen to this challenge. TRCs are in a unique position to tailor-make recommendations that fit the cultural, economic, and political context of the particular society where abuses have occurred.

What forms of redress should corporations provide to victims?

Under international law, as already noted, there are different forms of redress: restitution, compensation, satisfaction, rehabilitation, and guarantees of non-repetition. In theory, any of them in isolation, or a combination of them,

74 This argument is explored at length in the transitional justice literature. See, for example, *Report of the Special Rapporteur on Violence against Women, its Causes and Consequences*, Rashida Manjoo, A/HRC/14/22, 23 April 2010, para.37; and Office of the High Commissioner for Human Rights, *Rule-of-law Tool for Post-Conflict States, Reparations Programmes*, 2008, pp.16–17.

could be provided by corporations. In practice, however, there are differences between what can be expected from corporations, on the one hand, and from states, on the other. Under international law, the preferred form of reparation is restitution; only when it is not possible or sufficient are other forms of reparation to be awarded.[75] In the case of corporations, as shown in this chapter, there is a tendency to prefer compensation over other forms of reparations when addressing the human rights violations they caused or facilitated. If economic resources are available, compensation is easier to implement than other forms of reparation. However, where monetary compensation is provided to victims it is important to consider carefully the political and cultural context, as well as the views of victims, in order to avoid further harm and victimization. To this end, it may be more practical for a corporation to provide redress by way of financial contributions to a domestic administrative reparation program so that it enhances the different forms of reparation that it includes. If no domestic administrative reparation program is set up, corporations must consider making financial contributions to a designated fund or be encouraged to consider other types of reparation, particularly restitution or a combination such as compensation and restitution.

While compensation is preferred over restitution, the latter can also be provided by corporations. For example, in the case of Colombia, where corporations, together with armed groups, have caused or been complicit in the internal displacement of people, it is feasible to consider that corporations should engage in a land restitution process. Over the last decade, the country has witnessed a growing production of palm oil, which, in turn, has led to internal displacement.[76] At the heart of displacement has been land dispossession. Here, adequate reparation requires land restitution unless issues of a safe return are at stake. In the context of a transition where the discrimination of a group occurred, it is also possible to request that corporations actively engage in the restitution of jobs in their particular economic activity, and even apply affirmative action measures trying to make right a historical wrong that affected a particular group of people.[77]

Satisfaction can also be provided by corporations in the form of an apology to a state and/or to surviving victims, as well as by building monuments. It is often the case that corporations agree to a settlement without the recognition

75 Permanent Court of Justice, *Factory at Chorzów*, merits, judgment No. 13, 1928, Series A, No.17, p.47.

76 Indeed, in the Magdalena region "there were 42,817 hectares of palm tree in 2000, which doubled in 2006 to 94,312. . . . Equally, internal displacement grew [in that region] from 1,598 persons in 1998 to 12,202 in 2007." Goebertus, J., 'Palma de aceite y desplazamiento forzado en Zona Bananera: "trayectorias" entre recursos naturales y conflicto', 67 *Colombia Internacional* 152–175 (2008).

77 As in South Africa with the implementation of black economic empowerment policies—for example, under the Broad-Based Socio-Economic Empowerment Charter for the South African Mining Industry (2002).

of legal liability. So, while apologies might seem simple, getting corporations to accept that they did something wrong and to apologize can prove difficult, particularly when they may fear litigation. In some of the clearest cases, such as *Wiwa v Shell* and *Wiwa v Anderson*,[78] despite the existence of evidence implicating Shell in human rights abuses, the public settlement was entered by the plaintiffs and the defendants on the basis that "[d]efendants denied the allegations of wrongdoing contained in the complaints in each of the Litigations and deny any wrongdoing or liability to Plaintiffs." It was moreover emphasized that "the parties are entering into this Settlement Agreement to eliminate the uncertainties, burden and expense of further protracted litigation."[79] This is problematic, since victims effectively renounce their right to reparation when they accept some kind of ex gratia payment that fails to recognize responsibility for the harm caused to them.

Rehabilitation—meaning the provision of physical and mental health services and other services needed by victims to provide them with full restitution to the situation they were in prior to the violation—is an elusive form of reparation. Its legal scope is not well defined, and the delivery of rehabilitation to victims brings with it different challenges.[80] Corporations, in some situations, might be well situated to provide certain services to victims, particularly when these services are part of a corporation's economic activity. For example, a corporation dealing with health services could be in a position to open a hospital. Corporations could also help the state provide rehabilitation services to the required standard. For example, they could contribute financially to a special fund for the state to invest exclusively in particular health services and medicines or education and vocational services for victims. This is compensation, but for a particular rehabilitation objective. Also, a corporation involved in the exploitation of natural resources, such as water, in a conflict situation could help by supplying clean and potable water to victimized communities to contribute to an adequate standard of living.

Guarantees of non-repetition can take multiple forms. Some need to focus on reforming state institutions that can have an impact on the way

78 *Wiwa v Royal Dutch Petroleum Company*, 226 F.3d 88 (2nd Circuit, 2000). For more information on these cases, see the website of the Centre for Constitutional Rights, http://ccrjustice.org/ourcases/current-cases/wiwa-v.-royal-dutch-petroleum or the website of The Case Against Shell, http://wiwavshell.org/wiwa-v-shell-victory-settlement/.

79 United States District Court, Southern District of New York, *Ken Wiwa et al (plaintiffs) v Shell Petroleum et al (defendants) and Ken Wiwa et al (plaintiffs) v Brian Anderson (defendant), and Ken Wiwa et al (plaintiffs) v Shell Petroleum Development Company of Nigeria Limited (defendant)*, Settlement Agreement and Mutual Release, 8 June 2009, http://wiwavshell.org/documents/Wiwa_v_Shell_SETTLEMENT_AGREEMENT.Signed.pdf.

80 C. Sandoval, *Rehabilitation as a Form of Reparation Under International Law*, Redress, London, December 2009, www.redress.org/downloads/publications/The%20right%20to%20rehabilitation.pdf.

corporations behave. For example, reforming audit commissions, competition commissions, or commissions that award licenses to trade could be crucial to provide the state with the mechanisms and tools needed to control and sanction corporate behavior. Such institutions could apply, for example, vetting measures in relation to corporations, such as forbidding them or their subsidiaries from bidding to carry out their economic operations in the country for a set period of time or in a specific region.

Additionally, by following Ruggie's UN Guiding Principles and setting up policies and processes to respect human rights, corporations would be contributing to the reparation of atrocities that already took place.[81] Furthermore, fully developing the due diligence dimension of Ruggie's UN Guiding Principles would provide a significant platform to avoid repetition of such atrocities in the future. Nevertheless, Ruggie's due diligence would need to be complemented by other measures, since it alone is insufficient to deal with non-repetition. For example, financial assurances that harm caused will be duly redressed by corporations, particularly in countries emerging from conflict or repression and in areas where there is an increased risk of human rights violations, should be adopted. These guarantees could include trust funds, surety bonds, insurance policies, and liens against real property. Such measures would ensure that if corporations are implicated in human rights violations, they will have to redress harm caused; in addition, they would help deter corporations from carrying out such violations in the first place.

Conclusion

There is no explicit legal rule under public international law or any of its branches stating that corporations can be held responsible for human rights violations, violations of humanitarian law, or international crimes by action or omission and that as a consequence they have the obligation to provide prompt, adequate, and effective reparation to victims. Nevertheless, an important reference framework—that of the Global Compact, the UN Norms, and the UN Guiding Principles—already exists that permits the assertion that corporations should provide redress for such violations to their victims. This framework, while not legally binding, reflects broad consensus on the existence of responsibility to remedy harms done by corporations. Transitional justice stakeholders have a major opportunity to define, make use of, and advance this framework, particularly the UN Guiding Principles, to help victims secure reparation for harm suffered.

The lack of a clear legal framework establishing that corporations, as opposed to just states, can violate human rights and that they must provide

81 Guiding Principles, n.1, principle 15.

reparations has not been a major obstacle for stakeholders to use transitional justice mechanisms to hold businesses accountable for harm caused and to try to obtain reparations. Indeed, as illustrated in this chapter, some truth commissions have addressed the responsibility of corporations and have gone as far as calling on them to provide reparations in specific ways. This is because the mandate of such bodies includes looking at root causes and consequences and various actors of conflict and repression. The role played so far by some TRCs cannot be taken to mean that there is a general trend in transitional justice to look at the responsibility of corporations; nevertheless, it is indicative of how transitional justice mechanisms could engage with corporate responsibility and reparations. Important practice in relation to the substantive and procedural dimension of the right to a remedy and reparation is beginning to emerge in this context.

TRCs, at least the ones studied in this chapter, have made the role of corporations in periods of conflict and repression visible, putting pressure on them to at least respect human rights. On the other hand, visibility has not translated into reparations for victims—with the exception of the South African TRC, where, even if in an inadequate manner, some corporations contributed money to a special fund that was used for development purposes.

This means that careful consideration must be given to how best and in what form to get corporations to provide redress to victims. In particular, transitional justice stakeholders need to examine what incentives might be necessary to get corporations to contribute to reparations and, more importantly, to acknowledge their responsibility for the harm done. This chapter has explored some possible answers to these questions. In relation to the substantive dimension of the right to a remedy and reparation, the chapter has noted that corporations could provide redress in the form of compensation by way of capital injections to either domestic reparation programs or to trust funds. Corporations can also provide redress using other forms of reparation, such as restitution, satisfaction, rehabilitation, and guarantees of non-repetition. Nevertheless, compensation appears to be a more natural way for them to deal with harm caused, since their business is to make a profit, and they could easily give the state or designated trustees money to be used in a way that helps victims.

In relation to the procedural dimension of the right to a remedy and reparation, both judicial and non-judicial venues need to be open to victims after periods of conflict or repression. However, domestic reparation programs and trust funds appear to be ideally placed to deal with the harm suffered by large numbers of victims and to do so in a more flexible, cheap, and fast way than courts. However, the role that litigation can play in obtaining redress cannot be forgotten, for on many occasions victims have been able to achieve some form of redress through, for example, settlements, simply because the "litigation threat" was costly, not only financially, for corporations. A good balance must be found between reparations through courts and those through non-judicial means. Victims, however, cannot be deprived of their right to use remedies, including of a judicial nature, to obtain redress.

Still, ensuring that corporations contribute to reparations will continue to be a challenge. Steps can be taken to ensure they are more receptive to the reparations process. For example, it is important to raise awareness of corporations' obligations within the transitional justice field by affirming the link between corporations, human rights violations, and corporations' obligation to provide redress. This will help guarantee that corporations are fully included in transitional justice mechanisms, such as truth commissions, prosecutions, reparations, and institutional reform. Ensuring their inclusion in some transitional justice mechanisms, such as the work of truth commissions, will, in turn, make it more likely that businesses are considered in any reparation schemes, including funding mechanisms for state-run administrative reparation schemes. The cases of Liberia and Timor-Leste offer good examples of where this model has been suggested, though the lack of program implementation had a negative impact on the role and responsibility that corporations ought to have had toward victims. States' lack of commitment toward the implementation of reparations programs, particularly toward making corporations redress the harm they have caused, leaves victims without tools to achieve redress. The power to allow corporations to work in their territory and profit from their resources lies with states. If states do not call on corporations to respond to the harm caused, they validate their behavior and permit them to continue to commit the same wrongs in the future.

Chapter 6

Corporate Accountability, Reparations, and Distributive Justice in Post-Conflict Societies

*Nelson Camilo Sánchez**

Introduction

The redistribution of power is perhaps the primary demand of any transitional process that has as a goal the democratic transformation of society.[1] Confronting power is, at the same time, one of the greatest challenges of a transition. During the last few decades, the field of transitional justice has, following peace negotiations or more coercive means of ending conflict, promoted transitions that fit into a framework of minimum international human rights standards and that, simultaneously, have had relative success in dismantling antidemocratic military power and promoting more open and equal political systems.[2] However, the economic forces that supported antidemocratic regimes or that benefited from them financially have often been excluded from assignments of responsibility during processes of transitional change.[3]

* The ideas presented in this text come, for the most part, from discussions with Rodrigo Uprimny, Director of the Center for the Study of Law, Justice, and Society (Dejusticia). I thank Professor Uprimny for his generosity with his ideas and his analytic guidance in developing the schematization that I present in this chapter. In addition, Sabine Michalowski made insightful comments and suggestions. The chapter has also benefited from research conducted by David Attanasio on civil litigation involving MNCs. Nicole Summers and Eva Maas also provided superb research assistance. Errors and omissions are mine.

1 A. Gross, 'The Constitution, Reconciliation, and Transitional Justice: Lessons from South Africa and Israel', 40 *Stanford Journal of International Law* 47–104 (2004), p.48; Z. Miller, 'Effects of Invisibility: In Search of the "Economic" in Transitional Justice', 2 *The International Journal of Transitional Justice* 266–291 (2008), p.267; P. Arthur, 'How "Transitions" Reshaped Human Rights: A Conceptual History of Transitional Justice', 31 *Human Rights Quarterly* 321–363 (2009), p.334.

2 See, for example, R. Teitel, 'Transitional Jurisprudence: The Role of Law in Political Transformation', 106 *The Yale Law Journal* 2009–2080 (1997), p.2016; N. Rouhana, 'Identity and Power in Reconciliation in National Conflict: The Israeli-Palestinian Case', in A. Eagly, R. Baron and L. Hamilton (eds), *The Social Psychology of Group Identity and Social Conflict: Theory, Application, and Practice*, APA Books, Washington DC, 2004 (272–294).

3 See, for example, J. Cavallaro and S. Albuja, 'The Lost Agenda: Economic Crisis and Truth Commissions in Latin America and Beyond', in K. McEvoy and L. McGregor (eds),

The notion of transitional justice is widely debated today. For the purposes of this chapter, transitional justice is defined as those processes by which a society undergoes radical transformation of its social and political orders: for example, the processes accompanying the shift from a dictatorial to a democratic regime, or from the end of violent internal conflict to a peaceful society. I understand these processes within a political and normative context that strives to balance the distinct goals of justice and peace. From this perspective, transitional justice is conceptualized as encompassing changes, whether from dictatorship or from conflict, to democratic governance and changes to society (a concept understood to be controversial). These processes involve a series of measures that seek to achieve pacification, disarmament, and reintegration, and at the same time the protection of victims' rights. Consequently, transitional justice has to confront the past and simultaneously think forward to decide how to construct the future.[4]

The protection of the rights of victims is nowadays a central concern in transitional processes.[5] This is in part due to the fact that international human rights law, particularly the right to reparations for victims of serious violations, contains a binding legal framework for states.[6] Nonetheless, private and corporate responsibility is difficult to address within this framework because many situations of corporate abuse lack an adequate legal-factual link that establishes responsibility: the evidence of a connection to the violations is weak or non-existent, or there is no legal harm that allows for the redistribution of resources to facilitate transition. Moreover, there is a latent political dilemma in every transition that effectively discourages discussion of these questions: if those with wealth are confronted, the most likely result is that these people, using their economic power, will block the democratization

Transitional Justice from Below: Grassroots Activism and the Struggle for Change, Hart Publishing, Oxford, 2008 (121–141).

4 For others who adopt a similar definition of transitional justice, see R. Teitel, *Transitional Justice*, Oxford University Press, Oxford, 2000, p.11; N. Kritz (ed.), *Transitional Justice: How Emerging Democracies Reckon with Former Regimes*, United States Institute of Peace, New York, 1995, p.xxxi.

5 R. Teitel, 'Transitional Justice Genealogy', 16 *Harvard Human Rights Journal* 69–94 (2003), p.90.

6 For comprehensive summaries of the evolution of international law related to reparations of gross human rights violations, see R. Falk, 'Reparations, International Law and Global Justice: A New Frontier', in P. de Greiff (ed.), *The Handbook of Reparations*, Oxford University Press, Oxford, 2006 (428–503); A. Buyse, *Post-Conflict Housing Restitution. The European Human Rights Perspective with a Case Study on Bosnia Herzegovina*, Intersentia, Leiden, 2007 (113–137). The evolution in the Inter-American Court of Human Rights has been remarkable. See J. Pasqualucci, *The practice and procedure of the Inter-American Court*, Cambridge University Press, Cambridge, 2003, pp.230–290. See also A. Carrillo 'Justice in context: The relevance of Inter-American Human Rights Law and practice to repairing the past', in P. de Greiff (ed.), *The Handbook of Reparations*, Oxford University Press, Oxford, 2006 (504–538).

of political power and the dismantling of military structures. As a result, the most sensible policy—when balancing what is desirable with what is possible—might be to promote political pacification and democratization first, and only later confront the issues of asset seizure and redistribution.[7]

As Pablo de Greiff has expressed, the transitional mechanisms that a society must implement in order to achieve the goals of transition—long, medium, and short term—must be designed and applied in a manner that will guarantee internal and external coherence.[8] An example can be used to illustrate the relationship between the different objectives of transitional justice in the case of assurance of corporate responsibility: if the ultimate objectives of transitional justice are civic trust and reconciliation, it is not hard to think of ways in which measures that aim to hold corporations to account for their role in the atrocities of the past can become tools to achieve reconciliation and to strengthen the functioning of the democratic institutions and the confidence therein. In this sense (focusing on the intermediate goals of transitional justice), accountability of powerful economic actors from the past can contribute to achieving recognition of the victims (of rights violations by corporate entities), trust (in a new state that confronts powerful economic actors), and political participation (in a society where economic asymmetries do not hinder participation). At the same time, taking measures to hold corporations responsible for violations of human rights allows us to reach more immediate goals such as uncovering the truth of the past, achieving justice for individuals whose rights have been violated, and offering sufficient economic resources to provide for reparations and to carry out institutional reforms and the reconstruction of a country in conflict.[9]

This chapter will develop a proposal that, based on the principles and mechanisms of the transitional justice framework, addresses the diverse ways in which economic forces, businesses, and corporations illegitimately accumulated assets during times of conflict or repression. The reflections, formulated from a practitioner's perspective, are a first attempt to address these difficult issues and suggest ways of tackling them. While it is clear that a model of transition that encourages implementing corporate accountability mechanisms—both coercive and voluntary—can and must promote the ultimate goals of democratic transition, such as civic trust, solidarity, and

7 See, for example, A. Schneider, 'Intersection of Dispute Systems Design and Transitional Justice', 14 *Harvard Negotiation Law Review* 289–315 (2009), p. 291; K. Franke, 'Gendered Subject of Transitional Justice', 15 *Columbia Journal of Law and Gender* 813–828 (2006), p.819.

8 P. de Greiff, 'Justice and Reparations', in P. de Greiff (ed.), *The Handbook of Reparations*, Oxford University Press, Oxford, 2006 (451–472), p.467.

9 For a more complete view on Pablo de Greiff's discussion of the short-term, intermediate, and long-term goals of transitional justice, see *ibid.*

recognition,[10] a deeper discussion of these general questions is beyond the scope of this chapter. I will instead concentrate on the specific questions that arise with regard to corporate responsibility in the context of transitional justice.

The first section of the chapter focuses on the context of economic power and corporate responsibility. The second section, using as examples initiatives that are currently being advanced in Colombia, presents three scenarios that address economic power and the role of corporate responsibility. The chapter closes with tentative conclusions encouraging further research and discussion.

Economic power, conflict, and transition: where do corporations fit in?

To start, it is appropriate to locate the subject of corporate accountability within the general context of economic power and conflict. During repression and conflict, economic power, rent capture, and accumulation of assets occur within complex and sophisticated structures that lie between the public and the private, the legal and the illegal. In between there are many gray areas in which the exercise of power is based on both public and private strategies and in which resources are extracted through both legal and illegal transactions.

The state is a primary actor that can drain resources from victims and from society in general. It will often do so by confiscating property[11] and/or using the dictatorship or conflict to accumulate public or private resources for the personal or private benefit of public officials, their political parties, or their families.[12] However, the main scenario of interest for the purpose of this chapter is that of private actors that directly or indirectly take advantage of the conflict to redirect economic resources and amass legal and illegal wealth. Three different types of actors can be involved here: armed groups, national and multinational corporations and businesses, and individuals. Above all, particular individuals such as local leaders, large landowners, etc. participate at the local level. An example of this is the so-called phenomenon of the "para-economy" in Colombia.[13]

10 *Ibid.*

11 L. Shelley, *Policing Soviet Society: The Evolution of State Control*, Routledge, New York and London, 1996, p.6.

12 See, for example, the work of the Philippine Commission, which successfully recovered US$680 million in ill-gotten assets of the family of Ferdinand Marcos hidden in banks in Switzerland, the United States, and other countries, www.assetrecovery.org/kc/resources/org.apache.wicket.Application/repo?nid=62506d95-a33e-11dc-bf1b-335d0754ba85.

13 The para-economy is not the money of the paramilitaries, but rather the economic networks that have benefitted, in their business dealings, from political and paramilitary violence, in which sectors of the legal economy are also involved. V. Franco and J. Restrepo, 'Empresarios Palmeros, Poderes de Facto, y Despojo de Tierras en el Bajo Atrato', in M. Romero (ed.), *La Economía de los Paramilitares*, Random House Mondadori, Bogota, 2011 (269–411), p.317.

Given the diversity of ways in which private actors can use conflicts to benefit themselves economically, it is nearly impossible to establish a schematization that clearly identifies all methods as either legal or illegal. Some companies, businesses, and corporations benefit legally, such as through legal confiscations or the transfer of monopolies and rents.[14] Others do so illegally—according to national law in place at the time, or international law, or both—or by using a combination of legal and illegal methods.

The involvement of palm oil companies in the Colombian conflict provides a strong example of the gray area between legality and illegality in which companies exploit conflict to profit economically. In the Urabá and other regions of Colombia, palm oil companies that legally bought land from which communities and individuals had been displaced (by conflict) had and continue to have direct links to the paramilitaries. More specifically, several of these companies are owned by paramilitaries operating under aliases.[15]

Many recent transitions around the globe have encompassed legal actions against businesses directly involved in the conflict that have engaged in activities whose legality is ambiguous.[16] In some cases, judicial processes have been started in national[17] or international[18] jurisdictions, while in others, corporations have voluntarily contributed to reparations efforts.[19] For the most part, these initiatives have had limited success due to problems with collecting and presenting evidence in court, as well as with establishing connections between the corporations and the events and between parent corporations and their subsidiaries.[20]

Defining mechanisms for wealth restoration based on degrees of responsibility and available evidence

The model proposed here considers two different perspectives: one based on factual observations and the other on theoretical considerations. On the one

14 For more on legal confiscation during times of conflict, see the example of Czechoslovakia in J. Renzulli, 'Claims of U.S. Nationals under the Restitution Laws of Czechoslovakia', 15 *Boston College International and Comparative Law Review* 165–190 (1992), p.165.

15 Franco and Restrepo, n.13, p.286.

16 For academic reflections regarding some of these experiences, see W. Kaleck and M. Saage-Maass, 'Corporate Accountability for Human Rights Violations Amounting to International Crimes. The Status Quo and its Challenges', 8 *Journal of International Criminal Justice* 699–724 (2010), p.702.

17 For an account of the Argentinian litigation experience, see J.P. Bohoslavsky and V. Opgenhaffen, 'The Past and Present of Corporate Complicity: Financing the Argentinian Dictatorship', 23 *Harvard Human Rights Journal* 157–203 (2010).

18 See *Mujica v Occidental Petroleum Corp.*, 381 F.Supp.2d 1134 (C.D. Ca 2005), p.1138; and *Sinaltrainal v Coca-Cola Company*, 578 F.3d 1252 (11th Circuit, 2009), p.1258.

19 J. Ruggie, 'The Theory and Practice of Learning Networks: Corporate Social Responsibility and the Global Compact', 5 *Journal of Corporate Citizenship* 27–36, (2002), p.33.

20 Chapter 3 of this book discusses many of these challenges in the context of the American ATS.

hand, the model is inspired by the Colombian experience. Specifically, it is informed by the existence of a complicated network of wealth transfer in the Colombian conflict, the general failure of international litigation to hold accountable MNCs that have participated in or benefited from the conflict, and the limited success achieved by the implementation of social corporate accountability mechanisms. In a way, the model is a proposal of means to confront the barriers to justice that have emerged in the Colombian context, and presumably also in other societies in conflict and transition. On the other hand, it is part of a theoretical elaboration of the concept of transformative reparations, as part of which a model of evidentiary proof is suggested that would serve to create different levels of accountability.

The idea of transformative reparations, a notion proposed by Dejusticia,[21] seeks to harmonize the imperatives of corrective and distributive justice in transitional contexts. This concept is an effort to combine the dominant concept of reparations, which in current legal theory is backward looking and grounded in corrective justice, with the concept of distributive justice, which is forward looking and takes into consideration current needs of the population.[22] The notion of transformative reparations is based on two main tenets: the purpose of reparations in this situation, and the scope that reparation programs should have. The first tenet holds that the purpose of reparations of massive human rights violations in unequal societies should not be to restore disadvantaged victims to their previous situation of poverty and discrimination, but to change or "transform" the circumstances in which they lived—circumstances that could have been one of the roots of conflict and that are moreover in themselves unjust. The second tenet holds that reparation programs must be grounded on corrective justice, because they have to address the suffering of victims, but that they should also respond to considerations of distributive justice. This means that the duty to give redress for a wrong inflicted on a victim should be considered as a principle or a prima facie obligation, but not as a strict rule or a definitive obligation. In that sense, victims' right to redress for a wrong inflicted exists, and states

21 C. Sanchez and R. Uprimny, 'Propuestas para una restitución de tierras transformadora', in C. Díaz (ed.), *Tareas Pendientes: Propuestas para la Formulación de Políticas Públicas de Reparación en Colombia*, International Center for Transitional Justice, Bogotá, 2010 (223–243); R. Uprimny and M. Saffon, 'Reparaciones Transformadoras, Justicia Distributiva y Profundización Democrática', in C. Díaz *et al.* (eds), *Reparar en Colombia: los Dilemas en Contexto de Conflicto, Pobreza y Exclusión*, International Center for Transitional Justice/Dejusticia, Bogotá, 2009 (34–43); R. Uprimny, 'Between corrective and distribute justice: Reparations to gross human rights violations in times of transition', Inaugural Address as Visiting Professor to the UNESCO Chair in Education for Peace, Human Rights and Democracy 2009, delivered on 21 October 2009 at Utrecht University, www.uu.nl/university/research/EN/international_collaboration/latinamerica/Documents/OratieRodrigoUprimny.pdf.

22 Uprimny and Saffon, *ibid.*

should make all efforts to satisfy it; but this obligation can be outweighed in certain circumstances by considerations of distributive justice.[23]

Based on that framework, a comprehensive strategy to restore illegally accumulated assets and redistribute the wealth that private agents collected during the repression or conflict must keep in mind two key factors. The first is the degree of responsibility of the actor that obtained the wealth. The second is the type of proof available to demonstrate such responsibility. With regard to the first factor, I propose to distinguish three levels of responsibility: high, medium, and low. High responsibility refers to direct responsibility, applying to cases in which a company directly committed illegal acts to obtain economic benefit or financed armed groups to create commercial or production advantages. Medium responsibility refers to indirect responsibility, in which a corporation conducted business with the knowledge that the conflict helped its commercial success, but in which the corporation did not directly support or participate in violations and violence. Lastly, low responsibility refers to those cases in which a company developed a successful business in a country suffering from violence and violations, but in which there was no causal nexus between the violence and the company's profits.

Some examples from the Colombian context can clarify these different degrees of responsibility. Regarding direct responsibility, Drummond and Coca-Cola have both been accused of paying paramilitary groups to violently resolve labor disputes, thereby suppressing the unions organizing the workforce and generating increased earnings from decreased labor costs.[24] In the *Drummond* case, Drummond, a mining company with operations in Colombia, was accused of using paramilitaries to suppress union activity at one of its mines. More specifically, the plaintiffs alleged that Drummond gave the paramilitaries and the regular military access to its facilities, as well as financial and material support, and that the paramilitaries tortured and murdered three union officials. In the *Coca-Cola* case, the plaintiffs alleged that Coca-Cola and its local subsidiary, acting through bottling companies, hired paramilitaries to torture, murder, kidnap, and intimidate labor leaders. The companies involved in these violations have a high degree of responsibility because they caused violence through their direct and conscious actions.

Medium or indirect responsibility can have various expressions. One of these may be present in the case of Chiquita Brands, an American company accused of giving money to armed groups so that they would allow Chiquita

23 Uprimny, n.21, p.18.

24 In 2002 and 2003, plaintiffs brought a suit against the Drummond Company, which went to trial in 2007 with a verdict for the defendants. This was the first ATS suit against a corporation to reach a jury, 256 F.Supp. 2d 1250 (N.D. Ala. 2003). With regard to Coca-Cola, plaintiffs brought a suit in 2008; the litigation concluded with a dismissal following an appeals court judgment in 2009, *Sinaltrainal v Coca-Cola Company*, 578 F.3d 1252 (11th Circuit, 2009).

operations in conflict zones.[25] Obviously, here it is difficult or impossible to link the company to all the violent actions undertaken by the armed groups, but it may not be too difficult to demonstrate Chiquita's indirect responsibility given the economic returns that it obtained through the protection allegedly granted by these groups. A link could be shown between the financial and material support Chiquita provided to the paramilitaries (estimated at US$3.2 million in cash alone, though it could be higher) and the violent actions undertaken by the paramilitaries in the areas where Chiquita wished to do business.[26] In this case of indirect responsibility, although the violent actions were not directly commissioned by the company (as was the case with Coca Cola and Drummond), a clear supportive link between the armed groups and the company is present. A second example of indirect responsibility is the inexpensive purchase of land by companies in conflict areas, made possible by large-scale forced displacement. For example, a local milk cooperative has been accused of purchasing great expanses of land at prices far below the market value.[27] Companies such as these are aware of how the conflict has affected the land market and have been known to take advantage of the situation by purchasing lands abandoned due to violence. The economic benefit is clear, but not the companies' direct participation in displacement.

Lastly, the cases of many Colombian banks exemplify low degrees of responsibility. Despite the state of conflict and massive property dispossession, many businesses have been prosperous in Colombia, including many financial institutions. While Colombian banks have suffered losses due to the global

25 The *Chiquita* litigation, concerns payments made to armed groups that then carried out torture and killings. Unlike the prior corporate litigation involving paramilitary attacks, the plaintiffs in the *Chiquita* litigation do not generally allege that Chiquita directly instigated the individual crimes. Instead, they allege that Chiquita, knowing of the nature of the paramilitaries, supported the paramilitaries economically and materially, making payments, and aiding arms imports and drug exports. Chiquita thus aided and abetted the paramilitaries, conspired with them, and used them as its agents. This financial and material support allowed the paramilitaries to engage in violence and was provided with the purpose that the paramilitaries would generally protect Chiquita's security and economic interests via violent means. The crimes allegedly committed as a result included murders, kidnappings, and torture. *In re Chiquita Brands International, Inc. Alien Tort Statute and Shareholder Derivative Litigation*, 2010 WL 432426 (S.D. Fla). The decision of the US Supreme Court in *Kiobel v Royal Dutch Petroleum Co.* (2013), 2013 WL 1628935, sheds serious doubts on the success of this litigation which relies on the exercise of extraterritorial jurisdiction by US courts.

26 M. Romero and D. Torres, 'Drummond, Chiquita, y Paramilitares: Adaptación y Negociación de Ventajas en Medio del Conflicto', in M. Romero (ed.), *La Economía de los Paramilitares*, Random House, Mondadori, Bogotá, 2011 (149–190), p.150

27 Superintendencia de Notariado y Registro (SNR), *Informe sobre el despojo de tierras en el Urabá Antioqueño y Montes de María*, Ley de Víctimas y Restitución de Tierras: Informe Ejecutivo de Gestión, Nov 2010 – Octubre 2011, SNR, Bogotá, 2011, www.supernotariado.gov.co/supernotariado/images/smilies/Noticias2011/infdestierras.pdf.

economic crisis, they have not suffered any due to the country's internal conflict. Indeed, the financial transactions that have occurred during the conflict have benefited the banking business, as would a large-scale reparations program.[28] A significant number of people acquired bank loans that, because they became victims of displacement, they were unable to pay back. The large-scale restitution program that is being designed in Colombia assumes that property restitution must guarantee that the property returned is free of burdens such as taxes and debts.[29] Based on a classic version of responsibility for forced displacement, the state should assume the payment of debts, with the result that scarce public resources would benefit a sector that, even if it did not directly participate in the conflict, clearly benefited economically from the conflict. Banks—some of which are quasi-state entities, such as Fondo para el Financiamiento del Sector Agropecuario, Fondo Agropecuario de Garantías, and Incentivo a la Capitalización Rural—invested heavily in banana and palm oil companies that, as described in the case of Chiquita above, provided financial and material support to the paramilitaries, who violently displaced indigenous communities in the Urabá and Santa Marta regions in order to clear the land for the companies to do business.[30]

A second step of the proposal is to evaluate the evidence needed to measure harm impacts judicially or administratively, and to assess the administrative and judicial ability to deploy accountability mechanisms. From the point of view of establishing accountability through the adjudication of individual cases, for example, it is not enough to know who was directly responsible without having evidence to support the knowledge. In the transitional context, the lack of evidence constitutes a barrier that adds to the high threshold of substantive legal standards—for example, the need to show causation.

In spite of this, the lack of evidence is not an insurmountable barrier to the implementation of a model of justice that seeks to accomplish the objectives of a democratic transition. Table 6.1 summarizes this relation between responsibility and evidence, as well as possible ways to establish transitional programs that, based on theories of justice tied to the paradigmatic objectives of transitional justice, allow for procedures that reassign assets and recognize responsibility. Again, this box formalizes a set of proposals that are currently being designed and promoted in the context of the "transition" in Colombia.

The first row of the table summarizes the classical version of international human rights law that provides the basis for the dominant modern notion of transitional justice: it employs the idea of corrective justice on which the legal right to reparations is based. The principle of integral reparation requires

28 R. Uprimny and C. Sanchez, 'Los Dilemas de la Restitución de Tierras en Colombia', 12 *Estudios Socio-Jurídicos* 305–342 (2010), p.325.

29 *Ibid.*

30 Romero and Torres, n.26, p.169.

Table 6.1 Responsibility degrees and evidence

Degree of responsibility	*Available evidence*	*Theory of justice*	*Forfeiture mechanisms*
High: participation in violence	Direct	Corrective	Coercive/restitution and fines/ forfeiture of concessions/ cancellation of monopolies/ economic sanctions
Medium: no direct support or participation	Indirect	Corrective/ distributive	Dynamic burden of proof/ additional probative mechanisms/limited restitution/promotion of voluntary mechanisms
Low: no participation	Not available or exculpatory	Distributive	Solidarity mechanisms/ progressive tax liability/ promotion of voluntary mechanisms such as affirmative action

that all victims of serious human rights violations receive full reparations, or at least reparations proportional to the seriousness of the violation and injury that they suffered. Thus, reparation is guided by the idea of full or complete restitution, which implies that the state must make all possible efforts to erase the effects of the crime and undo the damage caused, with the aim of restoring the victim to his or her condition before the crime.[31]

Establishing responsibility and correcting the illegal actions is possible when there is a sufficient degree of certainty about what happened. This is why applying these standards requires a minimum amount of evidence to support reparation decisions. That is, a case-by-case adjudicatory model requires evidence to determine the facts, responsibility, and legal consequences. The best examples of this model are the judgments about criminal responsibility (for individuals) and civil responsibility (for corporations) issued in international legal systems or those of other countries (such as with ATS litigation in the United States).[32]

In any process of transition, dealing with all cases through adjudication will be impossible. However, this does not mean that it is necessary to give up on a mechanism that seeks to adjudicate responsibility in some of the

31 M. Auckerman, 'Extraordinary Evil, Ordinary Crime: A Framework for Understanding Transitional Justice', 15 *Harvard Human Rights Journal* 39–97 (2002), p.78.

32 See, for instance, *In re South African Apartheid Litigation*, 617 F.Supp.2d 228 (S.D.N.Y. 2009). For a case description, see L. Dhooge, 'Accessorial Liability of Transnational Corporations Pursuant to the Alien Tort Statute: The South African Apartheid Litigation and the Lessons of Central Bank', 18 *Transnational Law & Contemporary Problems* 247–297 (2009), p.273. See also chapters 3 and 8 of this book.

cases, particularly the most prominent and important. The general idea of transitional justice represented by the slogan "trials are important"[33] applies here. In the case of corporations and economic powers, as well as in the case of atrocious crimes, some corrective/criminal justice will be useful and necessary for the transitional process.[34]

Other traditional mechanisms could become useful here as well. First, truth commissions can establish who caused dispossession and enriched themselves, which could motivate the creation of voluntary and involuntary reparation mechanisms. The final report of the TRC of Sierra Leone is a good example of this. The report recommended specific reforms of the country's mining sector, including transparency of earnings, protection against corruption, certification of diamond origins through a strict chain of custody (known as the Kimberley Process), and the investment of a portion of diamond revenue in rural development.[35]

Second, societies have created funds with the illegal earnings obtained from repressors. Among these were those created from US$9 million seized from Augusto Pinochet, US$97 million from Alberto Fujimori, and US$2 billion from Ferdinand Marcos.[36] Although the funds have been more symbolic than substantial, and have been limited exclusively to the earnings of dictators and their allies, they provide a model to develop a form of corporate accountability. Following similar principles, the recent Ley de Víctimas in Colombia has stipulated that money used to compensate victims will partially come from those who have been condemned for organizing, promoting, arming, or financing paramilitary groups, relative to the amount justified in the "economic chain," as well as from businesses that have financed paramilitaries, relative to the extent to which the conflict was exacerbated by the businesses' financial support.[37] A further step would be to give victims the right to some of the corporations' illegal earnings reaped as a product of displacement and conflict.

33 See Teitel, n.5, p.75.

34 See W. Lambourne, 'Transitional Justice and Peacebuilding after Mass Violence', 3 *The International Journal of Transitional Justice* 28–48 (2009), p.30.

35 See E. Harwell and P. Le Billon, 'Natural Connections: Linking Transitional Justice and Development Through a Focus on Natural Resources', in P. de Greiff and R. Duthie (eds), *Transitional Justice and Development: Making Connections*, International Center for Transitional Justice, New York, 2009 (282–330), p.301.

36 *Ibid.*, p.302.

37 See Artículo 177, Ley de Víctimas, www.minjusticia.gov.co/Library/News/Files/CARTILLA%20LEY%20DE%20V%C3%8DCTIMAS%20Y%20RESTITUCI%C3%93N%20DE%20TIERRAS70.PDF. These obligatory payments are part of the overall compensation pot, which is also funded by private donations from individuals who choose to give a voluntary contribution upon finalizing a bank transaction or supermarket purchase. Damages paid by paramilitary groups and individuals from legal actions taken against them are also part of the fund.

Lastly, disqualifying state functionaries can be effective mechanisms for dismantling the corruption that exists between corporations and public concessions. Similar processes could also provide the means to remove concessions and monopolies that favor corporations that, with the help of the regime, had captured public and private rents.

These mechanisms would obviously have to be complemented with other ways of addressing past events. The second and third rows of the above table try to respond to this challenge. In the second scenario, the most pressing question is the following: what to do when certain corporations are known to have acted illegally but the available evidence is insufficient for successful judicial proceedings? That is the case, for example, of Chiquita Brands and its involvement in the Colombian conflict. Even though the company was fined US$25 million as part of a settlement with the US Department of Justice for having ties to Colombian paramilitary groups, in Colombia, the Attorney General's Office recently closed the case by saying that Chiquita was a victim of extortion.[38] In this sense, while under the public eye Chiquita bears responsibility for its actions, there is no available cause of action to take the company to a court of law.

Complementarily, how should a society redirect scarce resources for reconstruction and reparations from those whom the conflict indirectly enriched? Here there are no unique or easy formulas, as with almost all tasks in a transition. However, one could think about designing mechanisms, voluntary and coercive, that respond by jointly applying the principles of corrective and distributive justice, and thus simultaneously restore victims to their previous position and enhance their economic, political, and social power by applying redistributive principles. In this area, there are several promising but still incomplete examples currently under consideration in Colombia. Among them, the Ley de Víctimas establishes a judicial presumption that people who transferred property in an area of generalized violence did so because of the violence:[39] a current occupant of the property who opposes the restitution claim must prove his or her good faith and lack of fault in occupying the land.[40] The law also provides for a victims' fund that, as explained before, partially comes from money collected from businesses that have financed armed groups.

A common question in the Colombian conflict has been the concentration of cultivable land through the forced displacement of persons. Estimates indicate that 11 per cent of the country's cultivable land changed hands

38 D. Montero, 'Las cosas que no vio el fiscal que precluyó la investigación de Chiquita Brands', *Lasillavacia.com*, 29 March 2012, www.lasillavacia.com/historia/las-cosas-que-no-vio-el-fiscal-que-precluyo-la-investigacion-de-chiquita-brands-32405.

39 Ley de Víctimas, L.1448/11, 10 June 2011, 40.096 Diario Oficial, articles 77–78 (Colom.).

40 *Ibid.*

during the last 15 years of conflict.[41] Companies engaged in various productive activities (wood, meat, and biofuels, primarily African palm) acquired much of this land for derisory prices.[42]

In Colombia, the means that activists and scholars have considered for reversing this illegitimate accumulation of wealth, as noted previously, combine corrective and distributive justice. For example, in the case of large-scale land dispossession, some have proposed including flexible evidence mechanisms that allow land and territory restitution without requiring the victims to prove the intention, bad faith, or participation of companies in acts of violence. One of these proposals seeks to create zones in which it will be presumed that all land transactions during the conflict were illegitimate. A competent authority could establish such zones in those areas where land possession, value, use, accumulation, and other relations to rural or urban land had manifestly changed hands as a result of intimidation or armed action. The logic that sustains this means of repair is simple: because it was publicly known that the conflict altered the land market, corporations cannot invoke lack of knowledge. The decision to participate in land transactions like these consequently makes them complicit in displacement, and, as a result, they must accept certain consequences. One of them is to reverse certain legal transactions. Some activists, including lawyers, have advocated for stronger measures—supported by distributive justice—that limit or eliminate indemnifications for corporations even when they have shown that they became secondary land occupants in good faith. These proposals simultaneously address the past injustice (unfair appropriation of land) and confront distributional issues by setting a precedent that severely limits corporations' abilities to appropriate land in times of conflicts.[43] Thus, there can be overlap between corrective and distributive justice.

A second problem is that national and multinational companies have been involved in the Colombian conflict, but there is very limited evidence to

41 Comisión de Seguimiento, *Cuantificación y Valoración de las Tierras y los Bienes Abandonados o Despojados a la Población Desplazada en Colombia*, 5 January 2011, p.7 (reporting that 6.6 million hectares have been dispossessed since 1980); L. Garay *et al.*, *El Reto Ante la Tragedia Humanitaria del Desplazamiento Forzado: Reparar de Manera Integral el Despojo de TierrasyBienes*,Volume5,2009,p.57,www.internal-displacement.org/8025708F004CE90B/(httpDocuments)/9C9025369DCE9579C12575E0005439CA/$file/Vol_5_TIERRAS.pdf (reporting that 5.5 million hectares have been dispossessed since 1998).

42 Sistema Nacional de Atención Integral a la Población Desplazada (SNAIPD), *Informe del Gobierno Nacional a la Corte Constitucional sobre la Superación del Estado de Cosas Inconstitucional Declarado Mediante la Sentencia T-025 de 2004*, 1 July 2010, p.86 (citing numbers from the Registro Unico de Población Desplazada as of April 2010); Consultoría para los Derechos Humanos y el Desplazamiento CODHES, '¿Salto estratégico o salto al vacío?', Boletín informativo 76, 27 January 2010 (reporting the total number of people displaced in the last 25 years).

43 Sanchez and Uprimny, n.21, p.243; see also Uprimny and Saffon, n.21, p.65.

support judicial proceedings, and those that have begun have had little success. The failed attempts to litigate in US courts through the ATS are typical. While the lawsuits themselves have so far not led to awards of compensation,[44] the information retrieved in these suits has shed some light on the conflict. This information indicates that some companies provided material and economic aid to armed groups and took advantage of the conflict to maintain or advance their position in the labor market, their monopolies in production areas, and the security of personnel and property, among other things.[45] These advantages may have made the companies more competitive and, as a result, their businesses more profitable. This problem may be addressed by applying the common mechanisms contained in the legal framework of corporate responsibility, supported by documents such as the OECD Guidelines for Multinational Enterprises, the UN Global Compact, and the work of Professor John Ruggie and the UN Human Rights Council.[46] In particular, applying the mechanisms against unfair competition may be an appropriate response in light of the illicit advantages obtained by the companies involved.

These means must be complemented by institutional reforms aimed at preventing a repetition of events. An example of such a reform is the Liberia Forest Initiative, which reformed the country's forestry legislation in 2006 as a condition of removing economic sanctions. The reform included regulations on competitive bidding for contract allocation, community involvement in decision-making, disclosure requirements, comprehensive public access to information, and a chain-of-custody (COC) system to track the origin of timber from stump to export in order to ensure legality and the payment of taxes, among other things.[47] We hope to promote a similar model in Colombia for restitution, which will focus not only on return and property restitution but also on ways to reverse the concentration of land holdings and to revise the current rural development model that favors industrial exploitation at the expense of small- and medium-scale economic activity. Given the role of corporations in contributing to past injustices and the broader unjust distribution of land, as explained above, Colombia should use

44 It is worth noting here that the US$25 million fine mentioned earlier was paid by the company to the US government, but none of that money was later redirected to the Colombian government or the Colombian victims.

45 The Drummond Company and Coca-Cola litigation have shed light on the use of paramilitaries to suppress union activity; and the Chiquita litigation has put together evidence that shows how companies, knowing the nature of the paramilitaries, supported such groups economically and materially, making payments, aiding arms imports, and aiding drug exports.

46 All documents produced by Mr Ruggie in connection with his mandate can be found within the Business and Human Rights Resource Center's website, www.business-humanrights.org/SpecialRepPortal/Home.

47 Harwell and Le Billon, n.35, p.314.

these initiatives to hold corporations accountable for their past actions and set limits on their power.

Lastly, the third row of the table presents a strategy to establish a model of corporate responsibility in transitional processes when responsibility is even less clear. This happens when there is insufficient evidence to establish any degree of responsibility (even the negligence discussed above) or when there is evidence that exculpates corporations. The ethical and legal justification for requiring these corporations to contribute to the transitional process is not corrective justice, but instead distributive justice, based on solidarity with public burdens. This statement does not imply that legitimate businesses must right the wrongs of the individuals and companies that caused the damages. On the contrary, this idea highlights the fact that distributive justice, considered a legal principle by many societies, provides for a legal duty of society to assist individual members in proportion to: (i) the individual's needs, contribution, and responsibility; (ii) the resources available to the society; and (iii) the society's responsibility to the common good.[48] In that sense, what is proposed here is a way to connect principles of corrective justice with distributive justice duties.[49]

In Colombia, civil society organizations are supporting some mechanisms of this type. Returning to the topic of the Colombian financial system and its influence on the conflict and, most importantly, the transition, even though it may be possible to determine whether particular financial organizations played a role in violations, assume for now that there are no such relationships or that they are impossible to demonstrate. Do we want to say that this establishes that financial corporations are free of obligations to contribute to the transitional reconstruction and reparation process, and that any efforts that they undertake must be understood as voluntary? The Colombian Constitutional Court has ruled that, in the model of state established by the Colombian Constitution, participation is more than simply a moral duty.[50] Thus, for example, in applying the principle of solidarity, the Court has ordered banks to freeze loans, thereby not allowing interest to accumulate or banks to demand payment, in cases where, due to the violence, people, such as displaced, disappeared, and kidnapped persons, are unable to meet their

48 K. Jackson, 'Global Distributive Justice and the Corporate Duty to Aid', 12 *Journal of Business Ethics* 547–551 (1993), p.160.

49 For a similar proposal, see Uprimny, n.21. For a different view, which prefers the use of distributive justice considerations over corrective justice justifications, see P. Kalmanovitz, 'Corrective Justice vs. Social Justice in the Aftermath of War', in M. Bergsmo, C. Rodríguez-Garavito, P. Kalmanovitz and M. Saffon (eds), *Distributive Justice in Transitions*, Torkel Opsahl Academic EPublisher, Oslo, 2010 (71–96).

50 This initiative is nothing new in the comparative context. In fact, the South African TRC recommended the imposition of "contributions" on corporations, primarily in the mining sector, that benefited from apartheid, see Harwell and Le Billon, n.35, p.306, and chapter 8 of this book.

obligations. We propose to extend this principle of solidarity to a principle of distributive justice, thereby requiring, for example, that banks forgive the loans of displaced persons. Proposals of this type, based on distributive justice, have been included in the national Programa de Restitución de Bienes, based on the recognition that restitution of titles alone has been an insufficient response to reverse the effects of massive displacement. Instead, more robust mechanisms are needed to ensure just reparations and enjoyment of land of the displaced populations, and to prevent further displacement. The fact that banks have benefited significantly from this conflict and have played a role in furthering displacement, as described above, further bolsters the justification for debt relief.[51]

Conclusion

In this chapter, I have tried to indicate some possible ways to build bridges between the long- and short-term goals of democratic transition and corporate complicity in acts of violence and repression. There are multiple challenges to building these bridges. They come both from the nature of transitions and the limited interest that practitioners and theorists have devoted to the topic. Despite these challenges, however, there have been some valuable initiatives in this area worth considering.

The task, then, is to determine how to think about the problems confronting local efforts to use transitional justice mechanisms to hold powerful economic groups accountable without creating an atmosphere of vengeance and without preventing international financial investment aimed at economic and democratic development. In my opinion, strategies for addressing corporations during the transition process should be designed and implemented while taking into account the overall context of the transition and seeking to ensure that they reinforce one another. Some of these measures should be based on principles of corrective justice, others on principles of distributive justice, and yet others on a mixture of both. Moreover, these initiatives should be implemented by coercive—that is, legally enforceable—means that will probably spontaneously generate voluntary "corporate social responsibility" initiatives, as companies will attempt to prevent legal action from being taken against them.

In any case, attempts to construct a typology of cases and possible routes should consider the common risks faced when implementing transitional measures. Experience has conclusively shown that transitional justice must favor measures arising from the local context and consensus, and must avoid a cookie-cutter approach. A second rule from experience, and relevant in this

51 Comisión Nacional de Reparación y Reconciliación (CNRR), *Programa de Restitución de Bienes*, Bogotá, 2 July 2010, p.67.

context, is the need to assess the historical moment at which the measures are going to be implemented and the need to generate public support—both nationally and internationally—for the measures. Lastly, experience shows that a model that seeks a lasting democratic transition should avoid the temptation to pursue quick economic recovery at the expense of long-term democratic governance. To that extent, even though some measures that address corporations, especially transnational economic punishment, may be undesirable, allowing the perpetuation of undemocratic practices that benefit the wealthy at the expense of the general welfare of the population does not facilitate the non-repetition of events and might even endanger the already-settled elements of transition in a democratic transformation.[52]

52 For more on how the experiences of Rwanda, Cambodia, Sierra Leone, and East Timor support this view, see Lambourne, n.34; R. Mani, *Beyond Retribution: Seeking Justice in the Shadows of War*, Polity Press, Cambridge, 2002; R. Duthie, 'Towards a Development-Sensitive Approach to Transitional Justice', 2 *International Journal of Transitional Justice* 159–168 (2008).

Chapter 7

A New Avenue Towards Corporate Accountability

The Optional Protocol to the Covenant on Economic, Social and Cultural Rights

Sylvain Aubry

Introduction

While the impact of corporations on human rights has mainly been dealt with in the framework of civil and political rights,[1] such as the rights to be free from torture and arbitrary killing, and in the context of labor-related rights, such as the right to work and the right to unionize, companies may equally be involved in violations of the full range of ESCR.[2] A study of the SRSG on a sample of 320 allegations of corporate abuses demonstrates this close link between businesses and ESCR.[3] For instance, abuses of the right to an adequate standard of living, including the rights to adequate food, clothing, and housing, was alleged in nearly 40 per cent of the cases reviewed.[4] There are therefore good reasons to address the impact of companies on ESCR.

Besides, ESCR infringements not only constitute violations of international human rights law; they are also often the root cause of gross civil and political rights violations involving companies, and they create tensions within societies that lead to conflicts. For instance, in the case of the crisis in Nigeria in the mid-nineties, which involved the oil company Shell, Daniel Aguirre notes that it was "[t]he repudiation of ESCRs" that caused "the slide towards violence, miscarriage of justice and killing," due to the international community's failure "to condemn the government and Shell for

1 Even when the cases address economic and social issues, see for instance A. Nolan, 'Addressing Economic and Social Rights Violations by Non-State Actors through the Role of the State: A Comparison of Regional Approaches to the Obligation to Protect', 9 *Human Rights Law Review* 225 (2009), p.253.

2 See generally D. Aguirre, 'Multinational Corporations and the Realisation of Economic, Social and Cultural Rights', 35 *California Western International Law Journal* 53 (2004–2005), pp.60–63.

3 Special Representative of the United Nations Secretary-General on Business and Human Rights, *Addendum: Corporations and human rights: a survey of the scope and patterns of alleged corporate-related human rights abuse*, A/HRC/8/5/Add.2, 23 May 2008, para.19.

4 *Ibid.*, para.25.

environmental degradation and the denial of development and lack of revenue filtering back to the local community from natural resource exploitation."[5] It has similarly been argued that the exploitation of cotton in a way that violates ESCR is the bedrock of Uzbekistan's authoritarian regime,[6] with companies playing a key role in the abuses. In the context of transitions, using the ESCR framework thus permits a view of the economic, social, and cultural background that causes, facilitates, or aggravates the repression or conflict. By including an analysis of state economic policy, an ESCR approach furthermore provides a unique basis to achieve distributive justice, whose importance is shown in chapter 6 of this book. In this respect, highlighting ESCR violations holds the potential to bring a fresh and more holistic perspective on transitional justice.[7]

In addition to these theoretical reasons to look more in detail at companies' impact on ESCR, the recent adoption of the Optional Protocol to the International Covenant on Economic, Social and Cultural Rights (Optional Protocol), which creates new international complaint mechanisms for alleged violations of the International Covenant on Economic, Social and Cultural Rights (ICESCR), provides great opportunities to address corporations' ESCR abuses.

The Optional Protocol was adopted unanimously by the UN General Assembly on 10 December 2008,[8] after almost 20 years of negotiation.[9] It entered into force on 5 May 2013, three months after the tenth state ratified it.[10] The Optional Protocol creates three new mechanisms to monitor states'

5 Aguirre, n.2, p.63.

6 Environmental Justice Foundation, *White Gold: The True Cost of Cotton: Uzbekistan, Cotton and the Crushing of a Nation*, Environmental Justice Foundation, London, 2005.

7 See generally R. Mani, 'Dilemmas of Expanding Transitional Justice, or Forging the Nexus between Transitional Justice and Development', 2 *International Journal of Transitional Justice* 253–265 (2008).

8 UNGA Res.63/117, 2008.

9 See notably C. Mahon, 'Progress at the Front: the Draft Optional Protocol to the International Covenant on Economic, Social and Cultural Rights', 8 *Human Rights Law Review* 617 (2008); M. Langford, 'Closing the Gap? An Introduction to the Optional Protocol to the International Covenant on Economic, Social and Cultural Rights', 27 *Nordic Journal of Human Rights* 1 (2009); C. Albuquerque, 'Chronicle of an Announced Birth: The Coming into Life of the Optional Protocol to the International Covenant on Economic, Social and Cultural Rights – The Missing Piece of the International Bill of Human Rights', 32 *Human Rights Quarterly* 144 (2010); A. Vandenbogaerde and W. Vandenhole, 'The Optional Protocol to the International Covenant on Economic, Social and Cultural Rights: an ex ante assessment of its effectiveness in light of the drafting process', 10 *Human Rights Law Review* 207 (2010).

10 See http://treaties.un.org/Pages/ViewDetails.aspx?src=TREATY&mtdsg_no=IV-3-a&chapter=4&lang=en. See also the *Provisional rules of procedure under the Optional Protocol to the International Covenant on Economic, Social and Cultural Rights*, adopted by the Committee on Economic Social and Cultural Rights at its forty-ninth session, E/C.12/49/3, 15 January 2013.

compliance with the ICESCR. The most promising mechanism is the possibility for individuals or groups of individuals to bring a case before the UN Committee on Economic, Social and Cultural Rights (CESCR), the body charged with monitoring states' compliance with the ICESCR, for an alleged violation of their ESCR. The two other mechanisms created by the Optional Protocol are an interstate communication procedure (article 10) and an inquiry procedure (article 11). While these two latter procedures could potentially be of interest in the context of corporate accountability, they are available only if a state, upon ratification of the Optional Protocol, specifically recognizes the CESCR's competence in this respect. It therefore remains doubtful that a significant use of these mechanisms will be made, and this chapter will focus primarily on the individual complaint mechanism.

So far, no academic reflection on how the Optional Protocol can be used to hold corporations accountable has been undertaken. This chapter will attempt to outline preliminary strategies on how the new mechanisms created by the Optional Protocol could be used to advance corporate accountability for human rights violations, particularly in transitional states. The Optional Protocol is unlikely to make businesses directly accountable, since the ICESCR defines only state obligations, and only states can be found to violate the Covenant. Nevertheless, this chapter argues that the Optional Protocol can be used as a catalyst for progressive legal thinking about corporate accountability, and it introduces some possible strategic approaches to the instrument's use in the context of corporate accountability. The chapter also presents some observations on how these strategies could be applied in the context of transitional justice.

To discuss these points, this chapter will examine the status of existing international human rights law, but it will also rely on relevant soft law and doctrine, in order to infer how the CESCR might interpret the Optional Protocol. Reference will be made in particular to the work of the SRSG, John Ruggie, which is described in detail in chapter 4. Although Ruggie's reports are not legally binding, and have been argued to provide a relatively conservative interpretation of the law,[11] they constitute a useful basis for reflection, as they have received broad support from states and companies alike.

Addressing corporate abuses under the ICESCR

Under the Optional Protocol, the CESCR has the competency to consider alleged violations of the rights set forth in the ICESCR. Article 2 of the

11 See, e.g., the various submissions of major international human rights organizations available at www.business-humanrights.org/SpecialRepPortal/Home/Protect-Respect-Remedy-Framework/GuidingPrinciples/Submissions, or the statement made by FIAN International and 27 other non-governmental organizations after the Guiding Principles were issued: 'Statement to the Delegations on the Human Rights Council 2011, 17th Session, Agenda Item 3', 30 May 2011, www.globalpolicy.org/images/pdfs/humanrights.pdf.

ICESCR requires states to take steps to progressively realize the rights protected under the Covenant to the maximum of their available resources, without discrimination. Under the now well-established triptych of obligations used by the CESCR since issuing its General Comment 12, states must respect, protect, and fulfill ESCR.[12] The *obligation to respect* requires states not to take any measures that result in denying or limiting the access to some of the Covenant's rights; the *obligation to protect* requires them to take measures to prevent third parties from interfering with the rights of the Covenant; and the *obligation to fulfill* requires them to adopt appropriate measures toward the full realization of ESCR. State parties to the ICESCR have both "progressive" and "immediate" obligations,[13] including some minimum core obligations.[14]

As a human rights text, the ICESCR defines only states' obligations,[15] and "only States are parties to the Covenant and are . . . ultimately accountable for compliance with it."[16] As a result, it is highly unlikely that private companies will be found to violate one of its provisions.[17] However, it has been argued that state responsibility actually "plays a seminal role in achieving corporate responsibility for fundamental human rights."[18] As expressed by the SRSG, the human rights treaty bodies' focus "is on the protection of rights – whether the violation is caused by a State organ, a business entity or any other private

12 CESCR, General Comment No.12: *The right to adequate food*, U.N. Doc. E/C.12/1999/5, 12 May 1999, para.15. See also the CESCR General Comments 13 to 19 and 21. See generally M. Langford and J. King, 'Committee on Economic, Social and Cultural Rights', in M. Langford (ed.), *Social Rights Jurisprudence*, Cambridge University Press, New York, 2008 (477–516), pp.484–486.

13 CESCR, General Comment No.3, *The nature of States Parties obligations*, U.N. Doc. E/1991/23, 14 December 1990, para.9. See generally on the types of duties I.E. Koch, 'Dichotomies, Trichotomies or Waves of Duties?' 5 *Human Rights Law Review* 81 (2005).

14 See notably M. Sepúlveda, *The Nature of the Obligations under the International Covenant on Economic Social and Cultural Rights*, Intersentia, 2002, and more recently Langford and King, n.12.

15 See generally N. Rodley, 'Can Armed Opposition Groups Violate Human Rights?' in K. Mahoney and P. Mahoney, *Human Rights in the Twenty-first Century: A Global Challenge*, Nijhoff, Dordrecht/Boston/London, 1993 (297–318).

16 CESCR, General Comment No.12, n.12, para.20.

17 E.g. *ibid.*, para.20. See also Nolan, n.1, p.229; A. Clapham, *Human Rights Obligations of Non-State Actors,* Oxford University Press, Oxford, 2006, p.240; J.L. Černič, *Human Rights Law and Business: Corporate Responsibility for Fundamental Human Rights*, Europa Law Publishing, Netherlands, 2010, p.240. See also the view of the SRSG, *Report of the Special Representative of the Secretary-General on the issue of human rights and transnational corporations and other business enterprises*, A/HRC/4/35, 19 February 2007, para.44.

18 Černič, n.17, p.119. See also J.A. Hessbruegge, 'Human Rights Violations Arising from Conduct of Non-State Actors', 11 *Buffalo Human Rights Law Review* 21–88 (2005), pp.31–32.

actor seems less relevant than the result (the protection and promotion of human rights)."[19]

Since companies do not have direct obligations under the ICESCR, in order to use the Optional Protocol to advance corporate accountability, businesses' responsibilities will have to be addressed indirectly through states' obligations. As will be discussed in the next section, there are a number of circumstances under which a state can be in violation of its treaty obligations as a result of the activities of a company. It is in those circumstances that a communication or an inquiry can help move forward corporate accountability. Though only states will be found to violate the ICESCR, such communications or inquiries could detail the abuses committed by the company targeted, with the aim of getting the CESCR to highlight in its conclusions the corporation's role in the violations committed by the state. The CESCR could do so based on the information made available to it—for example, in amici curiae briefs[20] and shadow reports—and could draw inspiration from soft-law instruments that provide authoritative guidance on the issue, such as the UN Guiding Principles on Business and Human Rights.[21] In a strong case where the available information is solid enough, the CESCR could potentially even make a bold statement explicitly asserting the direct contribution of a company to the abuse and its responsibility for it, or the CESCR could denounce the benefits that the private actor received from the violation—though it should be careful to take a balanced approach to ensure that its conclusions are not used to excuse the state's own role.[22]

Thus, the Optional Protocol could constitute a mechanism to shed light on, and perhaps get an authoritative comment on, states' obligations and companies' responsibilities to guarantee human rights. The views of the CESCR would provide legal arguments and political weight to further litigation and campaigning work, whether at the national or international level, that will be needed to translate the outcome of proceedings that are foremost geared at determining state responsibility into findings of concrete corporate accountability. Since ESCR litigation represents a relatively recent

19 J. Ruggie, *State responsibilities to regulate and adjudicate corporate activities under the United Nations core human rights treaties: an overview of treaty body commentaries*, A/HRC/4/35/Add.1, 13 February 2007, para.29.

20 Albuquerque, n.9, p.173.

21 J. Ruggie, Report of the Special Representative of the Secretary-General on the Issue of Human Rights and Transnational Corporations and Other Business Enterprises, *Guiding Principles on Business and Human Rights: Implementing the United Nations 'Protect, Respect, Remedy' Framework*, U.N. Doc. A/HRC/17/31, 21 March 2011.

22 Nolan, n.1, p.254. The SRSG also notes that even in conflict zones, states are at no point discharged from their obligation to protect against all corporate abuse within their jurisdiction: *Report of the Special Representative of the Secretary-General on the issue of human rights and transnational corporations and other business enterprises, John Ruggie*, A/HRC/8/5, 7 April 2008, para.49.

avenue for corporate accountability at the international level, this may open new perspectives on how to conceptualize corporate accountability. This could thereby help shape transitions by providing a tool to investigate corporate responsibility regarding the violation of ESCR.

Possible strategies for using the Optional Protocol to highlight corporations' impact on ESCR

As mentioned above, in the context of the Optional Protocol, corporate responsibility can be addressed only indirectly through state obligations. This section reviews four possible approaches whereby state obligations can be used to advance corporate accountability through an individual communication. The first three relate to territorial obligations, meaning that a communication concerns events that took place in the state against which the communication is brought. The fourth approach examines how these three strategies can be applied to states' extraterritorial obligations.

Corporate conduct directly attributable to the state

Under certain circumstances, the activities of corporations, which have a legal personality distinct from the state, can be directly attributed to the state, whose obligation to respect the ICESCR may thus be engaged by the corporate activities. The exact conditions under which the acts of a non-state actor can be attributed to a state are listed in the Draft Articles on Responsibility of States for Internationally Wrongful Acts (Draft Articles) of the International Law Commission. The Draft Articles "seek to formulate, by way of codification and progressive development, the basic rules of international law concerning the responsibility of States for their internationally wrongful acts"[23] and are generally considered to reflect existing customary international law.[24]

According to article 8 of the Draft Articles, companies acting on the instruction or under the direction or control of a state can engage the responsibility of that state. The company's acts will be attributed to a state only if its conduct "was directly part of the State instruction or control and not where it was only incidental to it."[25] The state's level of control over the company

23 Report of the International Law Commission, U.N. GAOR, 56th Sess., Supp. No.10, pp.43–59, U.N. Doc. A/56/10,2001, ILC Commentary, p.31.

24 The United Nations General Assembly resolution 56/83 "commended [the articles] to the attention of Governments without prejudice to the question of their future adoption or other appropriate action." U.N. Resolution adopted by the General Assembly, 56/83 Responsibility of States for Internationally Wrongful Acts, A/RES/56/83, 28 January 2002.

25 R. McCorquodale and P.C. Simons, 'Responsibility beyond Borders: State Responsibility for Extraterritorial Violations by Corporations of International Human Rights Law', 70 *Modern Law Review* 601 (2007), p.608. See ILC Commentary, n.23, Commentary to article 8, p.47, para.3.

will have to be assessed in each case, but, as noted by the SRSG, "[w]hen the treaty bodies do discuss State-owned enterprises, they hold States responsible for abuse carried out by such enterprises even where the State argues that it has minimum control over the enterprise's daily decision-making."[26] The CESCR notably mentions in two of its general comments the obligations of "State-owned facilities" as part of states' obligation to respect ESCR;[27] thus, it may be possible to obtain a progressive interpretation from the CESCR to this effect in the context of an individual communication under the Optional Protocol.

Regarding companies exercising elements of governmental authority, article 5 of the Draft Articles addresses the situation where an entity is not formally an organ of the state but where it "is empowered by the law of that State to exercise elements of the governmental authority." In such situations, the acts of this entity shall be considered an act of the state under international law. The exact criteria for determining which entities qualify have yet to be defined,[28] but the International Law Commission did mention that a company's status as public or private is "not decisive" as a criterion.[29] In addition, the International Law Commission indicates that the aim of article 5 is to "take account of the increasingly common phenomenon of parastatal entities, which exercise elements of governmental authority in place of State organs, as well as situations where former State corporations have been privatised but retain certain public or regulatory functions."[30] However, very few cases at the national or international levels address states' ESCR obligations in the context of privatization,[31] despite the CESCR regularly stressing this issue.[32] Litigation under the Optional Protocol could be a catalyst for progress in this area, in particular when a pre-transition government has privatized some of its activities—for instance, education or water services—as part of its oppressive strategy.

26 Ruggie, n.19, para.79.

27 CESCR, General Comment No.14, *The right to the highest attainable standard of health*, E/C.12/2000/4, 11 August 2000, para.34; CESCR, General Comment No.15, *The right to water*, E/C.12/2002/11, 20 January 2003, para.21.

28 ILC Commentary, n.23, p.43, para.6.

29 *Ibid.*, p.43, para.3. Hesbruegge, n.18, argues that the source of financing could define whether a private entity carries out a public function, p.60.

30 ILC Commentary, n.23, p.42, para.1.

31 M. Langford, 'The Justiciability of Social Rights: From Practice to Theory', in M. Langford (ed.), *Social Rights Jurisprudence*, Cambridge University Press, New York, 2008 (3–45), p.18.

32 E.g. General Comment No.14, n.27, para.35; General Comment No.16, *The Equal Right of Men and Women to the Enjoyment of All Economic, Social and Cultural Rights (Art.3 of the Covenant)*, E/C.12/2005/4, 11 August 2005, para.20; General Comment No.18, *The Right to Work*, E/C.12/GC/18, 6 February 2006, para.25; General Comment No.21, *The right of everyone to take part in cultural life*, E/C.12/GC/21, 21 December 2009, para.50.

Such cases where a company's activities that harm human rights can be directly attributed to a state would entail the state's violation of its obligation *to respect* human rights.[33] As such, these cases offer an excellent avenue to hold corporations accountable under the Optional Protocol. Scholars Robert McCorquodale and Penelope Simons have argued that "cases brought before international human rights treaty bodies may have some chance of success if those bodies attribute the actions of the corporations to the state, on the basis that they are acting on the instructions of the state."[34] Although the state is the entity considered to have violated human rights, it is the behavior of the company that will be reviewed and assessed by the CESCR, and findings of responsibility could provide a strong basis for further advocacy work.

Obligation to protect and the general obligation to respect

The second category concerns the duty to protect and the duty to respect where corporate conduct is not directly attributable to the state. The obligation to protect can engage the responsibility of a state if it fails to prevent, regulate, or remedy a wrongful act committed by a private actor.[35] For instance, violations of the right to health "can occur through the direct action of States or other entities insufficiently regulated by States."[36] The duty to protect is well established in international law and has consistently been used by the CESCR.[37] Jurisprudence on the obligation to protect exists with regard to civil and political rights and to ESCR.[38]

Cases in this category could include situations where a private company supports a paramilitary group whose actions adversely affect ESCR—for instance, the right to food, by taking over the land that farmers use to feed themselves—and the state does not take the necessary steps to protect ESCR.[39] Another example could be when a regime condones discrimination

33 Ruggie, n.19, para.10.

34 McCorquodale and Simons, n.25, p.610.

35 See generally D.M. Chirwa, 'The Doctrine of State Responsibility as a Potential Means of Holding Private Actors Accountable for Human Rights', 5 *Melbourne Journal of International Law* 1 (2004). See also Ruggie, n.19, fn.13; CESCR General Comment No.12, n.12, para.19.

36 CESCR General Comment No.14, n.27, para.48.

37 SRSG, n.17, para.18; and Ruggie, n.19, para.19.

38 See Nolan, n.1; McCorquodale and Simons, n.25, p.618.

39 State responsibility for paramilitaries' involvement in human rights violations, including ESCR-related issues, has arisen, for instance, in Colombia, though not involving businesses: Inter-American Court of Human Rights, *Ituango Massacres v Colombia*, Preliminary Objection, Merits, Reparations and Costs, Judgment of 1 July 2006, Series C No.148. Still in Colombia, but not directly involving a paramilitary group, a palm oil company was

by private companies—for instance, allowing a private hospital or a private school to discriminate on ethnic or other grounds—potentially for the state's political purposes.[40] It will be interesting to see whether the CESCR will outline criteria to define the scope of the obligation. Treaty bodies have suggested that it is important for states to promote human rights awareness for business enterprises,[41] and it may be argued that a failure to do so could, where a company is harming ESCR, constitute a sufficient gap to constitute an ESCR violation of the state's obligation to protect.

While the obligation to protect does not permit holding private actors directly accountable, a finding of the CESCR that a state breached its obligation to protect necessarily means that some wrong was done by a private party, for which the state is responsible at the international level. The underlying message could constitute a solid basis for civil society and domestic judges to achieve accountability of the private actor at the national level. Thus, the obligation to protect, "although insufficient on its own, may play an important role as an instrument of mobilisation to change perceptions within society that may accelerate the implementation of the rights."[42]

Finally, there could also be cases where the state not only failed to regulate a company but has laws or policies that directly facilitate abuse by business enterprises. Again, it would be a company harming human rights, but the state would be violating the ICESCR by actively inviting the harmful activities—for instance, by encouraging companies to discriminate against certain groups or to use labor standards below those outlined in the ICESCR.[43] Such cases would constitute a violation of the obligation to respect,[44] but the distinction would probably not make much difference in terms of the use of the Optional Protocol and subsequent advocacy. As with the cases involving the obligation to protect, they could be used to hold accountable the companies that deliberately agree to follow laws or policies involving the abuse of ESCR.

alleged to harm the right to food of a community, which was evicted by the state police, which could equally constitute a violation of the obligation to protect ESCR, see R. Syal and S. Brodzinsky, 'Body Shop ethics under fire after Colombian peasant evictions', *The Observer*, 13 September 2009, www.guardian.co.uk/world/2009/sep/13/body-shop-colombia-evictions; and Christian Aid, 'Body Shop decision praised as it cuts ties with Colombian palm oil supplier', October 2010, www.christianaid.org.uk/whatwedo/partnerfocus/body-shop-praise-for-cutting-ties-with-palm-olive-supplier.aspx.

40 A similar example, but regarding the obligation to respect, can be found in CESCR, General Comment No.14, n.27, para.50.

41 Ruggie, n.19, para.10.

42 Sepúlveda, n.14, p.223.

43 Similar cases can be found, for example, in Uzbekistan: Environmental Justice Foundation, n.6.

44 Ruggie, n.19, para.10.

Obligation to provide access to remedies

The right to a remedy is not expressly enounced in the ICESCR, but the Covenant defensibly imposes a number of obligations regarding access to remedies and accountability.[45] According to the CESCR, states must "investigate" and "examine" or "address" alleged violations.[46] States must provide access to effective remedies, which need not be judicial,[47] although there is a strong presumption that judicial remedies are needed[48] and even sometimes "indispensable," such as with regard to the obligation of non-discrimination.[49] In the case of administrative remedies, they "should be accessible, affordable, timely, and effective."[50]

Where a company is abusing ESCR, the state must at least ensure that appropriate processes are in place to assist rights-holders in bringing claims against corporate abuse.[51] Though this is an open question to be specified by jurisprudence, whether the remedy is provided by the company itself or the state will probably be less important than whether it is an *effective* remedy (which is itself open to interpretation). In the context of the Optional Protocol, and particularly in situations of transition, this duty could prove to be very relevant for holding corporations accountable. For example, there could potentially be a valid case under the Optional Protocol where states create a general amnesty for the acts committed by companies during the pre-transition period in a context where these companies do not provide any adequate remedy themselves, or where states investigate and acknowledge abuses committed by a company—for instance, via a truth and reconciliation commission—but do not provide for adequate reparations.

Extraterritorial obligations

Extraterritorial human rights obligations refer to states' obligation to guarantee human rights outside their territorial boundaries. In the context of this book, the concept is particularly relevant for cases where a company

45 See e.g. General Comment No.9, *The Domestic Application of the Covenant*, E/C.12/1998/24, 3 December 1998. See also generally UN General Assembly, *Basic Principles and Guidelines on the Right to a Remedy and Reparation for Victims of Gross Violations of International Human Rights Law and Serious Violations of International Humanitarian Law*, Res. N.60/147, 16 December 2005; SRSG, n.22, para.82; and UN Guiding Principles, n.21, principle 25.

46 CESCR, General Comment No.20, *Non-Discrimination in Economic, Social and Cultural Rights*, E/C.12/GC/20, 2 July 2009, para.40; CESCR, General Comment No.21, n.32, para.72; Ruggie, n.19, para.52.

47 CESCR, General Comment No.9, n.45, para.9.

48 *Ibid.*, para.3.

49 *Ibid.*, para.9.

50 *Ibid.*

51 See the interpretation of the duty to protect in UN Guiding Principles, n.21, principle 25; Ruggie, n.19, para.57.

based in a state party's territory is or was involved in human rights violations in another country that is undergoing a transition. This could be used, for instance, to assess the responsibility of Sweden, Austria, and Malaysia for the role played by the oil companies based in their jurisdiction for their ESCR abuses in Sudan.[52] There are strong arguments for defending the affirmation that state parties have extraterritorial obligations, particularly under the ICESCR. Article 2(1) of the ICESCR does not mention any territorial or jurisdictional limitations, and makes direct reference to international assistance and cooperation. This has led some commentators to affirm that "the extra-territorial nature of the ICESCR obligations is clear."[53] The CESCR has also repeatedly argued that state parties to the ICESCR have extraterritorial obligations,[54] and it goes as far as stating in its General Comment No. 14 on the right to health that:

> States parties have to . . . prevent third parties from violating the right in other countries, if they are able to influence these third parties by way of legal or political means, in accordance with the Charter of the United Nations and applicable international law.[55]

This suggests that the CESCR could be open to finding a state in violation of human rights if a company based in its jurisdiction harms human rights in another state.

The content and scope of extraterritorial obligations in the area of ESCR were detailed at an expert meeting in Maastricht in September 2011, where the Maastricht Principles on Extraterritorial Obligations of States in the area of Economic, Social and Cultural Rights (ETO Principles) were adopted.[56] These principles seek to codify existing international law and thus constitute

52 European Coalition on Oil in Sudan (ECOS), *Unpaid Debt: The Legacy of Lundin, Petronas and OMV in Block 5A, Sudan 1997–2003*, ECOS, Utrecht, 2010, p.10.

53 C. Courtis and M. Sepúlveda, 'Are Extra-Territorial Obligations Reviewable under the Optional Protocol to the ICESCR?' 27 *Nordic Journal of Human Rights* 54 (2009), p.63.

54 CESCR, General Comment No.12, n.12, para.36; General Comment No.14, n.27, para.39; General Comment No.15, n.27, para.31; General Comment No.19, *The right to social security*, E/C.12/GC/19, 4 February 2008, para.53.

55 CESCR, General Comment No.14, n.27, para.34. See also General Comment No.12, n.12, para.36, General Comment No.15, n.27, para.33, and General Comment No.19, *ibid.*, para.54. The SRSG suggested that "[i]t is not clear what types of steps should be taken, including whether an exercise of extraterritorial jurisdiction is considered necessary under the Covenant", Ruggie, n.19, para.87.

56 September 2011, www.rtfn-watch.org/uploads/media/Maastricht_ETO_Principles__EN.pdf. For the February 2012 Commentary of the Principles by the drafting committee, composed of Olivier de Schutter, Asbjørn Eide, Ashfaq Khalfan, Marcos Orellana, Margot Salomon, and Ian Seiderman, see http://danton1066.files.wordpress.com/2012/03/maastricht-principles-commentary.pdf.

a useful guide for identifying what the CESCR's jurisprudence could be regarding extraterritorial human rights obligations.

The general idea detailed in the ETO Principles is that the state's responsibility is engaged when the state impairs or nullifies the enjoyment of ESCR extraterritorially and when such impairment or nullification was a foreseeable result of the state's conduct (principle 13). This concept thereby extends the three types of state obligations related to corporate activities, discussed above, beyond states' national borders in situations where the effect on human rights of state conduct was foreseeable. For instance, if a corporation controlled by the state in which it is based (the home state) harms human rights in another country (the host state), the home state could be violating its extraterritorial obligation to respect human rights if the harm was foreseeable (principle 12). Equally, states must take all necessary measures—whether through regulations, public procurement, international diplomacy, or other means—to ensure that the companies that they are in a position to influence do not harm ESCR abroad (principles 23–26); and home states must ensure that an effective remedy is available if host states do not provide for it (principles 36–37).

However, this is a delicate issue to litigate under the Optional Protocol. Two particular difficulties arise. First, the complainant has to prove the existence of a causal link between the action or omission of the state party and the alleged violation abroad. This difficulty in proving the causal link between an action or omission and a rights violation exists in virtually any litigation before an international human rights body, but it may be particularly arduous to prove when the action takes place abroad. Second, the Optional Protocol adds a condition that was not explicitly present in the Covenant: the alleged victim must be "under the jurisdiction" of the state party against which the complaint is brought (article 2),[57] and it may be difficult to demonstrate that a victim is under a state's jurisdiction if the victim is not on the territory of this state. As reminded by Magdalena Sepúlveda and Christian Courtis, "claims involving extra-territorial violations of the ICESCR cannot be addressed validly under the communications procedure, unless a clear demonstration that a State party has jurisdiction beyond its territory is provided."[58]

Nonetheless, the success of a case alleging a state's failure to comply with its extraterritorial obligations cannot be ruled out,[59] and there are solid arguments to defend the idea that a state party has jurisdiction beyond its territory. Principle 9 of the ETO Principles defines the scope of jurisdiction

57 C. Courtis, *Commentary on the Optional Protocol to the International Covenant on Economic, Social and Cultural Rights*, Inter-American Institute of Human Rights/International Commission of Jurists, 2008, p.53; Courtis and Sepúlveda, n.53, pp.55–56.

58 *Ibid.*

59 For support of this view, see Courtis, n.57, p.53.

by considering that a state has an obligation to respect, protect, and fulfill economic, social, and cultural rights in any of the following scenarios:

a) situations over which it exercises authority or effective control, whether or not such control is exercised in accordance with international law;
b) situations over which state acts or omissions bring about foreseeable effects on the enjoyment of economic, social and cultural rights, whether within or outside its territory;
c) situations in which the state, acting separately or jointly, whether through its executive, legislative or judicial branches, is in a position to exercise decisive influence or to take measures to realize economic, social and cultural rights extraterritorially, in accordance with international law.

This would mean, for instance, that an individual based in Sudan whose ESCR are impaired because of the activities of a Sweden-, Austria-, or Malaysia-based company could fall under the jurisdiction of one of these three countries if an omission (such as the relevant state's failure to regulate its companies, particularly if there are credible indications that decisions made on its territory allegedly contributed to ESCR violations) that brought about foreseeable effects on the enjoyment of ESCR can be shown[60]—though the petitioner(s) will bear the burden of proof to demonstrate that they are indeed under the relevant state's jurisdiction.[61] Partly because the ICESCR is one of the human rights treaties to impose the most explicit extraterritorial obligations,[62] and partly due to the willingness shown by the CESCR to address these obligations,[63] it is conceivable that the CESCR may accept this definition of jurisdiction, and the individual communication procedure under the Optional Protocol could thus prove to be a promising mechanism to address extraterritorial obligations.

However, extraterritorial-obligation cases will have to be extremely well prepared, preferably litigating a flagrant violation of ESCR in a situation where strong evidence demonstrates that the alleged victim is under the jurisdiction of the home state. In addition, such cases should be brought at an advanced stage of the functioning of the Optional Protocol, when there is a wider consensus among states on extraterritorial obligations.[64]

60 ECOS, n.52, p.10.
61 Courtis and Sepúlveda, n.53, p.58.
62 *Ibid.*
63 The SRSG for instance noted that "CESCR says slightly more on the topic": Ruggie, n.19, para.86.
64 The SRSG has suggested that the follow-up group or expert mandate to be created after his mandate clarify certain legal international standards, including the question of "when the

A case may be stronger, and litigation easier, when the company accused of the wrongdoing abroad is owned by the state, or exercises elements of governmental authority. Such cases could involve states' obligations to respect and to protect. McCorquodale and Simons give the example of the Australian Wheat Board, a former government agency that was privatized but retains sole responsibility for the marketing and export of Australian wheat around the world. The Australian Wheat Board allegedly harmed the right to food of Iraqis while it was active in the Iraqi Oil-for-Food Programme managed by the UN, which could be a human rights violation attributable to the Australian state.[65] A case before the Optional Protocol could have demonstrated that Australia violated its obligation to protect the right to food beyond its borders, giving additional arguments for holding the Australian Wheat Board accountable and pressuring the Australian government to make the necessary structural adjustments and adopt regulation. McCorquodale and Simons equally argue that export credit agencies would qualify as companies exercising elements of government authority.[66]

They have also interestingly pointed out two other situations where it can be asserted that states have constructive knowledge that corporate nationals may harm human rights standards in their extraterritorial operations, which are directly relevant for transitional situations. The first situation is "where corporate nationals invest, or intend to invest, in conflict zones, failed states or repressive regimes, and engage in a business relationship with host state governments or a non-state actor party to a civil conflict."[67] For example, when oil companies invested in 1997 in Sudan to extract petrol from a disputed territory, they ran the risk of being involved in the abuse of ESCR, such as the right to housing and the right to food.[68] In a case such as this, victims could potentially litigate under the Optional Protocol. The home states of those companies—Sweden, Austria, and Malaysia—could have been found to violate their obligation to protect ESCR, which could have motivated their governments or national courts to hold the corporations to account.

Second, "where a home state of a TNC [transnational corporation] negotiates a bilateral investment treaty (BIT) with a non-industrialised state," and a company based in the home country benefits from this treaty to invest in the host country and harms human rights in the process, the home

extension of jurisdiction abroad may be appropriate, and the acceptable bases for the exercise of such jurisdiction": SRSG, "Recommendations on follow-up to the mandate", February 2011, p.4, www.business-humanrights.org/media/documents/ruggie/ruggie-special-mandate-follow-up-11-feb-2011.pdf.

65 McCorquodale and Simons, n.25, p.607.

66 *Ibid.*, p.608.

67 *Ibid.*, p.620.

68 ECOS, n.52, pp.9–10.

state could be seen as facilitating extraterritorial harm perpetrated by the corporate national, and may be more likely to be found in violation of the ICESCR.[69] Depending on the situation and the terms of the BIT, the home state's adoption of the treaty might in itself be enough to place this state in breach of its obligation to respect ESCR extraterritorially—or it could at least add weight to a case alleging a failure to protect from harm caused by the corporate national in the host country. If jurisdiction can be shown, such situations could constitute ideal cases for developing the jurisprudence regarding extraterritorial obligations before the CESCR.[70]

Applying the Optional Protocol to situations of transition

A number of difficulties arise when using the Optional Protocol in the context of transitional justice.[71] It would, for example, be problematic if the company caused the harm before the Optional Protocol came into force in the state against which the case is brought (home or host state). This situation is common in the context of transition; authoritarian regimes are often reluctant to commit to human rights obligations, whereas post-transition governments are eager to break with the past and show their goodwill by ratifying international instruments, which may include the Optional Protocol. The CESCR would then normally not have jurisdiction over the violations that took place before the Optional Protocol was ratified, as it would lack jurisdiction *ratione temporis*.

However, there may be exceptions, under the doctrine of continuing violation. This concept has been used by some international human rights bodies to assess violations that started before the treaty over which the body has jurisdiction entered into force if these violations continue after the treaty becomes binding in a state.[72] The principle was first used by the Permanent

69 McCorquodale and Simons, n.25, p.621.

70 It may be noted that McCorquodale and Simons also explore the concept of state complicity, using Draft Articles, article 16 as a potential avenue to hold corporations accountable for their wrongdoings abroad, *ibid.*, pp.611–615.

71 It could, for instance, be questioned whether truth and reconciliation commissions constitute a remedy that should be exhausted.

72 See generally K. Altiparmak, 'The Application of the Concept of Continuing Violation to the Duty to Investigate, Prosecute and Punish under International Human Rights Law', 21–25 *Turkish Yearbook of Human Rights* 3–50 (2003); P.A. Ormachea, 'Moiwana Village: The Inter-American Court and the Continuing Violation Doctrine', 19 *Harvard Human Rights Journal* 283 (2006); J.M. Pasqualucci, *The practice and procedure of the Inter-American Court of Human Rights*, Cambridge University Press, Cambridge, 2003, pp.110–113; A. Van Pachtenbeke and Y. Haeck, 'From De Becker to Varnava: The State of Continuing Situations in the Strasbourg Case Law', 1 *European Human Rights Law Review* 47–59 (2010).

Court of International Justice[73] and subsequently codified by the International Law Commission in article 14 of the Draft Articles. It has been applied by the European Court of Human Rights,[74] the Inter-American Court of Human Rights,[75] and the UN Human Rights Committee.[76] The Optional Protocol clearly leaves open this possibility by specifying in its article 3 that the facts that took place prior to the Protocol's entry into force would be inadmissible *unless* "those facts continued after that date."[77]

It is not clear which violations can be considered as continuing, particularly regarding ESCR for which there is little international jurisprudence. According to the International Law Commission, "[w]hether a wrongful act is completed or has a continuing character will depend both on the primary obligation and the circumstances of the given case."[78] Furthermore, it is not sufficient that the consequences of the wrongful act continue—"[i]t must be the wrongful act as such which continues."[79] However, alleged violations relating to events that occurred prior to a treaty's entry into force but "which have effects which themselves constitute violations" after the treaty becomes applicable constitute a continuing violation.[80]

It is likely that the failure to provide effective remedies constitutes a continuing violation of international human rights law, as suggested by the UN Human Rights Committee.[81] It is not clear, however, whether considering the failure to provide effective remedies as a continuing violation would be applicable to the ICESCR, as the treaty lacks a specific provision establishing the obligation to provide effective remedies, contrary to regional human rights conventions and the International Covenant on Civil and

73 *Italy v France*, PCIJ, Series A/B No.74.

74 E.g. *De Becker v Belgium*, Application No.214/56, Judgment of 27 March 1962, para.8; *Papamichalopoulos and Others v Greece*, Application No.14556/89, Judgment of 24 June 1993, para.40; *Loizidou v Turkey*, Application No.15318/89, Judgment of 23 March 1995, para.102.

75 Inter-American Court of Human Rights, *Moiwana Community v Suriname*, Preliminary Objections, Merits, Reparations and Costs, Judgment of 15 June 2005, Series C No.124, paras.39–43; Inter-American Court of Human Rights, *Serrano Cruz Sisters v El Salvador*, Preliminary Objections, Judgment of 23 November 2004, Series C No.118, paras.67 and 94; Inter-American Court of Human Rights, *Blake v Guatemala*, Preliminary Objections, Judgment of 2 July 1996, Series C No.27, paras.39 and 40.

76 E.g. *Ivan Somers v Hungary*, Communication No.566/1993, U.N. Doc. CCPR/C/53/D/566/1993 (1996), para.6.2; *Patrick Holland v Ireland*, Communication No. 593/1994, U.N. Doc. CCPR/C/58/D/593/1994 (1996) para.9.2.

77 See also Langford, n.9, p.23, who argues that continuing violations which started before the date of entry into force of the Protocol could be reviewed by the CESCR.

78 ILC Draft Articles with Commentary, n.23, article 14, p.60, para.4.

79 *Ibid.*, para.6.

80 *Lovelace v Canada*, Official Records of the General Assembly, Thirty-sixth Session, Supplement No.40 (A/36/40), annex XVIII, communication No.R.6/24, p.172, para.11 (1981).

81 UN Human Rights Committee, General Comment 31, *Nature of the General Legal Obligation Imposed on States Parties to the Covenant*, CCPR/C/21/Rev.1/Add.13, para.19.

Political Rights, which the UN Human Rights Committee oversees. The Optional Protocol could be an occasion to test this aspect. A case where a state's lack of legislation has allowed companies to infringe rights protected under the ICESCR—and where the legislative gap continues after the state's ratification of the Optional Protocol—may equally qualify as a continuing violation.

Nevertheless, it is uncertain whether the CESCR would be ready to consider as continuing violations issues such as the poor state of health, grave lack of access to education, or massive discriminations caused or contributed to by corporations before the Optional Protocol was applicable. For example, it will be interesting to see whether the CESCR is ready to consider cases such as that of the Achuar communities in Peru, who live with the legacy of the abuses allegedly committed by Oxy, a petrol company that operated in the country between 1970 and 2000, before the transitional process. This legacy is exemplified by "extreme pollution of their lands and waterways, disruption of their ability to fish, hunt, and raise crops, and persistent health problems, including widespread lead and cadmium poisoning."[82]

Alternatively, a case could also be brought to obtain a decision about current violations, but making reference to past violations in the hope that the CESCR might include a statement about the impact of past events on the subsequent violations. Although a petition specifically focused on time-bound facts that occurred before the entry into force of the Optional Protocol would be inadmissible, the CESCR may nonetheless take some of these "past" facts into account if they have effects on the current situation. It could follow the jurisprudence of the European Court of Human Rights, which has established that the Court may "have regard to the facts prior to ratification inasmuch as they could be considered to have created a situation extending beyond that date or may be relevant for the understanding of facts occurring after that date."[83]

If the continuing violations doctrine were accepted by the CESCR, it should be used and applied with extreme care. Pablo Ormachea remarks that while this theory has allowed the Inter-American Court of Human Rights to do justice in cases of human rights violations that would otherwise have remained ignored, the Court applied it cautiously, in order not to undermine its authority and not to discourage hesitant countries to recognize its jurisdiction.[84] These considerations are all the more valid in the context of the Optional Protocol.

82 EarthRights International, Racimos de Ungurahui, Amazon Watch, *A Legacy of Harm: Occidental Petroleum in Indigenous Territory in the Peruvian Amazon*, 2006, p.8, www.earthrights.org/sites/default/files/publications/A-Legacy-of-Harm.pdf.

83 Case of *Skrzynski v Poland*, Application No.38672/02, Judgment of 6 September 2007, para.41.

84 Ormachea, n.72, p.288.

Alternatively, if the state where the harm is done has not ratified the Optional Protocol, one could consider bringing a case against another state that has ratified it and has extraterritorial obligations over the activities of a company operating in the country where the harm is done. If, for instance, Burma went into a transition, there could be benefits to bringing cases against the home states of the petrol companies that made profits in the country for years and contributed to financing the military regime's oppression and, in doing so, abusing ESCR. Such cases could be used to eventually hold the companies accountable and allow Burmese society to move forward. Under the Optional Protocol, the home states of the companies could be found to have violated their obligation to respect and/or protect ESCR in Burma, which could trigger processes at the national level to examine the role and responsibilities of companies in the Burmese dictatorship. This process could not only help fulfill victims' needs for justice but also contribute to shaping the post-transitional society. By uncovering the beneficiaries of the dictatorship regime and shedding light on the economic system that supported it, it would allow various actors—including political authorities, the courts (both in Burma and in home countries), and international organizations—to try to address and correct past injustices. In particular, through targeted remedies, courts could help build a fair and peaceful society. For instance, they could request that companies pay compensation to groups economically marginalized by the dictatorship, to make apologies, or to participate in the material reconstruction of the country, with a focus on the most affected groups. The Optional Protocol could provide the starting point for inspiring original and well-crafted remedies.

Conclusion: why use the Optional Protocol?

As discussed above, one cannot expect corporations to be held directly accountable under the Optional Protocol. Only states can violate the ICESCR, and companies' responsibilities will have to be demonstrated through states' obligations. It should also be kept in mind that UN treaty bodies usually face a low level of compliance with their decisions. Therefore, it is rather unlikely that the CESCR's views will bring direct reparations to the victims[85]—

85 See e.g. the analysis by H.J. Steiner, 'Individual Claims in a World of Massive Violations: What Role for the Human Rights Committee?' in P. Alston and J. Crawford (eds), *The Future of UN Human Rights Treaty Monitoring*, Cambridge University Press, Cambridge, 2000 (15), p.49; J.L. Cavallaro and S.E. Brewer, 'Reevaluating Regional Human Rights Litigation in the Twenty-First Century: The Case of the Inter-American Court', 102 *American Journal of International Law* 768 (2008), p.785; C.J. Borgen, 'Transnational Tribunals and the Transmission of Norms: the Hegemony of Process', 39 *George Washington International Law Review* 685 (2007), pp.744–745; C. Heyns and F. Viljoen, 'The Impact of the United Nations Human Rights Treaties on the Domestic Level', 23 *Human Rights Quarterly* 483 (2001), p.488; L.R. Helfer and A.-M.

although this is a legitimate expectation that should be advocated for. In addition, particularly in the context of transitional justice, there are a number of technical difficulties in using the Optional Protocol, not least fulfilling the admissibility criteria for the individual complaint procedure.

Nevertheless, even if the Optional Protocol may have limited direct legal influence, it could still play an important role in changing the global approach to corporate accountability. As Beth Simmons puts it, with the Optional Protocol "we are not in the world of litigation, but instead in the world of communication and persuasion."[86] This chapter has suggested that the Optional Protocol holds high potential for unlocking legal and political thinking on business and human rights. For instance, as others have also argued, effective determination of states' responsibilities at the international level could force them to put pressure on companies.[87] It may help to create the necessary "effective guidance" at the international level called for by the SRSG in order for states to "achieve greater policy coherence." According to Ruggie, "[t]he human rights treaty bodies can play an important role in making recommendations to States on implementing their obligations to protect rights vis-à-vis corporate activities."[88]

The CESCR could thus become a useful source for determining companies' involvement in human rights violations. The CESCR's work under the Optional Protocol could influence the content of future general comments of the CESCR. It could also be a model for domestic legislative work, providing governments with a basis for enacting and enforcing adequate laws, and giving legitimacy to judges to issue progressive decisions. A number of commentators have made similar arguments. David Marcus, for example, has suggested that supranational tribunals' jurisprudence can play an important role in convincing national courts to enforce ESCR, particularly the obligation to protect.[89] Malcolm Langford has argued that the adoption of the Optional Protocol "could prompt greater national litigation and constitutional reform by virtue of its requirement that domestic remedies first be exhausted and its role in promoting awareness of the potential justiciability of ESC rights."[90]

Slaughter, 'Toward a Theory of Effective Supranational Adjudication', 107 *Yale Law Journal* 273 (1997), p.367.

86 B.A. Simmons, 'Should States Ratify? Process and Consequences of the Optional Protocol to the ICESCR', 27 *Nordic Journal of Human Rights* 64–81 (2009), p.71.

87 V. Engström, *Who is Responsible for Corporate Human Rights Violations?* Institute for Human Rights, Abo Akademi University, Finland, 2002, p.20, www.abo.fi/media/24259/report2.pdf.

88 SRSG, n.22, para.43.

89 D. Marcus, 'The Normative Development of Socioeconomic Rights through Supranational Adjudication', 42 *Stanford Journal of International Law* 53–102 (2006), p.89.

90 M. Langford, 'Domestic Adjudication and Economic, Social and Cultural Rights: A Socio-Legal Review', 6 SUR 11, 91–121 (2009), p.92.

If employed strategically and carefully, the Optional Protocol could have a crucial impact in the context of transitional justice. It could shed light on the abuses committed by a company during a dictatorship, demonstrate the company's responsibilities, and influence the post-transition public debate. An individual complaint or an inquiry could help gather information about a company's involvement in human rights abuses and create the necessary momentum to hold the company accountable before national tribunals. Other supranational courts have played such a role before. Clara Sandoval, for instance, has shown how cases related to the dictatorship in Peru brought before the Inter-American Court of Human Rights have not only empowered people to fight impunity but also provided legal operators with important evidence and arguments, which were of utmost importance in the trial against the former Peruvian dictator Fujimori.[91] Though perhaps to a lesser extent, in addressing corporate accountability from a new perspective, one could hope that the Optional Protocol would equally have the potential to open a new chapter in the sinuous path toward corporate accountability, which could lead states and international actors to rethink how they deal with corporate complicity for past abuses.

91 C. Sandoval, 'The Challenge of Impunity in Peru: The Significance of the Inter-American Court of Human Rights', 5 *Essex Human Rights Review* 1–20 (2008), p.16.

Part II

Linking Transitional Justice and Corporate Accountability: Examples and Case Studies

Chapter 8

Lessons from the South African Experience

*Charles P. Abrahams**

Introduction

Transitional justice traditionally uses mechanisms such as truth commissions to deal with past systematic abuses of civil and political rights. One of its aims is to unearth the truth, and a means to achieve this is to grant amnesty to those having perpetrated the crimes, in exchange for full disclosure. Prosecutions are largely pursued only in the most egregious cases or where perpetrators have not been forthcoming with the truth to qualify for an amnesty. However, the ultimate aims of transitional justice mechanisms are to promote reconciliation between perpetrators and victims,[1] provide justice and reparations, and bring closure to the past, in order to enable the new regime to embark on a new direction of policy and institutional reform.[2]

In most instances, transitional justice is aimed at the abuses committed by individuals, with hardly any consideration given to the role of corporate actors as aiders and abettors of the human rights violations. Only very few of the many truth commissions established worldwide since 1974 appear to have expressly engaged with the role of corporations in facilitating violations of civil and political rights, socioeconomic rights, and economic crimes.[3]

Just as the inclusion of socioeconomic rights violations within the framework of transitional justice remains contentious,[4] states and the international community have also been slow to recognize corporate accountability as a means of achieving the goals of transitional justice. They often envisage corporate actors as playing a key role in their efforts to rebuild post-conflict societies, particularly with regard to achieving the new regime's

* Many thanks to Lisa Hecht for her assistance with earlier drafts of this chapter.

1 For a recent analysis of the justice-versus-reconciliation debate in the African context, see I. Eberechi, 'Who will save these endangered species? Evaluating the implications of the principle of complementarity on the traditional African conflict resolution mechanisms', 20 *African Journal of International and Comparative Law* 22–41 (2012).

2 For further discussion, see chapter 1 of this book.

3 R. Carranza, 'Plunder and Pain: Should Transitional Justice Engage with Corruption and Economic Crimes?' 2 *International Journal of Transitional Justice* 310–330 (2008), p.315.

4 I. Muvingi, 'Sitting on Powder Kegs: Socio-Economic Rights in Transitional Societies', 3 *International Journal of Transitional Justice* 163–182 (2009).

socioeconomic or developmental objectives. As a result, transitional justice mechanisms have often been granted only limited powers over corporate actors, notwithstanding evidence of their complicity with the former regime.

Attempts to achieve legal accountability of corporations under private law for their role as accomplices in crimes committed in times of conflict and oppression face serious hurdles, as the long and complicated history of the South African apartheid litigation[5] as well as the recent blow to the exercise of extraterritorial jurisdiction by the US Supreme Court's *Kiobel* decision demonstrate.[6]

South Africa's transition from apartheid to democracy in 1994 encapsulates all of these complex challenges that make corporate accountability a difficult tool for transitional justice. This chapter focuses on the manner in which South Africa's TRC dealt with the issue of corporate complicity under apartheid, and on the potential and problems of using the courts to hold corporations liable to redress the shortcomings of the TRC's approach and the government's implementation of the TRC's recommendations.

Caught between a rock and a hard place

The TRC as the Main Transitional Justice Mechanism

The TRC was established in 1995, pursuant to the TRC Act.[7] Amongst other things, it was tasked with establishing "as complete a picture as possible of the causes, nature and extent of the gross violations of human rights which were committed during the period from 1 March 1960 to the cut-off date."[8] This included considering the antecedents, circumstances, factors, and context of such violations, as well as the perspectives of the victims and the motives and perspectives of the persons responsible for committing the violations. The TRC could facilitate—and, where necessary, initiate or coordinate—inquiries into gross violations of human rights, including violations that were part of a systematic pattern of abuse, and into the identity of all persons, authorities, institutions, and organizations involved in such violations. The work of the TRC was carried out primarily by means of investigations and hearings.[9]

The overall objective of the TRC was to promote national unity and reconciliation in South Africa. It was empowered to achieve this goal by

5 *In re South African Apartheid Litigation*, 346 F.Supp.2d 538 (SDNY 2004); *Khulumani v Barclay National Bank, Ltd.*, 504 F.3d 254 (2nd Circuit, 2007); *American Isuzu Motors, Inc v Ntsebeza*, 553 U.S. 1028 (2008); *In re South African Apartheid Litigation*, 617 F.Supp.2d 228 (SDNY 2009).

6 *Kiobel v. Royal Dutch Petroleum Co.* (2013), 2013 WL 1628935.

7 Promotion of Reconciliation Act 34 of 1995.

8 The initial cut-off date was 6 December 1993, but it was later extended to 10 May 1994.

9 TRC Act, section 3(1)(a).

facilitating the granting of amnesty to persons who made full disclosure of all the relevant facts relating to acts associated with a political objective.[10] The work of the TRC thus brought together the objectives of truth, justice, and reconciliation. According to Professors Jeremy Sarkin and Erin Daly, the relationship between these objectives must be carefully balanced, and efforts to combine them are not always free of conflict. Attaining all may be "a luxury that many countries recovering from traumatic political transitions cannot afford,"[11] and the achievement of justice might rather often cause serious practical problems. To punish the perpetrators could potentially create tensions in transitional and often unstable societies, particularly, as will frequently be the case, if those who are most culpable stay politically and economically powerful. On the other hand, if the perpetrators remain unpunished and receive impunity, this might adversely affect the new regime's break with the past and the creation of a democratic society based on the rule of law and human rights principles.[12] It could moreover lead to deep dissatisfaction with the new regime on the part of victims.

Furthermore, as Sarkin and Daly point out, reconciliation programs are problematic, as "[r]econciliation is so easily invoked, so commonly promoted, and so immediately appealing"[13] that policymakers often overlook the serious questions they raise. In particular, policymakers frequently pay insufficient attention to how reconciliation might affect other aims of transitional justice, such as "the possibility of justice after 'radical evil,' the re-distribution of wealth, the creation of civil society, and the relevance of the past to the present and the future."[14]

The TRC's treatment of the issue of corporate accountability highlighted the very complex relationship between truth, justice, and reconciliation. In order to understand these linkages in the South African context, one needs to consider the scope of the TRC's powers in general, and in relation to corporations that were complicit with apartheid in particular.

Section 20(2) of the TRC Act limits the type of applicants who are eligible for amnesty to individuals—for example, members of political organizations and liberation movements, or employees of the state and security officials. According to section 20(1)(b), amnesty could be granted only if "the act, omission or offence to which the application relates is an act associated with a political objective committed in the course of the conflicts of the past." Section 20(3) sets out the criteria that determine whether an act is associated

10 *Ibid.*, section 3(1)(b).

11 J. Sarkin and E. Daly, 'Too Many Questions, Too Few Answers: Reconciliation in Transitional Societies', 35 *Columbia Human Rights Law Review* 661–728 (2003–2004), p.669.

12 *Ibid.*, p.670.

13 *Ibid.*, p.664.

14 *Ibid.*

with a political objective. These include the person's motive; the context within which the act, omission, or offense occurred; the legal and factual nature of the act; whether it was executed pursuant to an order; and the relationship between the act, omission, or offense and the political objective pursued. As the references to "person" and "employee" in sections 18 and 20 of the TRC Act show, amnesties were available only to individuals. Thus, notwithstanding any disclosure by a corporation of its involvement or complicity in acts of gross human rights violations, it would not have been entitled to amnesty. This is reflected in the findings of the special amnesty panel of the TRC's Amnesty Committee that suggested that the amnesty applications by 27 African National Congress (ANC) leaders did not comply with the requirements of the TRC Act. In that case, the leaders applied for amnesty not in their own name but instead on behalf of their members. In this respect, the panel held that:

> in so far as the applicants seek to apply for amnesty for acts committed by their members on the basis of collective political and moral responsibility, their applications fall outside the ambit of the . . . act and accordingly they do not require to apply for amnesty.[15]

The business community did not regard its participation in the business institutional hearings before the TRC as applying for amnesty. According to the TRC, the business community participated, rather, in order to promote "understanding of the role of business under apartheid and to explore ways where business failed to press for change—both at a political and at an organizational level."[16] Business participation also seems to have been motivated by the desire of businesses to distance themselves from any participation in gross human rights violations.[17] For that reason, Old Mutual, a South African insurance corporation, stated in its opening submission to the TRC that "in principle, the mandate of the Commission which focuses on gross violations of human rights would almost certainly exclude Old Mutual from having to make any submission."[18] Indeed, the business community to some extent portrayed itself as a victim, as apartheid made conducting business more costly, eroded the skills base, and undermined long-term productivity and growth.[19]

The TRC devoted a whole chapter to the role of businesses under apartheid.[20] It considered various submissions made by diverse groups,

15 www.justice.gov.za/trc/media/1999/9903/s990304k.htm.

16 Truth and Reconciliation Commission South Africa, *Final Report*, Volume 4, Chapter 2, 1998, p.21.

17 *Ibid.*

18 *Ibid.*, p.20

19 *Ibid.*, pp.20 and 38–39.

20 *Ibid.*, Volume 4, Chapter 2.

including the South African Communist Party, the Congress of South African Trade Unions, the South African Chamber of Business, the Afrikaner Handelsinstituut, and the South African Chamber of Mines. The TRC noted that at the heart of the business and labor hearings lay the complex power relations of apartheid, the legacy of which continued to afflict post-apartheid society.[21] It found that the degree to which corporations became complicit in sustaining the apartheid regime varied from "engaging in activities directly associated with repressive functions to simply benefiting from operating in a racially structured society in which wages were low and workers were denied basic democratic rights."[22] In order to capture the different degrees of culpability, the TRC distinguished between first-, second-, and third-order involvement of businesses with the apartheid regime.

Companies that played a central role in helping design and implement apartheid policies were categorized as having first-order involvement.[23] The TRC singled out mining companies and the South African Chamber of Mines (the Chamber) as falling into this category. According to the TRC, rather than:

> relying simply on the forces of supply and demand, the mining industry harnessed the services of the state to shape labour supply conditions to their advantage . . . and due to the monopolistic power of the Chamber . . . black wages . . . were lower . . . than they would almost certainly otherwise have been.[24]

The TRC found the submission of the Anglo American Corporation, the largest gold mining corporation in South Africa, to be flawed,[25] as it blamed race politics for "depressing black wage levels,"[26] without taking responsibility for "the active measures taken by mining magnates to ensure the continued supply of cheap migrant labour."[27]

Businesses categorized as having had second-order involvement were those "*knowing* that their products or services would be used for morally unacceptable purposes."[28] For example, companies that provided arms and ammunition, military technology, and transportation fell within this category. The TRC found that "[t]he moral case against the armaments industry is that business willingly (and for profit) involved itself in manufacturing products that it

21 *Ibid.*, p.18.
22 Truth and Reconciliation Commission South Africa, *Final Report*, Volume 6, Chapter 5, 2003, p.140.
23 TRC Report, n.15, p.24.
24 *Ibid.*
25 *Ibid.*
26 *Ibid.*, p.34.
27 *Ibid.*
28 *Ibid.*, p.25.

knew would be used to facilitate human rights abuses domestically and abroad."[29] The Armaments Corporation of South Africa, the apartheid regime's parastatal corporation in charge of manufacturing and procuring arms and ammunition during apartheid, was expressly mentioned as an example of this type of involvement.[30]

Lastly, businesses engaged in third-order involvement were those that benefited indirectly from the repressive regime through the very fact of operating within the racially structured context of South African society.[31] Third-order involvement was therefore intricately linked to the fact that the concentration of wealth in the hands of the white minority—which gave these businesses structural advantages that persisted after the end of apartheid—was secured through the way in which business could be conducted under apartheid.[32] The white agricultural industry, for example, "benefited from its privileged access to land."[33] For the TRC, condemning such businesses "suggests that all who prospered under apartheid have something to answer for, in that they took advantage which depressed the earning of black South Africans, whilst boosting their own."[34]

The TRC determined that business in general benefited financially and materially from the policies of apartheid. For example, the TRC concluded that white-owned large-scale agricultural, farming, and agribusiness enterprises benefited from exclusive white land ownership and the low wages of black workers, and that the extractive industry benefited from a cheap migratory labor force. Furthermore, it stated that:

> the manufacturing industry benefited from cheap electricity generated through the exploitation of cheap labour in the coal mines. The arms industry benefited from the military requirements of the apartheid regime, resulting in internal repression and external destabilisation. Those banks and financial institutions that bankrolled the mineral-industrial complex and the mineral-energy complexes benefited vicariously.[35]

All in all, the TRC formed the opinion that business played a central role in sustaining the economy during apartheid.[36]

In light of these findings, the TRC devoted an entire chapter of its final report to *Reparations and the Business Sector*. Some of its key recommendations

29 *Ibid.*, p.36.
30 *Ibid.*, p.37.
31 *Ibid.*, p.25.
32 *Ibid.*, p.26.
33 *Ibid.*, p.58.
34 *Ibid.*, p.26.
35 TRC Report, n.21, p.141
36 *Ibid.*, p.140.

were the imposition of a once-off wealth tax on South African business and industry, reconsideration of the repayment by the new government of the apartheid regime's odious debts, and the establishment of a business reconciliation fund to which businesses could contribute to fund small black entrepreneurs.[37] The TRC described its recommendations as based on "at the very least, a moral obligation [of businesses] to assist in the reconstruction and development of post-apartheid South Africa."[38]

The TRC's recommendations regarding corporations cut across all business sectors and were not linked to the nature of a business's involvement with apartheid. Unlike with regard to individuals, where the TRC had the power to make decisions itself and grant amnesties where appropriate, its findings on corporate responsibility resulted only in recommendations. This indicates the TRC's limited powers over corporations.[39]

In some instances, the TRC pointed not only to moral but also to legal responsibility on the part of corporations. This was the case with regard to the role played by banks.[40] The TRC found that Swiss banks, in particular, "played an instrumental role in prolonging apartheid from the time of the debt crisis in 1985 and onwards."[41] Moreover, it argued that "banks that gave financial support to the apartheid state were accomplices to a criminal government that consistently violated international law."[42] It went as far as to make a case for reparations against Swiss banks on several grounds: these banks "benefited over several decades from the exploitation of black mine-workers" in the South African gold mines, ignored calls for sanctions against the apartheid regime, "continued to enrich themselves through the gold trade and lending . . . [and] played an instrumental role in prolonging apartheid from the time of the debt crisis in 1985 onwards"[43] by supplying the government with the necessary financial means to contribute to its continued existence.

The TRC expressly recognized bases for civil and criminal liability of certain businesses for their actions, including for aiding and abetting the crimes committed by the apartheid regime. It also suggested the existence of legal grounds for instituting a claim for reparations based on the unenforceability of contracts that had been contrary to public policy.[44] This seems to have been aimed particularly at the claims of lenders for funds supplied to the apartheid regime that were regarded as against public policy, since they financed an immoral and illegal regime. The TRC consequently suggested

37 *Ibid.*, p.143.
38 *Ibid.*, pp.143–144.
39 TRC Act, section 20(1).
40 TRC Report, n.21, p.146.
41 *Ibid.*
42 *Ibid.*, pp.146–147.
43 *Ibid.*, p.146.
44 *Ibid.*, pp.146–147.

that to the extent that such loans had already been repaid, reparations claims might exist against the lenders. Loans that still had to be repaid, on the other hand, were regarded as potentially odious and therefore unenforceable, as they were "incurred by illegitimate parties for illegitimate purposes."[45]

The TRC's consideration of the role played by corporations during apartheid is a clear indication that, notwithstanding its own limited mandate, it certainly did not regard businesses to be immune from either criminal prosecution or civil litigation.

Position of the South African Government Regarding Accountability of Corporations for their Role during Apartheid

The South African government did not implement any of the TRC's recommendations concerning businesses. Not requiring businesses to make reparations was in line with the general policy that reparations were not to be provided by the perpetrators and beneficiaries of apartheid but rather to come out of the President's Fund established under section 42 of the TRC Act. However, while the TRC had recommended reparations of up to R2.8 billion,[46] the government decided to provide only a one-time payment of R30,000 to the 19,000 designated victims.[47]

The South African government's approach to the recommendations of the TRC was clearly influenced by its Growth, Employment and Redistribution (GEAR) policy.[48] This policy, which has since been abandoned in favor of the New Economic Growth Path (NEGP),[49] acknowledged the importance of fast economic growth and job creation as "the only way out of poverty, inequality, and unemployment."[50] Foreign and local private-sector investment were regarded as crucial for achieving these goals, which is why the government tried to avoid and remove potential obstacles to investment. Already, in the run-up to the first democratic elections in 1994, the ANC tried to reassure

45 *Ibid.*, p.147.

46 C. Waterhouse, 'The good, the bad and the ugly: moral agency and the role of victims in reparations programs', 31 *University of Pennsylvania Journal of International Law* 257–294 (2009–2010), p.284.

47 Thabo Mbeki, President of South Africa, *Statement to the National Houses of Parliament and the Nation at the Tabling of the Report of the Truth and Reconciliation Commission*, 15 April 2003, p.7, www.nftc.org/default/ussabc/Mbeki_Sp.pdf.

48 Department of Finance, Republic of South Africa, *Growth, Employment and Redistribution. A Macroeconomic Strategy*, www.treasury.gov.za/publications/other/gear/all.pdf.

49 www.info.gov.za/view/DownloadFileAction?id=135748.

50 Ministry: Justice and Constitutional Development Republic of South Africa, Maduna, *Declaration to Judge Sprizzo regarding the position of the South African government toward the South African apartheid litigation pending in US courts* (Maduna Declaration), 11 July 2003, para.8.1, www.nftc.org/default/ussabc/Maduna%20Declaration.pdf.

foreign investors that no expropriations or nationalizations would take place and that the new regime would guarantee the free repatriation of their profits and dividends.[51] The focus on attracting investment is evident from the conclusion of 41 BITs from 1994 to 2006.[52]

Corporate social investment programs were regarded as a useful tool to improve the lives of the formerly disadvantaged and to further reconciliation. The government's attention thus clearly focused on economic growth as a remedy for the nation's apartheid legacy, which resulted in a policy of non-confrontation toward corporations and a lack of political will to follow the TRC's recommendations regarding the accountability of corporations for their role in apartheid. Instead of obligating corporations to provide reparations to apartheid victims, the South African government complimented businesses for their voluntary contributions to the Business Trust Fund that was established in 1999 as a voluntary initiative by businesses with the purpose of creating jobs, building capacity, and reducing poverty.[53] In a partnership between the government and businesses, the Business Trust Fund was said to have "improved the lives of 2.5-million disadvantaged South Africans through focused programmes of human capacity building and employment creation."[54]

The tension between the TRC's recommendations and the government's approach is indicative of the difficulties in attending simultaneously to justice and reconciliation—a tension that, to this day, continues to permeate post-apartheid South Africa. Thus, for example, the avoidance of confrontation with the apartheid legacy of corporations might be inconsistent with the aim of achieving justice for victims of their complicit behavior. By focusing on growth and capacity building, the government could be accused of confusing the rights and entitlements of victims with the constitutionally guaranteed socioeconomic rights of all disadvantaged citizens. While both claims are important, it could be argued that claims of victims of certain violations of civil and political rights, such as torture or the killing of a close family member, should not be conflated with general claims of all victims of apartheid to be lifted out of apartheid-related poverty and social exclusion.[55] However, in a context of such structural inequality and social deprivation as that caused by apartheid, it is unsatisfactory to limit the victim status, and

51 L.E. Peterson, *South Africa's Bilateral Investment Treaties – Implications for Development and Human Rights*, Friedrich Ebert Stiftung, SAIIA & IISD, Dialogue on Globalization, Occasional Paper No.26, November 2006, p.6.

52 *Ibid.*

53 www.btrust.org.za/resources.html.

54 Maduna Declaration, n.49, para.9.

55 For a discussion, see also S. Wilson, 'The myth of restorative justice: Truth, reconciliation and the ethics of amnesty', 17 *South African Journal on Human Rights* 531–562 (2001), p.557.

accordingly the question of reparations, to civil and political rights violations alone. Indeed, one must also look at the violations of ESCR suffered by all victims of the racist policies.[56] The question should then not be one of whether these violations need to be addressed in the context of transitional justice. Instead, it needs to be asked whether redress for violations of economic, social, and cultural rights should be harmonized with the objectives of transitional justice, or whether it should be pursued at the expense of justice and reparations for victims of corporate complicity in apartheid crimes.

Applied to the problem of corporate accountability in the context of the South African transition, the debate centered on whether corporations should be brought to justice for their complicity in human rights violations, or whether they should receive absolution in order to further economic development. While the government clearly favored the latter approach, many victims were unsatisfied with the government's implementation of the TRC findings regarding corporations, as well as with its reparations policy more generally.[57] As a consequence, in 2002, several lawsuits were filed in New York on behalf of South African victims against a variety of multinational corporations for aiding and abetting or otherwise participating in the international law violations committed by the apartheid regime. This litigation, which should be understood as "a logical continuation of the outcome of the TRC,"[58] exemplarily illustrates the consequences of the political tensions between justice and reconciliation with regard to corporations.

Litigating apartheid wrongs

In 2002, the Khulumani Support Group, a South African victims' organization, together with 93 of its members, filed a civil complaint under the ATS in the Eastern District Court of New York[59] against 23 multinational corporations and banks for having aided and abetted the apartheid regime. The apartheid litigation came about against the backdrop of a long-running campaign by the global movement Jubilee 2000 to cancel the sovereign debt of the former apartheid regime.[60] It is estimated that by 1994, the overall foreign debt of

56 See, for example, K. Asmal, 'Truth, Reconciliation and Justice: The South African Experience in Perspective', 63 *Modern Law Review* 1–24 (2000).

57 G. Thompson, 'South Africa to Pay $3,900 to Each Family of Apartheid Victims', *New York Times*, 16 April 2003, www.nytimes.com/2003/04/16/world/south-africa-to-pay-3900-to-each-family-of-apartheid-victims.html.

58 C. Abrahams, 'The TRC's unfinished business: reparations', in C. Villa-Vicencio, F. du Toit (eds), *Truth & Reconciliation in South Africa: 10 Years On*, New Africa Books, Claremont, 2006 (34–36), p.36.

59 The *Khulumani* lawsuit was initially filed in the Eastern District Court of New York. In 2003, the Multi-District Litigation Panel ordered the transfer of the case to the Southern District Court of New York.

60 For an overview of Jubilee South Africa's position on apartheid debt, see C. Rustomjee, *Jubilee South Africa. A case study for the UKZN project entitled: Globalisation, Marginalisation*

the former apartheid regime stood at approximately US$14.6 billion,[61] most of which was owed to Swiss and German banks. In line with the TRC's findings in this respect,[62] activists deemed the debt *odious*, meaning that it was contracted without the consent of the people of the country, that it was not contracted for their benefit, and that the creditors were aware of the odious nature of the debt.[63] Jubilee South Africa argued that a failure to cancel the apartheid debt was tantamount to black South Africans paying twice for their own oppression and called on Swiss and German banks to cancel the debt as an act of reparations in favor of the people of South Africa.[64] Despite this prolonged campaign, Swiss and German banks steadfastly refused to heed the call for cancellation.

The new democratic, ANC-led government refused to unilaterally stop paying the debts for fear of sending the wrong signals to the global financial markets and thereby jeopardizing its policy of development through private-sector investment. As a consequence, Jubilee South Africa considered its legal options for bringing Swiss and German banks to account. However, legal avenues for challenging the validity of sovereign debts not only are hard to find but also require complex and innovative argumentation.[65] The movement therefore changed its strategy and considered using the ATS to bring an action in the United States. Under the ATS, foreign nationals can bring a legal action for violations of international treaties to which the United States is party or of the law of nations that occurred outside the United States, provided that the perpetrators (or aiders and abettors) are jurisdictionally present in the United States.[66] Such actions do not question the validity of the debt or of debt repayment claims but rather demand compensation for harm caused to specific victims by the defendant's complicit behavior.

The argument was that Swiss and German banks had aided and abetted the former apartheid regime, particularly its security forces, in the commission of gross human rights violations, resulting in many people's injury and death. However, international banks were not alone in aiding and abetting the former apartheid regime; other industries, such as arms and ammunitions,

and New Social Movements in post-Apartheid South Africa, 2004, pp.9–13, http://ccs.ukzn.ac.za/files/Rustomjee%20JSA%20ResearchReport.pdf.

61 C. Abrahams, *The Doctrine of "Odious Debts"*, LLM thesis, Leiden, NL, 2000, p.62, http://jubileescotlandwiki.wikispaces.com/file/view/Abrahams+-+The+Doctrine+of+%E2%80%98Odious+Debts%E2%80%99.pdf.

62 TRC Report, n.21, pp.146–147.

63 A. Sack, *Les Effets des Transformations des États sur leurs Dettes Publiques et Autres Obligations Financières*, Receuil Sirey, Paris, 1927, p.163.

64 Rustomjee, n.59, pp.9–13.

65 See, for example, S. Michalowski and J.P. Bohoslavsky, 'Ius cogens, Transitional Justice and Other Trends of the Debate on Odious Debts: A Response to the World Bank Discussion Paper on Odious Debts', 48 *Columbia Journal of Transnational Law* 61–120 (2009).

66 28 U.S.C. § 1350. For a detailed discussion of the ATS, see chapter 3 of this book.

fuel and transportation, security and military forces, and military technology industries, had equally been complicit in apartheid. The banks provided the finances that made aiding and abetting possible in these areas.

It can thus be seen how the legacy of apartheid and the South African way of conducting its transitional justice processes were at the root of this litigation. The government's refusal to implement the TRC's findings and recommendations against corporations, including banks, led activists and victims to seek other avenues for pursuing their claims for justice and reparations.

Since the Khulumani Support Group was a partner organization of Jubilee South Africa, the two organizations agreed that the Khulumani Support Group and its members would file a claim for damages against a number of multinational corporations and banks for aiding and abetting the apartheid regime and thereby causing injury and death to its members. Jubilee South Africa provided civil society support to this action.[67]

The claimants relied on the legal theory of secondary liability for aiding and abetting crimes, averring that the corporations and banks aided and abetted the apartheid regime in the commission of the crimes of apartheid, forced labor, genocide, extrajudicial killing, torture, sexual assault, unlawful detention, and cruel and inhuman treatment. In legal terms, aiding and abetting liability under the ATS requires showing that the defendants knowingly or intentionally[68] provided the principal offender with "practical assistance, encouragement, or moral support which has a *substantial effect* on the perpetration of the crime."[69] The claims that had a political and moral origin thus needed to be rephrased to meet the pleading standards under the ATS.

In order to show how the defendants' actions had factually aided and abetted the crimes committed by the apartheid regime, the original complaint submitted in 2002 by the Khulumani plaintiffs[70] argued that:

> the participation of the defendants, companies in the key industries of oil, armaments, banking, transportation, technology, and mining, was instrumental in encouraging and furthering the abuses. Defendants' conduct was so integrally connected to the abuses that apartheid would not have occurred in the same way without their participation.[71]

67 Rustomjee, n.59, pp.13–14.

68 US courts are split on the appropriate *mens rea* standard. See, e.g., *Presbyterian Church of Sudan v Talisman Energy, Inc.*, 582 F.3d 244 (2nd Circuit, 2009), applying a *mens rea* standard of primary purpose, and *Doe v Exxon Mobil Corp.*, 654 F.3d 11 (D.C. Circuit, 2011), holding that the *mens rea* standard in international law is that of knowledge.

69 *In re South African Apartheid Litigation*, 617 F.Supp.2d 228 (SDNY 2009), p.257. See also *Presbyterian Church of Sudan v Talisman Energy, Inc.*, 374 F. Supp. 2d 331 (S.D.N.Y. 2005), pp.337–338 and 340; *Doe v Unocal Corp.*, 395 F.3d 932 (9th Circuit, 2002), p.951.

70 Khulumani complaint, 11 November 2002, www.khulumani.net/attachments/259_Khulumani%20Complaint.pdf.

71 *Ibid.*, para.3.

When the case was first heard in the Southern District of New York in November 2004, the complaint was dismissed on the grounds that liability for aiding and abetting could not be invoked under the ATS.[72] However, the Second Circuit Court of Appeal disagreed with the District Court's analysis. Judge Katzman, writing the *per curiam* decision of the court in an opinion handed down on 12 October 2007, concluded that "the recognition of the individual responsibility of a defendant who aids and abets the violation of international law is one of those rules that States universally abide by, or accede to, out of a sense of legal obligation and mutual concern."[73] The court allowed the plaintiffs to amend and specify their complaints and remanded the case to the District Court.

The amended complaint, submitted in October 2008, reduced the number of defendants to eight so that a more specific case could be presented. They came from four strategic sectors—armaments, technology, transportation, and banking—that were identified as having been of particular importance for assisting the apartheid regime in its crimes, including apartheid itself; extrajudicial killing; torture; prolonged unlawful detention; and cruel, inhuman, and degrading treatment.[74]

Given that the litigation historically originated from campaigns against banks for their role in financing apartheid, and for the cancellation of the resulting debt that democratic South Africa was left to pay, the following brief overview of some of the legal challenges faced in the litigation will concentrate on the claims against the banking defendants. Barclays and UBS were accused of aiding and abetting the apartheid regime in the commission of its crimes by having made large-scale funding available to the apartheid regime.[75] It was suggested that without this assistance, "the apartheid regime could not have maintained control over the civilian population to the same degree, nor could it have maintained and expanded its security forces to the same degree."[76] The claim also alleged that the banks had provided funds directly to the South African security forces "that carried out the most brutal aspects of apartheid."[77] Without these funds, the growing costs of policing the apartheid state could not have been met by the government.[78]

The court started its analysis of the liability of the banking defendants by considering that "simply doing business with a state or individual who

72 *In re South African Apartheid Litigation*, 346 F.Supp.2d 538 (SDNY 2004), p.550.

73 *Khulumani v Barclay National Bank*, 504 F.3d 254 (2nd Circuit, 2007), p.270.

74 First Amended Complaint, *In re South African Apartheid Litigation*, 617 F. Supp. 2d 228 (SDNY 2009) (Civ. No. 03-cv-04524), para.145, www.hausfeldllp.com/content_documents/9/KhulumaniClassActionComplai.pdf.

75 *Ibid.*, para.150.

76 *Ibid.*, para.151.

77 *Ibid.*, para.152.

78 *Ibid.*, para.169.

violates the law of nations is insufficient to create liability under customary international law" and that "aiding a criminal 'is not the same thing as aiding and abetting [his or her] alleged human rights abuses.'"[79] For business transactions to give rise to aiding and abetting liability, the quality of the assistance provided to the primary violator was crucial:

> The provision of goods specifically designed to kill, to inflict pain, or to cause other injuries resulting from violations of customary international law bear a closer causal connection to the principal crime than the sale of raw materials or the provision of loans.[80]

As a consequence of the court's approach to liability,[81] all claims that were based on what resembled ordinary business transactions were dismissed. With regard to loans, the court specified that:

> supplying a violator of the law of nations with funds—even funds that could not have been obtained but for those loans—is not sufficiently connected to the primary violation to fulfill the *actus reus* requirement of aiding and abetting a violation of the law of nations.[82]

This stands in stark contrast to the TRC's view on the moral and legal liability of banks for their loans to the apartheid regime. The only claims that remained were those where the court found that the goods or services provided by the defendant corporation had provided the direct means for carrying out the violations, such as the sale of vehicles with military specifications[83] or the design of computer software to implement the policy of "geographic segregation and racial discrimination."[84]

The defendants appealed the District Court's decision. One of the key issues argued before the Second Circuit Court of Appeal was whether international law extends the scope of aiding and abetting liability to corporations. Judgment in this case was pending at the time of writing. After the Second Circuit Court of Appeal answered this question in the negative in *Kiobel v Royal Dutch Petroleum Co.*[85] the apartheid litigation lay on ice while the US Supreme Court decision in *Kiobel* was pending. The Supreme Court, however, did not address this issue in *Kiobel,* but instead dismissed the case

79 *In re South African Apartheid Litigation*, 617 F.Supp.2d 228 (SDNY 2009), p.257.
80 *Ibid.*, p.258.
81 For a critical discussion, see S. Michalowski, 'No complicity liability for financing gross human rights violations?' 30 *Berkeley Journal of International Law* 451–524 (2012).
82 *In re South African Apartheid Litigation*, 617 F.Supp.2d 228 (SDNY 2009), p.269.
83 *Ibid.*, pp.264 and 266.
84 *Ibid.*, p.265.
85 *Kiobel v Royal Dutch Petroleum Co.*, 621 F.3d 111 (2nd Circuit, 2010).

based on other grounds. The majority held that because of the presumption against an extraterritorial application of legislation, the ATS does not apply to violations that occurred outside of the US.[86] It concluded that "even where the claims touch and concern the territory of the United States, they must do so with sufficient force to displace the presumption against extraterritorial application."[87] This decision has a direct impact on the future of the apartheid litigation as it seems difficult to establish such a link in cases of companies not based in the US. To what extent the courts will find a sufficient link where claims are directed against US companies remains to be tested.

The South African government's position toward the litigation

When the litigation started, the South African government chose to oppose the lawsuits and submitted a declaration to the court in July 2003 urging it to dismiss the case. The declaration, which has since become known as the Maduna Declaration,[88] set out the government's opposition in great detail, the main argument being that the litigation interfered with South Africa's sovereignty.[89] The government contended that the new democratic South Africa deliberately avoided a "victors' justice" approach to the crimes of apartheid and opted instead for a transitional justice process based on "reconciliation, reconstruction, reparation and goodwill."[90] It quoted an address made by then President Mbeki to the South African Parliament in April 2003, in which he considered it to be "completely unacceptable that matters . . . central to the future of our country should be adjudicated in foreign courts which bear no responsibility for the well-being of our country."[91] The declaration stressed the government's aim to achieve a:

> fundamental transformation of South African society . . . attempting to rehabilitate the lives of the previously disadvantaged through the promotion of non-racialism, equality and social justice . . . through wide ranging legislative reforms. . . . In other words, what the government is attempting to do is to repair the damage caused by the apartheid system through a broad programme of socio-economic reparations.[92]

86 *Kiobel v Royal Dutch Petroleum Co.*, (2013), 2013 WL 1628935, para.9.
87 *Ibid.*, para.10.
88 So named after the former Minister of Justice and Constitutional Development, Penneul Maduna, who filed it on behalf of the South African government.
89 Maduna Declaration, n.49, para.2.
90 *Ibid.*, para.3.2.1.
91 *Ibid.*, para.3.2.3.
92 *Ibid.*, para.4.

The government regarded the litigation as an attempt on the part of the claimants to act as a "surrogate government" and to undermine the governmental policy on reparations.[93] It considered the remedies claimed before the US courts to be inconsistent with the government's strategy of achieving reparations and social transformation through economic growth in partnership with private actors, including corporations.[94] The litigation was portrayed as primarily political in nature and intruding on and disrupting South Africa's attempts "to achieve reconciliation and reconstruction."[95] The government feared, in particular, that the litigation could have a negative effect on foreign investment, thereby "undermining economic stability."[96]

The government's claim was strongly contested by former TRC commissioners, who filed an amicus brief with the Southern District of New York in support of the claimants.[97] Their brief argued that civil litigation against corporations for aiding and abetting apartheid crimes was unlikely to affect investment decisions and would instead have the positive effect of deterring "future threats to radically inequitable economic growth in South Africa and elsewhere."[98]

The brief clarified the former commissioners' conviction that the TRC was not "meant to be, nor was it, an exhaustive effort to redress and repair the ravages of apartheid."[99] Instead, they highlighted that it had always been clear that additional measures to address past injustices would be necessary, of which the apartheid litigation was one example. They pointed out that TRC proceedings precluded litigation only against perpetrators who had been granted amnesty. However, none of the defendants in the litigation before the US court had received an amnesty by the TRC. In fact, none of them even participated in the business hearings before the TRC.[100] As the defendants were neither given an amnesty nor entitled to it (since the TRC did not even have the power to grant amnesty to corporations that participated in the hearings), the commissioners forcefully emphasized that "[t]here was absolutely nothing in the TRC process, its goals, or the pursuit of the overarching goal of reconciliation, linked with truth, that would be impeded by this litigation."[101]

93 *Ibid.*, para.7.
94 *Ibid.*, para.10.
95 *Ibid.*, para.11.
96 *Ibid.*, para.12.
97 Brief of *Amici Curiae* former Commissioners and Committee Members of South Africa's Truth and Reconciliation Commission in support of appellants to the United States Court of Appeals for the Second Circuit in *Khulumani v Barclay National Bank*, www.sdshhlaw.com/Apartheid/pdfs/TRC_Amicus083005.pdf.
98 *Ibid.*, p.16.
99 *Ibid.*, p.3.
100 *Ibid.*, p.4.
101 *Ibid.*, p.14.

In clear disagreement with the government's view that the litigation was inconsistent with the South African approach to transitional justice, the commissioners concluded that the continuation of the litigation was in line with the goals of transitional justice: "by giving voice to those harmed by multinational corporations aiding and abetting apartheid, it assists the healing and reconciliation process."[102]

One day after Judge Scheindlin's decision in the Southern District Court of New York, the South African government, through its Minister of Justice and Constitutional Development, Jeff Radebe, submitted a letter to the judge informing her of the South African government's change of position in relation to the litigation. The letter advised that:

> the Government of the Republic of South Africa, having considered carefully the judgment of the United States District Court, Southern District of New York is now of the view that this Court is an appropriate forum to hear the remaining claims of aiding and abetting in violation of international law.[103]

This change of opinion was explained by the fact that the South African government's opposition to the litigation had been prompted mainly by the concern that it undermined the government's approach to the TRC's recommendation with regard to the role of businesses in apartheid. When the court dismissed the claims that were considered to be based solely on the fact that the defendant corporation had been doing business with the apartheid regime, and upheld only those claims that referred to corporate aiding and abetting in the commission of serious crimes under international law, this concern no longer persisted.

However, the U-turn of the South African government seemed to mark a broader policy shift in its position, which occurred after the change in presidency from Thabo Mbeki to Jacob Zuma. The Zuma administration adopted a new economic policy, NEGP, mentioned above.[104] Just like its predecessor, GEAR, the NEGP policy seeks to reduce inequality and defeat poverty by placing an emphasis on job creation. However, unlike GEAR, NEGP is based on a state-led developmental approach that does not place its trust primarily in free-market policies. It rather stresses the need to "align market outcomes with development needs."[105]

While the government's shift in economic policy may not be the only or even the main reason for changing its stance on the apartheid litigation, it

102 *Ibid.*, pp.15–16.

103 www.khulumani.net/attachments/343_RSA.Min.Justice_letter_J.Scheindlin_09.01.09.PDF.

104 NEGP Framework, www.info.gov.za/view/DownloadFileAction?id=135748.

105 *Ibid.*, para.3.4.1.

does suggest that rediscovering the role of the state in economic development means that there is less of an incentive to support the interests of business and thus to oppose litigation against corporations.

Other challenges in the aftermath of the TRC

The changed attitude of the South African government toward economic policies and corporate accountability might open new possibilities for reconciliation and justice in post-apartheid South Africa. Nevertheless, that the apartheid legacy persists in parts of the corporate domain, and still holds big potential for social injustice and unrest, was highlighted by the very tragic developments in recent South African history. On 16 August 2012, the South African police opened fire on protesting mine workers at the Lonmin gold mine in Rustenberg, killing 34 miners and wounding many others.[106] The tragedy has since become known as the Marikana massacre. The miners had been protesting against low wages and bad living and working conditions. The protests reflected not only miners' discontent with current conditions in South African goldmines but also dissatisfaction with an inherently exploitative system that has prevailed in the gold mining industry for more than 100 years and that, post-apartheid, has not seen any fundamental change. The TRC, as indicated above, had been critical of the role played by the South African gold mining industry in designing and benefitting from the exploitative migrant labor system,[107] which to this day has remained largely unchanged.

The apartheid legacy in the mining sector has moreover led to litigation against South Africa's largest gold mining companies, AngloGold Ashanti Limited, Harmony Gold Mining Company Limited, and Gold Fields Limited. At the heart of this litigation are miners' claims for damages for having been exposed to silica dust in South African gold mines and, as a consequence, having suffered occupational lung disease. The TRC had drawn attention to the fact that the migrant labor system allowed gold mining companies to repatriate miners suffering from occupational lung disease,[108] who would then "die slow and painful deaths, living on meagre pensions without the necessary medical treatment."[109] Though no reliable statistics exist, research done by Anna Trapido[110] estimates that almost half a million former mine

106 www.bbc.co.uk/news/world-africa-19292909.

107 TRC Report, n.15, p.34.

108 TRC Report, n.21, pp.151–155.

109 *Ibid.*, p.154.

110 A. Trapido, *An Analysis of the Burden of Occupational Lung Disease in a Random Sample of Former Gold Mineworkers in the Libode District of the Eastern Cape*, Thesis submitted to the Faculty of Health Sciences, University of the Witwatersrand, in fulfilment of the requirements for the degree of Doctor of Philosophy Uitzicht, 2000, http://wiredspace.wits.ac.za/bitstream/handle/10539/10093/Trapido_A.pdf%201.pdf?sequence=1.

workers in Southern Africa, having worked in South African gold mines, suffer from occupational lung disease and that the total amount of unpaid compensation amounts to about R2.8 billion.

During apartheid, the mining companies thus blatantly violated the rights of workers, who continue to suffer consequences to this day. However, even though the TRC recognized that a claim for reparations could be brought against mining companies such as Anglo American, the government did not act on this. As a consequence, just like with the *Khulumani* claimants, victims ended up seeking justice in court, suing mining companies AngloGold Ashanti Limited, Harmony Gold Mining Company Limited, and Gold Fields Limited for compensation for having exposed the workers to occupational lung diseases such as silicosis and tuberculosis.[111]

At the same time, it is interesting to note different tensions that can arise when relying on private-sector investment for redressing the injustices and inequalities of the past. The case of *Piero Foresti v The Republic of South Africa* provides an example of this. In that case, a group of investors from Italy and Luxembourg filed a claim with the International Centre for Settlement of Investment Disputes against the South African government for breach of the provisions of BITs between South Africa and Italy and Luxembourg.[112] The investors were holders of certain mineral rights in South Africa that were affected by the Mineral and Petroleum Resources Development Act, which came into force in 2004 and aimed to further South Africa's policy of "black economic empowerment" by, among other things, substantially expanding "the opportunities for historically disadvantaged persons . . . to benefit from the exploitation of the nation's mineral and petroleum resources."[113] The legislation transferred all mineral rights in South Africa to the state, meaning that land can be owned privately but that mining activities on that property require permission from the state. Mineral exploitation rights were made subject to a government-issued license whose granting depends on whether the mining firms fulfill a number of objective conditions laid down in the law. These include, inter alia, generating employment equity for and increasing procurement from historically disadvantaged South Africans, and the transfer of 26 per cent of shares in the mining sector into the hands of black investors by 2014.[114]

111 Three class certification applications were issued out of the South Gauteng High Court on 21 August 2012: *Dyamara January Jibhana & Others v Gold Fields Limited & Others* (case no: 31324/2012); *Zonisele Jan Nkompela & Others v Harmony Gold Mining Company Limited & Others* (case no: 31326/12); and *Bangumzi Bennet Vilakazi & Others v AngloGold Ashanti Limited* (case no: 31327/2012).

112 ICSID Case No ARB(AF)/07/1.

113 Mineral and Petroleum Resources Development Act, section 2(d).

114 As required by the Broad-Based Socio-Economic Empowerment Charter for the Mining Industry of South Africa (2002).

The investors argued a violation of the "fair and equitable treatment" and "national treatment" provisions of two BITs, as well as expropriation.[115] Claimants discontinued the proceedings when South Africa granted them a license without requiring them to sell 26 per cent of their shares to historically disadvantaged South Africans.[116] This dispute highlights the potential problem faced by a government that provides far-reaching protection of investors' rights to advance its policy of fighting inequality through economic growth: investor rights can conflict with the state's obligation to address the socioeconomic inequalities of the past, as in the form of black economic empowerment policies. Indeed, the fact that foreign corporations challenged the South African government's policies aimed at addressing past socioeconomic injustices not only suggests an attitudinal view of business-as-normal entitlement but creates further legitimacy challenges for the government in its reconciliatory approach toward business.

Conclusion

Despite South Africa's successful political transition, the government's reconciliatory approach toward business has raised numerous questions. Holding corporate actors accountable for past conduct that resulted in either direct or indirect human rights violations cannot be addressed simply through voluntary initiatives or commitment by corporations to invest in the post-conflict society. Even though the establishment of the Business Trust Fund by South African businesses could be seen as helpful in the broader transitional justice project, it dwarfs in comparison to the benefits they received from apartheid, whether directly or indirectly. It appears that the South African government's policy orientation with regard to corporations is aligned more toward reconciliation than toward maintaining a balance between truth, justice, and reconciliation.

The selective overview of some of the experiences of South Africa regarding corporate accountability in the context of transitional justice presented in this chapter has shown the tensions that transitional societies face when trying to break free from the past and construct a changed society. Corporations clearly

115 For a discussion, see, for example, M.W. Chow, 'Discriminatory equality v. nondiscriminatory inequality: the legitimacy of South Africa's affirmative action policies under international law', 24 *Connecticut Journal of International Law* 291 (2009); A. Friedman, 'Flexible arbitration for the developing world: Piero Foresti and the future of bilateral investment treaties in the Global South', 7 *Brigham Young University International Law & Management Review* 37 (2010).

116 ICSID Case No ARB(AF)/07/1, p.20: they were "deemed to have complied with the Mining Charter by (i) making a 21% beneficiation offset (i.e., beneficiating – processing and adding value to the quarried stone – in South Africa 21% of the stone that it mined in South Africa); and (ii) providing a 5% employee ownership program for employees of the Operating Companies."

benefited from—and in some instances more actively participated in—the crimes of the apartheid regime, yet the incoming democratic government saw corporations primarily as necessary partners for reconstruction and development rather than culprits who should provide victims with reparations. The analysis of the apartheid litigation in the United States demonstrates some of the consequences of such an approach, as victims might seek alternative avenues, even abroad if necessary, if their sense of justice is not satisfied by the transitional justice processes in their country.

As can be seen from the *Khulumani* case, litigation does have a role in holding corporations accountable, but it is invariably a narrow one. This type of litigation faces inordinate legal challenges, as can be seen from the *Kiobel* judgment. Time is also a further challenge in these types of proceedings. Ten years have passed since the lawsuit was originally filed in the Eastern District Court of New York. Since then, it has been on appeal to the Second Circuit Court of Appeal, on application for Certiorari before the US Supreme Court, back to the Eastern District Court and then again on appeal before the Second Circuit Court where it is still pending.

Chapter 9

International Criminal Law and Transnational Businesses

Cases from Argentina and Colombia

*Wolfgang Kaleck**

Introduction

Drawing on post-colonial theories, representatives of "Third World approaches to international law" criticize current international law as an amalgam of Eurocentric doctrines and principles that evolved in the particular setting of European history and experience and was extended to include the non-European world without considering its distinct history. Another point of criticism is that many Western human rights organizations emphasize civil and political rights while overlooking ESCR. These organizations are accused of consciously ignoring the ideological basis of the human rights discourse—that is, the advancement of democracy and free trade—in order to pledge political neutrality.[1] This ideology is reflected in activities of both institutional and non-governmental organizations in the area of international criminal law and transitional justice that neglect the underlying contradictions of this particular type of justice: war crimes and crimes against humanity are structural and systemic injustices, perpetrated by a repressive (state) apparatus, while ordinary criminal law deals with the liability of individuals.[2] Consequently, international criminal lawyers tend to focus their efforts on particular problems of criminal law—for example, the problem of superiors'

* Translated from German by Lisa Hecht.

1 M. Mutua, 'The Transformation of Africa: A Critique of the Rights Discourse', in F. Gomez and K. De Feyter (eds), *Human Rights and Diversity: International Human Rights Law in a Global Context*, University of Deusto, Bilbao, 2009 (899), http://ssrn.com/abstract=1526734; A. Angie, 'The Evolution of International Law: Colonial and Post-Colonial Realities', 27 *Third World Quarterly* 739–753 (2006), where Angie retraces the colonial roots of international law and points to dominating legitimizations for interventions in the internal affairs of states labelled as "uncivilized." On this topic, see also I. Wallerstein, *European Universalism: The Rhetoric of Power*, The New Press, New York, 2006.

2 M. Drumbi, *Atrocity, Punishment and International Law*, Cambridge University Press, Cambridge/New York, 2007.

liability[3] or the question of whether widespread and systemic attacks against civilians are crimes against humanity[4]—while ignoring the political, social, and economic factors that led to violations of international criminal law. Their engagement with human rights violations is only phenomenological, and their subjects of inquiry are the observable effects that can be placed into criminal law categories, and not their underlying causes.

In contrast, social movements of the southern hemisphere have developed a more differentiated understanding of law and a political practice that goes beyond existing legal categories. For them, law is a means to solve social problems and conflicts, and judicial proceedings and their outcomes accordingly serve as a means to an end. Societal changes and the elimination of social injustices are at the core of their efforts. The achievement of such objectives requires an approach that links the traditionally separate areas of civil and political rights and economic, social, and cultural rights.[5]

Good examples of this inclusive approach can be found in lawsuits in Argentina and Colombia that were filed in the aftermath of unionist persecutions under military rule (Argentina) and at the beginning of the twenty-first century in the context of corporate complicity in dictatorships or conflict (Argentina and Colombia). One of these cases is that of 16 unionists of the Mercedes-Benz factory in González Catán, located in the province of Buenos Aires, Argentina, who disappeared in 1976–1977. Other cases deal with repressive measures in the periphery of the Argentinian agribusiness Ledesma and a murdered Nestlé unionist in Colombia.

The chapter begins by introducing the historical background of the military dictatorship in Argentina and the legal treatment after its demise. It then highlights repression against unionists, in particular those occurring at Mercedes-Benz and Ledesma. The third section deals with legal efforts in Argentina, Germany, and the United States to hold those responsible to account and to obtain reparations for the victims of Argentina's dictatorship. The fourth section turns toward criminal proceedings initiated in Switzerland against Nestlé managers for their complicity in the persecution

3 See, for example, V. Nerlich, 'Superior responsibility under Article 28 ICC Statute: for what exactly is the superior held responsible?' 5 *Journal of International Criminal Justice* 665–682 (2007).

4 See for example, A. Cassese, *International Law*, Oxford University Press, Oxford, 2005, pp.439–442.

5 This is evident in the activities and publications of human rights organizations such as Human Rights Law Network (India), www.hrln.org; Saligan (Philippines), www.saligan.org; Khulumani Support Group (South Africa), www.khulumani.net; Proyecto de Derechos Económicos, Sociales y Culturales – Prodesc (Mexico), www.prodesc.org.mx; and Colectivo de Abogados Jose Alvear Restrepo – CAJAR (Colombia), www.colectivodeabogados.org. The New York-based Center for Constitutional Rights uses a similar approach, http://ccrjustice.org/.

of unionists in Colombia. Finally, the concluding section offers an outlook on the future.

Military rule in Argentina and the fight against impunity

On 24 March 1976, General Jorge Rafael Videla led a coup in Argentina that installed one of the most brutal regimes of the last century. Tens of thousands of people were tortured, and up to 30,000 are estimated to have disappeared.[6] This military regime was a response to the political conflicts in the early 1970s. The fragile compromise between the government and large companies, on the one hand, and the labor movement, on the other, which had offered remarkable social security to the Argentinian workforce, broke apart, while the (often corrupt) unions promised social peace. At the company level, workers' councils campaigned for better remuneration and working conditions, and unions provided political representation of workers' interests. In response, the country slowly took an authoritarian turn. In 1974 and 1975, numerous unionists, journalists, and lawyers were murdered by death squadrons.

The terror unfolded fully from March 1976 onwards. Argentina's system of repression had at its center secret torture centers and paramilitary abduction units. The regime did more than simply persecute members of the armed and militant left wing; rather, oriented toward the United States, it adopted the Cold War strategy of anti-communism and counter-insurgency. Its "Doctrine of National Security" declared "Jewish-Marxist Subversion," with its support base in international communism, the main threat to internal security. In practice, this doctrine included all groups opposing the military regime's political and economic project.[7] Already then, critics of the military rule pointed to a close link between the regime and worsening economic conditions. In his famous open letter written one year after the coup, author Rodolfo Walsh noted his concern over the regime's restructuring of the economy, the 40 per cent decrease in real wages, and the enormous loss of purchasing power that affected the poor in particular. Walsh criticized the regime's economic policies as the worst among all its

6 General information can be found in Argentine National Commission on the Disappeared (CONADEP), *Nunca Más (Never Again)*, Editorial Universitaria, Buenos Aires, 1984. See also W. Kaleck, *Kampf gegen die Straflosigkeit. Argentiniens Militär vor Gericht*, Klaus Wagenbach Verlag, Berlin, 2010.

7 W. Heinz, 'Konsequenzen der Demokratisierung für die Streitkräfte in Argentinien, Brasilien und Uruguay', in H. Tobler and P. Waldmann (eds), *Staatliche und parastaatliche Gewalt in Lateinamerika*, Vervuert Verlag, Frankfurt, 1991 (265–316), p.267; D. Pion-Berlin, 'Political Repression and Economic Doctrines: "The Case of Argentina"', 16 *Comparative Political Studies* 37–66 (1983), pp.46 and 61.

human rights violations, since they deliberately condemned millions of people to poverty.[8]

After losing the Falklands/Malvinas War in 1982, the military's power decreased notably.[9] One year later, it ceded power to Raúl Alfonsín, who had won the democratic elections held by the regime. Alfonsín then initiated criminal prosecutions of the regime's leading figures. In the lawsuits of 1985 and 1986, several members of the *junta* were sentenced to life imprisonment or long detention.[10] However, the military objected to the far-reaching prosecution of its officers and soldiers, and threatened violent opposition. Against this background, the government issued extensive amnesty and decriminalization laws.[11] The long years of impunity began.

Nevertheless, thanks to the efforts of human rights organizations and associations of victims' relatives, particularly the Mothers of Plaza de Mayo, the investigation and punishment of crimes remained an issue. The efforts of committed prosecutors and judges, as well as the 2003 election of President Kirchner, resulted in the annulment of the amnesty laws in 2005–2006.[12] This led to an avalanche of about 1,000 criminal investigations and trials, which are currently under way, and to 200 sentences for police and military officers so far.[13] It is worth noting that the investigations and trials are limited to crimes of torture, murder, and enforced disappearances—in other words, cases of direct repression. However, the repressive state apparatus—with its secret prison and torture centers, disappearances, and child abductions—could not have been maintained without the direct and indirect complicity of civilians, such as judges, court clerks, civil servants, and ministry officials. Yet these individuals have not had to face charges. The same applies to individuals who partook in the military's property offenses. During the days of military rule, it was common practice not only to confiscate property of the detained and disappeared but also to blackmail victims and their relatives in order to acquire their property rights to factories and estates. This part of the authoritarian legacy still awaits investigation.[14] Similarly,

8 R. Walsh, 'Open Letter to the Military Junta', in D. Link (ed), *El Violento Oficio de Escribir*, Planeta, Buenos Aires, 1995, p.415.

9 J.S. Elias, 'Constitutional changes, transitional justice and legitimacy', 31 *Hastings International and Comparative Law Review* 587–646 (2008), pp.592–593.

10 For an interesting discussion, see *ibid.*, pp.609–613.

11 Punto Final or Full Stop Law: Law No. 23492, 24 December 1986, A.L.J.A. 1100; Ley Obedencia Debida or Due Obedience Law: Law No. 23521, 8 June 1987, A.L.J.A 260.

12 'Simón, Julio Héctor y otros s/ privación ilegítima de la libertad, etc. – causa No. 17.768', Fallos 328:2056; see also M. O'Donnell, 'New Dirty War Judgements in Argentina: National Courts and Domestic Prosecutions of International Human Rights Violations', 84 *New York University Law Review* 333–374 (2009), pp.333–334.

13 For up-to-date statistics, see www.cels.org.ar/wpblogs/.

14 One case in which these issues play a role is that of Papel Prensa, a paper factory that was sold during the dictatorship to the biggest media groups; see Secretaría de Comercio Interior,

the complicity of corporate managers in the repression of independent unionists and members of workers' councils has yet to be examined.

Repression against the labor movement: the cases of Mercedes-Benz Argentina and Ledesma

Organized labor was one of the main targets of repression under the Argentinian military regime. In order to impose its economic model, the military was keen to silence union leaders.[15] Globalization critic Naomi Klein uses the military regimes in Argentina and Chile as examples of what she labels a *shock doctrine*. These regimes sought to immobilize societies through repression and torture in order to introduce rampant capitalism outside the control of unions and state institutions.[16] Klein quotes Orlando Letelier, a Chilean who was murdered for his opposition to the regime: "Concentration of wealth is no accident, but a rule; it is not the marginal outcome of a difficult situation . . . but the base for a social project, it is not an economic liability but a temporary political success."[17] It was no coincidence that, as the truth commission "*Nunca Más*" (Never Again) inaugurated by President Alfonsín determined, 48.1 per cent of the disappeared were part of the country's organized labor force.[18]

A systematic study of union persecution in Argentina, as well as a compilation and analysis of individual cases, is still missing. However, taken together, these cases reveal a specific pattern: the industrialized areas of Buenos Aires, Rosario, Córdoba, and the agricultural industry of Jujuy were at the center of the repression. Campo de Mayo, one of the country's biggest prisons and torture centers, was located in the province of Buenos Aires. The majority of the prison's 5,000 detainees, most of whom were later executed, had previously been active in the labor movement. About a hundred unionists on the wharfs Astilleros Astara, Mestrina, and Forte were detained there, among them a large majority of the work council members. Furthermore, dozens of the work council members of car manufacturers Ford and Mercedes-Benz, both located in the province of Buenos Aires, were imprisoned at Campo de Mayo.[19] Unionists of the construction company Acindar were detained and tortured in a provisional camp on the company site at Rosario.[20]

Ministerio de Economía y Finanzas Públicas, Presidencia de la Nación, *Papel Prensa, La Verdad* (2010), www.mecon.gov.ar/basehome/pdf/papel_prensa_informe_final.pdf.

15 N. Klein, *The Shock Doctrine. The Rise of Disaster Capitalism*, Metropolitan Books, New York, 2007, pp.75–97.

16 *Ibid.*

17 *Ibid.*, p.86.

18 *Ibid.*, p.106.

19 Kaleck, n.6, p.80.

20 G. Fuertes, 'Oyarbide consideró que en Acindar se cometieron delitos de lesa humanidad', *Tiempo Argentino*, 20 November 2011.

Ford followed a similar strategy,[21] and the situation at the site of sugar monopolist Ledesma was just as notorious. The night of 21 July 1976, the so called "*Noche de Apagón*" (Night of the Power Cut), became a particularly infamous date of the military regime. With technical assistance from Ledesma, electrical power was turned off that night in the entire municipality. Using military vehicles as well as those of the company, about 400 people, mainly unionists, were arrested. Among the arrested was Luis Aredez, a company doctor who had advocated better work conditions. Fifty-five people remain disappeared since that night.[22]

Following the example of Spain, German activists founded the organization 'Coalition against Impunity: Truth and Justice for Disappeared Germans in Argentina'. In the name of German torture victims and their relatives, the coalition filed criminal complaints against members of the Argentinian military regime.[23] Although initially hesitant, the Nuremberg-Fuerth public prosecutor conducted thorough investigations, which eventually resulted in international arrest warrants and extradition requests for ex-dictators Jorge Videla and Emilio Massera.[24] Inspired by these activities, the Latin America-based German journalist Gaby Weber researched the cases of the disappeared unionists of Mercedes-Benz. She describes her motivation as follows:

> I wanted to research where the real power was concentrated. And this is not the military and its retired generals. All those Pinochets and Videlas, and whatever their names might be, have served their purpose and have already been condemned as evildoers by the international press cartel. Accusing those people and criticizing the amnesty laws is hardly a novelty or a sign of bravery and morals. The wide reaching network of professional human rights organizations already attends to these tasks. Donations can be tax exempted and business is a welcomed sponsor. I was looking for a German company . . . that had a skeleton in the cupboard.[25]

Her research was first presented in a radio broadcast in August 1999 and later published as a book. Based on her research, a criminal complaint was filed in 1999 in the name of the surviving unionist Héctor Ratto against Juan Tasselkraut, former production manager of the Mercedes-Benz factory in González Catán, for aiding and abetting murder. On 12 August 1977, the day of his arrest, Ratto was detained in Tasselkraut's office and later taken

21 G. Weber, *Die Verschwundenen von Mercedes Benz*, Assoziation A, Berlin, 2004, p.19.

22 See www.ecchr.de/index.php/argentina_cases/articles/case-against-argentinian-sugar-company-ledesma.html.

23 See www.koalition-gegen-straflosigkeit.de.

24 Kaleck, n.6, pp.65–66.

25 Weber, n.21, p.12.

away by the military. On this occasion, he overheard Tasselkraut reveal the address of work council member Diego Núñez to the police. The following day, Núñez was found at this address and abducted. Ratto himself disappeared and was tortured with electrical shocks and has been suffering a hip complaint since then. Both men were detained in the Campo de Mayo prison, along with other colleagues from the factory, where they were tortured.[26] While Ratto was eventually released, Núñez and the other unionists disappeared without a trace. In total, 16 unionists of Mercedes-Benz Argentina were abducted in 1976–1977, of whom only two survived.[27]

These abductions were a reaction to severe disputes between workers and managers at the factory in González Catán. Workers had previously formed an independent work council to distance themselves from the corrupt car manufacturers' union, SMATA. Through strikes and campaigns, the work council showed its opposition to dismissals at the factory. In 1975, a town guerrilla unit abducted the German factory manager Heinrich Metz and released him upon payment of ransom. In reaction to this abduction, the factory's management provided military authorities with a list of unionists. Apart from Ratto's testimony, there was a series of further evidence of the factory's collaboration with repressive state institutions. Former police commissioner Rubén Lavallén worked as security chief at the factory from 1978 until the end of the regime.[28] Prior to that, he headed the police station Ramos Mejía, which was located in the factory's proximity and was used to detain and torture unionists. After the demise of the regime, Rubén Lavallén was one of the first to be criminally convicted of forcibly taking custody over a child of murdered dissidents.[29]

Legal proceedings in Germany, the United States, and Argentina

During the one-and-a-half decades in which impunity reigned in Argentina and Chile, the Argentinian human rights movement undertook efforts to initiate investigations and legal proceedings in Europe. Their aim was not only to pursue the conviction of individual torturers abroad but also to pressure the Argentinian and Chilean judiciaries to take legal action in their own countries. As part of this strategy, and using the passive personality principle as a legal base, relatives of French, German, and Italian victims initiated criminal prosecutions in their home countries.[30] In Spain, the

26 *Ibid.*, pp.49–56.
27 Kaleck, n.6, pp.65–66.
28 Weber, n.21, p.98.
29 Kaleck, n.6, p.66.
30 *Ibid.*, pp.31–47.

principle of universal jurisdiction offered a basis for far-reaching inquiries,[31] which eventually resulted in the arrest of former Chilean dictator Augusto Pinochet in London on 16 October 1998. This case motivated human rights organizations and lawyers worldwide to initiate similar proceedings against those involved in torture and crimes against humanity. Among the accused were low- and high-ranking officials, including both former and current members of the government. French and Italian courts convicted several Argentinian and Chilean defendants in their absence. German and Spanish courts issued arrest warrants against dozens of military officials. Germany even went as far as to request the extradition of former *junta* leader Jorge Rafael Videla.[32]

Although these various proceedings resulted in only one conviction—that of Adolfo Scilingo, a former military official, in Spain[33]—they were arguably still a success. The jurisprudence of the Inter-American Court of Human Rights also provided important legal arguments against impunity.[34] Alongside the persistent legal and political efforts of the Argentinian human rights movement, of which the Mothers of Plaza de Mayo was at the forefront, the legal proceedings contributed to a reconsideration of Argentina's amnesty and impunity laws. The annulment of those laws triggered criminal investigations in all parts of Argentina, resulting in about 200 convictions to date. This interrelationship came to be known as the "Pinochet effect" or "Videla effect": Where local remedies are not available (as was the case when Argentina's amnesty laws were in effect), plaintiffs will resort to global remedies.[35] It is worth noting, however, that almost all of the lawsuits were filed against direct perpetrators of torture and murder. The structural background of the Argentinian dictatorship and the involvement of various economic actors did not play a role in the investigations. Even most human rights organizations and relatives of victims did not consider this an issue, instead focusing on those with more direct responsibility for the crimes committed.

The lawsuit against Mercedes manager Juan Tasselkraut in 1999 therefore constitutes an exception. The Nuremberg-Fuerth public prosecutor initiated investigations, which led to interviews of many witnesses at the German Embassy in Buenos Aires. However, in November 2003, the prosecution

31 E. Rojo, 'National legislation providing for the prosecution and punishment of international crimes in Spain', 9 *Journal of International Criminal Justice* 699–728 (2011).

32 Kaleck, n.6, pp.65–66.

33 Rojo, n.31, p.707.

34 Inter-American Court of Human Rights, *Case of the "White Van" (Paniagua-Morales et al.) v Guatemala*, Merits, Judgment of 8 March 1998, Series C No.37, para.173; Inter-American Court of Human Rights, *Case of Bulacio v Argentina*, Merits, Reparations and Costs, Judgment of 18 September 2003, Series C No.100, para.120.

35 N. Roht-Ariaza, *The Pinochet Effect: Transnational Justice in the Age of Human Rights*, University of Pennsylvania Press, Philadelphia, 2005.

suspended the proceedings for lack of sufficient evidence. The prosecution declared Ratto's testimony contradictory, and the defendant, Tasselkraut, denied the charges. Furthermore, the prosecution stated that the murder of unionist Diego Núñez could not be proven since his fate had not been verified.[36] This is explained by the fact that the Rome Statute of the International Criminal Court entered into force only on 31 July 2002. Before that date, crimes against humanity—and thus the crime of enforced disappearances—did not constitute an offense under German law. Thus, defendants were usually charged with murder, which made it difficult to satisfy the legal requirements regarding the crimes under investigation, as in many cases the death of the person could not be proved but only assumed.[37] The suspension of legal proceedings in these cases demonstrates the need for national criminal law norms that are modeled after the Rome Statute and that apply to crimes with an international dimension. Nevertheless, in the case of Diego Núñez, the prosecution could well have reached the decision that there was, in fact, sufficient evidence for murder. Núñez had been last seen at one of the infamous torture centers, and for the subsequent 30 years his whereabouts were unknown.[38]

Due to legal restrictions, only one manager of Mercedes-Benz Argentina had to face charges in Germany as an accessory to murder. In contrast to other European countries, German criminal law does not provide for corporate liability. Thus, like in the Nuremberg Trials,[39] the only actors who can face charges are individuals whose direct involvement in crimes, including in the form of aiding and abetting, is proven. This has serious disadvantages where a business cooperated with a repressive regime, but where evidence for the involvement of individuals cannot be produced. The public prosecutor of Buenos Aires used this as an argument for suspending proceedings against leading Mercedes-Benz employees.[40] In Germany, because the relevant crimes had been committed before the Rome Statute took effect, criminal accusations had to be based on murder rather than crimes against humanity in the form of forced disappearances, which did not adequately reflect the injustice and complexity of the crimes.

A significant side effect of the litigation in Germany was the formation in Argentina of a group of former Mercedes-Benz unionists[41]—which shows how important legal proceedings can be, regardless of their outcome. This group ensured that the events of 1976–1977 became known in Argentina;

36 Kaleck, n.6, pp.66–67.
37 *Ibid.*, pp.66–69.
38 *Ibid.*, pp.66–67.
39 See, for example, the *Farben* case, *United States v Carl Krauch, et al.*, Law Reports of Trials of War Criminals, Vol.X, 1949, p.52.
40 Kaleck, n.6, pp.66–67.
41 *Ibid.*, pp.69–70.

organized the installation of memorial plaques in places where disappearances had occurred; and, in 2002, filed a lawsuit with the Public Prosecutor's Office in Buenos Aires. On the basis of evidence established by the La Plata truth tribunal, Mercedes-Benz Argentina, the politician Carlos Ruckauf, the corrupt union SMATA, and the military were accused of having constituted a criminal enterprise that aimed to kidnap and murder undesired unionists. After five years of investigations, the prosecution concluded that certain leading figures of Mercedes and SMATA had had knowledge of the crimes. Nevertheless, it could not establish sufficient evidence. At this point, the proceedings were transferred to the Federal Court of San Martín in the province of Buenos Aires because the abductions had been committed in the area of the court's jurisdiction. The same court has jurisdiction over cases of persecution of workers' council members of the Ford factory in Pacheco. But investigations in both cases have practically come to a standstill. In a last move, unionists' lawyers requested that the proceedings be transferred to the more active Federal Court of Buenos Aires.[42]

It is noteworthy that in none of the cases of persecuted unionists at Mercedes, Ford, and Ledesma were accusations raised against accomplices within the companies. To the extent that criminal trials and convictions took place, they concentrated on the direct perpetrators—that is, military and police officers. This is partially due to the fact that the courts handling these cases, the federal courts in San Martín and Jujuy, are infamous for their tendency to reduce all proceedings to a minimum. But one could also suspect political motives behind this. Although the federal government is generally committed to seeking justice for past crimes, its attitude toward corporate complicity may be more lax out of fear of hampering these companies' economic activities.

Nevertheless, these cases helped initiate a debate on the role of civil and economic actors in the crimes of the regime. In 2004, a group of relatives and surviving unionists filed a civil lawsuit in the United States against DaimlerChrysler AG, requesting compensation for the victims of gross human rights violations committed by the company. While the court of first instance regarded the claim as inadmissible, the appeal court allowed the proceedings to continue[43] which was a remarkable success for the plaintiffs, even though it remained open whether and how the court would address the substantive issues involved.

Claiming compensation and punitive damages in civil proceedings in the United States is thus seen as an alternative way of dealing with extraterritorial human rights violations—and as a complement to criminal proceedings,

42 See the website of investigative journalist Gaby Weber for further information, www.gabyweber.com/prozesse_mba.php.

43 *Bauman v DaimlerChrysler Corp*, 644 F.3d 909 (9th Circuit, 2011).

which are the principal legal remedy in Europe. However, civil litigation is often a lengthy process, sometimes lasting for more than ten years. Furthermore, even in the few cases in which defendants have been ordered to pay damages, these orders have rarely been implemented. Such proceedings should therefore be regarded merely as a supplement to criminal proceedings that are taking place in other countries. Nevertheless, the value of civil litigation should not be underestimated—for example, it can serve to pressure a company to reach an out-of-court settlement with the plaintiffs in order to avoid negative press coverage and reputational harm that might be triggered as a result of the proceedings. The US Supreme Court decision in *Kiobel v Royal Dutch Petroleum Co.* of 17 April 2013, which severely restricts the extraterritorial application of the Alien Tort Statute (ATS)[44] and accordingly limits jurisdiction of US courts in cases of gross human rights violations that occurred outside of the US, is thus highly regrettable.

After focusing for many years on the prosecution of direct perpetrators of torture and disappearances, Argentinian human rights organizations are now undergoing a paradigm shift. This has become apparent in the rising number of organized events and debates that question the roles of civil and economic actors under the country's authoritarian rule. It is also reflected in the fact that the former regime is now often referred to as a civic-military regime. In addition, this paradigm shift is evident in new types of criminal proceedings that human rights organizations are bringing against economic actors. An interesting example relates to Ledesma's involvement in the regime's crimes in the province of Jujuy. Two Ledesma executives—Pedro Blaquier, long-term company manager, and Alberto Lemos, former executive director—have been formally summoned to court hearings.[45] In August 2012, the prosecutor requested the detention of Blaquier.[46]

Nestlé in Colombia and Switzerland

Colombia is home to one of the highest levels of attacks on unionists in the world, accounting for half of unionist murders worldwide.[47] Over the last 25 years, about 2,500 unionists have been murdered in Colombia.[48] By far,

44 2013 WL 1628935. For a discussion see chapter 3 of this book.

45 See European Center for Constitutional and Human Rights, Press Release, 'Argentine managers summoned for questioning on complicity in dictatorship-era crimes', 15 May 2012, www.ecchr.de/index.php/argentina_cases/articles/case-against-argentinian-sugar-company-ledesma.html.

46 A. Dandan, 'Nuevas pruebas y pedido de detención para Blaquier', *Pagina 12*, 12 August 2012, www.pagina12.com.ar/diario/elpais/1-200942-2012-08-13.html.

47 IACHR, *Second Report on the Situation of Human Rights Defenders in the Americas*, OEA/Ser.L/V/II, 31 December 2011, para.262; EscuelaNacionalSindical (ENS), *2.515 o esa siniestra facilidad para olvidar*, Ediciones ENS, Medellin, 2007, p.11, www.ens.org.co/aa/img_upload/45bdec76fa6b8848acf029430d10bb5a/cuaderno_19.pdf.

48 *Ibid.*, p.11.

the majority of these killings occur at the hands of paramilitary and state security forces. At the same time, the level of impunity is high. Regardless of the efforts to demobilize paramilitaries between 2003 and 2006, unionists are still being threatened and killed by paramilitaries, and they continue to be victims of killings and arbitrary prosecutions by state security forces. Amnesty International suspects a coordinated strategy of military and paramilitary forces that aims to undermine the work of unions by means of threats and public defamations.[49] These strategically planned and wide-reaching attacks against unionists constitute massive human rights violations and international crimes.

The government of Colombia is either unable or unwilling to protect unionists adequately. Even after repeated interventions of the Inter-American Commission on Human Rights,[50] the government failed to take the requested steps to protect threatened unionists.[51] An emblematic case is the murder of unionist Luciano Romero who, on 10 September 2005, was murdered by paramilitaries. Romero had been working for the Nestlé subsidiary Cicolac for several years.[52]

Legal investigations of this crime are underway in Colombia, and five lower-level paramilitary members have been convicted of murder.[53] In addition, investigations and criminal proceedings have been initiated against other paramilitaries, as well as informants and members of the former Colombian secret service, DAS (Departamento Administrativo de Seguridad).[54] In one of the rulings in this case, justice Nirio Sánchez ordered the prosecution to investigate the company's role. He suggested that the proceedings:

> revealed that the deceased had been preparing to testify about the practices of the transnational corporation Nestlé Cicolac in front of the Permanent People's Tribunal in Bern, Switzerland which was to take place from 29 to 30 of October 2005. And [it was furthermore revealed] that under similar circumstances union leaders of Sinaltrainal and former

49 Amnesty International (AI), *Colombia: Killings, arbitrary detentions, and death threats – the reality of trade unionism in Colombia*, London, July 2007, p.3, www.amnesty.org/es/library/info/AMR23/001/2007.

50 The Inter-American Commission on Human Rights has granted precautionary measures in favour of several trade unionists, *Precautionary measures of Marta Cecilia Díaz Suárez and María Mancilla Gamboa-ASTEMP*, 22 September 2006, www.cidh.org/medidas/2006.eng.htm; *Precautionary measures in favour of Francisco Eladio Ramírez Cuellar,* 29 October 2004, www.cidh.org/medidas/2004.eng.htm; *Precautionary measures in favour of Álvaro Vélez Carriazo et al.,* 19 May 2004, www.cidh.org/medidas/2004.eng.htm.

51 AI, n.49, pp.15–16.

52 *Ibid.*, pp.40–41.

53 European Center for Constitutional and Human Rights (ECCHR), *Special Newsletter on the Criminal Complaint Against Nestle in the Case of the Murdered Colombian Trade Unionist Luciano Romero*, 6 March 2012, p.6, www.ecchr.de/index.php/nestle-518.html.

54 *Ibid.*

> Cicolac workers, namely Victor Mieles, Alejandro Martinez Toribio de la Hoz and Harry Laguna, were murdered.[55]

Investigations against employees of the Colombian company have not progressed since 2007.[56] Because the investigations that took place in Colombia did not include questions regarding the criminal liability of actors in Switzerland, this question has now been raised in criminal accusations placed with the Swiss criminal investigation authority in order to instigate an investigation of the responsibility of the Swiss parent company.[57]

In order to fill the gap in domestic Colombian investigations, in March 2012, the European Center for Constitutional and Human Rights and the Colombian union Sinaltrainal filed a criminal complaint against Nestlé AG and several of its leading figures before the Public Prosecutor's Office in Zug, Switzerland.[58] The defendants are accused of having negligently caused Romero's death by omission. As managers, it was their duty to act to prevent the crimes. Romero's murder took place in the context of an armed conflict in which unionists and other social groups were subject to systematic persecution by paramilitary and state forces. In the years prior to his murder, local Nestlé representatives wrongly defamed Romero for being a guerrilla combatant. In Colombia, such defamations can be tantamount to a death sentence. Furthermore, local Nestlé representatives were linked to paramilitary circles on several levels. Nestlé received supplies from landowners who closely collaborated with the paramilitaries. There is also evidence suggesting that the local subsidiary made payments to the paramilitaries. The Swiss management knew about the risky behavior of its Colombia-based executives and about the corresponding dangers for the subsidiary's unionists. It nevertheless remained inactive, claiming that these issues had been delegated to the responsibility of the Colombian subsidiary.

Whether the investigations will result in criminal charges depends on the quality of the investigations and on the legal stance taken by the prosecution. Although regulations on corporate liability have entered into force as part of Swiss criminal law, they have not yet been applied in practice, let alone in cases of extraterritorial human rights violations. Corporate liability according to article 102(1) of the Swiss Criminal Code is clearly distinct from common criminal concepts. It is an offense against the administration of justice and is relevant only if the crime was perpetrated from within a company in which there is no identifiable individual who can be held to account. Often, individuals cannot be identified due to a lack of organization, surveillance, or

55 Criminal Court of the District of Bogota, Judgment in proceedings against Jose Ustariz Acuna and Jonathan David Contrera Puella, 26 November 2007, p.106 cont.

56 ECCHR, n.53, pp.6–7.

57 *Ibid.*

58 *Ibid.*

documentation. Thus, the company is punished for lack of organization rather than for the crime perpetrated.[59] The justification for punishment in such cases is not the company's responsibility to prevent crimes but rather its responsibility not to hinder criminal investigations, which means that even where a sentence accrues, it cannot adequately reflect the gravity of the crime.

Regardless of the outcome of these criminal proceedings, human rights organizations that supported the Swiss litigation hope that the analysis of corporate behavior according to criminal law standards will contribute to the development of human rights standards for corporate activity in regions of armed conflict or in weak states. The significance of the criminal proceedings around Romero's death thus goes beyond providing justice in the individual case. Rather, the proceedings will support multinational corporations active in regions of armed conflict or in weak states with regard to the necessary risk assessment. At the same time, they will contribute to further defining the *corporate responsibility to respect*, as postulated by the former SRSG in the UN Guiding Principles.[60]

Conclusion

The opportunities for strategic lawsuits that seek to enforce human rights have improved considerably in the last two decades. Human rights organizations from around the world have pressed criminal charges against perpetrators of human rights violations before European, US, and other courts.

Máximo Langer, an Argentinian legal academic, closely studied the outcome of approximately 1,000 criminal proceedings conducted in different European countries according to the principle of universal jurisdiction. He concluded that only proceedings with low political costs—that is, Nazi crimes, crimes in former Yugoslavia, and crimes in the African continent—resulted in convictions.[61] The decision of the US Supreme Court in *Kiobel*, however, constitutes an important drawback, in severely restricting

59 This solution is satisfactory only in part, for it continues to view individual criminal liability as the norm. Large companies often operate in a decentralized manner and with divided tasks. This allows companies to escape criminal liability by appointing nominal directors who do not actually attend to any managerial tasks of their division. They do, however, take responsibility in criminal proceedings in order to unburden the company as a whole. Those nominal directors are then financially compensated for any inconvenience occurring in the course of the proceedings.

60 J. Ruggie, Report of the Special Representative of the Secretary-General on the Issue of Human Rights and Transnational Corporations and Other Business Enterprises, *Guiding Principles on Business and Human Rights: Implementing the United Nations "Protect, Respect and Remedy" Framework*, U.N. Doc. A/HRC/17/31, 21 March 2011, principle 11.

61 M. Langer, 'The diplomacy of universal jurisdiction: the political branches and the transnational prosecution of international crimes', 105 *American Journal of International Law* 1–49 (2011).

the possibility of suing corporations under the ATS for gross human rights violations where this would involve the exercise of extraterritorial jurisdiction.[62]

Criminal and civil proceedings against corporations for complicity in human rights violations face both practical and legal difficulties. Political interventions in favor of the accused companies constitute another challenge. All these problems can be observed in the cases discussed in this chapter. Unlike most of the crimes perpetrated by state actors, the events of the 1970s at the Mercedes-Benz factory are not documented. Other evidence is difficult to obtain due to the long period of time that has passed since then. This is complemented by insufficient legal regulations to deal with these questions in countries such as Germany and the United States, where related legal challenges have therefore failed. However, it might have been possible to overcome the legal problems raised by this type of litigation—just as it would potentially be possible to overcome them now in the United States and Argentina, where cases are currently pending—if the economic power of the defendant companies did not have an impact on proceedings.

Nevertheless, the experiences of the aforementioned cases demonstrate that the judicial outcome is not the only measure of these cases' success. Documentation and reporting of the cases established a new narrative in German, Argentinian, and Latin American societies. This new narrative goes beyond the previous human rights mainstream. Often, an important and necessary first step toward ending impunity is to investigate cases of direct involvement in human rights violations. After the eventual establishment of a narrative and jurisdiction that accepts the occurrence of human rights violations as a fact, it is then reasonable to inquire into the political and legal responsibility of economic and political actors. The authoritarian rule in Argentina and Chile ended a long time ago, and the main actors were no longer in power when the judicial inquiry of past crimes began. However, legal proceedings in Europe, and later in the transitional countries themselves, can serve as models for human rights organizations and prosecutors all over the world. In Argentina and Colombia, the dynamics of criminal proceedings led to public discussions, academic research, and artistic engagement with the topic. In the course of these discussions, people also began to inquire into the underlying reasons for the regime's ruthless activities. The proceedings also contributed to a reorganization of unions, which presents another form of coming to terms with the past.

62 *Kiobel v Royal Dutch Petroleum Co.*, 2013 WL 1628935.

Chapter 10

Another Brick in the Uruguayan Transition

Financial Complicity

*Juan Pablo Bohoslavsky**

Introduction

One of the thorniest questions for the transitional justice community has been whether and to what extent economic factors of past atrocities should be incorporated into the transitional justice universe (be it for interpreting and dealing with the past[1] or for including social and economic rights in the transitional agenda).[2]

Within this debate, there is one particularly underdeveloped area: the role of lenders in supporting criminal regimes. While arguments for holding lenders—private, bilateral, and multilateral—accountable for complicity because of their substantial contribution to criminal regimes are being explored,[3] tailored avenues for channeling this type of accountability within the context of transitional justice have yet to be developed.

Deepening the analysis of this financial dimension of gross human rights violations would further the understanding of the causal link between finance and human rights violations, render it more visible, and assist with elaborating

* The author wishes to thank the following individuals for commenting on drafts of this chapter and sharing materials: Paola Azar, Jorge Errandonea, Louise Mallinder, Aldo Marchesi, Vania Markarian, Sabine Michalowski, Jorge Notaro, Mariana Rulli, Thomas Scheetz, and Jaime Yaffé. He also wishes to thank Gabriel Delacoste for his research assistance and Carla Bellota from the UN Office at Geneva Library for her efficiency and dedication. A longer version of this chapter has been published in Spanish in 21 (2) *Revista Uruguaya de Ciencia Política* 153–179 (2012). The views and conclusions reflected in this chapter are those of the author alone and are in no way intended to reflect the views of any of the institutions with which the author is affiliated.

1 J. Barnard-Naudé, 'For Justice and Reconciliation to Come: The TRC Archive, Big Business and the Demand for Material Reparations', in F. du Bois and A. du Bois-Pedain (eds), *Justice and Reconciliation in Post-Apartheid South Africa*, Cambridge University Press, Cambridge, 2008 (172–205).

2 L. Arbour, 'Economic and Social Justice for Societies in Transition', 40 *Journal of International Law and Politics* 1–28 (2007–8); D. Sharp (ed.), *Justice and Economic Violence in Transition*, Springer, Springer Publications, New York, 2013 (forthcoming).

3 See S. Michalowski, 'No complicity liability for funding gross human rights violations?' 30 *Berkeley Journal of International Law* 451–524 (2012).

adequate legal answers in a context of transitional justice. All of these seem to contribute to the transitional justice goals of creating a narrative, establishing justice, providing reparations, and achieving deterrence.

Given both the theoretical complexity and the important practical implications of these issues, they are best explored in the context of a case study. To this end, the experience of the Uruguayan dictatorship (1973–1984) is a goldmine: it offers a scenario of gross human rights violations in contravention of *ius cogens* norms,[4] an active role played by lenders during the dictatorship, and accessible data on public debt and military expenditures.[5] Moreover, the country's transitional justice mechanisms are still in progress, as the President revoked the administrative resolutions that impeded investigating and prosecuting the criminals[6] and the Amnesty Act was annulled by Statute, though the Supreme Court held this Act to be unconstitutional, a decision questioned by the Inter-American Court of Human Rights.[7]

This chapter adopts a holistic approach to analyzing the link between massive human rights violations and sovereign finance. Such an approach requires considering not only micro-relations (such as those established between death squadrons, their funders, and the victims) but also the more general structures, processes, and dynamics of the authoritarian regime. Hence, this case study considers political, social, economic, financial, and budgetary features of the Uruguayan dictatorship in order to shed light on whether and how lenders assisted this regime, and whether they should be subject to transitional justice mechanisms based on the notion of responsibility for complicity.[8]

To this end, the chapter begins by exploring the political context of the Uruguayan dictatorship, the seriousness and volume of the crimes perpetrated during this period, and public knowledge about these abuses. The following section analyzes Uruguay's macroeconomic performance during those years, paying particular attention to lenders' role in politically and economically supporting the regime, thereby facilitating its capacity to buy loyalties and repress the population. Because military expenditures are at the core of the regime's repressive policies, special consideration is paid to

4 Inter-American Court of Human Rights, *Gelman v Uruguay*, Merits and Reparations, Judgment, 24 February 2011, Series C No.221, paras.75, 99, 183 and 223.

5 *Ibid.*

6 Consejo de Ministros N°323, 30 June 2011, www.presidencia.gub.uy/wps/wcm/connect/presidencia/portalpresidencia/comunicacion/comunicacionnoticias/presidencia-remitio-suprema-corte-justicia-resolucion-revocatoria.

7 Act N°18.831, 27 October 2011, derogating the Amnesty Act N°15.848 passed on 28 December 1986. Supreme Court of Justice of Uruguay, M.L., J.F.F., O. – Denuncia – Excepción de inconstitucionalidad Arts. 1, 2 y 3 de la Ley N° 18.831, 22 February 2013. IACHR, *Gelman v Uruguay*, Supervisión de Cumplimiento de Sentencia. Resolución de la Corte Interamericana de Derechos Humanos, 20 March 2013.

8 J.P. Bohoslavsky and V. Opgenhaffen, 'The Past and Present of Bank Responsibility for Financing the Argentinian Dictatorship', 23 *Harvard Human Rights Journal* 157–203 (2010), p.160.

their budgetary evolution. Thereafter, the chapter explains the United States' position toward the Uruguayan dictatorship, focusing on US policies tying aid to human rights considerations. It then goes on to explore the absence of financial complicity considerations in the transitional justice measures taken in Uruguay since 1985 and proposes some specific transitional justice mechanisms for further discussion. The last section presents concluding remarks on the Uruguayan challenge of dealing with economic accomplices.

Political context: seriousness, volume, and public knowledge of the crimes

During the 1960s and 1970s, several countries in the Southern Cone suffered military coups and dictatorships. These regimes arose in Brazil in 1964, in Argentina in 1966 and 1976, and in Uruguay and Chile in 1973.[9]

During the first half of the twentieth century, Uruguay enjoyed consistent democratic rule and economic prosperity. It was also integrated as a society,[10] which is why the country was often referred to as the "Switzerland of the Americas."[11] However, in the early sixties, the breakdown of the import-substituting industrialization model, a deep economic crisis, and a loss of real income prompted new social conflicts and political tensions.[12] Violence became part of Uruguayan political life long before the coup in 1973, beginning during the 1960s and reaching extreme levels in 1971 and 1972. This spiral of violence, along with the increasing radicalization of political groups, set the stage for the coup.

The military sector became progressively involved in Uruguayan political life, particularly the fight against the guerrillas.[13] By 1973, military forces had defeated the armed revolutionary groups,[14] but nevertheless remained in the political scenario, implementing their own agenda[15] and using the "left threat" as an argument to implement a national security doctrine.

9 G. O'Donnell, 'Reflections on the Patterns of Change in the Bureaucratic-Authoritarian State', 13(1) *Latin American Research Review* 3–38 (1978), p.6.

10 M. Prats, 'Uruguay', in AA.VV., *Las víctimas y la justicia transicional. ¿Están cumpliendo los Estados Latinoamericanos con los estándares internacionales?*, Fundación para el Debido Proceso Legal, Washington, D.C., 2010, p.219.

11 H. Daly, 'The Uruguayan Economy: Its Basic Nature and Current Problems', 7 *Journal of Inter-American Studies* 316–330 (1965).

12 See generally H. Finch, *A Political Economy of Uruguay since 1870*, St. Martin's Press, New York, 1981, pp.220 and 246; G. Varela Petito, 'El golpe de Estado 1973, revisitado', in A. Marchesi *et al.*, *El presente de la dictadura. Estudios y reflexiones a 30 años del golpe de Estado en Uruguay*, Ed. Trilce, Montevideo, 2003, p.91.

13 W. Heinz and H. Fruhling, *Determinants of Gross Human Rights Violations by State and State-Sponsored Actors in Brazil, Uruguay, Chile, and Argentina (1960–1990)*, Kluwer Law International, The Hague, 1999, p.255.

14 C. Demasi, 'Un repaso a la teoría de los dos demonios', in A. Marchesi *et al.*, n.12, p.67.

15 Prats, n.10, p.220.

The civic-military government committed massive human rights violations, including illegal detentions, torture, disappearances, extrajudicial executions, and assassinations.[16] Between 1973 and 1984, at least 116 people were assassinated for political reasons. Most of these victims were murdered in Uruguay, while 25 were killed in Argentina and one in Chile.[17] Even with its limited inquisitive powers and scope,[18] Uruguay's Commission for Peace (COMPAZ), created in 2000, proved 172 cases of detained-disappeared.[19] The Commission found that arrests took place not only in Uruguay but also in Argentina, Bolivia, Chile, and Colombia, confirming the effectiveness of *Plan Cóndor*, a repressive agreement among the dictatorships of the Southern Cone.[20] An estimated 250,000 Uruguayans (around 14 per cent of the population) emigrated due to a combination of economic, social, and political reasons between 1972 and 1980, while the number of politically exiled persons between 1973 and 1977 is estimated between 28,000 and 62,000.[21]

According to the *Nunca Más* report published by the NGO Servicio Paz y Justicia (SERPAJ), during the dictatorship, 4,933 people were arrested and imprisoned for political reasons and subjected to legal processes, while 3,700 were arrested and imprisoned without any legal process. Ninety-nine per cent of the prisoners interviewed by SERPAJ had been tortured.[22] In a broader study, the Universidad de la República concluded that at least 5,925 political prisoners were being held in state prisons, while 67 babies were born in jail.[23] During those years, it was public knowledge that Uruguay had the highest per capita ratio of political detainees in Latin America[24] (50,000–60,000 victims out of 2.9 million inhabitants).[25]

16 Heinz and Fruhling, n.13, p.283.

17 Universidad de la República, *Investigación histórica sobre la dictadura y el terrorismo de Estado en el Uruguay (1973–1985)*, Ed. Cruz del Sur-Tradinco-CEIU, Montevideo, 2008.

18 J. Errandonea, 'Justicia transicional en Uruguay', 40 *Revista Instituto Interamericano de Derechos Humanos* 13–69 (2008), p.40; E. Skaar, 'Legal Development and Human Rights in Uruguay: 1985–2000', 8 *Human Rights Review* 52–70 (2007), p.60.

19 Comisión para la Paz, *Informe Final*, 10 April 2003.

20 See generally P. McSherry, *Predatory States*, Rowman & Littlefield Publishers, Lanham, 2005.

21 C. Aguiar, 'La migración de uruguayos a la Argentina', 1 *Revista Ciencias Sociales* 23 (1986).

22 Servicio de Paz y Justicia (SERPAJ), *Uruguay: Nunca Más. Informe sobre la violación a los derechos humanos (1972–1985)*, Montevideo, 1989.

23 Universidad de la República, n.17, pp.22 and 39.

24 See US Department of State, *Report on Human Rights Practices in Countries Receiving U.S. Aid*, submitted to the Committee on Foreign Relations, US Senate, and Committee on Foreign Affairs, US House of Representatives, 8 February 1979, p.334; Foreign Affairs and National Defense Division, Congressional Research Service, *The Status of the Human Rights in Selected Countries and the U.S. Response*, prepared for the Subcommittee on International Organizations of the Committee on International Relations, US House of Representatives, 25 July 1977, p.62.

25 Heinz and Fruhling, n.13, p.283.

While such crimes contributed to spreading terror among Uruguayans, the civic-military government tried to control and organize society according to its own political objectives. The suffocating penetration of military power into all aspects of social and personal life meant that universities, labor unions, political parties, student organizations, mass media, cultural activities, religious activities, and family relationships (even abroad) were dramatically affected.[26] This situation has been described as "the closest approximation in South America of the Orwellian totalitarian state."[27]

Linking macroeconomics, finance, military expenditures, and human rights abuses

To remain in power and carry out a massive campaign of human rights violations, an authoritarian government must be capable of implementing policies that secure a minimum level of political support or enable the repressive machinery to function efficiently in order to control and repress.[28] Financial resources are therefore necessary to sustain this policy for a certain period. In a context of fiscal deficit and a deteriorating national economy, a regime's options for funding are reduced, rendering the procurement of financiers even more critical for the regime (and with important implications for those who suffer under it).[29]

Economy and the purchase of loyalties

The economic stagnation suffered by Uruguay after 1955 prompted a range of measures.[30] Devaluation, fiscal deficit, and external indebtedness were the first official reactions, but they naturally fueled high inflation. In an attempt to stop this vicious circle, the government took some interventionist measures

26 See especially Universidad de la República, n.17, volumes II and III; Inter-American Court of Human Rights, *Informe sobre la situación de los Derechos Humanos en Uruguay*, OEA/Ser.L/V/II.43, 31 January 1978; Amnesty International, *Latin America*, 11 February 1977, XI (6).

27 Lawyers Committee for International Human Rights, *The Generals Give Back Uruguay: A Report on Human Rights*, New York, 1985.

28 On this trade-off between loyalty and repression, see generally B. Bueno de Mesquita, A. Smith, R. Siverson and J. Morrow, *The Logic of Political Survival*, MIT Press, Cambridge, MA, 2003. Elaborating on rational choices of authoritarian regimes and financial complicity, see J.P. Bohoslavsky, 'Tracking Down the Missing Financial Link in Transitional Justice', 1 *International Human Rights Law Review* 54–92 (2012); J.P. Bohoslavsky and A. Escriba-Folch, 'Rational Choice and Financial Complicity with Human Rights Abuses: Policy and Legal Implications', in J.P. Bohoslavsky and J. Cernic (eds), *Making Sovereign Financing & Human Rights Work*, Hart Publishing, Oxford, 2013 (forthcoming).

29 On the internal political role of the financial assistance received by the Brazilian dictatorship (1964–84), and its current legal implications, see J.P. Bohoslavsky and M. Torelly, 'Financial Complicity: The Brazilian Dictatorship under the *Macroscope*', in Sharp, n.2.

30 Heinz and Fruhling, n.13, p.231.

after 1968.[31] By 1971, however, its counter-inflationary strategy had failed, and during the first months of 1972 Uruguay was unable to repay its debt in foreign currency.[32] As a result of the country's poor economic performance, competition among social groups to maintain their real income levels intensified, resulting in political violence.[33]

The economic plan designed by President Bordaberry in 1972 had a clear neoliberal profile, with restrictive monetarist policies, salary limitations, fiscal policies aimed at reducing the public deficit, exchange measures to reduce inflation, broad trade and financial openness, incentives for hosting foreign direct investments, and promotion of traditional agro products exports.[34] Because the coup was launched in 1973 by a constitutional president with military support,[35] these policies continued after the coup.

Uruguay's neoliberal economic policies attached significant importance to exports and public sector demand,[36] provoking a transfer of resources from the wage-earning (workers) and passive sector (pensioners) to capital owners. These resources were distributed among domestic corporations through an array of instruments, which helped the regime, in its first years, build a solid base of political and social support.[37] This corporate support translated into a general backing of the economic plan implemented from 1974 onward.[38]

31 Such as wage and price freeze, J. Notaro, 'Estrategia de desarrollo, política económica y actores sociales. Uruguay 1968–1984', 9 *Boletín de Historia Económica* 31–40 (2010), p.32.

32 J. Notaro, 'La batalla que ganó la economía. 1972–1984', in R. Bertoni *et al.*, *El Uruguay del siglo XX. La Economía*, Instituto de Economía – Ediciones de la Banda Oriental, Montevideo, 2003, p.104.

33 Finch, n.12, p.235.

34 L. Faroppa, *Política para una economía desequilibrada: Uruguay 1958–1951*, Ediciones de la Banda Oriental, Montevideo, 1982.

35 A. Rico, 'Sobre el autoritarismo y el golpe de Estado. La dictadura y el dictador', in C. Demasi *et al.*, *La dictadura cívico militar. Uruguay 1973–1985*, Ediciones de la Banda Oriental, Montevideo, 2009, p.206.

36 H. Finch, 'El régimen militar y la clase dominante en Uruguay', in AA.VV. (various authors), *Uruguay y la democracia*, volume II, Ediciones de la Banda Oriental, Montevideo, 1985, p.79.

37 J. Notaro, *La política económica en el Uruguay (1968–1984)*, Ediciones de la Banda Oriental, Montevideo, 1984, p.94. See, for example, the speech given by the de facto president Bordaberry in 1975 addressed to the president of the Chamber of Industries, stating that, "the Chamber of Industries, under your presidency, has been and is a main actor and a preponderant factor in this work and this opportunity is favorable to highlight it," 'Bordaberry: La industria debe crecer hacia afuera', *El Diario*, 12 November 1975. Along this same vein, in a 1974 interview, the president of the Chamber of Industries explained that "the economic policy of minister Vegh Villegas is what allowed that abroad we are seen with other eyes. There is trust, therefore, more loans are gotten," *La Mañana*, 13 November 1974.

38 G. Caetano, 'Partidos, Estado y cámaras empresariales en el Uruguay contemporáneo (1900–1991)', in AA.VV., *Organizaciones empresariales y políticas públicas*, CIESU-FESUR, Montevideo, 1992, p.36; Notaro, *ibid.*, pp.94–95.

The massive entrance of foreign capital helped finance more imports and investments, which translated into moderate economic growth for the country.[39] This phenomenon went hand in hand with a huge increase in sovereign external indebtedness and a wide structural trade deficit. In the labor sector, the effects of the regime's repression were notable: in both the private and public sectors, real wages fell considerably during the dictatorship.[40]

The financial aid received by Uruguay provided the necessary funds to implement an aggressive policy of subsidies, fiscal privileges, and credit advantages to specific areas of the industrial sector and to primary producers.[41] The political support that the regime obtained in exchange for promoting greater industrial development helped moderate social discontent while the regime carried out a broad repressive campaign.[42] Here, it is useful to remember that 1973–1980, the period in which these economic policies were implemented, were also the bloodiest years of the dictatorship.

In 1978, the civic-military government began making efforts to control inflation, implementing a rigid scheme (known as *la tablita*) of periodical preannouncements of the rate of nominal devaluation. At the same time, the deregulation of Uruguay's financial system and its international trade, and the extensive dollarization of the economy were deepened.[43] This new policy resulted in fewer profits for industrial and raw material exporters, as well as lower internal economic demand, which eventually led to an internal, and later external, financial crisis.[44] With the higher cost of credit and the drop in sales, primary exporters gradually began to suffer.

Capital flight and the 1982 crisis unleashed the system's structural flaws, which caused a worsening of the country's unemployment rate, fiscal deficit, indebtedness, and GDP. Devaluation was then a logical consequence. In the midst of this crisis, the government's main goal was to keep the financial system afloat: this explains why the Central Bank of Uruguay bailed out

39 Banco Central del Uruguay, *Boletín Estadístico*, Montevideo, 1970–1990, www.bcu.gub.uy.

40 W. Cancela and A. Melgar, *El desarrollo frustrado*, Centro Latinoamericano de Economía Humana- Ediciones de la Banda Oriental (CLAEH-EBO), Montevideo, 1986, p.17.

41 Finch, n.36, p.78.

42 In 1976, the president of the Chamber of Industries stated that "the eloquence of the figures reflect not only the dynamism in the industrial sector but also, I must say, the support of the national government through incentives to exports, reimbursements, pre-financing and financing of exports, approval of the industrial promotion act, etc., . . . jointly with the labor peace reached, were the decisive factors to build the very much needed trust in the industrial sector . . . Our motto: active industry, prosperous country", 'Manderini: se ha creado conciencia exportadora de magníficos frutos', *La Mañana*, 12 November 1976.

43 J. Yaffé, 'Proceso económico y política económica durante la dictadura (1973–1984)', in C. Demasi, n.35, p.130.

44 Notaro, n.32, p.110.

national and foreign banks, buying their non-collectable credits for US$1.141 million.[45] Economic stagnation, inflation, and the financial crisis eroded the limited social support enjoyed by the military government, creating favorable conditions for a democratic transition.[46]

The wane in public support for the regime started to become evident with the national referendum of 1980, in which the civic-military government received only 41.9 per cent of the vote.[47] By 1984, this loss of support was undeniable: a broad social, political, and economic coalition (*Comisión Nacional Programática*) representing all but the military and banking sectors began to demand a democratic exit.

Political and economic role of external financial aid

What role did external financial assistance play in strengthening and stabilizing the Uruguayan regime and facilitating an effective repressive apparatus to perpetrate the crimes? Answering this question requires a macroeconomic analysis.[48] Such an analysis should consider the volume of loans in proportion to national economic performance, the country's financial dependency on foreign aid, and the economic instruments used by the government to buy loyalties. Public finance, which influences a range of social and economic actors across the country and, more specifically, military expenditures, which arguably have a more direct effect on human rights violations, should also be part of this analysis. The budget and the repressive apparatus will reflect, to some extent, the regime's repressive capacities and policies.

Because Uruguay's trade balance and fiscal account were negative during almost the entire dictatorship, an alternative financial source was necessary; this was found in the inflow of international capital, which massively financed the Uruguayan economy (see tables 10.1 and 10.2).[49] Public indebtedness helped implement a monetarist policy,[50] keep the financial system flowing, secure a minimum political support for the regime,[51] and finance

45 Yaffé, n.43, p.135.

46 S. Haggard and R. Kaufman, *The Political Economy of Democratic Transitions*, Princeton University Press, Princeton, 1995, p.95; Notaro, n.32, p.104.

47 G. Caetano and J. Rilla, *Historia Contemporánea del Uruguay: de la colonia al siglo XXI*, Editorial Fin de Siglo, Montevideo, 2005, p.560.

48 Bohoslavsky, n.28.

49 Yaffé, n.43, p.107.

50 In other words, the economy's performance is determined almost entirely by changes in the money supply.

51 See Yaffé, n.43, p.122.

Table 10.1 Debt stock evolution (US$ millions)[52]

	1971	*1973*	*1975*	*1977*	*1979*	*1981*	*1983*	*1985*
Public debt stock (including undisbursed)	363	469	1,034	1,205	1,416	1,931	3,066	3,287
Private nonguaranteed debt	29	31	52	83	185	326	158	60

Table 10.2 Principal ratios[53]

	1971	*1973*	*1975*	*1977*	*1979*	*1981*	*1983*	*1985*
Debt outstanding and disbursed/GNP (%)	10.6	11.9	17.8	17.9	13.2	12	49.5	55.5
Debt outstanding and disbursed/exports of goods and services (%)	137.2	93.1	135.4	104.8	72.9	73	170.3	200.3

Table 10.3 Composition of Uruguay's public debt (US$ millions)[54]

	1971	*1973*	*1975*	*1977*	*1979*	*1981*	*1983*	*1985*
Multilateral	113	156	260	241	346	583	601	731
Bilateral	95	165	234	193	153	225	216	193
Private creditors	155	149	540	771	917	1,123	2,249	2,363

public expenditures (including those of the military). The figures in tables 10.1 and 10.2 vividly show the state's increasing financial dependency on external aid, which became crucial for the country's political and economic well-being.

As the figures show, official (both bilateral and multilateral) aid had an active role in financing the Uruguayan state during the first years of the dictatorship. In later years this aid kept on flowing, but its relevance in the Uruguayan finance was gradually superseded by private loans. This is important from a legal perspective, as private lenders' contributions toward the commission of human rights abuses open the door to considerations of corporate responsibility for complicity.[55]

52 World Bank, *World Debt Tables, External Debt of Developing Countries*, several issues, http://data.worldbank.org/.

53 *Ibid.*

54 *Ibid.*

55 See also chapter 3 of this book.

This change in the composition of creditors followed a general tendency in international markets, in which multinational banks played a leading role in sovereign financing due to the phenomenal development of the Eurodollar market and the recycling of petrodollars.

During the dictatorship, public expenditures grew not only in absolute terms but also relatively (15.2 per cent of the GDP in 1973 compared with 20.5 per cent in 1984).[56] These increases were accompanied (except in 1979 and 1980) by a continuous fiscal deficit because the rhythm of the economy did not generate sufficient revenues to cover those expenditures (see discussion in previous subsection). Public indebtedness helped finance public account and commercial deficits.[57]

Interestingly, the Uruguayan dictatorship managed to maintain a budgetary policy that benefited not only broad corporate sectors of the national economy and the international banks but also, very clearly, the military sector. This seems to have allowed the state to carry out a massive campaign of crimes and an effective and overwhelming social control in a context of fiscal deficit, negative trade balance, and low growth rates.[58] In other words, the external financial aid received by the civic-military government provided the funds to buy key loyalties from the domestic elite, thus helping moderate social discontent, and to finance an efficient repression. Due to its central role during the dictatorship, the financial sector was deemed a "new social actor" in Uruguay.[59]

Once the economy was liberalized and subsidies and other state financial incentives were suppressed, borrowing became more expensive and the recession started to spread. From 1980 onward, the industrial and farming sectors gradually left the governmental coalition, and the financial sector took their place. As the crisis would later dramatically show, the financial sector was already playing a leading role in the economic life of the country.

Military expenditures and the repressive apparatus

The physiognomy of state violence and social control had to be in line with the political features and objectives of the Uruguayan civic-military regime. Particularly during the first phase of authoritarianism (1973–1975) and the subsequent trend toward totalitarianism (1975–1978),[60] the state needed an effective and efficient bureaucratic apparatus capable of keeping civil liberties and political opposition under strict control. As with other dictatorships in

56 On state budget and expenditures, see generally P. Azar, M. Bertino, R. Bertoni, S. Fleitas, U. García Repetto, C. Sanguinetti, M. Sienra and M. Torrelli, *¿De quiénes, para quiénes y para qué? Las finanzas públicas de Uruguay en el siglo XX*, Fin de Siglo, Montevideo, 2009.

57 Yaffé, n.43, p.155.

58 Notaro, n.32, p.96; Yaffé, n.43, p.125.

59 Notaro, n.32, p.110.

60 Rico, n.35, p.231.

Latin America, this phenomenon can be observed in the evolution of Uruguay's public budget, specifically its military expenditures.[61]

During the 1960s, military expenditure[62] as a percentage of the GDP was lower than 2 per cent.[63] This ratio rose considerably during the 1970s, alongside the military's increasing role in Uruguayan political life. Military expenditures amounted to 1.9 per cent of the GDP in 1970; 2.4 per cent in 1973; 2.7 per cent in 1978; 4 per cent in 1982; and 2.4 per cent in 1985.[64] This budgetary evolution seems to follow the civic-military government's expectation that increases in defense would increase political stability.[65]

In general, the functions of military expenditures evolve according to the military's role in society.[66] For example, a country whose military sector focuses on domestic stability instead of defense against external aggressions will spend more resources in line with this function. Thus, it is not surprising that while military expenditures as a whole rose during the Uruguayan dictatorship,[67] the budget line for arms imports (linked to the defense of the territory against external aggressions) did not follow this same pattern,[68] indicating that the increased military resources were spent largely on functions related to internal security.

It is also not surprising that the size of the Uruguayan Armed Forces and the Ministry of Defense, in a context of freedom from external aggression, grew continuously during the dictatorship. The armed forces numbered 17,000 in 1970; 25,000 in 1975; 28,000 in 1978; and 30,000 in 1983.[69] In addition, police were closely involved in the repression both before and after the coup, which helps explain why the size of the police force also increased steadily

61 M. Grindle, 'Civil-Military Relations and Budgetary Politics in Latin America', 13 *Armed Forces & Society* 255–275 (1987), p.262; T. Scheetz, 'Gastos militares en Chile, Perú y la Argentina', *Desarrollo Económico* 315–327 (Oct.–Dec. 1985), p.319.

62 According to the Stockholm International Peace Research Institute, these figures in principle include, among other things, expenditures on defense ministries and other governmental agencies engaged in defense projects, current military and civil personnel, operations and maintenance, procurement, military research and development, and military construction. See www.sipri.org/research/armaments/milex/resultoutput/sources_methods/definitions.

63 Stockholm International Peace Research Institute (SIPRI), 'World Armaments and Disarmament', *SIPRI Yearbook*, 1979, p.56.

64 SIPRI, 'World Armaments and Disarmament', *SIPRI Yearbook*, 1980, p.32; 1983, p.174; 1984, p.130; and 1990, p.200.

65 B. Blomberg, 'Growth, Political Instability and the Defense Burden', 63 *Economica* 649–672 (1996), p.649.

66 Grindle, n.61, p.262.

67 SIPRI, 'World Armaments and Disarmament', *SIPRI Yearbook*, 1983, p.174.

68 US Arms Control and Disarmament Agency, *World Military Expenditures and Arms Trade*, 1969–78, p.155; 1972–82, p.91; 1985, p.127; 1987, p.123; and 1988, p.107.

69 US Arms Control and Disarmament Agency, *World Military Expenditures and Arms Trade*, 1988, p.81.

during the 1970s, with a spectacular jump the year after the coup (1974). The number of Ministry of the Interior employees increased from 20,858 in 1970 to 21,661 in 1973 to 24,370 in 1974 and to 25,758 in 1978.[70]

Total public employment rose from 213,000 in 1969 to 241,000 in 1985. Almost all of this increase is accounted for by additions in military and police personnel. Within the central government (excluding *entes autónomos*) the defense and interior ministries accounted for 40 per cent of all positions (almost 43,000 and over 26,000 posts, respectively).[71]

The crimes suffered by Uruguayans implied the reconfiguration of the military sector's fundamental functions, in which internal security became more important than defense against external aggressions. The figures presented above are critical for understanding how the Uruguayan state was able to implement its spending policy, which included the maintenance of a wide, complex, and expensive bureaucratic apparatus in order to carry out the regime's criminal campaign of social and political control. The policy financed, for example, at least 50 centers or barracks in which tens of thousands were detained and tortured during the dictatorship, plus 11 clandestine camps.[72] It is thus not surprising that while in 1971 there were 7.1 military personnel for every 10,000 inhabitants, this ratio reached 10.3 by 1983.[73]

This budgetary expansion of the military sector was made possible in a context of public account and commercial deficits. This financial gap was (temporarily) filled by the provision of foreign currency operationalized through massive loans to the state.

As explained above, in order to better understand how finance and systematic campaigns of human rights abuses can be causally linked, further interdisciplinary analyses must be performed. Future research should consider not only microeconomic data but also macroeconomic data of the country and international markets; internal and external political and institutional processes; the social context; monetary, financial, budgetary, and fiscal policies; the human rights situation; and other relevant facts.

The US position and the recognition of the link between finance and human rights

As in other Latin American countries,[74] as a geopolitical implication of the Cold War and the fight against communism, the United States contributed

70 See Heinz and Fruhling, n.13, p.309.

71 M. Weinstein, *Uruguay: Democracy at the Crossroads*, Westview Press, Boulder and London, 1988, p.100.

72 Universidad de la República, n.17, p.39.

73 US Arms Control and Disarmament Agency, *World Military Expenditures and Arms Trade*, 1985, p.85.

74 M. Esparza, H. Huttenbach and D. Feierstein (eds), *State Violence and Genocide in Latin America: the Cold War Years*, Routledge, Oxford, 2009.

to the development of an authoritarian regime in Uruguay.[75] Militarily, the United States helped the Uruguayan government before the coup in 1973. This aid translated into military training, the sale of weapons and police equipment, intelligence capacity building, and economic aid.[76]

After the coup, Uruguay received mixed signals from the United States due to disagreements between US Congress and the executive branch.[77] Once Jimmy Carter assumed the presidency, human rights were incorporated into US foreign policy. The role played by American representatives and senators, US Assistant Secretary of State for Human Rights Patricia Derian,[78] and private organizations operating in the United States and Europe were key not only to publicizing the human rights abuses perpetrated in Uruguay but also to implementing governmental actions in order to stop these crimes.

After passing new regulations tying economic aid to human rights,[79] the Carter administration applied economic sanctions against regimes with records of gross abuses of human rights.[80] These regulations, coupled with widespread knowledge of Uruguay's human rights abuses,[81] led the secretary of state to announce reductions in US military assistance to Uruguay in 1977.[82] That same year, the United States raised the human rights issue in discussions within international financial institutions, when these institutions were faced with deciding whether to grant loans to Southern Cone authoritarian governments. The United States repeatedly voted against such

75 C. Aldrighi, *El caso Mitrione. La intervención de EEUU en Uruguay, 1965–1973*, Trilce, Montevideo, 2007.

76 Heinz and Fruhling, n.13, pp.313 and 357.

77 K. Sikkink, *Mixed Signals. U.S. Human Rights Policy and Latin America*, Cornell University Press, New York, 2004, p.127.

78 See US Department of State, *Country Reports on Human Rights Practices for 1979 and 1980*, submitted to the Committee on Foreign Relations, US Senate, and Committee of Foreign Affairs, US House of Representatives, 4 February 1980 and 2 February 1980.

79 International Development and Food Assistance Act of 1975, Pub. L. N° 94-161, S 310, 89 Stat. 849, 860; Act of May 31, 1976, Pub. L. 94-302, S. 211, 90 Stat. 591, 595; Act of October, 1977, Pub. L. N° 95-118, S. 701, 91 Stat. 1067.

80 In February 1977, Secretary of State Vance told a Senate subcommittee that the administration would reduce its aid request for Uruguay, specifically mentioning human rights abuses as the reason for this decision. US Congress, Senate, Committee on Appropriations, Foreign Assistance and Related Programs Appropriations Fiscal Year 1978, 95th Cong., 1st Sess., 1977, p.196.

81 *Ibid.*, p.296. As early as 1974, the US Congress put limitations on military aid to countries involved in gross violations of human rights (Foreign Assistance Act of 1974, Pub. L N° 93-559, S 46, 88 Stat. 1795, 1815–1816, adding S.502B to the Foreign Assistance Act of 1961). In 1976 (Pub. L. N° 94-329, S. 301(a), 90 Stat. 729, 748–750) and then in 1978 (Pub. L. N° 95-384, S 6, 92 Stat. 730, 731–732), the United States extended this legal limitation to security assistance as well.

82 T. Phelps, 'U.S. Cuts Foreign Aid in Rights Violations; South Korea Exempt', *New York Times*, 25 February 1977.

credits out of human rights concerns.[83] Nevertheless, the United States was outvoted, and these loans went forward.[84] With regard to its bilateral aid to Uruguay, the United States channeled its assistance exclusively through projects that directly benefited the poor.[85]

By 1978, the Ex-Im Bank[86] regularly refused to consider loan applications from Uruguay, informing the government that the refusals were based on human rights grounds.[87] The Overseas Private Investment Corporation had also adopted the policy of refusing to consider insurance applications for investments in countries engaged in egregious human rights violations, including Uruguay.[88]

The United States' linking of its lending policies to human rights—particularly its effort to ensure that aid had a positive impact in a context of widespread human rights violations—showed that financial aid can have a positive or negative impact on the human rights situation of any given country, depending on the circumstances.[89] Loans with the precise objective of building houses for the poorest, for example, are less likely to have negative impacts on human rights than are loans granted for general spending needs.[90]

The missing brick: some tools to bring truth, justice, and memory

As shown above, authoritarian regimes try to achieve a balance between loyalty and repression[91]—and for that, they need funds. To better understand whether and how lending to a regime can be causally connected to the crimes committed by that government, a holistic, interdisciplinary, and case-by-case analysis of the functioning of the state machinery and its context is necessary.

83 The United States opposed 12 of 13 loan requests made by Uruguay to international financial institutions during 1977–1980, see L. Schoultz, *Human Rights and United States Policy toward Latin America*, Princeton University Press, Princeton, 1981, pp.297–298.

84 R. Cohen, 'Human Rights Diplomacy: The Carter Administration and the Southern Cone', 4 *Human Rights Quarterly* 212–242 (1982), p.227.

85 International Development and Food Assistance Act of 1975, Pub. L. N° 94-161, Sec. 310, 89 Stat. 849 (codified at 22 USC Sec. 215n 1976).

86 The Export-Import Bank of the United States is the official export credit agency of the US government.

87 Schoultz, n.83, pp.311 and 320.

88 *Ibid.*

89 A. Cassese, *Study of the Impact of Foreign Economic Aid and Assistance on Respect for Human Rights in Chile*, E/CN.4/Sub.2/412, volume I, 1978, pp.3 and 18, http://alumnosmdag.blogspot.com/2010/12/informe-del-prof-antonio-cassese-sobre.html.

90 J. Walczak, 'New Directions in U.S. Food Aid: Human Rights and Economic Development', in V. Nanda (ed.), *Global Human Rights: Public Policies, Comparative Measures, and NGO Strategies*, Westview Press, Boulder, 1981, pp.29–57.

91 Bueno de Mesquita, n.28; R. Wintrobe, *The Political Economy of Dictatorship*, Cambridge University Press, Cambridge, 1998.

In a context of fiscal deficit and poor performance of the national economy, a state has limited options for funding, which renders the role of financiers even more critical. Ultimately, the regime must be capable of one or both of the following: implementing effective economic policies in order to obtain support from key political and economic actors in the country, and implementing a budget that supports an effective repressive apparatus, which usually translates into higher expenditures to benefit the military sector in charge of such a task. From a general perspective, while political institutions shape sovereign borrowing,[92] lending to sovereigns also shapes their political institutions, including those that are criminal in nature.

This chapter addressed these last variables by exploring the case of Uruguay, which—interestingly in the context of this book—actively involved private lenders. In light of the Uruguayan economy's poor performance, the civic-military government seemed to depend highly on foreign financial aid. The state was able to confront serious political and economic challenges and to buy key political support from the corporate elite because it received solid external financial resources that benefited this sector. The state was also able to implement a budgetary policy that specifically strengthened the military and police apparatuses.

The seriousness and volume of the crimes perpetrated by the civic-military government, as well as the relevance of the financial assistance in terms of ensuring the functioning of a system that perpetrated human rights abuses, became public knowledge during those years. In fact, the US government, during the Carter administration, recommended not lending money to the Uruguayan regime—as it did with other Southern Cone dictatorships—out of human rights concerns.[93] At the same time, however, official (multilateral and bilateral) lenders and, later, foreign private banks massively financed the Uruguayan state,[94] helping it meet its political and financial needs for a long period.[95] This assistance facilitated the dictatorship's budgetary policy of increasing military expenditures.[96]

Whether those collaborative lenders might be considered accomplices from a legal point of view is a question that needs further research. Such investigation must determine whether the requirements of legal responsibility (*mens rea*, *actus reus*, and causal link) are met.[97] However, when accountability is assessed through a transitional justice framework, factors that go

92 T. Oatley, 'Political Institutions and Foreign Debt in the Developing World', 54 *International Studies Quarterly* 175–195 (2010), p.176.

93 Schoultz, n.83. p.292.

94 See tables 10.1 and 10.2.

95 SIPRI, nn.64 and 67.

96 See table 10.3.

97 Bohoslavsky and Opgenhaffen, n.8, p.157; Michalowski, n.3, p.451. See also chapter 3 of this book.

beyond the narrow confines of legal responsibility for complicity might become relevant.[98] Thus, even where, as would be necessary in the legal context, the substantial effect of the loans or the necessary mental state of the lenders cannot be duly proven, in the transitional justice context, corporate involvement might nevertheless give rise to accountability.

Since 1984, when democracy was reinstated in Uruguay, a range of transitional justice mechanisms with limited scope have been implemented in the country.[99] Yet the role of economic, including financial, factors that contributed to the dictatorship has not been on the Uruguayan transitional justice agenda. How might the lenders' role during the dictatorship be incorporated into the Uruguayan transitional justice context? First of all, painting a vivid and more complete picture of financial actors' involvement in supporting a criminal regime and consequently facilitating gross human rights violations would make this narrative more compelling, and therefore the scope of transitional justice mechanisms would become broader. The virtuous circle of truth could thus be strengthened.

What are the available legal and institutional tools to make this practicable? First, a truth commission could be created with the aim of investigating the economic (and more specifically, financial) dimension of the dictatorship. Using the Cassese Report as a guide,[100] this commission could produce a report detailing the financial aid received by Uruguay and its impact in terms of supporting the regime and consequently facilitating human rights violations. The commission could also recommend further measures to be taken in order to reach goals related to justice, truth, memory, reparation, and non-repetition.

Second, since the international right to the truth[101] has been recognized under Uruguayan law,[102] if necessary, civil claims could be brought in order to establish the truth. Discovering more about the loans themselves (dates, volumes, contractual terms, goals, etc.), the lenders' public knowledge at the time, the officials involved in these transactions, how these funds were spent, and if and how they were causally connected to the perpetration of the crimes would provide steps toward a more complete archive of the past atrocities suffered by the people of Uruguay.

98 This section heavily relies on Bohoslavsky, n.28. See, also, chapter 6 of this book.

99 See above, section entitled 'Military expenditures and the repressive apparatus'.

99 See broadly Errandonea, n.18, p.13; P. Galain Palermo, 'The Prosecution of International Crimes in Uruguay', 10 *International Criminal Law Review* 601–618 (2010), p.601; Prats, n.10, p.219.

100 Cassese, n.89.

101 UN General Assembly, *Basic Principles and Guidelines on the Right to a Remedy and Reparation for Victims of Gross Violations of International Human Rights Law and Serious Violations of International Humanitarian Law*, Res. N° 60/147, 16 December 2005.

102 Representatives Chamber, Comisión Investigadora sobre la Situación de Personas Desaparecidas y Hechos que la Motivaron, *Final Report*, 8 November 1985; Amnesty Act 15.848 (1986), article 4; explanatory notes accompanying Decree 858/2000.

In addition, with the recently renewed surge in criminal trials against perpetrators of blood crimes,[103] investigations undertaken in the context of these trials could provide substantive information on how these crimes were supported and facilitated by a well-financed criminal machinery. This, in turn, might complete the narrative puzzle and make it possible to pursue a broader spectrum of justice in Uruguay. Such information could be achieved, for example, by asking the defendant military personnel whether they felt supported by economic actors and, if so, how this support affected their political decisions and criminal activities.[104]

Where the strict legal conditions of lender liability for complicity are met,[105] civil lawsuits against accomplices can be a potential compensatory measure. This is the judicial path being followed by victims of the Argentinian dictatorship, who are suing the banks that financed their executioners.[106] In the case of Uruguay—as in Argentina and many other countries[107]—legislation establishes a broad non-contractual responsibility for damages provoked negligently or wilfully, including for accomplices.[108]

Discussions about the validity of debts contracted during the dictatorship[109] can also contribute to attaining some of the goals of transitional justice. Emphasizing the connections between odious debts and past wrongs and injustices through repudiation may provide moral and political redress.[110]

In terms of memory, the lenders' role should be properly present in memorials, as is the case in the permanent exhibition at Argentina's Museum of Foreign Debt.[111] Here, the great challenge is to unravel the complex

103 See n.7.

104 Rafael Videla, one of the last infamous Argentinian dictators, in a recent interview highlighted the macro role of the foreign loans that the regime received at that time: 'No salimos a cazar pajaritos, sino al terrorismo y a los subversivos', *Cambio 16*, 4 March 2012, http://cambio16.es/not/1344/_ldquo_no_salimos_a_cazar_pajaritos___sino_al_terrorismo__y_a_los_subversivos_rdquo__/.

105 See broadly International Commission of Jurists, *Corporate Complicity & Legal Accountability*, volumes I–III, Geneva, 2008, www.icj.org/report-of-the-international-commission-of-jurists-expert-legal-panel-on-corporate-complicity-in-international-crimes/; Bohoslavsky and Opgenhaffen, n.8.

106 'Ibañez Manuel Leandro y otros casos/Diligencia Preliminar', Juzgado Nacional de 1° Instancia en lo Civil 34., Buenos Aires, N° 95.019/2009; 'Garramone, Andrés c. Citibank NA y otros', 2010, Juzgado Nacional en lo Contencioso Administrativo Federal N° 8, Buenos Aires, N° 47736/10.

107 J. Černič, *Human Rights Law and Business*, Europa Law Publishing, Amsterdam, 2010, pp.33 and 179.

108 Civil Code, article 1.319.

109 S. Michalowski and J.P. Bohoslavsky, 'Ius Cogens, Transitional Justice and other Trends of the Debate on Odious Debts. A Response to the World Bank Discussion Paper on Odious Debts', 48 *Columbia Journal of Transnational Law* 61–120 (2010), p.95.

110 A. Gelpern, 'Sovereign Debt Restructuring: What Iraq and Argentina Might Learn from Each Other', 6 *Chicago Journal of International Law* 391–414 (2005), p.407.

111 The exhibition is organized and sponsored by the University of Buenos Aires. See details on the museum at www.museodeladeuda.com/index2.php.

relationships that were involved in the regime's financing so that the role of lenders can be explained to a broad audience. Their historical economic role should also be incorporated into curricula, specifically history education.[112] Apologies and historical accountability acknowledgments from the accomplices would also contribute in terms of memory and might provide some redress to the victims.

It is also possible to reform regulatory laws in order to discourage future financial behaviors that might facilitate human rights abuses. This can be done, for example, by incorporating rules on the nullity of financial obligations contracted by the state during authoritarian regimes into national civil law, provided certain objective characteristics are present, but without any further evidence regarding the mental state of the lender (strict liability). Another possibility is establishing vetting processes aimed at screening public employees or candidates for public employment to determine whether their participation (as private actors or state officials) in those transactions warrants their exclusion from public institutions.[113] Financial accomplices could also be precluded from doing business in the transitional state.

Lastly, at the international level, if financial creditors are protected by bilateral investment treaties,[114] these norms should incorporate a clause[115] warning lenders that loans strengthening the host regime and facilitating human rights abuses will not be legally protected by these treaties.[116] Soft-law instruments regulating financial activities, such as the Equator Principles, could also elaborate on specific due diligence procedures and standards when dealing with human rights violators. In the transitional context, such norms could reinforce the idea of prevention and provide clearer standards for assessing financial actors' accountability.

112 E. Cole, 'Transitional Justice and the Reform of History Education', 1 *International Journal of Transitional Justice* 115–137 (2007).

113 See generally A. Mayer-Rieckh and P. de Greiff, *Justice as Prevention: Vetting Public Employees in Transitional Societies*, Social Science Research Council, New York, 2007.

114 This is indeed a real concern in Uruguay. See Treaty between the United States of America and the Oriental Republic of Uruguay Concerning the Encouragement and Reciprocal Protection of Investment (2005), Annex G, Section 1.

115 For suggestions regarding the incorporation of exception provisions into international investment agreements (IIA) in order to allow states to derogate from their IIA obligations under specified (economic and social) human rights conditions, see B. Choudhury, 'Exception Provisions as a Gateway to Incorporating Human Rights Issues into International Investment Agreements', 49 *Columbia Journal of Transnational Law* 670–716 (2010–11).

116 *Phoenix Action, Ltd. v The Czech Republic*, ICSID ARB/06/5, Award, 15 April 2009, para.78.

Conclusion

Since 1984, Uruguay has struggled to find a balance between justice and peace, domestic and international law,[117] and national sovereignty and legal globalization.[118] All of these factors have permanently influenced the complex and fluid process of justice in Uruguay.[119] The Uruguayan transition toward democracy has gone through different phases during the past 30 years,[120] and some legacies from the authoritarian regime remain. One matter still pending is whether and how to deal with the accountability of economic accomplices[121]—particularly financial accomplices, as was the focus of this chapter.

A complex assessment and balance—one that considers Uruguay's economic interests and external financial dependency, the advancement of justice, trade-offs between economic development and justice, and the mutual interaction between transitional measures—shapes the concrete transitional mechanisms to be implemented and determines their best sequence. This includes the possibility of using legal and institutional instruments to make financial accomplices accountable for their past wrongful behavior.

117 Skaar, n.18, p 60.

118 For some of this discussion, see R. Gargarella, '5 Comentarios sobre la Decisión de la Corte Interamericana en Gelman', 7 June 2011 and 'Se puede plebiscitar todo? (Gelman reloaded en parte)', 11 June 2011, www.seminariogargarella.blogspot.com/.

119 See broadly L. Mallinder, 'Impunity, Accountability and Public Participation: Uruguay's Evolving Experience of Amnesty Laws', Working paper from Beyond Legalism: Amnesties, Transition and Conflict Transformation project, Institute of Criminology and Criminal Justice, Queen's University Belfast, 2009, http://works.bepress.com/cgi/viewcontent.cgi?article=1000&context=louise_mallinder.

120 Galain Palermo, n.99, p.617.

121 Just a few days after the coup, the Uruguayan National Chamber of Commerce called for less state economic intervention and declared that "this National Chamber of Commerce shares, in its fundamental aspects, the development plans structured by the executive branch and is ready to provide full collaboration and face the corresponding responsibility once implemented the formulas that allow to co-participate in its execution," 'La Cámara Nacional de Comercio se dirige al país', *El País*, 14 July 1973.

Chapter 11

The Legal Framework for Private Investors in Kosovo

Implications for Environmental Protection in a Transitional Economy

David M. Ong

Introduction

As Alex Boraine observes, "In deeply divided societies where mistrust and fear still reign, there must be bridge-building and a commitment not only to criminal justice, but also to economic justice."[1] A link exists between socioeconomic institutional reform and the promotion of transitional justice in societies emerging from post-conflict situations like Kosovo, which will serve as a case study here. The creation of new (or perpetuation of old) socioeconomic asymmetries manifests itself in unequal opportunities for ensuring environmental protection for all members of the Kosovo polity. With regard to private investors who are expected to play a pivotal role in the socioeconomic reconstruction of Kosovo, there are questions as to whether the environmental impact of their activities is adequately regulated by the current institutional and legal framework. It will be seen that the emphasis on economic (re)development creates the potential to exacerbate prevailing inequalities within this ethnically and religiously divided society, necessitating redress through transitional justice mechanisms.

Within this context, an argument for the explicit inclusion of environmental considerations within the prioritized economic reconstruction of Kosovo is based on the universality of baseline human environmental quality needs, as opposed to contested notions of redistributive socioeconomic justice, especially within an ethnically divided transitional society. Basic human requirements for clean water, air, and soil, as well as sufficient and untainted food supplies, have been elevated to imperative goals within the international development agenda when tackling poverty in less developed countries, whether transitional or not. For example, the Millennium Development Goals provide, inter alia, for the eradication of extreme poverty and hunger (goal 1) and ensuring environmental sustainability (goal 7) through the integration of sustainable development principles into domestic policies and

1 A. Boraine, 'Transitional Justice: A Holistic Interpretation', 60 *Journal of International Affairs* 17–27 (2006), pp.23–24.

programs (Target 7.A).[2] Securing such basic environmental needs for the entire population of Kosovo without discriminating between majority and minority ethnic communities is therefore a fundamental baseline goal for the transitional environmental justice mechanisms examined here. The continuing legal challenge relates to how far these goals can also be enforced against private actors involved in Kosovo's socioeconomic reconstruction.

In this chapter, an examination of the institutional and legal frameworks for the provision of "environmental justice" is presented as an alternative perspective from which to address ethnic, social, and economic inequities either created or perpetuated by the drive toward socioeconomic reconstruction in Kosovo. The chapter will assess whether international, European, and domestic efforts to stimulate private investor involvement within Kosovo's reconstruction take account of the environmental threats from major infrastructure and privatization projects. The dominant narrative that describes jurisdictions in similar circumstances usually accords low priority to environmental protection. Socioeconomic reconstruction/development is apparently unable to take place without some form of concomitant environmental degradation. Even if environmental damage need not always occur,[3] private economic actor involvement is often perceived as a negative influence on the tendency of transitional societies to deprioritize environmental protection when reconstructing their economies.[4] Within this context, it should be noted that corporations are the main beneficiaries of this combination of the investor-friendly institutional framework and privatization policies, as well as weak enforcement of environmental justice mechanisms in transitional societies like Kosovo. The question then is how such corporations can be held accountable for their environmental impacts.

The first part of this chapter will examine the legal and institutional framework for the provision of financial and technical assistance in the post-conflict, socioeconomic reconstruction of Kosovo. The second section will examine the legal implications for environmental protection of the privatization process currently being undertaken within Kosovo. Lastly, the chapter will discuss the relevant environmental principles and procedural environmental rights derived from international environmental law, as well as the jurisprudence of the European Court of Human Rights, and related European Community/Union (EC/U) law. All these developments will be traced to their possible application within the reestablished Kosovo legal system, and

2 www.un.org/millenniumgoals/poverty.shtml.

3 S. Archibald, L. Banu and Z. Bochniarz, 'Market Liberalization and Sustainability in Transition: Turning Points and Trends in Central and Eastern Europe', in J. Carmin and S.VanDeveer (eds), *EU Enlargement and the Environment: Institutional Change and Environmental Policy in Central and Eastern Europe*, Routledge, London, 2005 (266–289), p.284.

4 R. Miller, *Globalizing Justice: The Ethics of Poverty and Power*, Oxford University Press, Oxford, 2010, p.3.

potential problems regarding their use and enforcement will be examined. The chapter will examine an apparent discrepancy between the international (UN/World Bank) and regional (European Union) institutions that are driving socioeconomic reconstruction efforts, and the relative paucity of effective domestic governmental structures within Kosovo, through the lens of prospects for transitional justice, especially *transitional environmental justice*.

International and EU institutional framework for investment in Kosovo

There is hardly another entity in the world today that exhibits so many of the classical features of both a transitional society and a fledgling state as that of present-day Kosovo. Yet Kosovo's international legal status still raises vexed questions that undermine efforts at final answers.[5] Despite its declaration of independence on 17 February 2008, Kosovo has been described as an "unfinished state,"[6] with only limited sovereignty and divided, de facto, into a Serb north and an Albanian south. Neither the United Nations Interim Administration Mission in Kosovo (UNMIK) nor the European Union Rule of Law Mission in Kosovo (EULEX) have so far been able to do anything to prevent its partition. While acknowledging the importance of these wider political issues for the people of Kosovo today, this chapter will focus on how the international and European institutional governance framework might prospectively address environmental justice issues in relation to private actors involved in the socioeconomic reconstruction of Kosovo.

Kosovo today is governed by a complex and arguably confusing amalgam of global and regional institutions, including the UN[7] and the European Union (EU),[8] with NATO in the form of the Kosovo Force[9] providing military support, and the World Bank[10] providing additional financial support.

5 For a recent assessment, see M. Weller, 'Kosovo's final status', 84 *International Affairs* 1223–1243 (2008).

6 V. Džihić and H. Kramer, 'Kosovo After Independence: Is the EU's EULEX Mission Delivering on its Promises?' *International Policy Analysis*, Friedrich Ebert Stiftung, Berlin, 2009, p.28, www.fes.de/ipa.

7 UN Security Council Resolution 1244/99, inter alia, establishing the UN Mission in Kosovo (UNMIK) is still the governing international law over Kosovo, http://daccess-dds-ny.un.org/doc/UNDOC/GEN/N99/172/89/PDF/N9917289.pdf?OpenElement.

8 The EU presence in Kosovo has been organized according to a three-way division of labor, encompassing a political commitment (the EU Special Representative in Kosovo), www.eusrinkosovo.eu/; the operational commitment (the EULEX Kosovo), www.eulex-kosovo.eu/; and the reform-driving commitment (the European Commission Liaison Office in Kosovo), www.delprn.ec.europa.eu/.

9 For information on the Kosovo Force's role and activities within Kosovo, see the KFOR/NATO website, www.nato.int/kfor/.

10 Kosovo was admitted into the World Bank Group, including the International Bank of Reconstruction and Development, the International Development Association, the

UNMIK was established as a temporary form of governance for the stakeholders to negotiate the final status of Kosovo. UN Security Council Resolution 1244 gave UNMIK the mandate to exercise civilian administration over Kosovo, but did not provide a clear end date to the mission. While UNMIK de jure operates as the interim civil administration in Kosovo, it has delegated certain functions to several other international institutions.

As significant and influential as these international institutions are, the domestic political bodies within Kosovo have now taken over much of the day-to-day government. The adoption of UNMIK Regulation 2001/9 on a Constitutional Framework for Provisional Self-Government defined the responsibilities relating to the administration of Kosovo as shared between the SRSG and the Provisional Institutions of Self-Government of Kosovo. This constitutional framework began the process of transferring powers to Kosovo's newly created institutions of self-government. Following the Declaration of Independence, a constitution was adopted by the Kosovo Assembly in 2008. Kosovo's main domestic political institutions comprise, inter alia, a representative legislature,[11] a presidency, and an executive central government, which in turn consists of a prime minister and relevant ministers within a cabinet.[12] Equally significant are the local (regionally based) municipal authorities elected to administer individual regions within the UN-designated Kosovo jurisdiction. Given the multitude of actors, Kosovo thus provides an interesting case of transitional justice.

The post-conflict social and economic reconstruction efforts in Kosovo have consistently aimed to create the legal conditions and social climate for a market economy. The agents in this process are typically envisaged to be small- and medium-scale enterprises, but larger infrastructure and capital-intensive projects are also being undertaken.[13] Evidence on the ground suggests that economic, and to a certain extent social, reconstruction efforts

International Finance Corporation, and the Multilateral Investment Guarantee Agency on 29 June 2009. Kosovo also joined the International Centre for Settlement of Investment Disputes on 29 July 2009. See Press Release No: 2009/448/ECA, http://go.worldbank.org/97H44AA7P0.

11 Information about the (Republic of) Kosovo legislative authorities can be accessed at www.assembly-kosova.org/.

12 Information on the domestic Kosovo government institutions can be accessed at www.kryeministri-ks.net/.

13 J. Sorensen, *State Collapse and Reconstruction in the Periphery: Political Economy, Ethnicity and Development in Yugoslavia, Serbia and Kosovo*, Berghahn, New York, 2009, p.11. According to an early World Bank assessment, there has been a recovery of economic activity and positive growth since 2000. However, the recent growth performance has been driven by a post-conflict boom financed by official aid flows and is unlikely to be sustainable. See World Bank, *Kosovo: Economic Memorandum*, Report No.28023-KOS, Poverty Reduction and Economic Management Unit, Europe and Central Asia Region, World Bank, 17 May 2004, http://siteresources.worldbank.org/INTKOSOVO/Data%20and%20Reference/20243120/KEM-5-17-2004%20with%20amendments.pdf.

are underway in Kosovo. While Kosovo's economic transition is largely managed by the World Bank and its sister agencies, its social reconstruction is coordinated by the EU.

EULEX's role in efforts aimed at restoring the rule of law arguably means that the EU is the most significant international organization operating within Kosovo.[14] The Kosovo government has established the (Kosovo) Agency for Coordination of Development and European Integration to assist with EU coordination of these international assistance efforts.[15] The Single European Market is one of Kosovo's main export markets, along with Southeastern Europe. Half of Kosovo's exports go to the EU.[16] Export growth is particularly evident in the newly privatized companies in Kosovo. As a recent report on the post-privatization performance of these companies notes, "There is strong orientation towards exports: 44% of (privatized) companies are export oriented."[17] Kosovo companies' continuing ability to export to the EU is significant, as the EU is becoming one of the most environmentally stringent markets to break into.

Thus, at least two significant international legal and institutional developments form the backdrop to Kosovo's socioeconomic reconstruction: (i) Kosovo's World Bank Group membership and its implications for both the public and private financing of socioeconomic reconstruction/development projects; and (ii) the all-encompassing EU presence in civilian matters within Kosovo. The goal prioritization and policy prescriptions of the international institutions operating within Kosovo tend to reflect the liberal, market economy-based approaches of these institutions' member states. This in turn represents the "internationally managed state-building" approach of the Western peace thesis,[18] which holds that liberal democracies are unlikely to be involved in violent conflict. On the basis of this assumption, international state-building projects aim to "build" liberal democracies in places defined as security risks,[19] such as Kosovo. As Jens Sorensen observes in relation to these Western liberal democratic efforts within the former communist/socialist

14 EULEX assumed its official role on 9 December 2008, www.eulex-kosovo.eu/en/.

15 See EU Commission Decision (2009) on a Multi-Annual Indicative Planning Document (MIPD) for Kosovo (under UNSCR 1244/99) 2009–2011, p.7, http://ec.europa.eu/enlargement/pdf/mipd_kosovo_2009_2011_en.pdf.

16 World Bank, *Kosovo – Unlocking Growth Potential: Strategies, Policies, Actions*, Report No. 53185-XK, Poverty Reduction and Economic Management Unit, Europe and Central Asia Region, World Bank, 29 April 2010, para.1.20, p.9.

17 M. Mustafa *et al.*, *Privatization and Post-Privatization in Kosovo: Glass Half Empty or Half Full?* Forum 2015, Prishtina, 2008, p.6.

18 R. Knudsen, *Privatization in Kosovo: The International Project 1999–2008*, NUPI Report, Norwegian Institute of International Affairs, Oslo, 2010, p.9.

19 For a summary of the liberal (democratic) peace thesis, see M. Doyle, 'Three pillars of the liberal peace', 99 *American Political Science Review* 463–466 (2005), responding to a critical assessment of this thesis by S. Rosato, 'The Flawed Logic of Democratic Peace Theory', 97 *American Political Science Review* 585–602 (2003).

transitional economies, "[t]he policy prescriptions are liberalization, privatization and structural adjustment."[20]

The World Bank's 2010 "Country Brief" for Kosovo emphasizes generating new sources of economic growth while ensuring associated *environmental* and social improvements. At the same time, however, it highlights the mining and energy sectors as potential key sources of future growth, noting that Kosovo has abundant natural resources, as well as duty-free access and relatively low transportation costs to the Single European Market. In particular, the utilization of Kosovo's lignite resources to attract strategic foreign investment could turn the energy sector into an engine of growth rather than a drain on public resources. But the environmental implications of this avowedly investment-driven, economic development-oriented policy prescription are hardly considered.[21] However, the two main objectives of the Bank's recently published Country Partnership Strategy for the Republic of Kosovo for 2012–2015 are: (i) to accelerate broad-based economic growth and employment generation; and (ii) to improve environmental management. The latter objective, acknowledged as having been less prominent in previous World Bank Group strategies, is now being given higher priority because of growing recognition that both the environmentally sensitive use of Kosovo's major natural resources and the cleanup of environmental hazards are critical elements for the improvement of health and living standards.[22]

World Bank Group assistance in the socioeconomic reconstruction of Kosovo

World Bank Group membership is of immense value as a catalyst for economic reconstruction efforts within Kosovo, whether in the public or private sectors of the economy, and its wider social implications for the reconciliation or reestablishment of the different communities within Kosovo cannot be underestimated. The World Bank provides assistance through investment loans, technical assistance, institutional development loans and credits, non-lending services, and partnerships.[23] The International Finance Corporation (IFC) assists business corporations operating within risky settings.[24] The

20 Sorensen, n.13, p.54.

21 World Bank, Kosovo, World Bank Country Brief, 2010, www.worldbank.org/.

22 See IDA, IFC and MIGA Country Partnership Strategy for the Republic of Kosovo for the Period FY12–FY15, Report No. 66877-XK, prepared and published by WB South East Europe Country Unit, Europe and Central Asia, and IFC, Europe and Central Asia, 1 May 2012.

23 For information about the World Bank Group and especially the International Bank for Reconstruction and Development services, see http://web.worldbank.org/WBSITE/EXTERNAL/EXTABOUTUS/0,,contentMDK:20103838~menuPK:1696997~pagePK:51123644~piPK:329829~theSitePK:29708,00.html.

24 For information on IFC services, see www1.ifc.org/wps/wcm/connect/CORP_EXT_Content/IFC_External_Corporate_Site/What+We+Do/.

World Bank's aim in Kosovo is to stimulate private individual and institutional foreign investment.

World Bank Group membership also brings with it opportunities for individuals and local communities to engage with the independent institutional accountability mechanisms for individual World Bank Group members. The Inspection Panel was established in 1993 for projects supported by the International Bank of Reconstruction and Development and the International Development Association. It is an independent, "bottom-up" accountability and recourse mechanism that investigates projects financed by these two entities to determine whether the Bank has complied with its own operational policies and procedures (including social and environmental safeguards) and addressed related issues of harm. It provides a forum for people who believe that they may be adversely affected by Bank-financed operations to bring their concerns to the highest decision-making levels of the World Bank.[25] The separately established independent accountability mechanism for the IFC and the Multilateral Investment Guarantee Agency—the two private-sector lending arms of the World Bank Group—is the Office of the Compliance Advisor Ombudsman (CAO). The CAO addresses complaints by individuals and communities affected by these two institutions' projects, with the aim of enhancing the social and environmental accountability of both institutions and thus fostering greater public accountability of these bodies. The CAO was established in 1999 and reports directly to the president of the World Bank Group.[26]

Negative impacts of World Bank-supported investment and privatization policies on environmental protection have arisen in the following areas:

- The transfer of polluting industries to relatively underdeveloped or transitional economies, such as Kosovo.
- The development of previously untapped natural resources, and the consequent environmental impacts.
- The cumulative impact of many small-scale polluting operations (such as greater amounts of urban transport due to infrastructure improvements, or better fuel distribution and retail networks).
- The exceptions from regulatory requirements that are sometimes part of the privatization transactions.[27]

25 World Bank Inspection Panel, http://web.worldbank.org/WBSITE/EXTERNAL/EXTINSPECTIONPANEL/0,,menuPK:64132057~pagePK:64130364~piPK:64132056~theSitePK:380794,00.html.

26 Compliance Advisor Ombudsman, www.cao-ombudsman.org/about/whoweare/index.html.

27 M. Lovei and B. Gentry, *The Environmental Implications of Privatization: Lessons for Developing Countries*, World Bank Discussion Paper No.426, World Bank, Washington D.C., 2002, pp.12–16.

In response to these negative impacts, the Bank has established certain basic elements of environmentally sound privatization within transitional economies like Kosovo, such as governmental commitment to including environmental considerations in sale negotiations and agreements; a domestic legal framework of environmental regulations, standards, and institutions; institutional capacity for, and commitment to, environmental enforcement; and investors' (domestic and foreign) environmental protection incentives and commitment.[28] Essentially, there are two specific environmental issues that are common to most privatization projects: responsibility and liability for the cleanup of past environmental damage and for the prevention of future environmental damage.

To minimize potential disruptions to the business models of recently privatized entities created by unpredicted and therefore uncertain environmental problems arising post-privatization, governments are enjoined by the World Bank to invest in the provision of environmental information for potential investors, address inventory problems, and develop remediation plans. However, research suggests that only a few of the Central European countries that have both undertaken large-scale privatization and experienced environmental problems arising from these exercises have adopted this advice. Moreover, merely providing information to potential investors is insufficient to spur remediation.[29]

Apart from the World Bank and its sister institutions, a number of EU member states, other public (and private) international finance institutions, international charity organizations, and bilateral donors are also active in Kosovo. Many investment projects ultimately rely on a mixture of public and private sources for funding and credit provision, especially when they concern the building and operation of large infrastructure projects. Thus, we should also consider the potentially environmentally supportive role played by private international finance institutions, in the context of project-financed socioeconomic reconstruction/development projects. For example, a significant aspect of the Equator Principles (explained below) applied by private banks is their close link with the promotion of environmental, social, and health and safety standards by state-funded multilateral and global financing institutions, such as the World Bank, when providing funding and technical support for socioeconomic development projects.[30]

28 *Ibid.*, p.16.

29 R. Bluffstone, 'Privatization and contaminated site remediation in Central and Eastern Europe: Do environmental liability policies matter?' 63 *Ecological Economics* 31–41 (2007), p.31.

30 C. Wright, 'Setting Standards for Responsible Banking: Examining the Role of the International Finance Corporation in the Emergence of the Equator Principles', in F. Biermann, B. Siebenhüner and A. Schreyrögg (eds), *International Organizations in Global Environmental Governance*, Routledge, Abingdon, 2009 (51–70).

Standing alongside the World Bank's Environmental, Health and Safety Guidelines,[31] the Equator Principles are a set of statements of social and environmental principles that have been agreed on and adopted by a large group of like-minded private commercial banks as applying to the "project finance" lending activities of these banks. These so-called "Equator Banks" undertake to provide loans only to projects that conform with the Equator Principles. The most significant by far for this chapter is principle 5, which requires the host government, borrowing company, or third party expert to consult with "affected communities" in a structured and culturally appropriate manner.[32] Moreover, for projects with significant adverse impacts on affected communities, the process will ensure their free, prior, and informed "consultation" as a means to establish, to the satisfaction of the Equator Banks, whether a project has adequately incorporated affected communities' concerns. In order to accomplish these consultation and disclosure requirements, the borrower is obligated to ensure that the project's strategic environmental assessment and action plan are made publicly available for a reasonable amount of time in the relevant local language and in a culturally appropriate manner. The borrower must also document the consultation process and its results. Finally, for projects with adverse social and environmental impacts, disclosure should occur early in the assessment process and be carried out on a continuing basis. These requirements, if implemented fully by the borrowing company, would provide far-reaching environmental protection. However, an important question is how far the Equator Bank concerned can actually both require and ensure the full implementation of this principle by the borrowing company situated in a different jurisdiction from its own. In a transitional society such as Kosovo, the appropriate domestic mechanisms for supervising or even monitoring these principles are currently limited, and corporate environmental accountability cannot be assured.

EU role in Kosovo

The EULEX is the largest civilian mission ever launched under the EU's Common Security and Defence Policy. The mission's central aim is to assist and support the Kosovo authorities in the rule of law, specifically in the areas of police, judiciary, and customs. It is a technical mission that implements its mandate through monitoring, mentoring, and advising roles, while retaining certain executive powers and responsibilities. EULEX works under the

31 Technical reference documents with general and industry-specific examples of good international industry practice performance levels acceptable to the IFC and considered to be achievable in new facilities at reasonable costs by existing technology, www.ifc.org/.

32 "Affected communities" is defined as "communities of local population within the project's area of influence who are likely to be adversely affected by the project."

general framework of UN Security Council Resolution 1244/99 and has a unified chain of command to Brussels.

Critical to the improvement of living conditions within Kosovo is the quality of the environment. On this issue, an EC report states:

> Kosovo's environment has been damaged by years of pollution and neglect. Kosovo's power plants are estimated to generate 25 tons of ash and dust per hour, or 74 times the level permitted by EU standards. . . . Improving Kosovo's environment is an imperative for improving the health of its citizens. Kosovo continues to make good progress in the legal transposition of EU standards. However, it lacks the capacity and resources to ensure adequate implementation. Less than 1% of the Kosovo budget goes to finance environmental activities.[33]

All EU financial assistance to countries with prospects for EU membership—including Kosovo—has been brought under the auspices of a single measure: the Instrument for Pre-Accession Assistance.[34] An EU Commission decision of 2009 identified *environmental considerations* as one of the major cross-cutting issues to be tackled in Kosovo, along with good governance, the provision of equal opportunities, the non-discrimination of minority and vulnerable groups, and the recognition of civil society organizations. All these issues are duly reflected in activities financed by the pre-accession instrument during 2009–2011, with specific actions dedicated to environmental protection, such as environmental impact assessments.[35] The EULEX mission represents the modality for ensuring the international accountability of domestic Kosovo institutions on all these issues for the foreseeable future. The establishment of viable environmental protection instruments as a significant criterion for continuing EU support will need to be taken into account by both domestic institutions and potential investors in Kosovo's economic reconstruction.

Kosovo privatization process: implications for environmental protection

Two issues need to be emphasized at the outset. First, privatization "has become *the* economic strategy of choice for international state-building projects, advancing it throughout the world as a self-evident part of the

33 *Kosovo – Fulfilling its European Perspective*, Communication from the Commission to the European Parliament and the Council, COM(2009) 5343, Brussels, 14 October 2009, p.11.

34 Council Regulation (EC) No.1085/2006 of 17 July 2006 establishing an Instrument for Pre-Accession Assistance (IPA).

35 See EU Comm Decision (2009) on a Multi-Annual Indicative Planning Document (MIPD) Kosovo (under UNSCR 1244/99) 2009–2011, Annex 4: Cross-cutting issues, p.26.

liberal peace thesis."[36] Second, the arguably unique character of the socialist model of the Yugoslav political economy should be acknowledged. Karim Medjad, for example, notes that in the former Yugoslavia, enterprises were neither private nor state-owned but in fact collective properties owned by their employees; they were known as "socially-owned enterprises."[37] This socialist form of ownership was the flagship of the Yugoslav model of self-management.

Following the establishment of UNMIK in 1999, the EU-led Pillar IV responsible for economic reconstruction and development made a key policy decision to embark on a privatization program to rebuild Kosovo's shattered economy.[38] Rita Knudsen suggests that since Kosovo's unresolved international status closed off avenues normally available to similar transitional economies hoping to benefit from international assistance and investment, internationally led privatization was in effect the *only* economic strategy for Kosovo.[39] Concerning the link between the different stages of Kosovo's privatization process and the relevant environmental principles, the preparation for sale of socially-owned enterprises entails environmental audits and risk assessments. This requires assessment of the previous and continuing environmental performance of existing socially-owned enterprises, their compliance record with environmental regulations, past contamination, the environmental risks of their continuing operation, recommended measures to improve compliance, and remediation of past environmental damage. Requests for bids to privatize socially-owned enterprises must include environmental references, baseline environmental information, and an indication of applicable environmental regulation requirements. During the due diligence period, environmental compliance (management) plans and environmental remediation plans must be drafted by the privatized entity and approved by the Kosovo authorities, which take into consideration environmental assessments, proposed investment plans, and input from the public. Negotiations for the privatization or sale of a socially-owned enterprise must include the environmental undertakings/agreements on compliance and remediation as an integral aspect of the final sale agreement. If an investor is asked to undertake remediation measures, the scope and cost of these measures and financing mechanisms must be agreed on. Performance bonds and other insurance mechanisms can be used to ensure implementation

36 Knudsen, n.18, p.10.

37 K. Medjad, 'The Fate of the Yugoslav Model: A Case Against Legal Conformity', 52 *American Journal of Comparative Law* 287–319 (2004), p.287.

38 Knudsen, n.18, p.33, citing D. Zaum, *The Sovereignty Paradox: The Norms and Politics of International Statebuilding*, Oxford University Press, Oxford, 2007, p.155. The recommendation was made in September 1999 by Joly Dixon, who was head of UNMIK's Pillar IV and Deputy SRSG in Kosovo.

39 Knudsen, *ibid.*

of environmental compliance (or even post-compliance) plans by the investor. Residual risks should be allocated (e.g. through governmental guarantee or indemnity). Post-privatization oversight involves environmental assessment of new investments, monitoring and enforcement of environmental regulations, and establishment of a dispute settlement mechanism to resolve any uncertainties about environmental liabilities (e.g. unforeseen damages and third party victims).[40]

An example of issues arising from the social and environmental assessment of a major privatization project in Kosovo is as follows: An initial US$5 million International Development Association grant was made to UNMIK in June 2007 to support the Kosovo Energy Corporation and the Kosovar authorities in cleaning up a gasification plant to enhance Kosovo's long-term electricity supply and to mitigate an urgent public health and environmental risk in Kosovo.[41] The IFC's Advisory Services were deployed in 2009 to assess and prepare the corporation for the possible unbundling and privatization of its electricity distribution functions via private-sector participation.[42] However, in 2011, a confidential complaint was made to the IFC's Compliance Advisor Ombudsman. The Kosovar complainants contended that access to information regarding the privatization was inadequate to allow people to address potential adverse impacts of the process, and that no appropriate social and environmental assessment—which would have contemplated project impacts on community members, the workforce, and the environment—had been conducted.[43] Initially, the CAO found the complaint eligible for further assessment and conducted two field trips to Pristina. Thereafter, the complainants informed the CAO that they considered their interests (and those of the Kosovar public) would be best served by the CAO's compliance function, and in January 2012, the case was formally transferred to the CAO's compliance team. The CAO's compliance function, which is separate from its ombudsman role, conducts internal assessments of the IFC's compliance with its own policies. Following an appraisal of the IFC's role in this project, the compliance function of the CAO concluded that an audit of the IFC's advisory services for the project was merited. Accordingly, since May 2012, the CAO has been conducting an investigation into the scope of the IFC's social and environmental due diligence review for this

40 Lovei and Gentry, n.27, pp.24–26.

41 *Project Name & Number*: Lignite Power Technical Assistance Project (IDA H2540).

42 *Project Name & Number:* Kosovo KEK (#29107). The project was approved by IFC in December 2009, with a budget of US$2,022,508. Information on this project is accessible at www.ifc.org/ifcext/spiwebsite1.nsf/0/852568b10055270d852576b0007a3338?opendocument.

43 *Case name:* Kosovo KEK-01/Prishtina; *concerns:* Social & environmental impacts of privatization; *date filed:* 25 August 2011, www.cao-ombudsman.org/documents/Kosovo_webtext_English_May2012.pdf.

project. This case study highlights the potential for World Bank Group compliance functions, such as the CAO and the Inspection Panel (noted above), to account for the social and environmental impacts of the infrastructure projects that the Bank financially supports. Moreover, where the Bank supports these projects alongside private investors, the investors will invariably be subjected to the same social and environmental protection standards as the Bank itself, especially if they are relying on loans from private international finance institutions such as the Equator Banks. However, unlike the CAO, which ensures the IFC's accountability for such standards, the Equator Banks can assert only limited accountability for social and environmental standards by the borrowing investor in project finance-type loan arrangements, and even less so on the newly privatized corporation established in a foreign jurisdiction like Kosovo as a result of the investment that was at least partly funded by this project finance.

Other environmental issues have arisen in the context of the Privatization Agency of Kosovo's privatization projects. The main form of Kosovo privatization so far is through auctions of small- and medium-scale enterprises that do not usually have serious past contamination problems. These smaller privatization projects also do not usually involve foreign investors, and therefore the international accountability mechanisms discussed above are not applicable. In this respect, Kosovo privatization has not differed from previous Central and Eastern European privatization exercises in the immediate aftermath of the fall of the Berlin Wall. A few of these privatized small and medium-scale enterprises do cause localized pollution—for example, petrol stations and dry-cleaning shops. Where these cases arose previously in Central and Eastern European privatizations, they were resolved by the provision of tailor-made regulations governing the specific enterprise activities. However, domestic Kosovo legislation, policy, and practice inadequately reflect these specific environmental concerns. In this respect, there is an accountability gap.

Moreover, when the post-privatization arrangements involve foreign investors for larger projects, such as that of the Kosovo Energy Corporation (above) or Trepça (see below), and these arrangements break down, the legal consequences can include litigation before an international arbitral tribunal established under the International Centre for the Settlement of Investment Disputes (ICSID) or the Energy Community Treaty, both of which Kosovo is now party to. Under these treaty-based dispute settlement mechanisms, foreign investors can sue the host state for threats to their investments posed by domestic measures, including new environmental regulations and higher environmental standards. A case study from the Bulgarian privatization program, *Plama v Bulgaria*,[44] highlights the potential litigation issues within

44 *Plama Consortium Ltd. v Republic of Bulgaria*, ICSID Case No. ARB/03/24, Award issued on 27 August 2008.

the Kosovo context. Plama Consortium Limited, a Cypriot company, acquired shares of Plama AD, a privatized Bulgarian oil refinery. In *Plama*, the claimant sued Bulgaria for approximately US$300 million, pursuant to the Energy Community Treaty. Its claims centered, inter alia, on allegations relating to the environmental liability of privatized entities, specifically the issue of the allocation of environmental cleanup and remediation costs for previous pollution damage. Plama claimed that the Bulgarian government was reneging on a prior commitment within their privatization agreements to shoulder liability for past pollution events. The tribunal considered the claims in view of the host state's Energy Community Treaty obligations with respect to fair and equitable treatment, constant protection and security, unreasonable and discriminatory measures, and expropriation. Specifically, the tribunal noted that under the fair and equitable treatment standard, the treaty does not protect the investor against any and all changes to the host country's (environmental) laws, unless the investor had reasonable and justifiable expectations in this regard. On the facts, and applying a "balanced interpretation which takes into account the totality of the [treaty]'s purpose," Bulgaria had not promised or made any representations to freeze its environmental laws in such a way as to have raised or created such expectations on the part of Plama.[45]

Thus, the Kosovo government should not necessarily be constrained when ensuring that investors in future privatization projects are subject to appropriate environmental regulation. This is significant because two of the largest prospective privatization projects have serious environmental and social implications. These include the putative privatization of the Kosovo Energy Corporation (see above) and the possible privatization of the most significant of all Kosovo small- and medium-scale enterprises—the large Trepça mining complex—which remains unresolved because of the political sensitivities raised by the location of the company site in Serb-dominated Northern Kosovo. In this regard, the Privatization Agency of Kosovo's recommendations for Trepça include the assignment of a special legal team to ensure that any reorganization plan for Trepça deals with ownership, social, and environmental issues,[46] especially environmental liability issues arising from more than 60 million tons of ore remains spread along the Ibar and other Kosovo river banks, according to the agency's 2010 annual report.[47] The resolution of these environmental issues through the environmental justice mechanisms outlined below is arguably representative of the wider challenge of holding both foreign and domestic investors to account within a transitional society like Kosovo.

45 *Ibid.*, Award, para.219, p.68.

46 Privatization Agency of Kosovo (PAK), Work Report, August 2008–August 2009, para.4.6, p.118, www.pak-ks.org/repository/docs/090904-English_Ver.pdf.

47 PAK Annual Report, January–December, 2010, p.17, www.pak-ks.org/repository/docs/raporti_anglisht_FINAL.pdf.

Striking a balance between stimulating investment and environmental protection in Kosovo

The most significant environmental principles for the achievement of "sustainable development" in Kosovo are as follows: the environmental impact assessment principle, providing that the environmental impact of proposed socioeconomic activities is fully accounted for; and the principle of public participation on environmental issues in decision-making processes relating to such socioeconomic development activities, including, for these purposes, access to justice. This latter set of principles is now established in the 1998 Aarhus Convention.[48] They are significant *procedural* requirements for the achievement of "environmental justice". Equally important to note is that the provision of procedural "rights" within these environmental principles stems from parallel developments in human rights law.

The potential application of these procedural environmental "rights" is crucial to the resolution of transitional "environmental justice" issues in Kosovo. At a practical level, the implementation of these principles is of utmost importance for ensuring that a local community not only has a voice but is confident that its voice will be heard. However, it should be noted that all three aspects of these principles—namely, environmental information, public participation, and access to justice—merely constitute the provision of procedural, rather than substantive, rights. A substantive right to a healthy or clean environment is not as well-established under international law as the procedural rights enumerated above. Such a right to a healthy environment would arguably establish a clear presumption against which any environmental interferences would have to be justified in explicit terms. Thus, it can be said that while a *substantive* human right to a clean or healthy environment has yet to be developed in international law, *procedural* environmental rights are now being progressively developed in the form of environmental impact assessments, as well as access to environmental information, public participation rights, and access to environmental justice (Aarhus).

Most Aarhus Convention rights are now part of EU law, which in turn is part of the European Community *acquis*. Access to information and participation in decision-making processes on environmental matters are legislated by EC/U directives. Although Kosovo has not signed the Aarhus Convention, its environmental legislation includes two pillars of the Convention: public access to environmental information and justice in environmental matters.

48 UN Economic Commission for Europe (UN-ECE) *Convention on Access to Information, Public Participation in Decision-making and Access to Justice in Environmental Matters*, adopted: 25 June 1998, entered into force: 30 October 2001. Serbia, which still considers Kosovo to be part of its territory, acceded to this Convention on 31 July 2009, www.unece.org/env/pp/treatytext.htm.

Access to information is also guaranteed by the Law on Environmental Protection (2009) and the Law on Access to Official Documents (2003). Public participation in decision making is enshrined in a number of other local laws, including the Law of Water (2004) and Law for Nature Protection (2005). However, implementation and enforcement of these laws has been slow, the public is not informed of its legal rights, and officials are often unaware of the obligation to share information.[49] As noted below, EU law has been interpreted by the European Court of Justice (ECJ) to apply equally to corporations that supply public utilities such as energy and water. Thus, insofar as these Kosovo laws reflect the relevant EU directives, they should similarly be applied to companies providing such public services in Kosovo.

Articles 22 and 53 of the 2008 Kosovo Constitution are also important here. They provide not only for the direct application of provisions from the European Convention on Human Rights but additionally for their application as interpreted by European Court of Human Rights jurisprudence. Article 52 of the Kosovo Constitution, on "responsibility for the environment," goes even further and provides for responsibility for nature and biodiversity protection, as well as the first and second pillars of the 1998 Aarhus Convention—namely, the right to be informed and participate (or in other words consulted) on environmental issues, and the environmental impact assessment principle. The relevant European Convention rights in the context of environmental issues are articles 2 (right to life) and 8 (right to privacy, family life, and home), and article 1 of Protocol I (right to property).

The most significant of these provisions is article 8, which has been interpreted by the European Court of Human Rights to include prevention from serious environmental interferences, rather than recognizing an intrinsic human right to a healthy, healthful, or clean environment, let alone any extended or additional state duty to ensure the protection of the natural environment.[50] As the Grand Chamber of the Court observed in *Hatton v UK*,[51] there is no explicit right in the Convention to a clean and quiet environment, but where an individual is directly and seriously affected by noise or other pollution, an issue may arise under article 8. Thus, in *Powell and Rayner v the UK*, where the applicants had complained about disturbance from daytime aircraft noise, the Court held that article 8 was relevant, since "the quality of [each] applicant's private life and the scope for enjoying the amenities of his

49 World Bank, Europe and Central Asia Region, Sustainable Development Department, *Integrating Environment into Agriculture and Forestry: Progress and Prospects in Eastern Europe and Central Asia*, Volume II, Kosovo Review, 2007, p.7.

50 L. Loucaides, 'Environmental Protection through the Jurisprudence of the European Convention on Human Rights', 75 *British Yearbook of International Law* 249–267 (2005), p.249.

51 *Hatton and Others v the United Kingdom* (GC), Judgment of 8 July 2003, (2005) 37 EHHR 28, para.96.

home [had] been adversely affected by the noise generated by aircraft using Heathrow Airport."[52] Similarly, in *López Ostra v Spain*, the Court held that article 8 could include a right to protection from severe environmental pollution, since such a problem might "affect individuals' well-being and prevent them from enjoying their homes in such a way as to affect their private and family life adversely, without, however, seriously endangering their health."[53] In *Guerra and Others v Italy*, which also concerned environmental pollution, the Court observed that the "direct effect of the toxic emissions on the applicants' right to respect for their private and family life means that Article 8 is applicable."[54] A significant recent case in this line of Court judgments is *Fadeyeva v Russia*,[55] where the Court accepted the applicant's claim that her prolonged exposure to excessive pollution levels from a nearby steel plant had "adversely affected the quality of life at her home" and that "the actual detriment to the applicant's health and well-being reached a level sufficient to bring it within the scope of Article 8 of the Convention."[56] These judgments have expanded the application of article 8 to cover serious environmental interferences.[57]

As noted above, these environmental principles and their derived procedural standards and rights are referred to in the Kosovo Constitution. They are elaborated by further and more specific environmental laws promulgated by the Kosovo Assembly, such as the Law on Environmental Protection (2009) and the Law on Environmental Impact Assessment (2009). Despite the progressive inclusion of these environmental principles and rights within the domestic legal framework, the overall domestic institutional governance for the implementation of these environmental laws and other laws still needs to be improved.[58]

Following from this and building on the fact that the Kosovo authorities are engaged in a long-term exercise to harmonize Kosovo's legal standards on environmental protection, we will focus on developments in ECJ jurisprudence on the potential horizontal direct effect of directives that afford opportunities for progress on environmental justice issues within Kosovo. Although these legal pathways for securing environmental justice are currently unavailable within the Kosovo jurisdiction, their potential application will be canvassed

52 Judgment of 21 February 1990, Series A no.172, para.40.

53 Judgment of 9 December 1994, Series A no.303-C, para.51.

54 Judgment of 19 February 1998, *Reports of Judgments and Decisions* 1998-I, para.57.

55 *Fadeyeva v Russia*, ECtHR, Judgment of 9 June 2005, (2007) 45 EHRR 10.

56 *Ibid.*, para.88.

57 This line of judgments has been confirmed by, inter alia, the following cases: *Giacomelli v Italy*, Judgment of 2 November 2006, (2007) 45 EHRR 38; *Tatar v Romania*, Judgment of 27 January 2009, Application no.67021/01, unreported; and recently, *Băcilă v Romania*, Judgment of 30 March 2010, Application no.19234/04, unreported.

58 EU Rule of Law Mission in Kosovo (EULEX) Programme Report 2010, p.25, www.eulex-kosovo.eu/en/.

here on the assumption that the EULEX "standards beyond status" strategy for Kosovo will ultimately prove successful and result in the progressive integration of Kosovo within the EU policy and legal framework,[59] if not quite EU membership in the foreseeable future. The following paragraphs therefore outline the potential "horizontal" effect of the EC/U directives implementing certain Aarhus Convention rights, especially against privatized utilities.

Under the ECJ doctrine of "direct effect," relevant EC/U treaty provisions and legislation that are precise and unconditional, and whose time limits for implementation by the member states have passed, have direct legal effects in that individuals can rely on these provisions directly against member state authorities within national courts. However, since directives are binding only as to the goal to be achieved by the directive concerned, it was thought that they could not be relied on directly by a private party against another private person. The question of the "horizontal" direct effect against another private actor under EU law is therefore problematic.[60] According to ECJ doctrine, EC/U directives do *not* allow horizontal or third-party legal effects. In the absence of domestic (member state) implementing measures, they do not usually allow individual claims against other private legal individuals, such as business corporations.[61]

However, both the ECJ and domestic courts have interpreted the term "public authority" broadly.[62] With much that was previously in the public sector now having been privatized, some privatized utilities may still be considered to be "emanations" of the state and therefore falling within the definition of "public authority" for the purposes of the application of an EC/U directive. Emanations of the state are bodies that provide "public services" and, in doing so, are able to exercise "special powers" not usually available to private bodies, and which are still under the "control" of the state. The seminal case *Foster v British Gas* before the ECJ on a preliminary reference request from the English High Court raised the possibility that privatized companies fulfilling public service functions, such as utilities (electricity, gas, and water) and waste treatment and disposal companies, may be subject to EU law,[63] including EC/U environmental directives.

59 M. Spernbauer, 'EULEX Kosovo: The Difficult Deployment and Challenging Implementation of the Most Comprehensive Civilian EU Operation to Date', 11 *German Law Journal* 769–802 (2010).

60 P. Craig, 'The Legal Effect of Directives: Policy, Rules and Exceptions', 34 *European Law Review* 349–377 (2009), pp.374–375.

61 The leading case is *Faccini Dori v Recreb*, C-91/92 [1994] ECR I-3325, para.20.

62 See *Marshall v Southampton and South West Hampshire Area Health Authority*, Case 152/84, [1986] ECR 723. For commentary, see A. Arnull, 'The incoming tide: responding to Marshall', *Public Law* 383–399 (1987).

63 *Foster v British Gas* [1990] ECR I-3313.

In *Griffin and others v South West Water Services Ltd. (SWW)*, also argued before the English High Court,[64] it was held that the defendant—a privatized water company—could be "horizontally" bound by EC employment directives, although the relevant provisions were ultimately not considered to be sufficiently clear, precise, or unconditional to be relied on by individuals for direct effect against the company.[65] According to Nigel Haigh, the High Court's finding that privatized water companies may be bound by the horizontal direct effect of employment directives could equally apply to environmental directives,[66] especially those implementing Aarhus Convention rights. Since Kosovo is obliged to strive to meet the relevant EU environmental standards under the Instrument for Pre-Accession Assistance, the possibility arises that once these procedural environmental rights are promulgated within Kosovo laws, they too will be interpreted (for example, by EULEX-appointed judges or prosecutors) as being applicable against any privatized entities permitted to run these services within Kosovo. Moreover, once remaining domestic institutional and personnel capacity issues are resolved, the influx of private actors within the fledgling Kosovo market economy will arguably be regulated to a similar degree to the rest of the Western European polity.

Conclusion: prospects for transitional environmental justice in Kosovo

It is still uncertain whether the international and EU-led socioeconomic reconstruction of Kosovo provides sufficient legal and institutional safeguards against environmental damage from the private investors and actors invited to participate in this project. In particular, EULEX efforts to strengthen domestic Kosovo institutions are crucial to the success or failure of this exercise. The relevant environmental principles and rights are now in place, along with legal avenues and techniques for ensuring the implementation and enforcement of these principles and rights. These hold real potential for addressing the possible negative environmental and social side effects of an unmitigated emphasis on the economic aspects of reconstruction efforts within Kosovo. Extrapolating from the Kosovo experience to inform other transitional polities suggests that both establishing and utilizing similar environmental and social rights to achieve *transitional environmental justice* is

64 [1995] IRLR 15. See J. Eady, 'Collective Dismissals, Consultation and Remedies: Griffen (sic) v South West Water Services Ltd (1994-G-no.3532; judgment 25.8.94) (Ch.D)', 23 *Industrial Law Journal* 350–354 (1994).

65 See *Griffin and others v South West Water Services Ltd. (SWW)* [1995] IRLR 15, paras.140–141.

66 N. Haigh, *Manual of Environmental Policy: The EU and Britain, The EC and Britain*, Cartermill Publishing, London, loose-leaf volume.

an important additional goal for all transitional societies. Significantly, environmental justice mechanisms are based on objective grounds and are non-discriminatory in their application, thereby ensuring that baseline environmental quality criteria are met for everyone. They are less likely to favor one ethnic community against another in an ethnically divided transitional society.

Moreover, the prospective inclusion of Kosovo into the EU legal framework should also exert an increasingly normative pull on domestic institutions and actors, including privatized utilities, as Kosovo strives to meet its EU pre-accession candidate requirements. The potential direct and even "horizontal" direct effect of EC/U directives, following doctrine developed by the ECJ, allows environmental justice mechanisms to be used against public institutions and private actors in cases where the private actors are deemed to be performing public service functions. Finally, the inclusion of higher environmental quality standards through further European integration acts as an additional spur to improve the environmental performance of all private actors investing and operating in Kosovo, whether or not they are deemed to be providing public services.

Chapter 12

Transitional States and the Flag of Convenience Fishing Industry

Darren Calley

Introduction

Conventional wisdom states that the corporations behind the flag of convenience[1] (FOC) fishing industry depend on weak and isolated states for their very existence and, correlatively, these states need the revenue generated by the FOC industry for their economic well-being. Many of the states currently listed as FOCs are states in transition: the International Transport Workers' Federation's list of 32 FOC states includes numerous states that are presently in the process of rebuilding their societies and economies after years of internal strife or external conflict.[2] This chapter will show, however, that far from being a relationship of mutual reliance and benefit, the relationship between transitional states and the FOC industry is uniquely exploitative and destructive, leaving only one side—the state—accountable for the harms caused. By countering the myth of symbiotic benefit, this chapter suggests that an alternative strategy of inclusion and lawfulness can have a much greater long-term benefit to transitional states that may be tempted to enter the FOC fishing industry.

It is worth stating, at the outset, the main argument posited here so that some valid and reasonable objections can be addressed. The central thesis is thus: many transitional states may see the FOC industry as an easy short-term solution to a pressing and immediate need for foreign investment. In this regard, the opening up of maritime registries to non-indigenous vessels is

1 As will be shown throughout this chapter, it is states' non-compliance with international laws that makes these states attractive to vessel owners. Thus, the slightly more apt term "flag of non-compliance" has recently found its way into the international fisheries discourse. Nonetheless, this chapter will use the more familiar and traditional term "flag of convenience."

2 The International Transport Workers' Federation recognizes 32 FOC states, of which many—Bolivia, Burma, Cambodia, Georgia, Honduras, Lebanon, and Liberia—have recently emerged from periods of internal unrest (see www.itfglobal.org/flags-convenience/flags-convenien-183.cfm). Inexplicably omitted from the Federation's list is Sierra Leone, which has historically been one of the most notorious FOC states.

thought to benefit states financially; for instance, larger FOCs have historically made sums of up to US$20 million per annum.[3] One might legitimately ask, therefore, what is wrong with states, particularly transitional ones, in need of foreign capital making the most of the opportunity to increase the size of their fishing fleets? The answer, as will be shown, is that the medium- to long-term repercussions of this practice can include states being subjected to painful trade embargoes that far outweigh the financial benefits of involvement with the FOC industry. One might nonetheless argue that these consequences are, on balance, a price worth paying if the state in transition also benefits from a large fishing capacity so that it can meet its obligations under article 11 of the International Covenant on Economic, Social and Cultural Rights to guarantee the right to food of its citizens. After all, a stable fishing industry is, according to the Food and Agriculture Organization of the UN, a very good thing. The global market for fish and fisheries products is worth an estimated US$93.9 billion,[4] and fish accounts for 15 per cent of the daily animal protein intake in the diets of three billion people.[5] Why would any state, not least of all a state in transition, not wish to partake of these benefits?

Yet, far from helping build developing states' capacities to feed themselves, the FOC industry often is destructive and undermines artisanal and coastal fishing entities; has been involved in serious breaches of human rights;[6] and negatively affects the sustainability of the entire fisheries sector.

Legal loophole that allows FOCs to flourish

According to the 1982 UN Convention on the Law of the Sea (UNCLOS)—the widely accepted[7] and authoritative instrument on the international law of the oceans—ships of all states have the right to use the high seas.[8] While on the high seas, provided that they are engaged in purely peaceful activities,[9] vessels are subject to very little authority other than the laws of

3 See, for instance, J. Swan, *Fishing Vessels Operating under Open Registries and the Exercise of Flag State Responsibilities – Information and Options*, Fisheries Circular No.90, FIPP/C980, UNFAO, Rome, 2002, Appendix 9, Table 3.

4 *The State of World Fisheries and Aquaculture 2010*, UN Food and Agriculture Organization, Rome, 2010, p.5.

5 *Ibid.*, p.64.

6 Not covered in this chapter, but see the International Transport Workers' Federation campaign against FOCs, www.itfglobal.org/flags-convenience/index.cfm.

7 UNCLOS currently has 161 state parties; see www.un.org/Depts/los/reference_files/chronological_lists_of_ratifications.htm#The United Nations Convention on the Law of the Sea.

8 UNCLOS, article 87.

9 UNCLOS, article 98.

the state of registry[10] and the (often rather vague) principles enunciated in the Convention itself. In terms of fishing, UNCLOS lacks detail, and the obligations imposed on states in this regard are simply to respect the rights of other states[11] and to cooperate to conserve stocks.[12]

Although the granting of a flag to vessels (the colloquialism used to denote registration) vests a great deal of power in the flag state (the state of registry), UNCLOS does not require a pre-existing connection between the state and the vessel: states can, and do, offer their flags to any vessel they choose.[13] The FOC industry thrives on this lack of regulation. While there are laws that bind some states, these laws are most often the product of states agreeing between themselves that certain detailed rules must apply on the high seas. International agreements adopted in the wake of UNCLOS—for example, the Fish Stocks Agreement,[14] the Compliance Agreement,[15] and measures enunciated under the auspices of regional fisheries management organizations (RFMOs)[16]—bind only states that are party to them, leaving the many states[17] that do not wish to subject themselves to these agreements free to disregard their rules.[18] Thus, unscrupulous vessel owners, by registering their vessels to states that are not party to these detailed agreements, can evade the laws to which "responsible" states subject themselves.

Inconvenient laws of the sea: bycatch and discards

The regulations evaded by the FOC fishing fleet include not only those seeking to protect seafarers or prevent the well-documented decline of

10 The most explicit exceptions are piracy (UNCLOS, article 105), narcotics (article 108), unauthorized broadcasting (article 109), and slavery (article 99). In these cases, the rights of seizure, arrest, and visit are vested in all states.

11 UNCLOS, article 87(2).

12 UNCLOS, articles 116–119.

13 UNCLOS, article 91.

14 *The United Nations Agreement for the Implementation of the Provisions of the Convention of 10 December 1982 Relating to the Conservation and Management of Straddling Fish Stocks and Highly Migratory Fish Stocks*, UN General Assembly, New York, 1995.

15 *Agreement to Promote Compliance with International Conservation and Management Measures by Fishing Vessels on the High Seas*, UNFAO, Rome, 1993.

16 RFMOs are the principal means of regional governance and are the organizations empowered by international agreements such as UNCLOS (article 118) and the Fish Stocks Agreement (Part III) to put the detailed provisions of oceans management in place.

17 For instance, while the Fish Stocks Agreement has 78 state parties, this represents less than 50 per cent of UNCLOS's membership. The Compliance Agreement is even more underrepresented, with only 39 state parties.

18 This legal idyll is, of course, subject to the political reality of the world order: as shown in this chapter, political pressure can, and often is, exerted on states to become parties to these Conventions and subjugate themselves to the laws contained therein.

fish stocks[19] but also those enacted to protect a diverse and degrading environment. For instance, a plethora of laws guard against the bycatch of non-target fish stocks and the "incidental mortality" of seabirds, sharks, dolphins, and turtles.[20] Avoiding these types of regulations puts FOC vessels at a competitive advantage—and in the cut-throat business of international fisheries, advantages count. For example, consider the serious threat posed to the marine environment by the common practice of discarding non-target fisheries (bycatch). Data suggests that 8 per cent of all fishery capture is thrown back into the ocean[21] simply because the catch is undesirable due to its size, species, or gender.[22] This problem has vexed the minds of the architects of fisheries policy for many years and has resulted in several international initiatives seeking to limit unnecessary discards. For instance, state parties to the UN Fish Stocks Agreement commit themselves to ensuring that their vessels comply with measures "aimed at minimizing catches of non-target species."[23] These measures (which apply only to those vessels flagged to states party to the Fish Stocks Agreement) are, by their very nature, often "inconvenient" to those actually engaged in the fishing industry, but are deemed necessary to prevent the decline of stock numbers or the unnecessary deaths of marine-dependent species.

Running a commercial-scale fishery is rarely an exact science. Despite advances in fishing technology, fishery requires luck and judgment in equal measure—quite simply, you place your net or line in the water and trust that what you catch is what you hoped for. Unmodified nets and lines can rarely discriminate between, say, mature tuna that is sought and juvenile tuna that cannot be marketed. Nor can they prevent the inadvertent trapping of turtles, dolphins, or seabirds. Recognizing the intolerably high level of bycatch, the international community has enacted numerous laws, as required by the Fish Stocks Agreement, to modify fishing practices so that equipment can be more discriminating. For instance, many RFMOs require that vessels fishing in "their" waters make efforts to avoid the bycatch of sea turtles.[24] Whilst

19 See, for example, UNFAO, *The State of the World's Fisheries and Aquaculture*, UNFAO, Rome, 2008, p.7.

20 For example, *The International Plan of Action for Reducing Incidental Catch of Seabirds in Longline Fisheries*, UNFAO, Rome, 1999; *The International Plan of Action for the Conservation and Management of Sharks*, UNFAO, Rome, 1999; *The La Jolla Agreement for the Reduction of Dolphin Mortality in the Eastern Pacific Ocean, Inter-American Tropical Tuna Commission*, La Jolla, 1992; *Guidelines to Reduce Sea Turtle Mortality in Fishing Operations*, UNFAO, Rome, 2009.

21 K. Keller, *Discards in the World's Marine Fisheries: An Update*, Food and Agriculture Organisation of the United Nations Fisheries Technical Paper 470, Rome, 2005, p.17.

22 *Ibid.*, p.5.

23 Fish Stocks Agreement, article 18(3)(i).

24 The global reported level of turtle bycatch between 1990 and 2008 was at least 85,000, but a more likely estimate of actual turtle mortality was calculated by Bryan Wallace to be "at least two orders of magnitude higher than this reported total." See B. Wallace, 'Global Patterns of Marine Turtle By-catch', *Conservation Letters* 1–12 (2010), pp.7–8.

analyzing each of these measures goes beyond the scope of this chapter, it is useful to consider one of them as an illustration. For example, the Inter-American Tropical Tuna Commission's (IATTC) Resolution to Mitigate the Impact of Tuna Fishing Vessels on Sea Turtles[25] requires all IATTC member states to ensure that their registered vessels adhere to the turtle mortality mitigation methods listed in the resolution. Thus, vessels should take positive steps to avoid the entanglement of turtles in nets or lines and should release any turtles that are entangled.[26] Additionally, states should implement observer programs[27] (whereby fishing vessels are monitored at sea) and adhere to the requirements of the FAO's Guidelines to Reduce Sea Turtle Mortality in Fishing Operations.[28]

From a financial cost-benefit perspective, which focuses on increasing productivity and reducing costs, every minute spent by a vessel's crew releasing entangled turtles from nets means a minute's lost productivity, and every dollar spent on new "turtle proof" nets is a dollar lost. Therefore, vessel owners may prefer to evade these inconvenient and unprofitable regulations by seeking a state of registry that is not bound to implement them. A vessel flagged, for instance, to Honduras (which is not an IAATC member) can fish in huge tracts of high seas in the Eastern Central Pacific while ignoring any measures established for sea turtle conservation, whereas vessels flagged, for example, to Costa Rica or the United States (both IAATC members) must adhere to the rules requiring the protection of sea turtles.

Benefits of international engagement: "turtle tourism"

Why should transitional states worry about the loss of a few sea turtles? One answer is that living sea turtles can be worth three times as much as dead ones, and it is often developing, coastal states that benefit from the tourism trade that follows such creatures.[29] Thus, any transitional state with the necessary geographical characteristics, a supply of living turtles, and a need for foreign investment might consider the fact that Costa Rica reaps almost US$9 million annually from its turtle tourism industry—nine times the revenue generated by the world's most lucrative FOC fishing registry, Honduras, during that registry's heyday.[30] This US$9 million has benefitted

25 Resolution C-07-03 of June 2007.

26 *Ibid.*, articles 6 and 7.

27 *Ibid.*, article 4.

28 *Ibid.*, article 1.

29 S. Troëng and C. Drews, *Money Talks: Economic Aspects of Marine Turtle Use and Conservation*, WWF International, Gland, 2004, p.22.

30 Of a total revenue of US$3.5 million generated by all FOC vessels (which include oil tankers, passenger liners, cargo vessels, etc.), Honduras's FOC fishing registry, whilst being the largest of all FOC states, generated a mere US$1 million; see Swan, n.3.

Costa Rica enormously and ensured that localities with few economic opportunities are able to satisfy the basic needs of far more of their people than are comparable locations that do not benefit from "turtle tourism."[31] Granted, the revenue generated by "turtle tourism" is negligible when compared to the Costa Rican and Honduran GDPs;[32] nevertheless, it is worth recalling that turtle mortality itself is merely one small portion of the larger problem of bycatch and discard, which, in turn, is just one of the global scourges created by unregulated fishing vessels. The point to be made, therefore, is not simply that turtles or eco-tourism—or, for that matter, any single issue—can resolve the financial problems faced by transitional states. Rather, whilst "selling" flags to unscrupulous vessel owners might be profitable, there is also revenue to be had by engaging with the international laws of the sea.

Negative impacts on states of FOC involvement: Honduras

For most of the twentieth century, Honduras formed, alongside Panama and Liberia, the so-called PanLibHon axis of FOC states that provided refuge for thousands of vessel owners seeking to evade state regulations concerning such diverse matters as alcohol prohibition, the neutrality of vessels in times of conflict, and labor relations.[33] Nonetheless, the Honduran experience of the late 1990s is perhaps one of the most telling examples of how a failure to engage with the international laws of the marine environment can result in real detriment to states. By the mid-1990s, Honduran-flagged fishing vessels were, according to the International Commission for the Conservation of Atlantic Tunas (ICCAT), fishing "in a manner which diminishes the effectiveness of the ICCAT bluefin tuna conservation measures." The Commission had, in 1996, attempted to engage with Honduras to no avail,[34] and so, in 1997, recommended that its members prohibit the importation of all Honduran-caught Atlantic bluefin tuna.[35] This process of prohibition was repeated, for the same reasons, in 2000 for all Honduran swordfish imports,[36]

31 Troëng and Drews, n.29, p.43.

32 US$35 billion and US$15 billion, respectively; see World Bank Country Data, http://data.worldbank.org/country.

33 See J. Wells, 'Vessel Registrations in Selected Open Registries', 6 *Tulane Maritime Law Journal* 221 (1981); B. Boczek, *Flags of Convenience: An International Legal Study*, Harvard University Press, Cambridge, MA, 1982.

34 See ICCAT Biennial Report 1996–1997, Part One (1996), Volume 1, Annex 7.3, www.iccat.es/Documents/BienRep/REP_EN_96-97_I_1.pdf.

35 Recommendation by ICCAT Regarding Belize and Honduras Pursuant to 1994 Bluefin Tuna Action Plan (Rec. 96/11), entered into force 4 August 1997.

36 *Recommendation by ICCAT Regarding Belize and Honduras Pursuant to 1995 Swordfish Action Plan* (Rec. 99/8), entered into force 15 June 2000.

and in 2001 for bigeye tuna imports.[37] Consequently, until these measures were removed in 2002,[38] following action by Honduran authorities to deregister many known offender vessels and subject the country's remaining fleet to greater regulation,[39] all Honduran exports of tuna and swordfish—and not just those consignments that could be traced to individual vessels engaged in deleterious activities—were denied entry to the markets of ICCAT members. Considering the scale of this lost market (ICCAT members include the United States, the European Union, and Japan[40]) and the benefits to the Honduran economy of fisheries exports, this was an arguably devastating blow.

Trade data for Honduras for tuna and tuna-like species during the period in which the ICCAT prohibition was in place, 1997–2002, is extremely difficult to come by. It is therefore not possible to estimate the price that Honduras paid for its unregulated FOC fishing fleet. It is, however, certain that the economic impact of the prohibition was felt by the Honduran government to such an extent that, as Honduran delegate Pedro Marcio Castellón informed ICCAT members during a special meeting in 2002, Honduras cancelled the registrations of 228 of its 269 registered fishing vessels.[41] This revocation by a state of its links to the FOC industry was, as will be shown below, the first of many public exercises in self-chastisement showing that the price for involvement in deleterious FOC activities was one not worth paying.

Like many underdeveloped countries, Honduras was, in the late 1990s, facing the biggest economic crisis in its history. Further, Hurricane Mitch, which swept through Central America in November 1998, aggravated Honduras's precarious financial situation by destroying many valuable crops and goods that would have been, under normal circumstances, destined for export.[42] To address this economic catastrophe, Sñr. Castellón announced that Honduras planned to develop a tuna fishing industry that contained only vessels over which Honduras could exercise control, so as to comply with ICCAT requirements. This "new" fishing industry would "generate

37 *Recommendation by ICCAT Regarding Belize, Cambodia, Honduras and St. Vincent and Grenadines Pursuant to the 1998 Resolution Concerning the Unreported and Unregulated Catches of Tunas by Large-Scale Longline Vessels in the Convention Area* (Rec. 02/18), entered into force 15 October 2001.

38 *Recommendation by ICCAT Concerning the Importation of Bluefin Tuna and Swordfish and Their Products From Honduras* (Rec. 01/15), entered into force 21 September 2002; *Recommendation by ICCAT Concerning the Importation of Bigeye Tuna and its Products From Honduras* (Rec. 02/18).

39 For further details see ICCAT, *Biennial Report 2002–2003*, Part One (2002), Volume 1, Annex 10, Appendix 5.

40 See ICCAT Contracting Parties, www.iccat.es/en/contracting.htm.

41 ICCAT, n.39, Volume 1, *Proceedings for the Special Meeting of the Commission*, p.74.

42 P. Morgan, *Honduras Fights Back After Mitch*, BBC News, February 1999, http://news.bbc.co.uk/1/hi/world/americas/276122.stm.

employment, revenue, and foreign currency."[43] If the generation of employment, revenue, and foreign currency required engagement with the international community, then what was the point of Honduras' involvement with the FOC industry in the first place? Consequently, one might ask, why—in the absence of any lasting financial incentive—might any state enter the FOC market?

FOC exodus from Central America

As previously noted, the turn of the millennium witnessed a mass expulsion of vessels from the Honduran registry. Adding to the 200-plus vessels expelled by Honduras, both Belize and Panama, for identical reasons (the ICCAT trade embargo), each purged up to 300 vessels from their respective registries.[44] These vessels did not cease to exist but instead found other states of registry. This section will chart the experiences of two of the states that hosted these vessels—Cambodia and Sierra Leone—to show that, like the case of Honduras, this dalliance with the FOC industry ultimately resulted in international condemnation and economic loss. The two states focused on below were not chosen because they are exceptional or unique: the section could equally have focused on any other of the many states providing a flag to ex-Honduran, Belizean, or Panamanian vessels. Cambodia and Sierra Leone were chosen simply because of their status as emblematic transitional states that felt the effects of international condemnation and economic sanctions particularly harshly.

Cambodia

Cambodia's turbulent history is well documented[45] and requires little explanation here. Nor do the problems of governance in Cambodia, following the fall of the Khmer Rouge in 1979, present any surprises. Riddled with corruption and incompetence following the "systematic destruction of the professional class" during the Khmer Rouge years, Cambodia's executive, legislature, and judiciary were in a terrible state of disarray at the turn of the millennium.[46] Years of civil war, several attempted *coups d'état*, and a residual

43 ICCAT, n.39, Volume 1, *Proceedings for the Special Meeting of the Commission*, p.74.

44 On the Belize expulsions, see D. Calley, *Market Denial and International Fisheries Regulation: The Targeted and Effective Use of Trade Measures Against the Flag of Convenience Fishing Industry*, Martinus Nijhof Publishers, Boston, 2012, pp.30–38.

45 K. Muddell, *Transitional Justice in Cambodia: Challenges and Opportunities*, International Centre for Transitional Justice and Human Rights Watch, Symposium Report, September 2003, http://ictj.org/sites/default/files/ICTJ-HRW-Cambodia-Symposium-2003-English.pdf.

46 *Ibid.*, p.4.

number of former Khmer Rouge members holding positions of political influence had left the state apparatus barely functioning.[47] Indeed, even as late as 2006, Cambodia's Deputy Prime Minister, Sok An, was forced to concede that his country still had more to do in order to achieve "perfect" law, order, and security.[48] The external view was slightly more damning: in the early years of the twenty-first century, wrote one observer, Cambodia lacked "anything resembling a legal culture, much less the rule of law."[49]

One potential explanation for Cambodia's attraction to the FOC industry might have been that "the voids and inconsistencies in the existing Cambodian Law provide[d] an abundance of opportunity for impropriety and perversion in the course of justice."[50] The lacunae in Cambodia's fisheries legislation were (and still are) quite apparent: article 51 of the Cambodian Law on Fisheries (itself not enacted until 2006) states simply that fishing and fisheries research, in international waters, shall respect national and international laws.[51] Absent from the Law on Fisheries are details on how such activities should adhere to international laws.

As well as lacking adequate domestic laws, Cambodia was devoid of any legal imperative to implement international laws of the sea. At the time of its entry into the international FOC industry, Cambodia was not engaged with the international "community of fisheries states." Although Cambodia indicated a willingness to abide by the more general provisions of UNCLOS by its signature of that Convention in 1983, it had not (and has not) become a party to the Fish Stocks Agreement or the UNFAO Compliance Agreement, both of which contain specific and detailed provisions regarding the fishing industry. Nor is Cambodia a member of any RFMO. Thus, despite the existence of international treaties governing how, where, and when high seas fishing operations can be undertaken, Cambodian flagged vessels—no matter how harmful and deleterious their actions—could not be held accountable under international law. As a non-party to international fisheries instruments, Cambodia was not obliged to apply any of their measures against its vessels, even if it had the capacity to do so.

The activities of the Cambodian fleet did not go unnoticed, however: Cambodian fishing vessels were, according to ICCAT, "fishing for tuna and

47 D. PoKempner, 'The Khmer Rouge Tribunal: Criticisms and Concerns', in *The Extraordinary Chambers*, the Open Society Justice Initiatives, 2006, pp.33–35, www.soros.org/initiatives/justice/articles_publications/publications/justice_20060421/jinitiatives_200604.pdf.

48 A. Sok, 'The Khmer Rouge Tribunal: What it Means for Cambodia,' in *The Extraordinary Chambers*, the Open Society Justice Initiatives, 2006, p.28.

49 PoKempner, n.47, p.34.

50 S. Linton, 'Safeguarding the Independence and Impartiality of the Cambodian Extraordinary Chambers', 4 *Journal of International Criminal Justice* 327–341 (2006), p.336, albeit the comment was made in a slightly different context.

51 Cambodian Law on Fisheries 2006 (Unofficial Translation), UN FAO, Rome, http://faolex.fao.org/docs/pdf/cam82001.pdf.

tuna-like species in a manner which diminishes the effectiveness of ICCAT conservation and management measures."[52] As a consequence, ICCAT recommended that its members—including the important import markets of the United States, Japan, Russia, China, and the European Union—"take appropriate measures . . . to the effect that the import of Atlantic bigeye tuna and its products in any form from . . . Cambodia . . . be prohibited."[53] Before these sanctions could bite, however, a seemingly chided and contrite Cambodian delegate appeared before the 2004 ICCAT meeting to explain his country's poor record of vessel management, stating:

> Cambodia has just emerged from more than two decades of civil war and internal unrest during the late 1990s. Thus, every effort has been made to reconstruct this war torn country from scratch especially the negative effects of the notorious Khmer Rouge regime. The country is now in the very busy process of rebuilding its lost human and physical resources to catch up with the developed world. On the other hand, it is the top priority of the Royal Government to reintegrate the country into the international community. . . .
>
> As a response to the trade ban, the Government has moved a step further by firing the Shipping Registry Company and the revocation of many registered vessels and the Government is taking the registration matter very seriously. . . . Cambodia will take any necessary measure to control its flagged vessels and to co-operate with the Secretariat to better implement the Convention.[54]

Seemingly content with this response, ICCAT lifted its tuna import prohibition against Cambodia that same year.[55] As the following section will demonstrate, Cambodia was not the only state to recognize the detrimental effects of its involvement with the FOC industry.

Sierra Leone

Sierra Leone, another notorious FOC state, also found itself questioning the gains to be had from allowing FOC vessels into its vessel registry. Unlike Cambodia, however, whose *volte-face* was almost exclusively driven by external factors such as the ICCAT trade embargo, Sierra Leone's reassessment of its fishing policy came about following a realization that even without external pressures, the FOC industry can negatively affect fragile transitional economies.

52 ICCAT Recommendation 00/15, Preamble.
53 *Ibid.*, article 1.
54 14th Annual Meeting of the Parties, Louisiana, 2004, ICCAT, *Report for the Biennial Period 2004–2005*, Part 1, Madrid, 2005.
55 ICCAT Recommendation 04/15.

Sierra Leone's dalliance with the FOC industry is remarkably similar to that of Cambodia, although on a slightly smaller scale. Like Cambodia, Sierra Leone was far from stable at the start of the twenty-first century and was not a participating member of the international community.[56] Although it had obligations under UNCLOS, which it signed and ratified in 1982 and 1994, respectively, in the context of the high seas, these obligations are little more than obligations to "co-operate and conserve."[57] Unlike Cambodia, however, Sierra Leone has put these obligations to cooperate into practice and become a member of a limited number of RFMOs—it has been a participant, for instance, in the Indian Ocean Tuna Commission[58] and ICCAT[59] since 2008. Furthermore, Sierra Leone has enacted numerous and detailed maritime and fisheries laws during its transition. The voluminous Merchant Shipping Act of 2003, for example, lists requirements for the granting of the Sierra Leonean flag to "foreign" vessels, and seemingly cognizant of the country's need to implement its obligations under UNCLOS, section 14 of the Act commits Sierra Leone to consult with foreign states to ensure that management and conservation plans are harmonized, and that arrangements are made to allocate fishing rights among interested states.[60]

In Sierra Leone's case, a rather bewildering picture begins to emerge. Despite its international commitments and domestic legislation, it is a participant in the FOC industry, with several of its registered vessels having been those that have moved from registry to registry whenever regulations appeared to stymie their activities. Of the fifty or so erstwhile Panamanian, Honduran, and Belizean vessels that, post-millennium, found refuge on the Sierra Leonean register,[61] a number are known and reported participants in illegal fishing: for example, vessels such as the *Gorilero*, a 43-year-old ex-Panamanian trawler that during its time as a Sierra Leonean vessel (2004–2007) was engaged in illegal fisheries in the North Atlantic,[62] or the *Sima Qian Baru 22* that, over a seven-year period, has engaged in numerous violations of the prohibition on fishing in certain areas of the South

56 For background on the status of Sierra Leone at the start of the millennium, see the *Report of the Security Council Mission to Sierra Leone*, UN Security Council, 16 October 2000, S/2000/992.

57 UNCLOS, articles 116–120.

58 See www.iotc.org/English/info/comstruct.php.

59 See www.iccat.int/en/contracting.htm.

60 The text of the Act and other noted legislation can be found at the FAO Fisheries and Aquaculture Department's FAO Lex, www.fao.org/fishery/countrysector/FI-CP_SL/5/en.

61 *Sea-Web Register of Ships*, www.sea-web.com/seaweb_key_features.html (subscription service).

62 The *Gorilero* was, and remains, listed by both the North East Atlantic Fisheries Commission and the Northwest Atlantic Fisheries Organization as engaged in fishing activities that undermine the effectiveness of conservation measures in the bodies' respective areas of competence. See www.neafc.org/blist and www.nafo.int/fisheries/frames/iuu.html.

Atlantic.[63] In fact, of the vessels with links to both Sierra Leone and one of the aforementioned Central American states, over 15 per cent are noted to have engaged in activities deemed to undermine fisheries conservation measures.[64]

As noted earlier in this chapter, there are some (relatively limited) fiscal advantages to be had for FOC states. In Sierra Leone's case, however, the opposite is true, and the FOC fishing fleet may actually cost the Sierra Leonean economy US$29 million per annum.[65] These losses consist of direct losses—for instance, "the value of the catches that could have been taken by the coastal state or licensed vessels if the illegal . . . [or unregulated] . . . fishing was not taking place"[66]—and indirect losses—for example, losses to the local economy stemming from less demand for ancillary services, such as fish processing works, or the manufacturing and service industries associated with the supply and maintenance of fishing boats.[67] Losses could also be of the environmental variety discussed earlier in this chapter (bycatch, discards, incidental mortality, etc.) or the varied and various socioeconomic losses that are concomitant with illegal fisheries, such as reduced food security for coastal communities and the physical conflicts that often result from the contiguity of illegal fishing vessels and local artisanal fishing communities.[68] Thus, Sierra Leone clearly has suffered the consequences of the flag of convenience industry, with foreign vessels routinely engaged in illegal fishing activities in its coastal waters, but unlike Cambodia, Sierra Leone has found itself cast as both a perpetrator and victim of the FOC industry. Why is this so?

To this question there are a number of possible answers, all of which share a common theme: Sierra Leone's transitional status and its inability to regulate its waters and fishing fleet. For instance, the Marine Research Assessment Group suggests that Sierra Leone's problems stem from the period of internal strife "when the government was unable to regulate and benefit from the fisheries," with the result that between 26 and 30 per cent of the fishing vessels operating in Sierra Leonean waters were doing so illegally.[69] Post-conflict, there may be slightly more political stability in Sierra Leone. While Sierra Leone may have the laws in place to tackle the problem of illegal

63 The *Huang He 22* has been listed by the Commission for the Conservation of Antarctic Marine Living Resources since 2004; www.ccamlr.org/en/node/77670.

64 This figure is arrived at by cross-referencing data contained on *Sea-Web Register of Ships* against the published "IUU" (illegal, unreported, and unregulated fishing) lists of RFMOs.

65 Environmental Justice Foundation, *Sierra Leone and Pirate Fishing*, www.ejfoundation.org/page370.html?gclid=CMOYmK7f1aYCFYMTfAod81fvMw.

66 Marine Research Assessment Group, *Illegal, Unreported and Unregulated Fishing*, Policy Brief No. 8, MRAG, London, pp.151–152.

67 *Ibid.*

68 *Ibid.*

69 *Ibid.*

fisheries in its own waters, it has only recently begun to find the resources to adequately implement and enforce them, thanks to assistance from the World Bank in the form of two new patrol boats.[70] This additional means of enforcement might assist Sierra Leone in overcoming its role as victim-state, but it does little to address the country's role as perpetrator-state. The problems caused by Sierra Leonean flagged vessels, conceded Fisheries Minister Joseph Koroma at a news conference convened to announce the closure of the of the Sierra Leonean international registry, was something that Sierra Leone should remedy. When Sierra Leone's FOC vessels depart Sierra Leonean waters for the high seas, there is, stated the minister, nothing that Sierra Leone can do about it. Consequently, Sierra Leone's international fishing registry would close.[71]

With the greatest respect to Minister Koroma, his assertion that "once the vessels enter the high seas there is nothing that Sierra Leone can do" is incorrect. In the same way that Cambodia might have been focused on purely "domestic" concerns, and less cognizant of its place in the international community following the country's lengthy period of internal strife, Sierra Leone appears to have overlooked two key issues. First, an ability to control vessels—even on the high seas—is required of states that are party to UNCLOS.[72] Second, Sierra Leone appears to have discounted the benefits of international cooperation. Members of RFMOs do not "go it alone" but instead act together to manage fisheries and protect the marine environment: they share resources and intelligence and, crucially, in many cases empower one another to take action against fishing vessels that violate the rules. As noted earlier, the general rule is that only the flag state can act against vessels engaged in infractions of fisheries laws on the high seas.[73] Members of the majority of RFMOs, however, explicitly authorize one another to take action against all vessels flying the flags of member states, when there are grounds to do so.[74] Additionally, RFMOs often mandate on-board observer schemes so that the integrity and provenance of the catch may be established, and observers are given powers to direct the ship's master to desist certain activities if they are incompatible with the RFMO's conservation and management strategies.[75]

70 S. Akam, *Sierra Leone Ends Flag of Convenience for Fishing Vessels*, Reuters, 28 October 2010.

71 *Ibid.*

72 UNCLOS, article 94.

73 See n.10.

74 See, for instance, Convention on the Conservation of Antarctic Marine Living Resources (CCAMLR) *Text of the CCAMLR System of Inspection*, article III; ICCAT Recommendation 08-05, *Amending the Recommendation by ICCAT to Establish a Multiannual Recovery Plan for Bluefin Tuna in the Eastern Atlantic and Mediterranean*, Annex 8; Northwest Atlantic Fisheries Organisation (NAFO), *Conservation and Enforcement Measures 2012*, Chapter VI.

75 See, for instance, ICCAT Recommendation 08-05, *ibid.*, Annex 7; IATTC Resolution C-03-04 on At-Sea Reporting; CCAMLR Convention, article XXIV(1).

Clearly, then, there *is* something Sierra Leone can do about its high seas fishing fleet, without having to go the way of Cambodia and Honduras before it. By complying with international and regional laws, it can prevent the painful and inevitable trade sanctions that follow an unregulated fishing fleet. Things are rarely simple, of course, and this chapter does not purport to suggest this. What transitional states can do with relative ease, however, is embark on an engagement strategy with international fisheries organizations. Despite their occasional use of options of last resort, such as trade restrictive measures, RFMOs are rarely so punitive as to ignore a state (especially a weak or developing one) that reaches out for assistance. For example, in addition to the aforementioned sharing of enforcement capacity, many RFMOs have enacted resolutions to provide financial assistance for training, capacity building, and participation within developing states.[76] Thus, by collaborating with RFMOs, transitional states may receive much of the necessary financial and technical assistance required to properly regulate their fleets, thereby avoiding—or at least lessening—the risk of sanctions.

Exploitation of "distracted" states?

The experiences of Honduras, Cambodia, and Sierra Leone clearly show that involvement in the FOC industry is not worth the price that must eventually be paid. What is obvious from the words and actions of these states is that while the short-term gains may act as a temporary allurement, the international sanctions and vilification that go hand-in-hand with the FOC industry are such a heavy price that few, if any, states can resist the international pressure to sever their links with the industry. What is slightly less clear, however, is why, having seen how international condemnation affected Honduras and Belize to such an extent that these "historical" FOCs closed their fishing registers to "foreign" vessels, states such as Cambodia and Sierra Leone might have thought that their own dalliance with convenient flags would end differently. Perhaps in this regard it is worth reconsidering the words of Cambodia's representative to the ICCAT conference in 2004 who, it will be recalled, noted that the state had to rebuild itself "from scratch" following the fall of the Khmer Rouge. Likewise, Sierra Leone, at the time of its first involvement with FOC fishing at the turn of the millennium, was more

76 IATTC Resolution C-11-11 on the Creation of the Special Sustainable Development Fund for Fisheries for Highly Migratory Species to Strengthen the Institutional Capacity of Developing Countries; IOTC Resolution 10/05 on the Establishment of a Meeting Participation Fund for Developing IOTC Members and Non-Contracting Co-operating Parties; the Convention of the South East Atlantic Fisheries Organisation, article 21; Convention of the South Pacific Regional Fisheries Management Organisation, article 19; Convention on the Conservation and Management of Highly Migratory Fish Stocks in the Western and Central Pacific Ocean, article 30.

concerned with domestic law and order than with its international fishing policy.[77] Of course, it would be both obvious and disingenuous simply to say that these states were mistaken and to point out—with the benefit of hindsight—that Cambodia and Sierra Leone should have spent more time considering their international commitments at the expense of rebuilding their internal infrastructures. A point to be made here, however, is that it is this very distraction that can allow the FOC industry to flourish: little or no effort is required on behalf of the state to create a fleet of "foreign" vessels, and often the registry itself is managed and maintained by strictly private entities.[78] Thus, often the already vulnerable transitional state—which may have entered the FOC industry in an ultimately misguided attempt to generate much-needed revenue, as a result of its ignorance of the risks associated with FOC fisheries, or simply because it lacked the capacity to adequately implement or enforce its own laws—will be left to take the fall. The extent to which private entities (vessel owners and registry management companies) can be held to account remains to be seen.

Perestroika: how the story began

Thus far, this chapter has portrayed typical transitional/FOC states as being fragile, impoverished countries, often coming to terms with internal conflict and/or making the transition from totalitarianism to democracy. Insofar as one contributor to the global FOC fleet is concerned, however, only the latter trait is relevant. With the breakup of the Soviet Union in the 1990s, the world witnessed one of the most drastic examples of transition and, of course, the socioeconomic and political consequences are well documented and need not trouble us here. It is, however, worth noting that some of the impetus behind the creation of the global FOC fleet was, in fact, the perestroika process.

To identify FOC vessels for the purposes of this chapter, the following methodology was adopted: first, the registration details of tens of thousands of fishing vessels were studied to identify links to Belize, Honduras, or Panama for the period 1995–2001. This process revealed that over 1,800 vessels were registered to one of these three FOC states and were subsequently deregistered when trade measures were enacted in 2001. While this might be inconclusive evidence of each vessel's involvement with illegal and unregulated fishing, in terms of identifying patterns of suspicious behavior, this methodology might raise certain questions about the propriety of the vessels' conduct. We have seen that after Belizean, Panamanian, and Honduran

77 Report of the Security Council Mission to Sierra Leone, UN Security Council, 16 October 2000, S/2000/992.

78 Even now the International Ships Register of Cambodia (ISROC) is a Korean concern, see www.isrocam.com/about/about01.php.

registration, many of these vessels registered with "new generation" FOC states, such as Cambodia and Sierra Leone—acts that can only reinforce any suspicions about the legitimacy of these vessels. After all, to be found on the registry of one FOC state during its heyday might be suspicious, but to move to another FOC during *its* heyday might come close to proof of wrongdoing.

Having identified these suspicious vessels, and having charted their histories after leaving their Central American registries, the author wished to study their longer-term histories, and the results of this analysis were illuminating. By far, the largest pattern of vessel movements between 1990 and 1995 were "new build" vessels that went straight from manufacture to Belize, Panama, or Honduras (705 vessels). The third largest was from the Soviet Union to these states (176 vessels). In isolation, this figure might not appear particularly large, but when compared to similar states—the United States or China, for instance—the Soviet figures do appear disproportionately high: of the 1,800 vessels, only 55 were former US-registered vessels and a mere 32 originated from China. Hence, it is suggested that the Soviet transition from communism to capitalism, with the concomitant social and economic change, began, albeit in a small way, the chain of events that ultimately led to the hardships felt by later FOC states such as Cambodia and Sierra Leone.

Corporate accountability

Just as had been the case a few years earlier when Panamanian, Honduran, and Belizean regulations threatened to impinge on FOC vessels' unfettered ability to make money, the closure of registries in Cambodia and Sierra Leone may have only marginally inconvenienced the vessels' owners. These owners simply find another state of registry and, to further disguise the vessel's provenance, often change the "on paper" ownership or management of the vessel and give the vessel a new name. These vessels then, almost certainly, carry on as before, undermining international and regional agreements aimed to prevent the degradation of the marine environment with seeming impunity and, in the process, harming the transitional states in which they are registered.

At this point in the chapter, therefore, the natural direction to follow would be to assess the ways in which international law can hold these corporations to account or, failing that, show how one-time states of registry could take punitive action against the companies whose fishing vessels engaged in deleterious fishing practices. Unfortunately, as the following section will demonstrate, there are at least two sizeable barriers to this analysis.

While some data on the ownership of vessels is available, this information is rarely of use in identifying the true owners of the vessel. Often, the named owner of a vessel is little more than that—a name to be used when required.[79] The real owners are rarely identifiable due to the limited publicly available information[80] and the reluctance of international courts to pierce the corporate veil.[81] As Lynden Griggs and Gail Lugten note, in the context of corporate accountability for violations of "non-high seas" fisheries regulations:

> Public International Law, with its focus on states, is inadequate to deal with the problems of private corporate regulation. Domestic corporate laws have promulgated the view of the separate legal entity, but they have failed to appreciate its potential for transnational violation and abuse.[82]

Hence, even if it were possible to apprehend the vessel itself—and on the high seas, this is impossible without the express agreement of the flag state—the most that any prosecuting state can do, for infractions in territorial seas or exclusive economic zones,[83] is to take action against the master and crew of the vessel and seize the vessel pending payment of a "reasonable bond or other security."[84]

Compounding the problem of untraceability is the fact that even if the vessel owners could be brought before a court, there is often no illegal activity with which to charge them. What the FOC vessel owners most often do is exploit the absence of law, not act in violation of law. A Cambodian-flagged vessel, for instance, has neither acted in violation of Cambodian law (because Cambodia has no specific laws governing high seas fisheries) nor breached any international laws (because these laws apply to *states*, which are obliged to exercise control over their fleets, and not to the vessels themselves). In both cases it is incumbent on the flag state to act, and, as we have seen throughout this chapter, it is the state's unwillingness or inability to act that makes flags of convenience so convenient for vessel owners. Transitional states, therefore,

79 "IUU fishing vessels are traditionally owned by 'front companies' which are themselves registered in international tax havens. These 'front companies' constitute the public face of a highly complex, transnational corporate structure that deliberately disguises the identity of the corporation's beneficial owners and corporations," L. Griggs and G. Lugten, 'Veil Over the Nets: Unravelling Corporate Liability for IUU Fishing Offences', 31 *Marine Policy* 159–168 (2007), p.160.

80 Although UNCLOS requires that states maintain a register of vessels, article 94(2)(a) of the Convention does not require publication of this information, nor does it require states to maintain a register of the often detailed and complex ownership arrangements of vessels.

81 Griggs and Lugten, n.79, p.165, who note that in relation to the *Volga Case (Russian Federation v Australia)*, Case No.11 of 23 December 2002, before the International Tribunal for the Law of the Sea, the Tribunal would not give credence to Australia's demand that the names of the actual owners of the vessel, the ownership details of the parent corporation, and its financiers be made public.

82 *Ibid.*, p.168.

83 See n.8.

84 UNCLOS, article 73.

are especially attractive havens for FOC activities because these particular states might, like Sierra Leone, lack the enforcement capacity to adequately implement their laws or, like Cambodia, claim ignorance of the problem. In all cases, however, the FOC industry will continue to target states so long as the state's cost-benefit analysis—however shortsighted it turns out to be—indicates that a quick profit might be made from the industry.

There is a further complicating factor: even if the flag state were to act against the vessel and its crew under national laws, what of the corporation that owns the vessel? UNCLOS does not require that the vessel-owning corporations have a legal presence in their states of registry,[85] and, notwithstanding any notional corporate presence in the flag state, the *real* corporate seat may well be in an entirely different jurisdiction—thus we return to the complex problem of piercing the corporate veil. For example, the author's analysis of 50 of the "Cambodian" vessels that fled from the registries of Belize, Honduras, and Panama revealed that whilst registered in Cambodia, only two vessels were listed as being "owned" by Cambodian companies.[86] The vast majority of these vessels were listed, in the relevant database, as being "owned," "operated by," or "managed by" entities based in South Korea, Japan, Russia, Panama, China, the Ukraine, Singapore, Honduras, the British Virgin Islands, and Malaysia. In many cases, a vessel's owner, manager, and operator were each based in different states; hence, even if the actual beneficial ownership of a vessel could be established, the jurisdictional problems of establishing where the "corporate offense" took place should not be underestimated.[87]

Conclusion

If we can learn anything from the experiences of Honduras, Sierra Leone, and Cambodia over the last decade, it is that involvement in the FOC industry may, at first glance, appear a tempting path to quick economic gain. To quote the old maxim, however, "If it seems too good to be true, it probably is." If this were not the case, and the transitional states studied in this chapter had, in fact, benefited from their involvement with the FOC industry, one might ask why they ceased their participation. The answer is, of course, that if there is a profit to be made from FOC fishing, the evidence suggests that

85 As a domestic condition of registry (not contingent on UNCLOS), many flag states do require a legal presence in the state of registry. This does not mean, however, that the corporation must be based in that state; often, the appointment of an agent will suffice.

86 Cognizant of the aforementioned point that any listed ownership details may simply be a "front company" and entirely unrepresentative of the actual ownership, see Griggs and Lugten, n.79.

87 *Sea-Web Register of Ships*, www.sea-web.com/seaweb_key_features.html (subscription service).

most of this money is more likely to fall into the pockets of shady and anonymous corporations than into those of any state. Consequently, the little fiscal benefits that the states receive in no way compensate for the wrath of the international community, the political pressure to comply with international norms, and the painful trade sanctions imposed.

There has, however, recently been a recognition by certain RFMOs that state sanctions, despite their efficacy, can be rather blunt instruments that fail to distinguish between legitimate and illegitimate fisheries[88] and that are too reactive in nature. Consequently, some RFMOs have begun to implement a "new generation" of more sophisticated market measures that, in many ways, remove the state from the loop and prevent, rather than punish, breaches of international and regional fishing regulations. Catch certificates and documentation schemes guarantee, insofar as it is possible to do so, compliance by *individual vessels* (irrespective of their flag) with RFMO regulations.[89] Thus, even a vessel registered with the weakest and most ineffective flag state must, under the new regime of market-related instruments, positively evidence compliance with regional regulations in order to sell its products within RFMO member states. As a result, the "do nothing" attitude that once made transitional and developing states so attractive to vessel owners is no longer viable. What will open up the lucrative markets of the developed states that are party to RFMO agreements is a "do something" attitude. Under these new market measures, it is increasingly the case that the requirement to "do something" falls on the vessel owners—and not on states that might be struggling to rebuild their economies and internal infrastructures and for whom compliance with international fishing regulations is, perhaps understandably, a distraction that cannot really be justified.

88 It will be recalled that *all* imports of tuna from Honduras, Belize, and Cambodia were prohibited by ICCAT—and not simply those that could be traced to FOC vessels.

89 For further on these catch certification schemes, see Calley, n.44, ch.5.

Conclusion

Sabine Michalowski and Ruben Carranza

The contributions in this book show the many facets of corporate involvement in repression and conflict, as well as the potential and challenges of achieving corporate accountability in the context of transitional justice. While conceptualizing corporate accountability in this context is clearly still in its infancy, several interesting trends have become apparent that make considering the connections between the two fields a timely enterprise. As shown in chapter 1, transitional justice theorists and practitioners more and more recognize that it is of crucial importance for achieving the goals of transitional justice that the transitional justice agenda is broadened to include considering root causes of conflict and repression. This to some extent requires a new approach to who should be held to account. Where the root causes are economic, addressing them could require tackling the role of economic actors, including corporations.

While transitional justice, and indeed international law, is traditionally state centered, trends in international law toward achieving corporate accountability (see chapters 1, 4, and 5) suggest that transitional justice equally needs to consider its stance in this context and take into account the changed realities of a globalized world in which corporations and economic interests are key players, operating beyond the boundaries of nation-states and without always being effectively regulated by them. At the same time, chapters 2 and 4 demonstrated that initiatives addressing the human rights accountability of businesses are flourishing. It is then no longer such a big step to bring both fields together and think about how transitional justice mechanisms can contribute to achieving corporate accountability in the particular context of transitions from conflict or repression, or, conversely, how the various means of holding corporations to account can be used in the transitional justice context.

One important conclusion to be drawn from the different chapters of this book is that it is impossible to identify one or several transitional justice or corporate accountability mechanisms as the "right" approach for achieving corporate accountability in the context of transitional justice. Instead, the various mechanisms must be seen as complementary, each having strengths and weaknesses. A lot, moreover, depends on the particular context in which they need to be applied.

With regard to the complementary relationship between TRCs and civil litigation taking place outside the transitional justice process, some interesting lessons can be learned from the experience of TRCs that have addressed the role of corporations. It is worth noting that whether an act gives rise to legal liability differs decisively from the definitions of responsibility as defined by TRCs (see, in particular, chapters 3, 5, 6, 8, and 10). As could be seen, the TRCs of South Africa, Liberia, and Timor-Leste found responsibility of corporations, but they examined it in the context of the events in the respective countries, and largely from a moral perspective. Where legal liability was suggested by a TRC, its basis was not clearly defined (see chapter 5). In civil litigation, on the other hand, liability is determined according to legal standards that were not designed for dealing with transitional justice or mass atrocities and that are applied by judges totally removed from the context of the transitional state (see chapters 3, 5, and 8).

Given that, unlike courts, TRCs are not bound by strict substantive and procedural legal rules, they can adopt a much more robust approach to corporate responsibility than courts can. This manifested itself particularly graphically in the conclusions of the South African TRC. The TRC found that even white businesses and landowners who did not contribute to the violations committed by the apartheid regime, but rather simply benefited from the structural advantages of operating within apartheid South Africa, should contribute to reparations programs (see chapter 8). This level of corporate responsibility would not usually give rise to civil claims of compensation.

Discrepancies between TRCs and courts in defining the standards of responsibility can be seen with regard to all areas of corporate activities. However, in this book, the issue came out particularly clearly with regard to the responsibility of banks for their role in human rights violations, the importance of which was forcefully demonstrated in chapter 10. The South African TRC made an especially strong case against banks and in fact regarded their responsibility as one of the few examples where corporate liability might have a legal, and not just a moral, basis. In the *Apartheid Litigation* case under the ATS, on the other hand, claims against banks were thrown out somewhat categorically on the basis of not meeting the requisite liability standards (see chapters 3 and 8). Nevertheless, chapter 6 presents interesting suggestions for breaching the gap between strict legal standards of corporate responsibility and the particular needs of transitional justice, both in general and with regard to banks, by suggesting a focus on legal remedies other than compensation.

The definition of who is to be recognized as a victim also depends decisively on whether a matter is dealt with by a TRC or a court. In civil proceedings, the notion of victim is related to who meets the procedural criteria to qualify as a plaintiff, while TRCs can adopt a definition of victim that is free from such constraints and tuned to the particular occurrences and transitional justice needs of the country where the violations occurred.

All of this reflects the different remits of TRCs as opposed to courts. TRCs have the task of furthering transitional justice goals, including determining the truth of what happened in the country during the period of conflict or repression. They can highlight the specific role played by corporations in the violations that occurred, but they might also uncover that, in some instances, businesses were the victims of a repressive regime, as was, for example, the case with coffee farmers in Timor-Leste.[1] Civil proceedings, on the other hand, aim to solve a specific problem between the parties of the litigation based on the relevant legal principles. Even though establishing the underlying facts is important for such proceedings, they are meant not to determine the truth broadly defined but rather to find the facts that are relevant for resolving the dispute before the court, based on the applicable standard of proof. Moreover, courts do not pursue the far-reaching objective of bringing social peace to a transitional society but the much less ambitious goal of resolving a disagreement between two parties. This means that the remit of courts is usually much narrower than that of TRCs. Nevertheless, there are many points of overlap, as well as complementarity. For instance, the South African example shows how the TRC's findings formed, to some extent, the evidentiary basis of future litigation (see chapter 8). At the same time, litigation can help shed light on what happened in a country where truth-finding was not achieved through transitional justice mechanisms (see chapter 3).

In many respects, TRCs seem to be best placed to establish corporate accountability in a way that meets the needs of the transitional society and to suggest remedies that are specific and sensitive to transitional justice. Nevertheless, several problems might make it necessary to consider litigation as an important complementary measure to TRCs. First, that TRCs have looked into the role of corporations does not mean that they will always be functionally able to address the role and responsibility of corporations. Indeed, one factor to bear in mind is that TRCs are politically weak institutions and often under-resourced. More importantly, they depend on governments to implement their recommendations, and this has proved to be a critical problem when it comes to achieving corporate accountability (see chapter 5). Indeed, the South African case showed rather clearly that the government, instead of following the TRC's recommendations regarding corporations, concentrated on their importance for bringing development and greater social equality to the new South Africa through corporate investment (see chapter 8).

1 Commission for Reception, Truth and Reconciliation in East Timor, *Chega! Final Report*, 2005, Chapter 7.9, paras.38–41.

Litigation might then be a means to overcome corporate impunity and achieve corporate accountability, for example, where, as in South Africa, the responsibility of corporations for human rights violations was established, but the government was unwilling to implement the TRC's recommendations regarding corporate reparations. It can also provide victims with reparations where reparations programs were regarded as insufficient (see chapters 5 and 8). Civil actions can also be important in situations where the role of corporations was not even part of the TRC's mandate or in societies where no comprehensive truth-seeking process has taken place.

A further advantage of certain civil litigation options is that they are available in countries with robust legal systems and economies, such as the United States, particularly in the case of the ATS (see chapter 3), and, to some extent, the UK (see chapter 2). Courts might then be less vulnerable to unlawful corporate responses to such litigation (such as bribery) or lawful reactions (such as threats to withdraw or withhold investments) than less independent judicial institutions in post-conflict and authoritarian settings and weakened economies might be (see also chapter 4).

However, litigation linked to transitional justice also raises problems (see especially chapters 2, 3, 5, and 8). First, transnational litigation in particular might be regarded as an intrusion on a transitional state's sovereignty and as inconsistent with that state's transitional justice approach. Moreover, the remedies available in lawsuits are usually limited to financial compensation, which is only one form of reparation that can be granted in the aftermath of mass atrocities. While these reservations are certainly important, and it must be borne in mind that litigation should, as much as possible, be pursued in sync with transitional justice processes, it is also obvious that litigation might in some instances be the only option for dissatisfied victims to pursue their own sense of justice.

Unlike civil litigation, criminal liability currently appears to be of limited relevance as a means of achieving corporate accountability in the context of transitional justice (see chapters 1, 3, and 9). One important reason for the marginal relevance of criminal law is that no corporate criminal liability exists at the international level, meaning that corporations could be held liable only indirectly through their directors or other individuals, which does not reflect the culpability of the corporation itself (chapters 3, 5, and 9). Where criminal corporate responsibility does exist, it is rarely used. Moreover, as the example of the criminal case against Nestlé in Switzerland shows, it might focus not on the actual violations that were committed but rather on organizational flaws within the corporation that made them possible, thereby not adequately reflecting the seriousness of the violations at stake from a transitional justice perspective (see chapter 9).

There are further reasons that might explain why civil liability is favored over criminal responsibility when it comes to establishing corporate accountability, even though such a trend goes against the usual tendency of transitional justice to focus primarily on criminal prosecutions. Civil litigation has the advantage of being able to be initiated by the victims themselves, instead of depending on the state's willingness to prosecute (see chapter 3). Another important factor might be the reparation function of civil proceedings against corporations that have the assets for large-scale compensation. Furthermore, the outcome of civil litigation does not have to be win-or-lose. While civil trials often end in settlements without a determination of responsibility or a decision ordering the payment of compensation which raises concerns from a transitional justice perspective, these settlements can nevertheless provide victims with some form of redress and recognition through the payment of compensation (see chapters 4 and 5).

This last point highlights that judicial decisions favorable to victims are not the only means to measure the success of litigation. Indeed, court proceedings, regardless of their outcome, might have lasting and positive effects for transitional justice by raising awareness of largely neglected aspects of the truth and triggering widespread debates in civil society. Chapter 9 shows how criminal proceedings in the context of the Argentinian and Colombian transitions changed the narrative in both countries through raising awareness of the economic dimensions and beneficiaries of the atrocities that occurred.

Judicial proceedings are not the only means through which corporate actors can become part of the transitional justice narrative. Indeed, a whole range of other measures, from soft law (see chapters 2 and 4) to individual communications under the Optional Protocol to the International Covenant on Economic, Social and Cultural Rights (see chapter 7) can also be used to bring the role of corporations in the context of transitional justice into the spotlight. Chapter 10 discusses a variety of measures that could be used to paint as complete a picture as possible of the causes and consequences of—as well as responsibilities for—past occurrences, be it through lobbying for transitional justice, litigation or relying on corporate accountability and regulation mechanisms.

Raising awareness of the complexities of the causes and consequences of conflict and repression, and the role of corporate actors in this context, is also important for influencing the growing debate on corporate accountability for human rights violations, in particular the discussion opened up by the UN Guiding Principles on Business and Human Rights (see chapter 4), but also other soft-law mechanisms, such as corporate social responsibility (see chapter 2). These mechanisms provide some potential for achieving corporate accountability in the context of transitional justice. However, so far, they have not risen to the challenge of defining corporate responsibilities arising in the specific scenario of conflict or repression. Transitional justice processes and debates can then contribute to defining corporate human rights responsibility and clarifying the evolving human rights standards, particularly regarding corporate activities in conflict zones. This is important from a corporate accountability perspective because it would help corporations avoid the particular risks involved in certain types of operations. At the same time, as could be learned from the discussion of the relationship between civil litigation and transitional justice mechanisms, from a transitional justice perspective it is crucial that when the UN Guiding Principles or other soft-law mechanisms are applied in the context of transitional justice, this is done with the particular demands of transitional justice clearly in mind—otherwise, there is a risk that transitional justice processes will be undermined rather than supported (see chapters 2, 4, and 5).

While soft-law mechanisms in general, and the UN Guiding Principles in particular, are discussed rather controversially in this book (see chapters 2, 4, 5, and 7), given their highly influential nature they are clearly important mechanisms to take into account and can serve several important functions. First, they can complement other means of corporate accountability, particularly tort litigation, but also contractual human rights protection, because of their focus on preventing future violations (see chapter 2). While other forms of accountability try to achieve a similar aim, primarily through deterrence, the human rights due diligence required under the UN Guiding Principles demands proactive steps on the part of corporations to identify human rights risks and to act on them, which goes beyond other forms of accountability. Another feature of soft law relevant for transitional justice is that, just like TRCs, it can establish responsibility beyond the narrow confines of the law. This means that the UN Guiding Principles and other soft-law mechanisms, on the one hand, and TRCs, on the other, could potentially draw on each other's experience when determining and refining corporate responsibility in the context of transitional justice.

The UN Guiding Principles' focus on remediation as one of their three pillars (see chapter 4) emphasizes the significance of reparations for victims of human rights violations. The vagueness of the UN Guiding Principles in this respect, as well as the failure to address the particular problems of reparations arising in the context of transitional justice, might be regarded as a weakness (see chapter 4). At the same time, however, this can offer opportunities for transitional justice stakeholders to contribute to the clarification of the relevant responsibilities—for example, by insisting on international human rights standards for their interpretation and, in the context of transitional justice, aligning them with the Basic Principles on Reparations (see chapter 5).

Chapter 5 demonstrates that the complementarity of transitional justice and corporate accountability mechanisms also prevails in the area of reparations. In the context of transitional justice, reparation programs are often designed by TRCs (or in the light of TRC findings and recommendations), and they need to find a careful balance between competing needs of individual victims as well as communities and the transitional society as a whole. Reparations for occurrences that are intimately linked to the transitional justice processes, but awarded outside of them, can potentially disturb this balance, such as by prioritizing the needs of those victims who could make avail of corporate remediation mechanisms or who qualify as plaintiffs in the context of litigation over other victims in a similar situation but who, for a variety of reasons, could not benefit from these ways to obtain corporate reparations (see chapters 4 and 5). While litigation and soft-law remediation mechanisms can have a positive effect on providing potential avenues for obtaining reparations where they are not forthcoming through transitional justice mechanisms, these alternatives must be approached with particular caution.

Adequate forms of corporate reparations need to be carefully chosen, both to achieve the deterrence effect that promotes non-recurrence and to reflect the needs of victims. Drawing on the experiences of TRCs and on recent Colombian legislation, chapters 5 and 6 show how corporate remedies might encourage innovative ways of designing reparation programs, including transformative reparations.

Another important question to address is that of how best to achieve the goal of non-recurrence. As pointed out in chapter 1, transitional justice mechanisms are meant to deal with extraordinary situations, while societies have ordinary regulatory tools in place to deal with corporate violations in a variety of different settings. Since corporate involvement in gross human rights violations in the context of conflict and repression often occurs as a byproduct of carrying out business transactions in affected zones, this might suggest that human rights violations committed in this context should be regarded as a general problem of corporate regulation and should be addressed outside the transitional justice framework through mechanisms directly geared at, and having experience with, corporate accountability and regulation (see chapter 1). However, as shown in chapters 2 and 4, regulation regarding corporate human rights violations is achieved primarily through soft law, largely without enforcement mechanisms controlled by state organs. Legal reforms that are being introduced at both national and international levels with respect to corporate conduct involve specific *crimes*—money laundering, drug trafficking, tax-related offenses—but not corporate human rights violations, either in general or in contexts of conflict and repression. It might then be worth considering whether the recognition that corporations can have a role in human rights violations that is relevant in transitional justice processes could require broadening the transitional justice outlook on institutional reforms which, as shown in chapter 1, has traditionally been concerned primarily with the security sector and judicial reforms. If holding corporations to account is to have a sustainable impact, it might be important to explore the possibility and desirability of reforms of state institutions that regulate corporate behavior (see chapter 5), and raise awareness of the importance of regulating the human rights impact of corporations in order to guarantee non-recurrence.

The significance of corporate accountability for transitional justice goes beyond redressing past wrongs and preventing recurrence. It also has an important role to play in shaping the design of the new society. Chapters 11 and 12 demonstrate that without adequate corporate accountability measures in place at the international level, transitional states that need corporate investment for economic reconstruction and development might risk that new violations of human rights, unrelated to the past atrocities but made possible because of the weak position such countries find themselves in, can and are likely to occur. Both chapters clearly highlight how the international law's focus on state responsibility does not always reflect the realities of the relationship between transitional states and powerful corporations; and that recent international and regional trends to achieve corporate human rights compliance need to be strengthened in order to assist transitional states with achieving reconstruction that does not invite new human rights violations.

Corporations play a role not only with regard to violations of civil and political rights but also with regard to violations of ESCR. The discussion about how to address this problem in the context of transitional justice is even less developed than its counterpart in the area of civil and political rights violations, as transitional justice generally shows a clear bias toward focusing on gross violations of civil and political rights. While the debate on whether and how to include ESCR in transitional justice processes in general, and how to link this to corporate accountability in particular, needs to be advanced further, the Optional Protocol to the International Covenant on Economic, Social and Cultural Rights might provide an interesting tool to bring the issue to the fore (see chapter 7).

This book clearly shows the importance of addressing corporate accountability for violations that occurred in the context of conflict and repression by linking such accountability to transitional justice, rather than approaching transitional justice and corporate accountability separately. Indeed, to the extent that corporations played a role in the occurrences of the past, attempts to address corporate accountability need to be approached with the needs and specificities of the transitional justice process in mind, to prevent corporate accountability measures from running counter to and possibly undermining the aims of transitional justice. As most chapters argued, if corporate accountability mechanisms are applied in a manner sensitive to transitional justice, they can be an important complement to the more traditional transitional justice mechanisms for establishing corporate accountability. At the same time, transitional justice mechanisms reveal important opportunities for addressing the specificities of corporate accountability in the transitional justice context, particularly by allowing for broader concepts of responsibility than those available in the legal realm.

Index